FACING
TED WILLIAMS

FACING TED WILLIAMS

PLAYERS FROM THE GOLDEN AGE OF BASEBALL RECALL THE GREATEST HITTER WHO EVER LIVED

EDITED BY DAVE HELLER

FOREWORD BY WADE BOGGS
AFTERWORD BY BOB WOLFF

SPORTS PUBLISHING

Sports Publishing books may be purchased in bulk at special discounts for sales promotion, corporate gifts, fund-raising, or educational purposes. Special editions can also be created to specifications. For details, contact the Special Sales Department, Sports Publishing, 307 West 36th Street, 11th Floor, New York, NY 10018 or sportspubbooks@skyhorsepublishing.com.

Sports Publishing® is a registered trademark of Skyhorse Publishing, Inc.®, a Delaware corporation.

Visit our website at www.sportspubbooks.com

10 9 8 7 6 5 4 3 2 1

Library of Congress Cataloging-in-Publication Data

Facing Ted Williams : players from the golden age of baseball recall the greatest hitter who ever lived / edited by Dave Heller ; foreword by Wade Boggs ; afterword by Bob Wolff.
    pages cm
(hardcover : alk. paper) 1. Williams, Ted, 1918-2002—Anecdotes. 2. Williams, Ted, 1918-2002—Friends and associates. 3. Baseball players—United States—Biography. I. Heller, David Alan.
GV865.W5F33 2013
796.357092—dc23
    2012048683

Print ISBN: 978-1-61321-769-6

Cover design by Brian Peterson
Cover photograph courtesy of the Boston Public Library

Printed in the United States of America

For my wife, Shelly. When she walks down the street,
they should say, "There goes the best damn wife there ever was."

CONTENTS

Foreword	1
Introduction	9
Section One: Pitchers	13
Dave Baldwin	15
Charlie Beamon	19
Ted Bowsfield	22
Dick Brodowski	25
Bob Bruce	27
Art Ceccarelli	29
Gene Conley	32
Glenn Cox	34
Bud Daley	36
Jim Derrington	40
Chuck Estrada	41
Bob Feller	46
Don Ferrarese	51
Bill Fischer	54
Paul Foytack	58
Bob Friend	62
Ned Garver	66
Jim "Mudcat" Grant	79
John Gray	82

Contents

Dick Hall	86
Jack Harshman	89
John James	97
Bob Kelly	99
Russ Kemmerer	102
Marty Kutyna	107
Don Larsen	109
Bobby Locke	113
Ralph Lumenti	116
Morrie Martin	118
Bill Oster	121
Duane Pillette	124
Tom Qualters	127
Hal Raether	130
Phil Regan	134
Marv Rotblatt	135
Bob Shaw	144
George Spencer	147
Dick Stigman	151
Wes Stock	152
Virgil Trucks	156
Ozzie Van Brabant	163
Vito Valentinetti	165
Jerry Walker	169
George Zuverink	172
Interviews:	175
Chuck Churn	177
Jerry Davie	178

Sonny Dixon   180

Bubba Harris   182

Don Johnson   183

Don Lee   185

Bob Savage   187

Carl Scheib   189

Bobby Shantz   192

Dave Sisler   195

Section Two: Catchers   197

Del Crandall   199

Jim French   202

Hal Keller   206

Hal Naragon   208

Neal Watlington   213

Interviews: 215

Bob Oldis   217

Red Wilson   219

Section Three: Infielders   221

Dr. Bobby Brown   223

Tom Carroll   227

Jerry Coleman   232

Billy DeMars   239

Gail Harris   240

Grady Hatton   241

Randy Jackson   242

Bob Johnson   245

Charlie Kress   248

Contents

Don Leppert 254

Al Naples 257

Herb Plews 259

J. W. Porter 261

Bobby Richardson 264

Art "Dutch" Schult 265

Jerry Snyder 268

Chuck Stevens 272

Wayne Terwilliger 283

Ray Webster 285

Interviews: 287

Bob Kline 289

Ted Lepcio 290

Gene Verble 291

Section Four: Outfielders 293

Chuck Diering 295

Joe Hicks 297

Jim Landis 298

Wally Westlake 301

Interviews: 303

Joe Durham 305

Jim McAnany 306

Roy Sievers 308

Afterword 311

Acknowledgments 319

Index 321

FOREWORD

TED WILLIAMS IS who John Wayne wanted to be when he grew up.

Growing up, I was a huge Ted Williams fan, and I mean *huge*. Coincidentally, I was drafted by the Red Sox in 1976. I wore No. 9 in high school and read *The Science of Hitting* my junior year. I never thought in my wildest dreams that I'd actually have the opportunity of meeting him.

Well, it did happen. The first time I met Ted was when I was starting out in the minors. It was my first spring training. I'm eighteen years old and standing in line at the movie theater two days into spring training, and standing two people behind me is bigger than life Ted Williams. I went up to Ted and introduced myself, said I was drafted the year before and played in Elmira,[1] and grew up admiring him as a hitter.

And he just went into this conversation about "how do you hold your hands, how do you do all of this"—right in line. Just firing off this and that, what kind of hitter was I in high school, and I thought I had just died and went to heaven. It was truly one of those monumental experiences that you are afforded in life, and for me, having had the opportunity to meet Ted, it was truly overwhelming.

So, I can imagine how these young pitchers felt when they got the opportunity to face Ted Williams. It had to be mind-blowing. And

---

[1] The Emira Pioneers (or Elmira Red Sox, as they were known) were a Red Sox affiliate in the New York–Penn League.

now I can see why Ted Williams walked so much—because guys were scared to pitch to him!

He was a John Wayne-esque figure; very intimidating, very brash. It was pretty much an R-rated conversation every time Ted would get going; definitely wasn't for Little Leaguers. But this is the way Ted carried himself. He had that aura about himself that very few people carry.

You knew right when he walked in the room, like in that old commercial: If E. F. Hutton is talking, you listen. Every time Ted would say something, the whole room would get quiet. That was the intimidating part about him. When you are young and impressionable, he really stands out. That was the great part about Ted.

During my minor league days, Ted would just sort of be roving around in a golf cart. He'd stop by maybe once during the day while I was in Double-A or Triple-A, and he'd stand behind the batting cage while guys were swinging and talk to various players. It was more of casual conversation than sit down and instruct.

"What did you do in the game yesterday, kid?"
"Two-for-three, Ted, with a walk."
"Where were your hits?"
"Line drive left-center base hit, ground ball in the hole for a base hit, grounder to short."
"You didn't pull the ball?"

Just certain conversations like that, rather than sitting down in the cage and doing it that way.

When I was in Triple-A, he said you have to get that 2–0, 2–1 pitch, and you just have to get those hips going and get those hands out in front. And that really wasn't my style. I stayed inside the ball and hit it the other way. I felt like when I did that, I rolled over a lot to second base and hit weak ground balls. I didn't have a good concept on how to pull the ball.

I sort of stuck to my guns, but it's tough when you're listening to the greatest hitter that ever lived, and he's telling you to do one thing, and then you're doing your own thing. It wasn't a thing of going against Ted Williams. Everyone has their own mechanical philosophy, and for me to try to change, I think that would have destroyed my whole swing.

I thought I was better utilized in Fenway Park if I could reach the wall rather than hit deep fly balls to right field for outs. It just didn't compute in my brain to where that made sense, and leaving the wall to didn't make sense.

But later on, Ted did say, you get that 2–0, 2–1 pitch, look for that pitch to drive. And I really did that. I hit the ball to left-center and it would be high off the wall. In Wrigley Field, that's a home run. In Houston,[2] that's a home run. And parks that didn't have the big 37-foot monster, you had the chance to hit the ball out of the park. It probably took some homers away, but it also gave you some hits. You could hit high fly balls to left field and then scrape the wall, which were outs in other parks.

Probably about 98 percent of the time I took the first pitch. There were instances when I'd jump on the first pitch and felt comfortable doing so, but I felt—another chapter out of Ted—that the longer you faced a guy, the more chances he was going to make a mistake. The more pitches I saw, I felt I had the upper hand, that the guy was going to make a mistake. He wasn't going to make that good pitch early in the count to get me out. If I had five, six, seven, or eight pitches, I had the upper hand. It's demoralizing for a pitcher to foul off a ball, foul off a ball, foul off a good pitch, and foul it off and not put it in play. He gets somewhat upset, makes a mistake, and that's when you capitalize on it.

---

[2] Boggs is speaking of the Houston Astrodome, which was home to the Astros from 1965–1999.

He would show up about once a year when I was with Boston. The Red Sox never had an old-timer's day, but Ted would make it a point to come up for a weekend series unannounced. He would just walk in. He'd be there for Friday, Saturday, and maybe a Sunday game, and then you wouldn't see him the rest of the year.

He always made sure to come over and find me, and then we'd sit down in front of my locker and chat. I have great pictures of us sitting in front of my locker, looking bright-eyed and very astute, with Ted doing his hand gestures. Those are very fond memories.

The funny part about it was, when he would come over, he'd never ever let any reporters eavesdrop on our conversation. He'd basically shoo them away and we'd talk for fifteen to twenty minutes. All the reporters would come up after, and their first question was, "Did you guys talk about hitting?" In actuality, Ted and I would talk fifteen to twenty minutes on nothing but fishing. During those chats, we would never, ever, talk about hitting. It was kind of funny. Every time we'd sit down, he'd want to know what kind of fish I caught in the offseason, what kind of line I used, where I was fishing, and various things like that. Hitting never really came up. He would like to talk about hitting with other players and young guys, but the majority of the time when Ted and I got together, it was non-stop fishing.

This is one of my worst regrets in life—that I had the opportunity to ask him to go fishing down in the Florida Keys and never did. But I never make the same mistake twice, because I had the opportunity to ask Curt Gowdy[3] to go fishing with me down in the Keys, and he graciously accepted. Although it wasn't Ted, I sort of got the same

---

[3] Curt Gowdy was the voice of the Boston Red Sox from 1951–1965, the host of *The American Sportsman*, and was elected into the National Baseball Hall of Fame in 1984. He was also a fishing partner of Williams.

thing, because Curt had a lot of stories about Ted. I didn't have Ted, but I had the next best thing. Listening to Curt recall fishing stories about time spent with Ted in the Keys, while sitting out back after a day of fishing, was just incredible.

But that is the one regret in life I do have; that I never pulled the trigger on asking Ted to go fishing. And I'm sure Ted would have accepted, and it would have been the greatest day ever, to bonefish with Ted down in the Keys.

Once I got to know him later in life, his voice started to calm down, but his presence was still there, and that was the great thing about him. All the way up until Ted passed away—I had seen him a couple months before he passed away—so from about the age of eighteen to Ted's passing, I had seen him periodically throughout the years.

Although Ted was basically a pull hitter throughout the majority of his career, he did hit the ball to left-center on some occasions. But I was more an inside-out hitter, and Ted was more hips ahead of hands, which enabled him to pull more balls than myself. So, our mechanical philosophies were different, but I think our cerebral philosophies were basically the same.

Work the pitch, get a good strike zone, work the counts, and if you don't get a good pitch to hit, then you accept the walk. All those points are the keys to being a disciplined hitter, and that's what Ted preached more than anything: Knowing the strike zone. And when you see the big strike zone in Ted's book, *The Science of Hitting*, you can see that the areas that gave him difficulty were basically bad pitches to swing at. But when you put the ball in the sweet spot, his average naturally went up.

And that was more or less my philosophy. If you put it in an area to where I can make solid contact, then I have an opportunity to hit the ball to the wall. And that's why I utilized Fenway Park for eleven years to my advantage, unlike Ted.

I mean, they had the very first shift on Ted, and he would beat the shift and still hit .400. I think that's what made it so amazing. They'd throw everyone on one side of the field, and he still hit .400. By the way, I've been an advocate that hitting .400 will never be done again . . . and Ted did back in 1941. Personally, to hit .400, I think those days are long gone.

There's very little that Ted hasn't done—serving our country during war and losing five years of a valuable career, just to come back, never missing a beat, and win another batting title. He's the greatest in my mind.

In 1986, Ted, Don Mattingly, and I were able to sit down over dinner one night with Peter Gammons to talk about hitting for an article he was writing for *Sports Illustrated*, and it ended up lasting for about five hours. We got to the restaurant at about 5:00 and I think we left between 10 and 10:30, and it was nonstop talking the whole time.

When I got inducted into Ted's Hitters Museum, Ted was still alive, and we had a couple of nights to sit down and talk about baseball and fishing. We actually talked more about baseball than we did during my playing days. Once I had retired, Ted and I would talk about various games, young players, and things of that nature. But I still told Ted about fishing trips in the offseason and catching sailfish. And now I'm into marlin, and Ted once caught a 1,000-pound marlin, and he said, "You have a ways to go if you want to catch me, kid."

But I have been over several times to his hitter's museum, and I have a cubicle of Red Sox stuff there. It's an extreme honor to even be in that museum. If anyone can get over to Tropicana Field and check it out, it's a wonderful museum and a tremendous place to go.

Speaking of Tropicana Field, when they had a ceremony for my 3,000th hit, Ted was there. That was very moving. We had sent out the invitation, and it came back that Ted wasn't feeling too well and wouldn't be able to make it. But lo and behold, I turn around in the clubhouse, and Ted walks in. It was very moving that he would come down and be a part of that. It was *extremely* special, it really was. And he tipped his cap to me. The greatest compliment a player could ever get is if Ted Williams tips his cap to you. That was '99 when he did that, the same year he had that moment at the All-Star Game at Fenway, which some of the former players in this book also talk about. I would have loved to have been there and wheeled him out. It was a monumental moment in baseball.

I have a lot of books in my library and pictures around the house of Ted's stuff. I have pictures of Ted in just about every room, so my house is somewhat of a shrine to him. He left me a shotgun, a fly-rod reel, and a spinning reel in his will when he passed away. I was completely shocked at that. Dave McCarthy, the curator of the Ted Williams Museum, called and said that Mr. Williams has left me some items in his will, and I was just overwhelmed that he would think of me and make such a gesture. That's goosebumpville.

And it would have been special, really special, if Ted could have been at my Hall of Fame induction, but he had passed away a few years earlier.

I was looking forward to reading this book; to see the psyche pitchers when a terrific hitter came to the plate. I know how they think now: They walk him and pitch to the next guy. That's why guys walk so much nowadays. It's not because they have a good eye, it's that guys just don't throw strikes to where they can swing the bat. They'd rather pitch to the guy behind him, who is either in a slump, isn't doing well, or isn't the same caliber of player.

In my opinion, *Facing Ted Williams* is a must-read because it's great to hear about the approach that pitchers, catchers, and fielders of that era dealt with a hitter like Ted Williams. I think facing Ted Williams as a young player would have been *so* intimidating. But when you look back at that era, there were a lot of intimidating players—just so many great players of that era—that pitchers were facing greats all the time. But it's always nice to read something about Ted.

It is extremely special, the journey I had with Ted. My dad's favorite player growing up was Ted Williams . . . well, Ted Williams and Mickey Mantle. Just having my dad sit down with Ted Williams during minor league and big league days, me sitting down and talking with him, making it to the Hall of Fame and being mentioned in the same breath as him, and wearing a Red Sox cap into the Hall of Fame—which Ted and I share—is extremely special.

I don't think Hollywood could have scripted anything better than a little, snotty-nosed kid from Tampa, Florida, who gets to be alongside his idol in the Hall of Fame and grow up to even be mentioned in the same breath as him.

It is an incredible journey. Growing up, I dreamed about being Ted Williams . . . that dream sort of manifested itself into myself. But there will never be another Ted Williams. His persona—not only on the field, but off—and to also be an American hero? I mean, wow. The legacy he left behind is what people aspire to, and it's a pleasure to have been able to know somebody like that.

—Wade Boggs, November 2012

INTRODUCTION

IS TED WILLIAMS the greatest hitter of all time? I believe that it's a question that will always be up for debate. I'm not sure there will ever be—or can be—a definitive answer. And who would know best, anyway? That is the purpose of this book; to find out from those whose opinions matter most: The people who went up against him.

But maybe I'm getting ahead of myself just a bit.

When I was in the sixth grade, I decided to replay a baseball season with my dice simulation of choice (APBA), and chose the 1941 American League. Certainly, it wasn't for the great pennant race, because there wasn't more than one team who was in it that year. (The Yankees won by 17 games, and there were only three teams at .500 or better in the AL.) Quite simply, it was the prospect of being able to replay the last time someone hit .400 in a season.[1] Later, when I was eighteen, I was fortunate enough to get a kind of backstage pass to the Hall of Fame induction ceremonies in Cooperstown. I got to see a lot of hall of famers make their entrance (and also got to taste rum for the first time, but that's another story), including Ted Williams. In fact, a friend I was with said he heard someone ask Williams what he'd hit if he were right-handed. Now, this guy could tell a joke with a straight face better than anyone, so I have no idea if this is true, but I did take a picture of Williams, and if I can recall correctly, he had a quizzical

---

[1] With two games left in the 1941 season (a doubleheader against the Philadelphia Athletics), Ted Williams had the choice of sitting out, as he had a .39955 batting average, which would have been rounded up to .400. That wasn't acceptable for Ted. Instead, he played in both games of the doubleheader, going 6–8 on the day, and finishing with a .406 batting average for the season.

look on his face. We've always heard theories from ballplayers about what it takes to be a great hitter. Rogers Hornsby used to say not to watch movies because it would hurt your eyes, and there are entire books written by the likes of Ted Williams and Tony Gwynn on the art of hitting.[2]

But what about the strategies of those who had to face him? How did they pitch to Williams? Did they play the Williams shift and, if so, did it really do any good? And how good was Williams, really?

Obviously, one of the issues in finding out these things is time. It has been over seventy years since Williams made his major-league debut (1939), and over fifty years since he had his last at-bat (a pretty famous home run, which is recounted within these pages). This means that many players from that era are no longer with us, including Williams, who died on July 5, 2002.

But there were over 236 former pitchers and ballplayers out there who I was able to get in touch with to chat about "The Splendid Splinter."

Those whom I spoke to had some great stories and memories. It really is kind of funny how certain themes would come across in the responses I got—like umpires not calling a strike on Williams if he didn't swing. And that's just one of many examples.

One of the first ballplayers I spoke with was Virgil Trucks, who recounted a home run Williams hit off him in 1940. After we were done talking, I went to verify what he had said, and discovered that, after seventy years, his details were spot-on. I mention this because, when I called one ex-pitcher and asked if he could share his memories against Williams, he told me, "That was over fifty goddamn years ago!" It wasn't said with malice or disgust, but rather just laying out the facts.

---

[2] Ted Williams' book, *The Science of Hitting*, came out in 1986 and is not only still in print, but continues to sell successfully.

While every former ballplayer in this book didn't have his details down pat like Trucks, I didn't feel it was my job to argue or confront these men with the "true" details. Because after all . . . this book is about their memories.

I do represent the true facts of game events that were incorrectly related. I don't do this to show up the ballplayers or to make them look bad, but rather to present an accurate, historical account.

And really, the details were usually correct. But minor things—like perhaps the situation (runners on base, inning, score)—weren't exactly the way it was. So he struck out Williams in the fourth inning, not the ninth, or there was no one on base, instead of two. The fact is, Williams did indeed strike out, so the memory of the pitches and the strikeout were, in my opinion, likely correct—just not the situation. And that's what's important.

And speaking of statistics, while the availability of stats has increased tremendously over the years, there are still some years in which box scores are not available (pre-1946 for the most part, plus some scattered games here and there post-1946). Thus, not all the statistics for Ted Williams vs. certain pitchers are complete. We've noted them within these pages, but have given the best representation possible.

While many of those who faced Ted in his prime are long gone, the ballplayers I spoke to were able to share their memories with me, and, in the end, gave wonderful stories that most of us would have never heard.

I hope you enjoy them as much as I did.

Section One: Pitchers

Dave Baldwin

Right-handed pitcher

1966–69:	Washington Senators
1970:	Milwaukee Brewers
1973:	Chicago White Sox
Career statistics:	6–11, 22 saves, 3.08 ERA

Note: Baldwin did not play against Ted Williams, but was managed by him in 1969 with the Senators.

WHEN THE WASHINGTON Senators went to spring training in Pompano Beach, Florida, in 1969, we had high hopes despite a dismal last place finish in '68. We had good reason to be optimistic. Our new manager was a legend, a baseball icon, a combination of Teddy Roosevelt, John Wayne, and Hercules. Our new manager was Ted Williams.

Ted was the perfect manager for the '69 Senators. Our roster was made up mostly of the '68 Senators team—not an encouraging situation—but Ted was bursting with confidence and that was infectious. We needed a leader who was authoritative and self-assured. Ted was that in spades. The players felt that just his presence in the dugout would be enough to lift a last place team into the first division.

Having those characteristics, Ted might be assumed to be egotistical, but his players didn't see him that way. He was focused on his team, trying to help each player become the best he could be. He demanded that his players have a can-do attitude. He was a larger-than-life, fifty-one-year-old cheerleader who convinced his team that they could be playing for the pennant. That was crucial to the Senators' success, but a manager must do much more for his team.

Ted realized he needed a coaching staff that would complement his abilities. First, he chose to retain Sid Hudson, a Red Sox teammate of

Ted's, for his pitching coach. He relied heavily on Sid's advice on all pitching matters. Then, Ted hired Joe Camacho to be his advisor on strategic and tactical decisions during games. Joe had been a senior instructor at Ted's baseball camp in Massachusetts. Ted's bullpen coaches were Doug Camilli and George Susce, two veteran catchers who were well acquainted with the Senators' pitchers.

Ted added veteran infielders Wayne Terwilliger (the manager of Buffalo in '68) and Nellie Fox to make our on-field operations run smoothly. Nellie also served another important function: at times he was a court jester, needling Ted to the amusement of the players. He goaded Ted more than anyone else dared. When Nellie looked at Ted, all he saw was a target. And there was Nellie, holding a handful of darts. "You know I had more hits than you did, don't you?" he would ask with a gleam in his eye. "And only about a third the strikeouts you had," he added, just to be sure he made his point.

Another thrust that always worked was "You would have been a hell'uva hitter if you could have gone to the opposite field." And his favorite jibe, "You were too predictable. I always knew right where to play you." This earned the perfect rustic yet colorful response from Ted.

This teasing by Nellie allowed Ted to look human and, therefore, approachable by his players. I don't know whether Nellie and Ted arranged for these little interactions for our benefit or whether they were acting on intuition, but it worked well, contrived or otherwise.

Whenever Ted expounded on any topic, he was an impressive show. Imagine a player asking him a question about hitting a baseball—his favorite subject. First, if Ted was sitting, he stood up—he had to be on his feet for this. Then, to make sure the player paid full attention, he would grow taller and lean back, the way he used to swing at a nickel curve. His audience would be awestruck. It was like driving past Mount Rainier. To emphasize his parameters, Ted would throw potent expletives and rapid-fire gestural metaphors at the player from all angles. *POW*, *BAM*, *ZAP*, and other cartoon interjections rattled windows as he punctuated his punctuations. Before long the player would be exhausted.

It *was* overwhelming, but this animated lecture could be an invaluable education for a pitcher. Ted was providing insight into how one of history's hardest-thinking batters thought about his business. The pitcher-batter battle was partly a mind-reading exercise and partly a guessing game. With Ted's enlightenment, it became more the former, less the latter.

Besides educating his pitchers, Ted was a great mentor for his hitters, of course. Eddie Brinkman was his prize pupil. Eddie batted only .208 over several seasons prior to '69, but under Ted's tutelage Eddie stopped uppercutting the ball so much and began to hit line drives instead of lazy fly balls. He hit .266, the highest batting average of his career.[1] In fact, the whole team hit much better under Ted. We had finished next to last in the American League in hitting in 1968 with a team average of .224. (Only the pathetic Yankees were worse. They had a season-long slump of .214, one of the poorest team batting averages in baseball history.) Under Ted, we improved to .251—tied with the Red Sox for third best in the 12-team league.

I wonder how often manager Williams thought, *Maybe I'll just take a few cuts.* Once, near the end of batting practice, he couldn't stand it any longer. He grabbed an unattended bat, shouted, "Let's see what you've got" to the pitcher (one of the coaches, probably Terwilliger or Fox) and stepped into the cage. Everyone in the park was transfixed as Ted hit nine or ten line drives against the right-field wall on as many pitches. He made perfect contact on every pitch. Although he was fifty-one, considerably hefty, and hadn't swung a bat in a game in nine years, he was still the best hitter on the team. He batted 1.000 that day, and that was the last time I ever saw him hit.

---

[1] Brinkman would hit .262 under Williams in 1970. He was traded to Detroit before the 1971 season and never hit higher than .237 again.

In that one incident, we saw conviction win out against the risk of pride. Ted was so sure he could pick up a bat and hit line drives cold it probably didn't occur to him he might look foolish in front of his whole team. No other manager was better at leading by example.

Charlie Beamon

Right-handed pitcher

1956–58: ....**Baltimore Orioles**
Career Statistics: ....**3–3, 0 saves, 3.91 ERA**

Ted Williams vs. Charlie Beamon

4-for-9, 1 double, 4 RBI, 0 walks, 0 strikeouts, 1 double play, .444 batting average, .444 on-base percentage, .556 slugging percentage

Charlie Beamon

YEAR	DATE	RESULT
1957	April 16	Fly out
	April 22	Fly out
1958	April 23	Fly out
		Single (1 RBI)
	May 9	Single (2 RBI)
		Single
	July 3	Double (1 RBI)
		Grounded into DP
		Ground out

IT WAS A serious situation [the first time I faced Williams]. I believe that I came in relief with a couple of men on. He just looked so relaxed. And I mean, I was really impressed; I had read so much about him, and this was the first time I had a chance to pitch against him.

I was pretty relaxed, though. I had a good sinker—a real good sinker—and Ted, to me, seemed to be a high-ball hitter from the few times I had seen him hit. So I just kept the ball down low on him. He hit it *very* hard, but it was right at somebody; you know, a ground ball.

But that was about it. I was very impressed with him, because he didn't waste any motion. When he moved, he swung the bat. I admired him more than anything from what I had read and seen.

If he wasn't going to swing, he wasn't going to [use] a lot of [motion]. But he picked that ball up real quick, and when he committed himself . . . boom! That was that. He was all about hitting. He wasn't about looking pretty and all that stuff, even though he did have a beautiful swing.

You had to watch him [when pitching], because he would move a little farther out of that on-deck circle to where he could really see the spin of the ball. When I came in and warmed up, he had moved over a little bit, but the umpire told him to get back in there—back in the on-deck circle.

But he was a keen observer of the game and had a real sharp mind; any advantage that he could get, he took. He was just tremendous.

When I got to the big leagues, I knew I was ready. I had been in the minors for three or four years and had pitched against some real good hitters in the Coast League—nothing like Williams—but I had faced some good hitters.

They didn't say too much [on how to pitch Williams], but the starting pitchers would talk about how they were going to pitch to hitters. So they didn't say too much to me; I just kind of observed and took it all in, picking up what I could. I knew what got me to the big leagues, and I was not going to change my way. I'd match my strength against any of them, including Ted Williams. I had an excellent changeup, too; so when I got behind, I'd throw changeups and different stuff.

[Our team used the Williams shift as well.] Waaaay over; the second baseman was almost next to the first baseman, and the shortstop was on the other side of second base (the right field side). But he was so quick; I mean [you knew] he was going to pull the ball. Half the time—even with the shift—he hit the ball so hard, he'd hit it right to them. It didn't matter.

I never got a chance to talk with him, but as far as talking with fans and kids—he really talked a lot with kids when I'd seen him. Sometimes coming into the ballpark, there he'd be, talking to three or four kids on the way into the park. He was quiet but very friendly to players and kids. I don't think he liked the media too much, but they were kind of weird anyway. Everybody wanted a story, which is okay; everybody has their purpose.

Ted was really something special. He was an outstanding hitter. He wouldn't swing at bad pitches and the umpires would not call a strike on him if he didn't swing. He was very patient, and he had a real good attitude about things, as far as the umpires and stuff like that. If they happened to call something he didn't think was a strike, he never said anything. All he needed was one pitch anyway, you know [laughs]. Yeah, he was a tremendous hitter.

He was alright. Ted was the man.

Ted Bowsfield

Left-handed pitcher

1958–60: ....**Boston Red Sox**
1960: ....**Cleveland Indians**
1961–62: ....**Los Angeles Angels**
1963–64: ....**Kansas City Athletics**
Career Statistics: ....**37–39, 6 saves, 4.35 ERA**

Ted Williams vs. Ted Bowsfield

0-for-2, 0 RBI, 0 walks, 1 strikeout, .000 batting average, .000 on-base percentage, .000 slugging percentage

Ted Bowsfield

YEAR	DATE	RESULT
1960	June 18	Strikeout
	July 24	Fly out

I ONLY FACED TED Williams twice in my career. In regards to my strategy against him, I don't think many teams had a strategy as far as how they were going to pitch to him. I think the general consensus was that you tried to get him out with your best stuff, whether it be a fastball or breaking ball. There was no point in trying to nibble around the plate, because if Ted took the pitch, the umpires generally called it a ball.

Generally, pitching to Williams was based on game situations. For example, when we played the Yankees in Yankee Stadium and in Boston, Jackie Jensen—a fine right fielder for the Sox—always hit in the No. 4 slot behind Williams. [Yankees manager Casey] Stengel, if the game were on the line, would always walk Williams and pitch to Jensen. I think the results were more favorable to the Yankees than they were to the Red Sox in those situations. Teams like Cleveland did use the Williams shift, but a lot of teams didn't, because he was such a great hitter that he'd usually hit the location of the pitch to any part of the field. This happened more as he got older.

Was he the toughest out I ever faced? Of course! I'm glad I didn't have to face him too often, but Al Kaline was the toughest batter for me.[2]

I faced a lot of great hitters [in my career]. Not all of them during regular season—some in spring training. But the likes of Willie Mays, Stan Musial, Mickey Mantle, Harmon Killebrew, Harvey Kuenn, Yogi Berra, Elston Howard—all of those players were great hitters. Mays was probably the best all-around player; Mantle would be a close second.

It was an honor to just watch Williams hit in 1958, '59, and '60, even as the years were getting on for him. In spring training, if we were left behind, we would pitch batting practice to Williams. For it to be a challenge, he would make the conditions always be Game 7 of the World Series, winning run on base, 3–2 on the hitter, and he would tell us to throw any pitch we wanted. I can remember Bill Monbouquette, and I did this several times with him. It was great fun and, of course, a great learning experience.

Ted was a good friend for a long time. Our paths continued to cross in Anaheim [while I was their traveling secretary] when he managed the Washington Senators, and in Seattle, when I managed the Kingdome [as the stadium director], he would stop by on his way to Alaska on fishing trips. The end of his life saddened me a great deal, because he was a wonderful man, not always understood. He didn't care for the press very much, but he was a wonderful teammate and treated everybody who played with him just great.

---

[2] In 34 plate appearances, Al Kaline went 8–25, with 1 home run, 5 RBI, 2 walks, 0 strikeouts, a .320 batting average, .370 on-base percentage, and .680 slugging percentage.

FACING TED WILLIAMS

Williams always said that it was easier to hit when you faced the same pitcher four times, like he did a lot in his early career. He maintained it was getting tougher to hit when he had to face three or four pitchers [in one game] later in his career.

The one thing he mentioned to me was that the pitchers who gave him the most trouble was the ones that had good control and changed speeds. The toughest pitcher he said he ever faced was Herb Score.[3] It's too bad that Herb has passed away, because I'm sure he would have had some great stories regarding their match-ups.

---

[3] In 34 plate appearances against Score, Williams went 6–25, with 4 home runs, 7 RBI, 9 walks, 2 strikeouts, a .240 batting average, .441 on-base percentage, and .760 slugging percentage.

Dick Brodowski

Right-handed pitcher

1952, 1955: ....Boston Red Sox
1956–57: ....Washington Senators
1958–59: .... Cleveland Indians
Career Statistics: .... 9–11, 5 saves, 4.76 ERA

Ted Williams vs. Dick Brodowski

1-for-1, 0 extra-base hits, 0 RBI, 2 walks, 0 strikeouts, 1.000 batting average, 1.000 on-base percentage, 1.000 slugging percentage

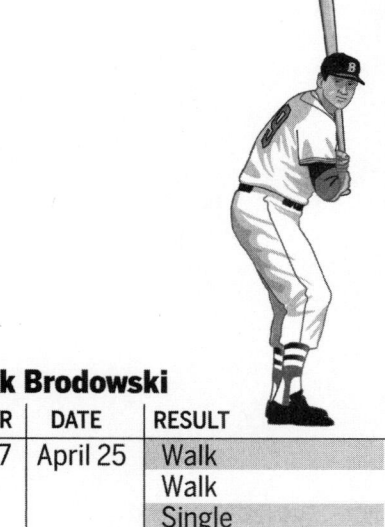

Dick Brodowski

YEAR	DATE	RESULT
1957	April 25	Walk
		Walk
		Single

MY MEETINGS WITH Ted were only a few, but they were very exciting, because I was nineteen years old and Ted was already a legend. He had a great personality and was a great guy.

I met him in the spring of 1952, which was my first opportunity to go to a major league spring training camp. In June of 1952, I came up to the Red Sox and he wasn't there—I believe he went to Korea in 1952.[4]

In spring training of 1955—I went into the military in 1952 and 1954 (drafted)—I always remembered that he would check every pitch the pitcher threw and what his

---

[4] Williams only played in six games in 1952 before being recalled to active duty to serve in the Korean War.

best pitch was, so if a pitcher was to get beat, he was to get beat on his best pitch. That made hitting much easier for him.

I remember facing him in spring training—I [think] in San Diego—but what we were doing there I don't know. I decided that I would throw pitches I didn't normally throw. I threw a nothing fastball, knuckleball slider, and fastball, and he hit a topspin ground ball through the right side. Also, the hit during the season was the same—which ain't bad for a "Triple-A" pitcher. I think we all used the Williams shift—he usually hit that way [right side]. The middle of every lineup was my toughest out.

I enjoyed the year of 1955; to watch Ted play ball for a full season . . . and it was an all-star season!

Bob Bruce

Right-handed pitcher

1959–61:	**Detroit Tigers**
1962–66:	**Houston Colt .45s/Astros**
1967:	**Atlanta Braves**
Career Statistics:	**49–71, 1 save, 3.85 ERA**

Ted Williams vs. Bob Bruce

2-for-5, 1 home run, 1 RBI, 1 walk, 1 strikeout, .400 batting average, .500 on-base percentage, 1.000 slugging percentage

Home Runs Allowed:

No. 505, June 30, 1960, at Boston

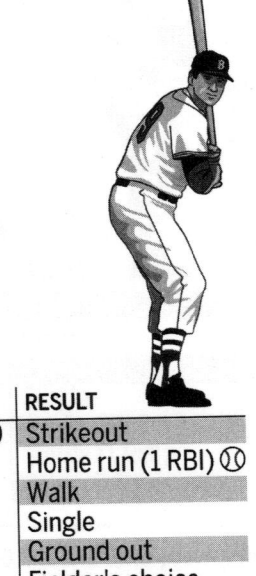

Bob Bruce

YEAR	DATE	RESULT
1960	June 30	Strikeout
		Home run (1 RBI) ⑩
	Aug. 31	Walk
		Single
		Ground out
		Fielder's choice

I REMEMBER TED WILLIAMS well. He was the best hitter I ever saw. I was a rookie with the Tigers when I first started against Boston.

Clem Labine and I were new teammates—I being a rookie and Clem a proven veteran. Clem was a locker mate of mine, and before the game, he leaned over and whispered, "Do you realize you and I are the only pitchers on the Detroit staff that Williams does not have in his book [referring to home runs]?" To make a long story short, I struck him out the first time up. The second at-bat, he hit the ball 400 feet for a homer.

Gene Conley

Right-handed pitcher

1952:	Brooklyn Dodgers
1953–58:	Milwaukee Braves
1959–60:	Philadelphia Phillies
1961–63:	Boston Red Sox
Career Statistics:	91–96, 9 saves, 3.82 ERA
National League All-Star:	1954, 1955, 1959

Ted Williams vs. Gene Conley in All-Star Games

0-for-1

1959: With the American League leading 3–1 in the fifth inning with one out and a runner on first, Williams struck out vs. Conley

Q. What was your strategy against Williams, and how do you think you fared?

A. Real good. Ha.

Gene Conley

YEAR	DATE	RESULT
1959	All-Star Game	Strikeout

I SPENT SEVEN YEARS in the National League. The year I was traded to the American League (1961), Williams had just retired. I was given his locker, however, right next to Frank Malzone.

He had left his bat and a few t-shirts in his locker. The bat was the [one he hit his] last home run on at the end of 1960. I gave the bat away to a kid in Rhode Island, and my wife didn't speak to me for a long time. (She read it was worth several thousand dollars later on. Ha. Oh well.)

It's hard for me to compare, as in the fifties there was some great hitters, which I'm sure you must know. From what I hear from [ballplayers] that I've talked to, he was probably the best of all the greats in the fifties. I feel like I didn't need the challenge.

Frank Malzone told me he played pepper[8] with him a lot. When Williams was finished with the pepper game, there would be just one spot on his bat where the ball always hit. I would say that must have been great hand-and-eye [coordination], especially playing pepper, when the throws weren't always strikes.

---

[8] Pepper is a game where one player hits ground balls to a group of fielders who are standing close by.

Glenn Cox

Right-handed pitcher

1955–58: ....**Kansas City Athletics**
Career Statistics: .... **1–4, 0 saves, 6.39 ERA**

Ted Williams vs. Glenn Cox

0-for-2, 1 walk (intentional), 1 strikeout, .000 batting average, .333 on-base percentage, .000 slugging percentage

Glenn Cox

YEAR	DATE	RESULT
1957	July 24	Ground out
	July 25	Intentional walk
		Strikeout

WHEN I PITCHED against Ted Williams, it wasn't the way that you have it here.[9]

I came in with no outs. The first batter who I pitched against was Ted Williams.[10] I'd heard that, from other pitchers, if the ball was not perfect—on the corner or something—that the umpire gave him a break.

So my first pitch was a fastball—a good fastball—right on the outside corner. The umpire called it ball one.

Well, I was young and cocky. So I wound up, and the next

---

[9] At the time of my letter to Cox, Retrosheet.org only had Williams' appearance against Cox on July 24, 1957. The other game—July 25, 1957—was missing from their data and was only recently added.

[10] In the game on July 24, Williams was the first batter Cox faced when entering the game. Williams grounded out to first base in that appearance. In the game on July 25, the at-bat Cox describes came with two out in the seventh inning.

pitch was beautiful, right on the outside corner, and Ted just looked at it. Ball two.

So I walked in, which you're not supposed to do, but I kept my mouth shut. I just walked in, and I think the umpire, I remember the name—well I did remember the name—but I walked in and got about five feet from home plate, and the umpire said, "You open your mouth punk and you're gone."[11]

I never said a word. And I walked a couple more feet and turned around and started back towards the mound. I turned around and Ted Williams was there, and I said, "Ted, I'm going to tell you what's coming, and you still can't hit me." This is all true. I said, "I'm going to throw you nothing but fastballs."

And I walked [back] to the mound. The next pitch was a little bit above the waist and he swung and fouled it off. And then he fouled off another pitch.

He didn't realize that I had a good screwball. And the next pitch, well, I made a perfect pitch and he swung and missed it. He just stood there and looked at me. I know he thought I threw him a spitter[12] or something, because that sucker just went *pshoo*. It's just like yesterday that it happened.

He was probably one of the great hitters that ever played the game. I just believed in myself, I guess.

---

[11] As per baseball-reference.com, the home plate umpire for the game was Larry Napp.
[12] Spitball

Bud Daley

Left-handed pitcher

1955–57: .... Cleveland Indians
1958–61: .... Kansas City Athletics
1961–64: .... New York Yankees
Career Statistics: .... 60–64, 10 saves, 4.03 ERA
American League All-Star: 1959, 1960

Ted Williams vs. Bud Daley

9-for-24, 2 doubles, 2 home runs, 7 RBI, 3 walks, 4 strikeouts, 4 hit by pitches, .375 batting average, .516 on-base percentage, 1.224 slugging percentage

Home Runs Allowed:

No. 502, June 21, 1960, at Kansas City
No. 503, June 21, 1960, at Kansas City

I DON'T KNOW IF you remember the old Kansas City ballpark, but it had two fences. It had one down below then a hill up, and a fence up on top, so people couldn't look in.

Anyway, I'm pitching one night and we score six runs in the first inning, and Williams is the first hitter in the second inning.[13] I called the catcher[14] out and said, "Hey, I've never thrown a slider and I've been working on it. Let's throw him a slider." So I threw him a slider and he hit it over the fence for a home run.

---

[13] On June 21, 1960, the A's scored five runs in the bottom of the first. Williams, who batted third, had hit in the first inning and grounded out. Daley retired the first eleven batters, with Williams coming up with two out in the fourth.
[14] Harry Chiti

Bud Daley

YEAR	DATE	RESULT
1957	May 22	Walk
		Single
		Hit by pitch
	June 20	Reached on error
	Aug. 22	Single (1 RBI)
1958	July 16	Strikeout
		Hit by pitch
	Sept. 18	Double
		Ground out
		Hit by pitch
		Ground out
1959	July 25	Single
	Aug. 19	Strikeout
		Fly out
		Strikeout
		Line out

YEAR	DATE	RESULT
1960	June 21	Ground out
		Home run (1 RBI)
		Home run (2 RBI)
		Single
	July 2	Foul out
		Foul out
		Walk
		Walk
		Double (2 RBI)
	July 15	Hit by pitch
		Ground out
		Ground out
		Single
		Strikeout
	Sept. 9	Ground out

So in the ninth inning he comes up, and the score is 10–1.[15] I told the catcher, I said I'm going to try that slider again. This time he hit it over the second fence. There've only been two homers hit over that fence.

The catcher comes out and says, "I think you better work on that pitch some more." I think that was the last slider I ever threw.

---

[15] It was actually the sixth inning with the score 8–1.

The first time I ever faced Ted Williams was in Boston, and I had two strikes on him. I threw a fastball right down the middle. He took it, and the umpire said ball.

So the next inning, I come out to bat. The catcher is out talking to the pitcher. I said to the umpire, "Hey, what was the matter with the pitch to Williams? It was right down the middle."

He says, "Son, let me tell you. People don't come here to see him strike out, they come here to see him hit."

I didn't realize he hit that much off of me, because I don't really remember him really hurting me in a ball game. [Actually,] I don't *ever* remember hitting him. That was the thing that really shocked me. I don't remember hitting him, and I'm sure I never hit him with a fastball.

I know he told me one time, "Your curveball is the hardest curveball to hit I've ever seen." He says, "Most curveballs come in and they kind of stop. Yours just keeps going and going and going." But I guess, apparently, he didn't have too much trouble.

One day we were warming up. You know how the pitchers catch the ball in for the outfielder during infield practice? Well, Williams is standing right behind me warming up, and I'm catching the balls from the outfield. He says, "Hey, Bud." I turn around and he says, "Watch this."

And he threw this little-bitty curveball that broke about three or four inches, and says, "You know what? I should have been a pitcher. I think I wasted a good career."[16]

---

[16] In his career, Ted Williams had one pitching performance. He pitched two innings, gave up three hits, one earned run, and one strikeout, finishing with a 4.50 ERA.

He was a heck of a nice guy. I really liked him. I think he's the best hitter I ever saw, [although] I wasn't as worried with him as I was with a couple [of] other guys.

I don't remember pitching to him too much, but when he came up, evidently I wasn't in a jam. But I would probably say that if I found myself in a jam, then I would have been really concerned . . . but hell, when you're up 10–1, you're not worried about it.

I always say that the best hitter I ever saw was Ted Williams; the most power was always Mickey Mantle; and the best all-around player I ever saw was Willie Mays.

Jim Derrington

Left-handed pitcher

1956–57: .... **Chicago White Sox**
Career Statistics: .... **0–2, 0 saves, 5.23 ERA**

Ted Williams vs. Jim Derrington

0-for-1, 0 RBI, 1 walk, 0 strikeouts, .000 batting average, .500 on-base percentage, .000 slugging percentage

THAT WAS A very long time ago. I do remember the time Williams grounded out to our first baseman, Walt Dropo. Williams hit it so hard that Dropo came by the mound and reminded me that he had a wife and family back in Chicago and to try and pitch Williams outside.

Our pitchers seemed to agree that the best way to pitch to him was to keep the ball low and hope he got a single. As you know, I only faced Williams twice [in my career]. For me, the toughest of the great hitters that I faced was Al Kaline.

Jim Derrington

YEAR	DATE	RESULT
1957	June 27	Walk
		Ground out

Chuck Estrada

Right-handed pitcher

1960–64: .... **Baltimore Orioles**
1966: .... **Chicago Cubs**
1967: .... **New York Mets**
American League All-Star: **1960**
Career Statistics: .... **50–44, 2 saves, 4.07 ERA**

Ted Williams vs. Chuck Estrada

4-for-7, 1 double, 2 home runs, 6 RBI, 2 walks, 1 strikeout, .571 batting average, .667 on-base percentage, 1.571 slugging percentage

Home Runs Allowed:

No. 514, August 20, 1960 (Game 1) at Baltimore
No. 515, August 20, 1960 (Game 1) at Baltimore

WELL, THERE'S A great story that I tell when I talk to different organizations about Ted.

What happened was, when I first got to the big leagues before my first start, I pitched in relief two or three times. So, I pitched in relief in Boston my third time out before I got my first start.[17] And we were in Fenway and had a six-run lead—a six- or five-run lead in the sixth inning and the phone rang and the manager of the team said just get some work in.[18] So I was just down there throwing.

Anyway, Boston ended up getting the bases loaded with nobody out. So as the story goes, they eventually called me in. Anyway, I struck out

---

[17] Estrada actually pitched in relief three times to start his career in 1960, then got two starts in early May before being used in relief in Boston on May 15, in the second game of a doubleheader.
[18] Baltimore led, 7–2.

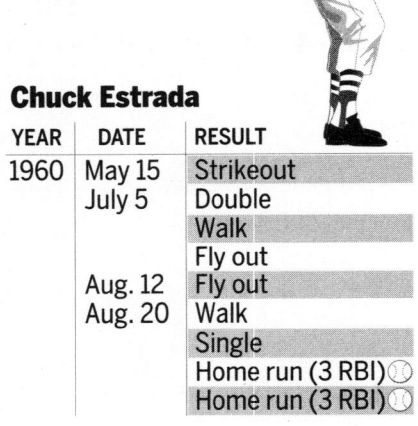

the first hitter and popped up the second hitter behind home plate.[19] And lo and behold I called time out and I was walking back to the mound and Brooks Robinson, our third baseman, came over and says, "Hey, Chuck, how are you going to pitch *this* guy?" I say, "what are you talking about?" He said, "Turn around." Well, it was Ted.[20] So I said, "Hell if I know, but I'm going to find out [laughs]."

So anyway, as the story goes, I got fortunate and struck him out with the bases loaded to end the inning. And the fans gave me a standing ovation for striking out the greatest hitter ever, right?

Chuck Estrada

YEAR	DATE	RESULT
1960	May 15	Strikeout
	July 5	Double
		Walk
		Fly out
	Aug. 12	Fly out
	Aug. 20	Walk
		Single
		Home run (3 RBI)
		Home run (3 RBI)

Well, that's not the funny part of the story.

The next day—they don't do this anymore—but during the infield, like they did in the old days, I was on the Boston side of the infield. And we were doing our infield drills warming up and I was shagging balls for the fungo hitter to left field. And all of a sudden I hear this voice.

"Hey, kid."

And I'm saying to myself, *I ain't no damn kid.* But anyway, that voice says, "Hey, kid!"

So now I get a little upset and I turn around and it's Ted. And he said, "I want to tell you one thing." And I said, "What?" And he said, "You're going to be one hell of a pitcher." And that's what I remember about Ted [laughs].

---

[19] Estrada relieved Hal Brown after Boston loaded the bases on two singles and an error. Estrada then struck out Lou Clinton and got Gary Geiger to pop to the second baseman.
[20] Williams was pinch-hitting for pitcher Dave Hillman.

But I was fortunate enough to see his last at-bat, hit the home run off of Jack Fischer. They say he tore his uniform off, went down the runway, and said that's it. But even at that age, whatever it was, I couldn't believe how quick a bat he still had. Even though I struck him out—of course I was blessed with a very good arm—but at that time I had no clue what was going on. I was just amazed at how fast his bat still was, because I was a fastball pitcher.

So anyway, that's the story I tell everybody. As I look back now as I'm an old man, and I say, that was quite a story. As far as I knew, I was just trying to get an out.

No, I didn't have a scouting report. I can still see the four pitches I threw. I went strike one away. I went strike two away. I threw him a high fastball that he swung at. And I swear to God I could just hear that bat, and he fouled it off. Then the next pitch I threw a fastball down and away and he took it for strike three.

I was just a raw kid. I'm a country boy. And I thought, *wow, this is something special.*

I was in the dugout [for Williams' last game]. He was amazing. It was just a beautiful swing. Well, most left-handers have that, but not like *him*. But he was a real treat to try to get out.

That was later in the year [he hit home runs off him]. Hey, he's the best ever. He's going to get you. To be perfectly honest with you, the wind was blowing out to right field and I thought they were just fly ball outs. And it got up into that wind and they ended up two home runs in the right-field bleachers in Fenway. So he got back at me.

I don't remember if we won the game or not, but the bottom line is I was fortunate enough to play against some really great players.[21]

---

[21] Estrada and Baltimore lost, 8–6, as Williams had a pair of three-run homers.

His numbers proved that. Amazing. I've just never seen anybody with that quick a bat. Even at *his* age, then. So I hate to guess what he was like when he was young. I faced some great players in my career before I got hurt, but Ted was the one I always remember.

I never talked to him. The one thing that Ted always did, though, especially at the end of his career, they used to have . . . he would send people over and say if you want an autographed picture of me I'll sign it. But I was totally against hitters then and I didn't. All the other players did. I said to hell with him. But it was a treat.

From all the stories, the shift didn't matter. They did shift, but they didn't play deep enough [laughs]. Because he defied you. He'd hit the ball so damn hard it would sink over your head. Most guys the ball would rise. But he would get topspin and it's amazing how he'd get a ball on the ground and it would pick up speed, because he had a great top hand. That always amazed me. Balls would just shoot through the infield. And I'd see balls go head high over the infield and just hook down into the ground because he had so much topspin. Those are the things I remember about Ted.

I'd hate to even guess what he was like even in the prime of his career.

When Ted hit the ball there was that sound, that sound that very few players had in the time I was there. You *knew* who was hitting. Just by the sound you'd say, oh, Ted is hitting [laughs] and you'd turn around and sure as heck.

I can tell you a funny story about Ted, though. We were playing a game in Baltimore and Piersall was playing center field. And Baltimore had a little quirky left field. Ted came in and the ball was hit down the left-field line. And if it got past the outfielder it would curve around the fence, you know. Well, Piersall never left center field. There was a ball hit down the line and Ted couldn't get to it. So he ran over and just stopped and the ball went around and Piersall still sat in center field. And they had a little discussion about not backing him up. I don't know if they got along very well.[22]

Yeah, I wish I could have played against him when he was in his prime. That would have been fun. I would have done what I did with everybody. First thing I found out was can they hit my fastball. That's the first thing I always did. I never listened to, this guy does this. I learned at a very young age find out for yourself. They say, well, you can't throw this guy a fastball. I found out early in my career that I'm going to find out if he can hit *my* fastball before I decide to throw other pitches. Because I got burnt.

I think that's what he did when he came up to pitch it. Because I was a rookie and they didn't know who the hell I was. When I came in with the bases loaded, he wanted to see what this guy has got, his history. And he found out [laughs]. The story that he told me the next day at the time I didn't think much of it, but now that I'm old I think it's pretty cool.

---

[22] Piersall was not on Boston in 1960, which was Estrada's rookie year, so this could well be a story told to him by someone else, or it was a different center fielder.

Bob Feller

Right-handed pitcher

1936–1941, 1945–1956: ....Cleveland Indians
Career Statistics: .... 266–162, 21 saves, 3.25 ERA
American League All-Star: 1938–1941, 1946–1948, 1950
Elected to the National Baseball Hall of Fame in 1962

Ted Williams vs. Bob Feller (incomplete data)

43-for-129, 10 doubles, 2 triples, 9 home runs,[23] 23 RBI,[24] 34 walks (5 intentional), 10 strikeouts, .333 batting average, .472 on-base percentage, .651 slugging percentage

Home Runs Allowed:

No. 131, May 4, 1946, at Boston
No. 141, June 12, 1946, at Boston
No. 203, May 9, 1948 (game one),[25] at Boston
No. 210, June 16, 1948, at Cleveland
No. 227, May 5, 1949, at Cleveland
No. 330, August 30, 1953, at Cleveland
No. 351, July 22, 1954 (game one), at Boston
No. 353, July 29, 1954, at Cleveland
No. 374, June 19, 1955, at Boston
No. 416, September 15, 1956, at Cleveland

---

[23] Of the known available box scores, Williams hit nine home runs off Feller. But the data is available for all of Williams' 521 career home runs, and he ended up with 10 off Feller.

[24] Retrosheet.org has more data of Williams vs. Feller, but does not include RBI. Baseball-reference.com lists Williams with 23 RBI in 72 at-bats (90 plate appearances) vs. Feller.

[25] This states that the home run in question was part of a doubleheader.

Bob Feller (data incomplete; missing 1939-'41, 1946-'47)

YEAR	DATE	RESULT
1948	May 9	Line out
		Home run (1 RBI)
		Walk
		Strikeout
	June 10	Walk
		Single
	June 16	Single
		Double
		Double
		Home run (2 RBI)
	July 31	Single (1 RBI)
		Walk
		Fly out
	Sept. 22	Fly out
		Fly out
		Line out
		Ground out
1949	May 5	Walk
		Grounded into DP
		Fly out
		Home run (1 RBI)
	June 1	Fly out
		Ground out
		Single
		Single (1 RBI)
	June 14	Walk
		Double (1 RBI)
		Strikeout
		Ground out
		Single (2 RBI)
	July 29	Walk
		Fly out
		Fly out
	Aug. 29	Single
		Ground out
		Double (RBI)
		Fly out
	Sept. 21	Sacrifice fly (1 RBI)
1950	May 3	Ground out
		Fly out
		Single
	June 2	Walk
		Fly out
	June 13	Intentional walk
		Single (1 RBI)
		Fielder's choice
1951	May 1	Strikeout
		Ground out
		Walk
		Ground out
	May 19	Grounded into DP
		Walk
		Single
		Single
	June 8	Ground out
		Fly out
		Walk
		Strikeout
	June 18	Fly out
		Fly out
		Single
		Fly out
		Walk
	July 17	Fly out
		Foul out
		Ground out
		Ground out
	July 28	Double (1 RBI)
	Aug. 26	Double
		Double
		Fielder's choice
1953	Aug. 30	Home run (1 RBI)
		Walk
		Fly out
1954	July 22	Fielder's choice
		Walk
		Home run (2 RBI)
		Walk
		Fly out
	July 29	Home run (2 RBI)
		Walk
1955	June 19	Home run (2 RBI)
	July 27	Strikeout
	Aug. 23	Intentional walk
1956	June 11	Double
		Walk
	Sept. 15	Strikeout
		Fly out
		Home run (3 RBI)
		Grounded into DP

WHEN HE FIRST came up, he was a dead low-ball hitter, and you had to pitch him high and tight. . . . And after he was up there about a year, why he got to be fouling off the high fastball. He always was a better low ball hitter throughout his career. You had to throw strikes to him. He would not swing at a ball unless it was over the plate—or he thought it was. He *seldom* ever took a called third strike that I know of.

If he got back too far [in the count], you'd try to throw a slider and catch the outside corner. . . . And you'd only throw the fastball inside to him so he couldn't get the barrel of the bat on the ball. He was a very good fastball hitter. Trying to throw a fastball by him was like trying to sneak a sunbeam past a rooster in the morning . . . very difficult. He might not hit it square, but he would certainly foul it back. He'd seldom miss. Most of your home run hitters are fastball hitters. He hit 10 home runs off me during his career, and his batting average against me was around .241 or .242, as far as I know.

Did our team use the Williams shift? Yes we did. [Actually,] we invented it, [though] it didn't effect him too much.[26] He'd hit those sinkers over the infield—those line drive sinkers—or hit one out of the ballpark.

The Boudreau shift didn't really hurt him any, as far as his average went. I only once saw him hit the ball to left field, which was a home run in Cleveland in our old ballpark—Old League Park. We had the shift on, the Williams shift, and he hit one purposely down the left field line about 10 feet fair for an inside-the-park home run.[27]

Was he the toughest out [I ever faced]? No, I had a dozen fellows that were tougher than Ted. A lot of left-hand hitters like Tommy Henrich and Taft Wright, Stan Spence and Roy Cullenbine, who was a switch-hitter, Johnny Pesky, Nellie Fox, Rip Radcliff—they were all tougher than Ted. DiMaggio hit me pretty good [as well]. He liked the ball away and he had a stance where you couldn't pitch to him inside, because he would have got hit if the ball got away from you. He would not move. He was anchored right there at the plate and he wouldn't get out of the way of the ball, so you had to be careful if you tried to

---

[26] The shift used against Ted was created by Indians manager Lou Boudreau after game one of a doubleheader between Cleveland and Boston in July of 1946. It was known as the "Boudreau" or "Williams" shift.

[27] On September 13, 1946, Williams hit an inside-the-park home run at Cleveland against Red Embree in the top of the first inning in a 1–0 Boston victory. It was the only inside-the-park home run of Williams' career.

pitch him inside, as you were very apt to hit him. He was very close to the plate.

Ted hit as well as any hitter in any [era]. He was very good in the clutch, like he was in the 1941 All-Star Game.[28] Williams went 4–4, including a three-run home run off a blooper pitch thrown by Pittsburgh's Rip Sewell in the bottom of the eighth inning during the 1946 All-Star Game in Fenway.

[Ted] was a good friend of mine. We were very friendly socially away from the ballpark and even at the ballpark before the game. He spent quite a bit of time at my museum out in Iowa and helped me raise money to finish the museum—he and his son, John Henry.

Ted was three months older than me. He came up in 1939, and I came up in 1936,[29] though I didn't start pitching regularly until 1937. I got in a month and a week in 1936, and I became a regular pitcher in 1937, even though I missed a month because I slipped during a wet opening day game in Cleveland and tore up some ligaments in my elbow. I was out about a month in 1937, so I didn't pitch all that much. My first complete year of pitching, taking my turn every day, was 1938.

I have no idea why he didn't hit a home run off me before the war, but he just didn't do it; though he hit 10 home runs off me in my last ten years.

I only struck him out two or three times that I can remember. The first time was in Cleveland. It was just after the war or just before the war. He was very difficult to strike out. I'd throw him a changeup around his ankles and he'd pull it foul, and then I'd throw a slider around his fists—right around his belly button, around the belt buckle—and that was a good pitch for him. I don't know how many times he struck out

---

[28] Williams hit a game-winning three-run home run off the NL's Clause Passeau in the bottom of the ninth inning to give the AL a 7–5 win.

[29] At the age of seventeen.

in his career, but it couldn't have been many.[30] DiMaggio was tough to strike out, too, but Ted was a much better hitter and had more power, but he was not much of an outfielder when you got him out of Boston. He was a good outfielder in Fenway Park.

He had good, quick wrists and was a big, strong guy, and he had a big, heavy bat that he could handle very well, like a toothpick. He could hit to left field if he wanted to, but he rarely wanted to.

He was seldom called out on strikes. The umpires respected him. I never thought that the umpires gave him the benefit of the doubt. I never had any problem with that, not at all. I always thought the umpires were calling it right when Ted was up to bat while I was pitching. As far as I'm concerned, he didn't get any favorable calls. He had a good eye and very good hand-eye coordination, which is what made him so great.

---

[30] Williams struck out 709 times in 9,791 plate appearances. He struck out over 50 times in a season just three times, and all of those occasions occurred prior to World War II, in three of his first four seasons in the majors.

Don Ferrarese

Left-handed pitcher

1955–57:	**Baltimore Orioles**
1958–59:	**Cleveland Indians**
1960:	**Chicago White Sox**
1961–62:	**Philadelphia Phillies**
1962:	**St. Louis Cardinals**
Career Statistics:	**19–36, 5 saves, 4.00 ERA**

Ted Williams vs. Don Ferrarese

1-for-7, 0 extra-base hits, 0 RBI, 2 walks, 1 strikeout, .143 batting average, .333 on-base percentage, .143 slugging percentage

Don Ferrarese

YEAR	DATE	RESULT
1956	June 30	Single
		Ground out
		Walk
	July 8	Line out
	Sept. 2	Fly out
1957	April 23	Ground out
1958	Aug. 21	Fly out
1959	July 18	Strikeout
		Walk

HE [TED] GAVE me a big picture that he signed, I'm looking at in my office right now, and on the bottom, it says, "Tell him he can stick his curveball up his ass."

In 1956, my first start was against Cleveland, and I struck out 13 and was a big hero. My second start, I had a no-hitter against the Yankees, beating them 1–0[31] and was on the Ed Sullivan show. My third start was against Detroit, and I again did well.[32] In my fourth start, I faced Ted in Fenway. Of course, he had just

---

[31] Ferrarese actually had a no-hitter through eight innings, but Andy Carey led off the ninth with a single. He finished with a two-hitter.

[32] Ferrarese had a shutout through eight innings, but he'd be pulled after allowing two runs in the ninth in an eventual 3–2 loss.

come back from the Marine Corps. As he was going out to left field, he passed me and said, "Hey, you're the kid I hear who has the good curveball."

So anyhow, we did the shift and Billy Gardner was our second baseman, playing way out in short right field. Ted comes up to bat, and I throw him a curveball, and he stood up there and didn't make a move. Just took it, strike one. And the second one, strike two. Never moved at all.

I'm sure other people have told you that when he was ready to swing, he swung; and if he didn't, he wouldn't lunge. No lunging. The third time, he hit the son of a bitch so hard that he knocked Gardner over, and he snow-coned it. The force of it knocked him over. He knocked the crap out of it. Gardner said, "Jesus, you sure didn't fool him, did you?"

And as he rounded first, he spit in the air and looked at me and said something. Mickey Vernon was our first baseman. I asked him, "What'd he say?" Vernon said, "Tell that little shit to stick his curveball up his ass."[33]

That was my story with Ted. I did know his dad, Sam, by the way. He passed away in Walnut Creek, California. My dad had a liquor store in Walnut Creek, and Sam used to get letters from Ted, and he used to share them with me. I was playing in the minors at the time and whenever Sam had a letter, he'd let me read it. I don't think they were very close, but they did communicate.

I didn't really know Ted because I only pitched against him a couple times. It's interesting that I pitched against him seven times. I didn't know that; I don't remember all that stuff. I didn't even know that I struck him out.

---

[33] The game Ferrarse is likely referring to was on July 8, 1956, when, in a 4–4 tie in the fourth inning with two out and runners on the corners, Williams is credited by retrosheet.org with a line out to second base. Mickey Vernon was the Red Sox first baseman that day (he never played for the Orioles); Gus Triandos was at first for Baltimore.

He sure was a hitter. His hitting was unbelievable. I'm sure they'll tell you, too, that the umpires had a hard time . . . you had a hard time striking him out. I mean, they wouldn't call him out. Ed Runge got his butt chewed out as a rookie umpire when he called him out on a called third strike. The commissioner[34] gave him hell because they came to see Ted hit. They didn't publicize that, but that was the story amongst the ballplayers.

Even the great pitchers—like I played with Robin Roberts—and Williams said that Roberts was known for his control, and he used to get pitches. You earn that, I guess, and he certainly earned it. But he was a hell of a hitter. He loved to talk hitting with the guys.

As far as pitching him, I remember Gary Bell of Cleveland when we were in Cleveland together. Gary had struck him out four times in a game that went extra innings, and Ted was on deck waiting to hit, and he was taking that bat and twisting it around like he was making powder out of the damn thing. He couldn't wait to hit against Gary Bell . . . and he ended up hitting a home run off of him.[35]

He was definitely a special guy.

---

[34] Ed Runge was a rookie umpire in 1954, and the commissioner at the time was Ford Frick.

[35] The game Ferrarese refers to is likely from August 3, 1958, when Williams hit a home run in the top of the ninth off Bell. (Bell only allowed one other home run to Williams, and it was in the third inning of a game on June 28, 1959.) However, Bell did not strike out Williams on August 3, 1958. He did strike Williams out twice on two occasions: June 24, 1958—Williams' last at-bat that day was a single in the seventh, and September 12, 1958—Williams' last at-bat that day was a single in the eighth. Retrosheet.org does not show Bell ever facing Williams in extra innings, and the only time he faced Williams in the ninth inning was then he hit the home run on August 3, 1958.

Bill Fischer

Right-handed pitcher

1956–58: .... **Chicago White Sox**
1958: .... **Detroit Tigers**
1958–60: .... **Washington Senators**
1960–61: .... **Detroit Tigers**
1961–63: .... **Kansas City Athletics**
1964: .... **Minnesota Twins**
Career Statistics: .... **45–58, 13 saves, 4.34 ERA**

Ted Williams vs. Bill Fischer

9-for-24, 2 doubles, 2 home runs, 7 RBI, 7 walks (2 intentional), 3 strike-outs, 1 double play, 1 sacrifice fly, .375 batting average, .516 on-base percentage, .708 slugging percentage

Home Runs Allowed:

No. 467, June 29, 1958, at Detroit
No. 473, July 29, 1958, at Detroit

Bill Fischer

YEAR	DATE	RESULT	YEAR	DATE	RESULT
1957	May 19	Single		Sept. 21	Grounded into DP
		Intentional walk			Strikeout
		Single			Double (1 RBI)
	June 27	Strikeout	1959	May 24	Walk
		Ground out			Ground out
	Aug. 3	Fielder's choice		May 29	Walk
1958	May 6	Intentional walk			Single
	May 25	Walk			Ground out
	June 7	Single			Fly out
		Single		July 2	Fly out
	June 27	Ground out			Ground out
	June 29	Home run (3 RBI)			Ground out
	July 18	Double	1960	Aug. 5	Pop out
		Walk		Aug. 30	Fly out
	July 28	Walk			
	July 29	Home run (3 RBI)			

HE WAS ONE of the greatest hitters of all-time they say, and I guess he was. He was the last guy to hit .400 and was a big and strong guy.

I pitched against him . . . oh, 1958, when I was traded to Washington from Detroit. I started a game in Fenway, and he came up to bat with the bases loaded and struck out. . . . And he was mad he struck out; he took the pitch and it was strike three. He made an imaginary swing after he was called out and then took his bat and threw it and it went over the Red Sox dugout and hit somebody in the stands. Well, they didn't know who it hit, but the umpires and both managers got together and said, "If we throw him out of the game, then he did it on purpose. Then whoever the bat hit could sue him." So they didn't throw him out of the game.

He then came up in the eighth inning and hit a two-run home run off me, and we lost 2–0.[36] When a guy strikes out, they throw the ball around and you wait to get the ball back. I didn't even really know what happened. That was an incident which was pretty big at that point in time.

I think he hit a couple of home runs off me . . . two, I believe. I know in Detroit, when I was with [the Tigers], he hit the ball above the second deck in old Tiger Stadium, where there was a wooden grandstand that people used to stand on.

He was always interesting to watch. One time when I was with the White Sox, he had three home runs in the game and came up the fourth time with nobody on base and two outs, and they walked him on purpose. [White Sox manager] Al Lopez said, "no one guy is ever going to hit four home runs against my team." So he walked him. I think the Red Sox won the game, 4–3.[37]

---

[36] The game took place September 21, 1958, in Boston. Williams struck out looking in the third inning and would later hit an RBI double in the sixth inning in a game Boston won, 2–0.

[37] The game was May 8, 1957, in Chicago. Williams hit three home runs, then was walked in the ninth inning with two out and a man on second. Boston would win 4–1.

When I coached with the Red Sox for seven years,[38] Ted was still [around the ballclub]. He used to come by spring training a lot and you'd see him during the season. When you'd see him coming, you didn't want to be around, because he'd ask these questions that you couldn't answer. Like, when do you start your curveball? Behind your head, in front, or wherever. It was never a question you could answer, because one guy would say this and another guy would say that. When he was around, he would talk loudly so that everybody knew he was there. . . . And he was always giving pointers on how to hit and how he would hit this guy. He was just fun to listen to. He was outspoken . . . very outspoken.

I know that the last time I saw him was with the All-Century Players [introduced at the 1999 All-Star Game at Fenway Park]. Then after that he got sick, but he was still around a lot. I got to know him very well. He never was a flashy dresser; sometimes you thought he didn't have any money at all. But he was a baseball man. When he talked, it was always about baseball.

The first time I faced him, I didn't strike him out; I know that.[39] In one game I saw in Detroit, Jim Bunning had a no-hitter with two outs [in the ninth], and Ted was at bat and Al Kaline was in right field. [Ted] hit a ball and Kaline had his back against the fence in right field. If he wouldn't have put his glove up, it would have gone into the bullpen. He just missed a home run.[40]

When facing Ted, I tried to keep the ball down so he'd [hit] the ball on the ground. If you pitched him up, he could hit the ball up in the air and get that backspin on the ball and it would just carry. The ball

---

[38] Fischer was Boston's pitching coach from 1985–91.
[39] Fischer first faced Williams on May 19, 1957, as a member of the White Sox. Williams singled to left field his first time up against Fischer.
[40] That no-hitter was July 20, 1958, in Boston.

would go up and you'd think, "well, it was a fly ball." Then you'd say, "oh my God, it's not going to come down right away."

But he was fun; the people enjoyed the way he played. The last year he didn't play a lot, because if he didn't feel right, he didn't play. But if [fans] knew he was playing, the stadium always had a few thousand more fans; so he was good for the game.

He was good at everything he did: fisherman, flyer, hunter, big-game hunter. He did everything 100 percent, full bore.

He was forty years old, thirty-five to forty when I faced him. He still had good reflexes and good eyesight. His strike zone was as big as a postage stamp. He got a lot of pitches that were strikes that the umpires gave him because he didn't swing. . . . And they didn't like to call him out. The fans wanted to see him swing. There ain't many of those guys around today, and it will be a while yet before there's another.

Paul Foytack

Right-handed pitcher

1953, 1955–63: ....Detroit Tigers
1963–64: .... Los Angeles Angels
Career Statistics: .... 86–87, 7 saves, 4.14 ERA

Ted Williams vs. Paul Foytack

12-for-45, 2 doubles, 4 home runs, 11 RBI, 11 walks, 3 strikeouts, .267 batting average, .404 on-base percentage, .578 slugging percentage

Home Runs Allowed:

No. 404, August 1, 1956, at Detroit
No. 438, June 30, 1957, at Boston
No. 450, August 27, 1957, at Detroit
No. 462, May 27, 1958, at Detroit

IT WASN'T FUN.

He was the greatest hitter that I ever faced, that's for sure. I talked to him about hitting, asked him why he stood with his right foot even with the front of home plate. He said, "Well, Paul, first of all, there's no one that can throw the ball by me." And I said, "Well, I can vouch for that." And he caught the curveballs and sliders before they got in too far on his hands. They didn't get a chance to get way in deep if you stand way in the box, and I guess they have a chance to get in on you, and he said, "I don't let that happen." And I said, "Oh boy, no wonder you're making more money than me, Ted." He was a great guy, but a tough, tough out.

My first concern when facing him was that I didn't want to get hit by a line drive. He hit me in the ankle one day and I'm hopping around, hopping around looking, and our first baseman said, "The ball

Paul Foytack

YEAR	DATE	RESULT
1955	June 22	Ground out
	July 29	Fly out
	July 31	Fly out
	Aug. 25	Ground out
	Sept. 7	Ground out
1956	May 15	Fly out
	June 6	Lined into DP
		Pop out
		Ground out
		Walk
	Aug. 1	Home run (3 RBI)
		Fly out
		Walk
		Fly out
1957	May 15	Fielder's choice
	June 30	Single
		Double
		Foul out
		Home run (3 RBI)
	July 13	Fly out
		Walk
		Walk
	Aug. 27	Single
		Ground out
		Home run (2 RBI)

YEAR	DATE	RESULT
1958	May 27	Fly out
		Home run (1 RBI)
		Ground out
		Ground out
	June 9	Single
		Walk
	June 12	Double
		Ground out
	June 29	Walk
		Fly out
		Single
	July 18	Fly out
		Walk
	Sept. 14	Ground out
		Flied into DP
		Ground out
		Foul out
1959	May 17	Strikeout
		Sacrifice fly (1 RBI)
	June 10	Pop out
		Foul out
		Single
	June 23	Walk
	Aug. 2	Line out
		Pop out
		Walk
		Walk
		Strikeout
1960	June 16	Walk
		Single (1 RBI)
	June 30	Strikeout
		Pop out

is right over there! The ball is right over there!" And I said, "I'm not looking for the ball, I'm looking for my foot!"

But as for trying to get him out, we just hoped that he would hit the ball at someone. He was a tough strikeout. That's all you could do. We weren't going to let him beat us in a ball game. We would intentionally walk him if we had to. We weren't going to let a hitter like that beat us in a ball game.

And I was good friends with Ted. Every time he'd take batting practice, it would be a 3–2 count, Tiger Stadium, ninth inning, two out—that's how he'd take his batting practice at Detroit. He was a great hitter, a great hitter.

He wouldn't [swing at a bad pitch], but the umpires had a tendency to sometimes give him a ball call when it was a strike only because he didn't swing at it. I said that's okay with me, don't ever swing at it! Like I said, the only thing you could talk about was don't let him beat you in a ball game if the score is tied or you're one run ahead or something. He was really something else.

We did not use the Williams shift that I could remember. He was certainly the toughest out. I never really thought about it. He wasn't going to hit the ball to left field anyhow. I don't know if that made him feel bad that he was going to give in and do that, but we really didn't have the shift that I can remember. And I didn't care, because all I thought about was, gee, I hope he doesn't hit me with a line drive.

One time—the only time I did this in my life—I don't know what the count was, but I got a little sweat from the back of my head and I threw him a spitter. It was wet, and halfway in he started to swing at it. I heard him say, "Oh, shit," and the ball hit the bat and bounced back to me. It was the only time I ever threw one. But he knew what it was right away when he saw it going down like it did.

He could see if you had the ball with the seams or across the seams and different things. He told me once, "Paul, if you had better control, you would win a lot of games." I was kind of a wild pitcher. Did I say kind of wild? I was very wild. I asked him about hitting one time. I said, "Did you hit a lot when you were in school?" He said there was a custodian at his school who would throw batting practice to him about an hour every morning before he went to class. I said, "Well, you big donkey, no wonder you can hit."

He was a good guy. He and I became real good friends, believe it or not. Talked about fishing one time and during the conversation, I mentioned that my uncle was the fly-tying champ of Pennsylvania; he used to make little flies for bait . . . make bugs and that. After that conversation, [Williams] invited me over to his hotel room. To cut a long story short, we called my uncle, and my uncle could not believe it and sent him about a dozen flies he had tied. And I swear, I thought Ted got the winning lottery number every month. That's how much he appreciated it. And he would *not* let me leave town without having dinner with him at least one night every trip.

We became good friends . . . but just during batting practice or right after a game. But no, he was not about to let up during a game. He was not that kind of person. He was going to hit and he didn't care who was on the mound.

He was something, boy. So good . . . and he did have a great eye. He would not swing at a bad pitch. He just didn't do it. If I had to throw one, and I threw it down the middle, oh boy. Almost wave bye-bye to it.

He hit .267 off of me. Actually, that's not too bad.

Bob Friend

Right-handed pitcher

1951–65: ....Pittsburgh Pirates
1966: ....New York Yankees
1966: ....New York Mets
Career Statistics: .... 197–230, 11 saves, 3.58 ERA
National League All-Star: 1956, 1958, 1960

Ted Williams vs. Bob Friend in All-Star Games

0-for-4

1956: First inning, 2 out, none on, tied 0–0, struck out; third inning, 2 out, runners on first and second, NL up 1–0, grounded out to first baseman Dale Long.

1958: Sixth inning, 1 out, runner on first, tied 3–3, reached on error by Frank Thomas.

1960: Second inning, 2 out, runner on third (after a balk and wild pitch), NL up 4–0, grounded out, Bill Mazeroski to Joe Adcock.

Bob Friend

YEAR	DATE	RESULT
1956	All-Star Game	Strikeout
		Ground out
1958	All-Star	Reached on error
1960	All-Star	Ground out

INEVER FACED HIM a hell of a lot, you know. Maybe spring training. Then you'd hear about how [he had] quick hands, a quick bat, and how he studied pitchers. After facing him, I agree with all of that.

But my strategy was not to get behind. Throw strikes and throw my best pitch, which was a hard sinkerball.

Okay, here's what happened in the all-star games: In 1956, I

He swung at a curveball on the last pitch.

pitched three innings and got the win. But in the third inning, the bases were loaded and Williams was up. I went 3–2 and struck him out swinging. He swung at a curveball on the last pitch. So that's a mistake there. He had runners on first and second with two outs in the third inning, and the NL leading 1–0, and he grounded out to first. No, sorry, he struck out. Bases loaded, I got 3–2 on him.[41]

I again faced him in 1958. He came up in the sixth inning with one out and the score tied 3–3, and Frank Thomas made an error on the play. It was a bouncing ball to Thomas that he just fumbled. We had a fantasy camp in Bradenton that year, and they had the All-Star Game on. The groundouts weren't hit that big. Like I said, it was a key spot in the '56 All-Star Game. Went down to 3–2 with the bases loaded, and that would have been the ball game. So I felt pretty good about getting him out in a key position. He probably hadn't seen me enough. I had pretty good stuff in those all-star games.

They always talked about Williams. You may get him out one or two times, but he was such a great study of pitchers that he'd have you figured out. Well, I didn't face him much; I didn't give him a chance.

As I didn't pitch in the American League, we never had to use the Williams shift. I think they probably fared pretty well with it, because it kept being used. He was probably one of the greatest hitters of all time, no question about it. I can't remember that [being used in the all-star game].[42]

It [the all-star game] was pretty important when we played in it. We'd pitch three innings unless we got knocked out. I had pretty good

---

[41] Listening to the broadcast from the 1956 All-Star Game, Williams struck out in the first inning with two out and no one on base, and in the third, he grounded out with two out and two on.

[42] Listening to the broadcast from the 1956 All-Star Game, the National League put shortstop Roy McMillan to the right side of second base and second baseman Johnny Temple halfway between first and second. First baseman Dale Long played four steps off the line. All three played deep on the outfield grass, while the outfielders were also shifted to the right.

luck in those games, as I won two and lost one with an ERA of probably one.[43]

He didn't get a hit off me—he got an error—and that wasn't bad. So I'll take it and won't comment on it anymore!

Was he the toughest hitter I ever faced? By reputation, yes. I had to go with my best stuff. You couldn't be scared of him; you had to stay ahead. And I had some pretty good luck with some pretty good hitters, and that's the way it was.

It's pretty tough to compare him [to other ballplayers] because he studied how to hit. He was really something. I think if you were going to look at the way to hit, you'd watch him up there. He's the one you wanted to [emulate]. Now someone else I faced a lot was Stan Musial. He had a different stance. He also put the wood on the ball and had a lot of infield hits and home runs.

Yes, [people in the National League talked about Williams] all the time. He studied hitting better than everybody. He knew the hitting, he knew all the pitchers, and he had a *great* memory. In fact, after I struck him out in the '56 All-Star Game, I ran into him at the Pompano racetrack down in Florida. I went over and introduced myself. "Bob Friend, Ted Williams, nice to see you."

He says, "Oh, I remember you. You struck me out with that curveball. I didn't think you were going to do it."

So that's the kind of mind he had with hitting and everything else . . . and that was twenty years later! That's the way he operated. He had a photographic memory and knew the pitchers.

Ed Bailey, my catcher, knew he was sitting on a fastball. You know, 3–2 in the All-Star Game; but I broke off a real good curveball, and he

---

[43] In 8.1 innings pitched over three all-star games, Friend had a 1.08 ERA.

swung and missed. I felt real good about it, but there was no reaction from him. I'm sure he was disappointed that he didn't get what he was looking for.

I didn't talk to him too much. I'd run into him a little bit and he was always nice. He was a ballplayer's guy; all the players liked him. Everything he did was first class. His service in the military flying jets, I mean, the guy did everything. He came back and was still playing well. The players definitely respected that.

Ned Garver

Right-handed pitcher

1948–52: ....**St. Louis Browns**
1952–56: ....**Detroit Tigers**
1957–60: ....**Kansas City Athletics**
1961: ....**Los Angeles Angels**
Career Statistics: ....**129–157, 12 saves, 3.73 ERA**
American League All-Star: **1951**

Ted Williams vs. Ned Garver (data incomplete)

40-for-97, 10 doubles, 9 home runs,[44] 26 RBI,[45] 27 walks (1 intentional), 6 strikeouts, 2 double plays, .412 batting average, .540 on-base percentage, .794 slugging percentage

Home Runs Allowed:

No. 213, June 27, 1948 (game two), at St. Louis
No. 245, July 22, 1949, at St. Louis
No. 272, May 7, 1950 (game one), at Boston
No. 282, June 9, 1950, at Boston
No. 337, September 17, 1953, at Boston
No. 375, June 21, 1955, at Boston
No. 385, July 31, 1955 (game one), at Boston
No. 422, April 30, 1957, at Kansas City
No. 436, June 23, 1957 (game one), at Boston
No. 459, April 30, 1958, at Boston

---

[44] Of the known available box scores, Williams hit 9 home runs off Garver. But the data is available for all of Williams' 521 career home runs, and he ended up with 10 off Garver.

[45] Retrosheet.org has more data of Williams vs. Garver, but does not include RBI. Baseball-reference.com lists Williams with 26 RBI in 84 at-bats (111 plate appearances) vs. Garver.

Ned Garver

YEAR	DATE	RESULT
1948	May 26	Strikeout
		Fly out
		Ground out
		Single
	June 3	Walk
		Walk
		Walk
		Double
	Aug. 4	Fly out
		Single (1 RBI)
		Out (unknown)
1949	May 8	Walk
		Strikeout
		Fly out
		Walk
	May 26	Walk
		Grounded into DP
		Fly out
		Walk
		Single (2 RBI)
	June 8	Walk
		Double
		Single
		Fly out
	June 23	Double
		Fly out
		Walk
		Double (RBI)
		Double
	Aug. 2	Single
		Ground out
		Double
		Walk
		Walk
1950	May 7	Walk
		Home run (1 RBI)
	May 25	Walk
		Sac fly (1 RBI)

YEAR	DATE	RESULT
	June 9	Home run (2 RBI)
		Ground out
		Double
		Fly out
	June 25	Ground out
		Single
		Single
		Fly out
1951	May 7	Walk
		Single (1 RBI)
		Line out
		Walk
	June 1	Single
		Ground out
		Fielder's choice
		Fly out
	June 16	Single
		Fly out
		Walk
	July 15	Walk
		Ground out
		Fly out
		Ground out
	July 31	Single
		Single
		Ground out
	Sept. 13	Walk
		Fly out
		Strikeout
		Strikeout
1953	Sept. 17	Fly out
		Foul out
		Foul out
		Home run (2 RBI)
1954	May 17	Walk
		Line out
		Ground out
		Intentional walk

YEAR	DATE	RESULT
	July 16	Foul out
		Double
		Walk
	July 30	Fly out
		Pop out
		Strikeout
		Line out
	Aug. 24	Fly out
		Single
1955	June 21	Fly out
		Foul out
		Walk
		Home run (3 RBI)
	July 31	Walk
		Ground out
		Home run (4 RBI)
	Aug. 25	Walk
		Double
		Single (1 RBI)
		Grounded into DP
1957	April 30	Single
		Ground out
		Double
		Home run (1 RBI)
1958	April 30	Fly out
		Walk
		Fly out
		Home run (2 RBI)
	June 13	Single (1 RBI)
		Ground out
		Single (1 RBI)
	Aug. 24	Single (1 RBI)
1959	May 21	Single
		Fly out
		Pop out
	Aug. 5	Single
1960	July 3	Walk

LET'S FACE IT, Ted Williams was the greatest hitter during my fourteen years in the big leagues. . . . The greatest hitter that I ever knew. So let's start out with that.

But the first time that you faced him as a pitcher—the first time you faced him—he had never seen you. That was the best chance you had of striking him out. So the first time I pitched against him, it so happens, he did strike out and went back to the dugout and hit his bat on something and cracked the bat.[46]

Our clubhouses in Boston [sic] were side-by-side. You had to go through their dugout to get to our clubhouse. So if you got knocked out of the game, you had to go through their dugout to get to the clubhouse! And there were two Orlando brothers who were the clubhouse men. So my trainer, who was Bob Bauman at the time with the St. Louis Browns, asked for that guy to give him that cracked bat and he did. He fixed it and put a couple of nails in it. He kept it from 1948 till about, maybe it was 2001 or something like that, when I made a trip to St. Louis to speak at the SABR[47] organization meeting. Bob knew I was going to be there and called me and said he was going to move into a smaller place and he needed to get rid of some stuff, and if I wanted, I could have the bat. I said yes and to bring it down to the ballpark—I was going to the Cardinals game—so he brought it down to the ballpark.

I ended up telling Ted about it. He was down in this town of Avon Park one time because he owned a part-interest in a fruit-shipping warehouse. He came to sign autographs and I went down to see him, and we had lunch. I told him that I had that bat. He said to bring it down next spring when I'd come and he'd sign it for me. So I did.

I brought it down and called him, and he invited me over to see his museum and to dinner. I got to spend several hours with him in the afternoon and have supper with him, and then he signed the bat.

I have three children, and I knew that the bat was pretty valuable, so I sold it after his death. But then last year, when I was down here in Florida, a guy from Miami, I think he's a lawyer, sent me some photos of that bat and the story that I wrote about the bat. He asked me if I'd notarize the letter and send it back to him. So I did. But then I asked him how much he paid for that bat, and he said $28,000. So that

---

[46] Garver first faced Boston on May 26, 1948, pitching eight innings in a 5–3, ten-inning loss at St. Louis. Williams went 1–4 against Garver with that strikeout.

[47] Society for American Baseball Research

was pretty interesting. That bat, the first time I ever pitched to Ted Williams, has now been sold for $28,000. That is something. And it was a cracked bat. A game-used bat is worth more than one that was not used.

For some reason or other, Ted was always nice to me. One time during a game, he got on third base and made a break like he was going to steal home. Well he wasn't, but he charged up the line. I didn't balk or anything like that, but then when he got back to third base, he looked back at me and gave a little smile. That made me feel at home, you know. For a big guy like that to horse around with you a little bit, that made you feel good. Made you feel like you belonged.

I have interviews where he was with [Fay] Vincent—that used to be commissioner—where he and [Joe] DiMaggio were being interviewed and Ted told them all that I could throw my glove out there and get him out and all that crap.

Well, I pitched against Ted an *enormous* amount of times. You played in each town four times a year. I pitched against Ted all four times in Boston, and if he came to bat three times, that would be twelve times a year, and I pitched against him for I'm sure ten years. That adds up to being a heck of a lot of at-bats—just pitching to him in Boston! And I pitched against him in St. Louis, too.

I think somebody up there in New England once sent me—and he paid me pretty well to sign them, too—but he was getting an autograph of every living pitcher that had thrown a home run ball to Ted Williams. He would send you the number of balls that he hit home runs off of you, with the date on there that he did it, and then wanted you to sign that, and I did. I think it was 10.

So he hit 10 home runs and still went on like he couldn't hit me. I will say this: He always hit the ball to left field on me. There were very few people that he tried to go to left field on. He used to say that he didn't want to start swinging at balls out of the strike zone just because he could hit them—like Yogi [Berra] did—because he said a guy like [Eddie] Lopat or Garver will keep leading you out, leading you out, and the next thing you'll forget what your strike zone is. But he'd go to left field on me and even hit a home run to left field in Fenway Park.

He had trouble hitting what I threw, see. He said I had a slider that he couldn't pick the spin up on. I had two sliders: one that I threw to right-handers that broke out and down, and another I threw to left-handers, which was pretty flat. But I held it like a football, and I would try to throw it just about waist high, so that when the ball would break, it would break in on their fists. I have a picture at home on my wall of Ted Williams breaking his bat on me. That means I had hit him on the fists. He hit a little pop-up to second base in that at-bat.

Well, now that's the reason I threw it that way. When I threw that flat slider to left-handed hitters, they couldn't adjust their hands back very far. They could only bring it back about so far, and that's why you could hit them on the fists and keep it in the ballpark. It wasn't a strikeout pitch, but it would do the job and kept them from hitting the long ball.

So he said he had trouble picking the spin up on that ball. In other words, most of the time, as soon as the ball left the pitcher's hand, he knew what it was going to do. He could pick the spin up on that ball. I threw him a dang-blum knuckleball one time after about eight or ten years, maybe twelve, I don't know. But anyway, I threw him a knuckleball, and I'll tell you, he just exploded out of that batter's box. He had never seen it; he didn't know what was going to happen, I guess. I don't know.

But as soon as that ball left your hands . . . I want to tell you; I watched him very closely when I was on the bench not pitching. And he could pick up the spin on the ball even [from] a left-handed pitcher. We had a little left-handed pitcher down there at St. Louis, and he kind of short-armed the ball, and I figured it was tough to pick up, as it would be coming out of the guy's uniform—old Sam Zoldak. But anyway, I'd see him relax before that ball got to home plate because he could see it was out of the strike zone, see it didn't have the spin on it to bring it back into the strike zone . . . and I want to tell you now that this all happened in a very short time; but I'm telling you, he did it. That's how good he was.[48]

But I loved pitching to guys like that. I loved to pitch against guys like [Mickey] Mantle and DiMaggio and people who were recognized as the great ones. If they got a hit off you, well, what the heck, he's supposed to get a hit; he's a great one. But if you got him out, then that was an accomplishment.

And I always figured that the fans came to see guys like Williams, DiMaggio, and Mantle. They were the ones that put the fans in the ballpark and they surely didn't come there to see them run bases or to field their positions. They came there to see them hit. That's why I never agreed with the fact that the manager would tell you before the series started, "Now be sure to get the ball over to Dominic DiMaggio or [Johnny] Pesky, don't walk those guys . . . but if you walk Williams, well, that will be all right."

What the heck? Walk Williams? People came from Arizona and Wyoming and places like that to see him hit when we were in Kansas City. They didn't come to see him walk to first. So I figured, what the heck, I ought to pitch to him.

That's just the way I wanted to do it, but I have to go by what the manager says. If he says to go out there and hit somebody, you hit them. If he says to walk Williams or pitch him nothing but screwballs off the plate, you throw it off the plate and outside. If he wants to let them hit, you let him hit. But that wasn't my way of doing things.

I tell that you one time I had played all year with a bad knee. It would pop out sometimes, and even my first baseman, Walt Dropo, would have to put it back. But we had a special brace to put on it, and the trainer would wrap it before the game. Because of this, players bunted a lot on me to try to have my knee go out. So after it came out about the second time, I'd have to come out of the game. But I played

---

[48] It depends on the speed, but a batter usually has 0.4 seconds to make the decision to swing.

all year with my knee like that. Then I was planning to go hunting in Wyoming in November, but I had to have my knee operated on. So we were in Boston, and Fred Hutchinson was our manager. He said to me, if you pitch here in Boston with two days' rest, I'll let you go [have surgery] when we're going back to Detroit. We're not going to be in the pennant race, and we have some minor-league people up here. So if you pitch here on two days' rest, when we go back home to Detroit, then I'll let you go and get your operation, so that you'll be able to go hunting in November.

So [laughs] I had them shut out 1–0 through seven innings. In the eighth, there was a man on second base and two out, and Williams was the batter. George Kell was their third baseman and their cleanup hitter at the time. The count was 2–1 on Williams, and I threw a pitch on the inside corner of the plate that I thought was a strike, but the umpire called it a ball, making it a 3–1 count. The umpires were not inclined to call a strike on Ted unless he swung at it. He knew his strike zone very well. But at the same token, that doesn't mean that there isn't sometimes that he ought to be called out.

But anyway, he took that pitch, and the catcher knows more than the pitcher, because the catcher is real quiet and the pitcher is out there moving around. Well anyway, I thought it was a strike and they called it ball three. I knew that Kell was a better hitter leading off an inning than he was with men on base. I always could lead him away—he might get a hit—but I could lead him off the plate with men on base because he was too eager to drive in runs.

So I decided that's it, I'm not pitching to Ted anymore with the count 3–1. I'm going to put him on base and pitch to George Kell.

Well, I didn't even take a sign. Frank House was my catcher. I just got the ball back and went into my stretch. You need to understand that Ted hardly ever swung at a ball that wasn't a strike. So I just come up and throw the ball at a pretty good speed up about shoulder high on the inside part of the plate. As I didn't have a sign with my catcher, he didn't know I was going to make a pitch out, but I didn't want to throw the ball to the backstop. I just threw it in there plenty bad and Williams stepped back and hit that sucker for a home run.

Now that's really the only home run I can remember beating me at the time. You know that Ted Williams can beat you, so you don't want to pitch to him if the game is at stake and you can pitch around him. But at the same token, I thought I had him at a 2–2 count, but the umpire said ball three, so now I'm trying to walk him and he hits a home run to make it 2–1 and win the ball game. He might have gotten suspicious when I didn't take enough time to get a sign. I never talked to him about that, but I wish I would have.[49] That was a big deal, the one he hit off of me, because I had them beat 1–0. I mean, it looked like I wasn't going to let him beat me, and then I let him beat me. That one sticks in my mind. I've given up a lot of grand slams, but I don't remember cussing one of them. I don't think they beat me in a ball game. I'm just grateful that I had the opportunity to pitch against him, I'll tell you that.

When he had a stroke, he was in a Gainesville hospital, and I was in Ohio. The paper where I read the story only said that he was in Gainesville, but didn't mention what hospital. So I wrote a letter and I addressed it to Ted Williams, baseball's greatest hitter, and sent it to Gainesville. That's all the address I put on it, and he got it.

So the next spring, the Major League Alumni were having a reunion over in St. Petersburg, Florida. In the hotel they had a whole bunch of us in a big room. Mickey Vernon was there, Bob Feller was there, the old third baseman from Minnesota who hit all the home runs— [Harmon] Killebrew—was there, Roy Sievers was there; there were a whole bunch of good old players. We were all in a circle and fans could buy a ticket and could come get everybody's signature that they wanted.

Well after a while, some big guy tapped me on the shoulder and said, "I'm John Henry Williams. My dad is back in another room making a television interview, but he'd like to see you." I supposed it might be

---

[49] That game was September 17, 1953. Garver retired the first two hitters in the eighth inning, then allowed a single to Jimmy Piersall before Williams homered.

because I sent him that letter saying he was the greatest hitter ever, but I didn't know for sure. But for him to single me out of that bunch, to ask me over there, to have me come over there and say hello, that made me feel pretty good.

I only pitched against DiMaggio for three years, and I'm sure he hit me well.[50] Of course I pitched to Williams a lot more years, but I consider [DiMaggio] a great hitter because he didn't have a weakness, though I still consider Williams to be the best. God gave him more ability than anybody else. He could see better than [most] people. But on top of that, he was so dedicated and worked exceptionally hard.

Mantle had a weakness. I had good luck against Mantle. I told him, "I wished I could [always] pitch against guys like you, as I'd be in the Hall of Fame."[51]

If [Ted] was going to be the second hitter of an inning, let's say the guy ahead of him was Pesky. Pesky wouldn't be up there at the plate measuring me on every pitch I threw, you know. But Williams would be. Williams would charge into that dugout, get a bat, and get up there. If he was going to be the second hitter, he was up there, watching my pitches, measuring me. He really was conscientious about getting prepared, getting the most out of what he had. And he, believe you me, worked at it.

He also knew the important things, too. Today, they put a left-hand pitcher in no matter who they got up there that's a left-hand hitter, but for Ted, he could hit anybody. He could hit Whitey Ford, he could hit Herb Score, he could hit 'em all. In fact, he probably bore down on them more than anybody. But at the same token, he could hit them because he knew his strike zone. He of course could pick up the pitches, but he knew his strike zone. He didn't swing at bad pitches. He knew what it took to be a hitter and he didn't deviate from it. I never saw Williams start a swing and foul it off or something

---

[50] Of the known data, Joe DiMaggio was 12–23 (.511) with 1 home run off Ned Garver.

[51] Mickey Mantle was 15–53 (.283) with 1 home run against Ned Garver.

like that and take a half-cut. No, no, when he swung at the ball, he swung at the ball. Baseball was so lucky to have a person like that.

When Boudreau managed us at Kansas City, he was a guy that he wanted to, you know, do unusual stuff. He'd have the pitcher hit eighth, crazy stuff like that. I don't know, I thought he couldn't play anymore, but he wanted his name in the paper once in a while. He'd also do stuff like [the Williams shift]. I'm not saying that's bad because Williams was a guy [laughs] where, if he wanted to, he'd get a hit every cussed time up with the shift on. I'm telling you the God's honest truth. But he wouldn't do it. You don't even see Jim Thome doing that. I don't understand why they don't learn to hit the ball to left field. They'd cut that crap out. Why, good Lord, Williams hit me to left field, so I know he could hit anyone to left field. If he hit to left field, then you're in trouble when you got that shift on. But then good Lord, if he hit a line-drive single to right field, your second baseman caught it. He hit that ball like a bullet time after time after time. What the heck, they could throw him out from right field. He hit that ball hard, and if the shortstop—who was playing by second base—didn't get it, the second baseman would be out there stationed toward the middle of right field, and he could field that ball and throw it to first and get him out. I'd get tired of getting thrown out on base hits.

Sure, the shift was a good idea, because he was bull-headed enough to try to hit into it all the time. So you'd take some base hits away. He didn't get any base hits as a result of that, by him hitting into the shift. The only way he got base hits is if he hit a little grounder toward third. But he wouldn't do it. He was just bull-headed enough that he was going to hit .400 no matter what he did.

He did some unusual stuff while he was in the service. He got a wounded plane back to base. And he never mouthed off, he never complained, he never did anything. He just went in there and was one of the best pilots that ever was, I'm sure. And that was probably another challenge for him, and that's why he did it so dang-blanged good.

But I can tell you one year, the first time he came back, it was against us in Detroit. We played a doubleheader, and I think he hit three home runs, one off Al Aber, a left-hand pitcher we brought in there.[52] He just hit that ball like . . . I mean, you thought, well, he's been gone all this time, he might not be so sharp. Holy crap, I mean, he took that out of your head in a hurry.

Briggs Stadium was a good hitting ballpark, especially for a left-hander, as it was kind of a short right field. He'd hit that ball into the upper deck like a bullet. He was just capable of doing great things. When you figure he was in that great big ballpark in Boston. Heck, how many balls did he hit in Boston that would have been out of the park in Briggs Stadium? Just an untold amount of balls. And I don't know what you would have had done. The managers would have probably had to say that you would walk him every time up, like Sparky Anderson did to George Brett.

One time against the Yankees, he had a couple of home runs off the Yankee pitcher, and Yogi complained because he called ball four on him, and the umpire said, "Well, at least I held him to one base." If you walked him, he only got to first. If you pitched to him, you didn't [know] what the hell was going to happen.

I have nothing negative to say about Ted Williams. There was a lot of controversy up there in Boston because the writers would write

---

[52] Wiliams's first game back from the Korean War was on August 6, 1953, in Boston, against the Browns. Williams played in three games against the Tigers in '53: September 2 (game one of a doubleheader); September 3 in Detroit; and September 17 (game one of a doubleheader), in Boston. The latter was the game Garver described previously, allowing a two-run homer to Williams in the bottom of the eighth inning of a then 1–0 game. Williams did homer twice in his career off Al Aber, both of those coming in 1955.

stuff—like when they had that first baby, how he wasn't home—and he got permanently aggravated at them. So he just wouldn't cooperate. I figure that I respect his decision there. If he decided he didn't want to talk to them because of the unfair abuse, well, I think that's his option.

Ted was, as far as I'm concerned, an inspiration. He showed it in his work ethic and *love* of the game of baseball; his complete dedication to the game. I mean, I loved the game of baseball. It meant a lot to me. I don't like to see people go out there like that dag-blammed [Johnny Damon], when he was playing for Boston, or that [Manny] Ramirez; they look like bums. I don't like to see the way they dress going to the ballparks now. You're a professional; you should act and dress like a professional. You ought to show a little respect for the game, that's the way I feel about it. . . . And Ted Williams did all of that. He never deviated from it. Now, [he] had the greatest ability of anybody, but he didn't take advantage of that and act like an idiot. These guys now, they get really good, they think they can do anything. They think they can mistreat anybody and act any way they want because they're not going to fire you. What the heck, they're not going to do anything to you because you're too good a player. Back in my day, those guys didn't act like that. DiMaggio, Williams, they didn't act like that. They were leaders, they led by example. And I take my hat off to 'em.

I'm pretty good friends with Bob Feller. I've had him come to where I live up north to speak and stuff like that. When I was over Ted's, I asked him who he considered the greatest pitcher he ever saw, and he immediately said Bob Feller. Now, he had hit against Lefty Grove; he hit against Lefty Gomez; he hit against Whitey Ford; he hit against that guy over there in Cleveland, that left-hander—Herb Score—he hit against all guys who were considered tough left-handers, and he said Bob Feller.

So I asked Bob Feller—the Major League Alumni had an event in Cleveland, and we had a get-together up there at the ballpark the night before, so Bob I and were at that and our wives were at the same table—so I asked him who he thought was the toughest hitter, and Bob said Ted Williams, just like that. So he'll tell you that Williams was the greatest.[53]

---

[53] While Bob Feller passed away in 2010, the interview with Ned Garver took place while Feller was still alive.

Jim "Mudcat" Grant

Right-handed pitcher

1958–64: .... Cleveland Indians
1964–67: .... Minnesota Twins
1968: .... Los Angeles Dodgers
1969: .... Montreal Expos
1969: .... St. Louis Cardinals
1970: .... Oakland A's
1970–71: .... Pittsburgh Pirates
1971: .... Oakland A's
Career Statistics: .... 145–119, 53 saves, 3.63 ERA
American League All-Star: 1963, 1965

Ted Williams vs. Mudcat Grant

9-for-26, 1 double, 2 home runs, 3 RBI, 4 walks (1 intentional), 1 strikeout, .346 batting average, .433 on-base percentage, .615 slugging percentage

Home Runs Allowed:

No. 486, June 27, 1959, at Cleveland
No. 507, July 22, 1960, at Boston

WHAT STOOD OUT when I faced Ted Williams? *Everything* stands out when I faced Ted Williams! The name Ted Williams [laughs]. I faced him a couple years. But his batting stance, his knowledge of the strike zone, all of that became evident as you worked against him.

I don't think he every really changed in terms of attacking the ball and stuff like that. In terms of what I saw when I was in the minor leagues years before then and stuff I had read about him, I didn't see any particular change in his approach to hitting.

Most of us guys back in those days, we were taught to throw strikes. We were taught to make the hitter hit the ball with something on it.

So the strategy was not to throw it in the zone where left-handers particularly like to hit the ball. And even though a lot of pitchers didn't do it, my thought was to pitch him up and in, no matter what he thought.

He was not only going to get the call, he was going to hit it if it was a strike. But you know, I look at pitchers from the time I retired to the time that I started, and part of the game was to try not to throw it in the area where they extended themselves to hit the ball. So I pitched him in most of the time, but he was devastating up and away. You knew he could see that ball real well. He was going to get a good part of the bat on the ball, so you sort of keep it away in that area. But nonetheless, you didn't try to be macho about it because it was Ted Williams. You tried to keep it in the areas where he didn't like it the most.

I remember walking him with the bases loaded. I was leading 3–1 and back in them days, if you had pretty good stuff, the manager didn't take you out. So I remember I had the bases loaded

Jim "Mudcat" Grant

YEAR	DATE	RESULT
1958	June 3	Double
		Ground out
	July 14	Reached on error
	Aug. 2	Single
		Single
		Ground out
		Fly out
	Aug. 21	Fly out
1959	May 15	Fly out into DP
		Ground out
		Fly out
		Line out into DP
	June 27	Fly out
		Pop out
		Home run (2 RBI)
	July 30	Fly out
		Strikeout
		Single
		Ground out
	Sept. 15	Single
1960	June 7	Walk
		Ground out
		Pop out
	July 22	Home run (1 RBI)
		Walk
		Walk
	Aug. 23	Ground out
		Single
	Aug. 25	Intentional walk
		Single

with two out, and I was leading 3–1, and walked him with the bases loaded. And I remember him gesturing [lowering voice], "Throw the ball over the plate." I said, "Go ahead, go ahead." And I struck out Jackie Jensen to end the game.[54]

We did use the shift, because I saw him bunt the ball. He bunted it down the third-base line. It was a rare occasion, but I remember once with the Cleveland Indians, he bunted against us and laughed all the way to first base.[55]

Well, he had to be up there among the great hitters. He has to be in the top three among the guys I played against.

You say that Ted hit two home runs off me? Man that was great. But I remember he was kind enough to sign a photo for me, "To Mudcat, thanks for helping me [get] in the Hall of Fame."

By the way, Mickey Mantle said the same thing in the photo he signed for me.

---

[54] It is unknown what game Grant could be referring to. Grant walked Williams four times in his career, and they all came in 1960. Jackie Jensen was not with the Red Sox in 1960.

[55] Williams bunted for a hit against Cleveland's Gary Bell in the first game of a doubleheader on July 24, 1960, in the bottom of the first inning.

John Gray

Right-handed pitcher

1954: .... **Philadelphia Athletics**
1955: .... **Kansas City Athletics**
1957: .... **Cleveland Indians**
1958: .... **Philadelphia Phillies**
Career Statistics: .... **4–18, 0 saves, 6.18 ERA**

Ted Williams vs. John Gray

1-for-7, 1 home run, 1 RBI, 2 walks, 1 strikeout, 1 double play, .143 batting average, .333 on-base percentage, .571 slugging percentage

Home Runs Allowed:

No. 365, September 9, 1954, at Boston

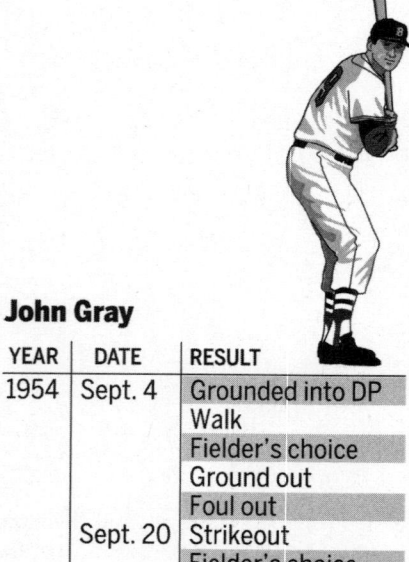

John Gray

YEAR	DATE	RESULT
1954	Sept. 4	Grounded into DP
		Walk
		Fielder's choice
		Ground out
		Foul out
	Sept. 20	Strikeout
		Fielder's choice
		Walk
		Home run (1 RBI)

I CAN REMEMBER FACING Ted Williams nine times. But I don't remember striking him out one time; I thought I struck him out four times. That's one thing I always remembered.

You see, Ted was a friend of mine. I used to run into him a lot. He used to run up and play golf with me from the Keys, and we used to have big discussions about why he never got any base hits off me to speak of.

He said something to me about it . . . I wish I could remember exactly what it was. When he came up to Kendall Lakes one time to play golf, he made some kind of remark about it. He was such a good person and very sincere. He said something like, "How come you don't ever throw the ball over the plate to me?"

And the one he did get off me was one of the craziest stories you've ever heard in your life, and if you were at the ball game, you probably would have jumped out of your seat. It was one of those runaway ball games, and Kerby Ferrell was the manager, who was an absolute dunce.

We go up to Boston to play, and I had real good luck against Ted. I never threw a fastball over the plate to him. I never got a ball over the plate. I bet I didn't throw three fastballs that ever hit that plate. And I had a pretty good fastball. But there isn't a man in the world that can throw a fastball by Ted Williams . . . nobody. I don't think there was ever a man born that could do it.

Anyway, I just kept pitching him in and out, in and out, and then I'd throw in my breaking ball where he'd have to [reach] after the ball. It was hard to get him to go after that one. He had the best eyes I've ever seen on a hitter. Shoot, if you were standing out there on the mound . . . I can remember him staring at me; it felt like I was being X-rayed; watching every move you made.

But how he got the home run: They had a runaway ball game, I don't know who was pitching that day. And they had the bases loaded or something—I can't exactly remember what it was—but Kerby asked me to go back in. Well, I didn't care. Back in those days, hell, I'd go in there every damn day if they asked me to pitch. We weren't prima donnas like they are today.

Anyway, I go out there and they kept calling [for the] fastball. Catcher says you have a great fastball. I said no. I'm standing out on the mound—you know how a pitcher will shake off a pitch with his left hand? I'm right-handed, so on my left hand was a glove, and I'd hang the glove down my side and shake it. Kerby was trying to call pitches.

So I got a strike on him or something, and they said throw the fastball, throw the fastball, got to get out of here. So he kept it up and I kept throwing the damn slider and the curveball, and then I'd waste the fastball because I was ahead of him. They come in with a fastball and I shake the glove off. I get down there and fastball again. I shake it off again. Finally he put the fastball down there again and I knew it had to be Kerby, because the catcher wouldn't fight with me. So I put my hand straight up in the air—my left hand—and I'm shaking in the middle of the stadium.

Kerby Ferrell comes running out, "What's wrong? What's wrong?" Well, I said, "To tell you the truth Kerby, I think my catcher's blind. I've been shaking him off down here and he didn't see it, so I thought if I stuck my hand way up in the air he might be able to see I was shaking off the pitch."

So finally he goes back in. I turn around and here comes the fastball again. I think I had a 3–2 count on him, I'm not sure. But I was so goddamn mad, I said, "Ah, fuck it," and I hauled off and threw the damn fastball.

We had Vic Power playing out in right field. Now Vic Power turns around and he runs back about three feet and stops, and he's hitting his glove hand—you know, hitting his fist in his gloved hand like he's going to catch the ball—then he backs up about four or five more feet, and he's hitting his gloved hand, thinking it's a big pop fly.

Well, in about another five or ten seconds, Vic Power is up against the fence, still pounding his glove, and that ball is still going up. I've never seen a ball hit that far or that high in my life.

And that's the only base hit he ever got off me.[56] It was comical, really. The crowd was going wild when I had my glove up in the air. I think that's the only fastball I threw him over the plate.

---

[56] Williams indeed did have just one hit off Gray, but Williams' hit—a home run off Gray—occurred September 20, 1954, when Gray was a member of the Philadelphia Athletics. The manager of that team was Eddie Joost. Gray started that game and allowed a leadoff homer in the seventh inning to Williams, with the score prior to the homer being 2–0 Red Sox. The right fielder in that game was Vic Power. Gray allowed just one home run as a member of the Indians in 1957, when his manager was Kerby Ferrell. It was a game on August 4 at Yankee Stadium against another left-handed Hall of Famer, Enos Slaughter. It was a two-out, three-run homer in the fourth inning to make the score 5–1. The right fielder in that game was Rocky Colavito.

I had watched him hit so many times, and like I said, any man that's got everybody on one side of the field 90 percent of the time when he's up to bat . . . how in the hell are you going to get a fastball by him?

He had the greatest eyes on any hitter I've ever seen. And you know what? He hit the golf ball like he hit that damn baseball. Boy, could he club it. He didn't score well, but he could hit it.

To me, he's the greatest hitter who ever walked out onto a baseball field. I couldn't imagine what he was like when he was younger before he went into the service, but I'll tell you, he was the greatest.

Dick Hall

Right-handed pitcher

1952–57, 1959: ....Pittsburgh Pirates
1960: ....Kansas City Athletics
1961–66: .... Baltimore Orioles
1967–68: .... Philadelphia Phillies
1969–71: .... Baltimore Orioles
Career Statistics: .... 93–75, 68 saves, 3.32 ERA

Ted Williams vs. Dick Hall

4-for-8, 1 double, 1 home run, 5 RBI, 1 walk, 1 strikeout, .500 batting average, .556 on-base percentage, 1.000 slugging percentage

Home Runs Allowed:

No. 506, July 3, 1960, at Boston

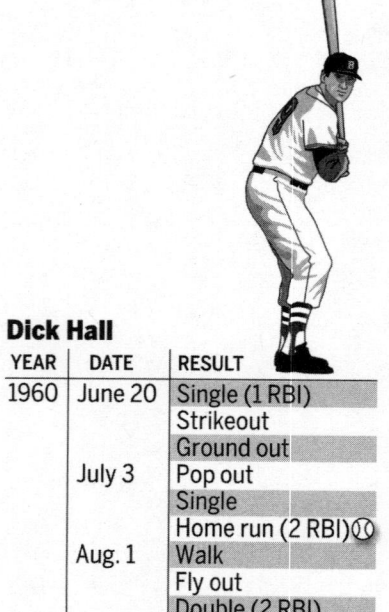

Dick Hall

YEAR	DATE	RESULT
1960	June 20	Single (1 RBI)
		Strikeout
		Ground out
	July 3	Pop out
		Single
		Home run (2 RBI)
	Aug. 1	Walk
		Fly out
		Double (2 RBI)

I CAN REMEMBER A lot of at-bats that Ted Williams had against me in 1960, the only year I faced him, because he was so noteworthy. I don't remember the double or the walk (maybe it was intentional).[57]

I started against Boston three times, first in Kansas City and then two times in Fenway. The first at-bat in Kansas City, he hit a fastball down and away for a line drive over the shortstop for a single. The next time up, I got two strikes on him and then threw my slider (the first I had

---

[57] The walk on August 1 was not intentional.

thrown him, all the other pitches the first two times up were fastballs) and backdoored it to the low outside corner (which is where I aimed it 99 percent of the time to left-handers—the slider was hard, with only a little break, and probably more resembled what is referred to these days as a cut fastball). Anyway, it was the first time he had seen it, and he just stood there and took it for strike three.

As for Fenway, the theory was that he was a little past his prime, so I started each at-bat with a high fastball and hoped he would swing at it and fly out to center field. Like Yogi Berra, I felt that the more pitches he saw off me in an at-bat, the better chance he had of getting a hit.

Well, in the later innings of a game in Boston, I started him again with a high fastball, but missed with it, as it was over the middle of the plate but up about even with his chin. He was famous for never swinging at bad pitches, but this time, because he was obviously (by hindsight) looking for a high fastball, he swung at it. *Problem*: He hit it into their part of the bullpen for a home run.

It was probably in the third game that I had faced him that for the first time I threw him my changeup (my changeup was good, though I didn't have control of it like I had of the other two pitches) and he was fooled and just took it for a strike. A couple pitches later, I threw him another one, and he was way out in front and dribbled a little foul roller toward the dugout. I threw him two or three fastballs low and away, which he fouled off. I then decided to throw the third changeup to him in that at-bat. He just calmly stroked a line drive into right field for a single. At that point, I decided throwing him three changeups in one at-bat was not a very good idea.

At the end of the season, I can remember thinking about having faced him and feeling that I had had pretty good success. Then I went through the at-bats and figured out that he had hit an even .500 against me. Oh!

He was known to study opposing pitchers, but what impressed me was that he had taken the time to try and figure me out. I wasn't over-powering at all, as I relied on good control and a funny delivery, but he had still taken the time to remember my pitch selection.

He was friendly with the other players to the extent he had contact with them. I remember an incident in Kansas City where he had just doubled, and we made a pitching change. We looked out at second and while the new pitcher was coming in, there was Williams, obviously giving a hitting lesson to Dick Howser, our rookie shortstop, which impressed all of us.

Jack Harshman

Left-handed pitcher

1948, 1950, 1952: ....New York Giants
1954–57: .... Chicago White Sox
1958–59: .... Baltimore Orioles
1959: ....Boston Red Sox
1959–60: .... Cleveland Indians
Career Statistics: .... 69–65, 7 saves, 3.50 ERA

Ted Williams vs. Jack Harshman

5-for-35, 1 double, 3 walks, 7 strikeouts, 2 double plays, .156 batting average, .229 on-base percentage, .188 slugging percentage

WE BOTH GREW up in San Diego. Of course, he's older than me, and I didn't really get acquainted with him there, but I did know of him. The very first time I ever had a chance to talk with Ted was in 1954, in our first meeting with the Red Sox in Chicago. He came and asked one of our players under the grandstand, where we both used the same entry out on the field—we'd stay down there and talk with the other players if we had an opportunity to—and he came to one of the White Sox players and asked about me, because he knew I had come from San Diego, but he obviously did not know me. And the player introduced me to Ted at the time. We stood there and talked, and he was as gracious as you could possibly be, and I really did appreciate his time, to take time out to talk with me. He didn't have to, but he certainly was nice enough to do that.

Then, as far as how I was able to pitch against him, as far as my strategy was—if you can have one—let me say this: Of all the hitters I watched hit, in a category of 1 to 10 with Ted being a 10, I think the next best hitter would be an 8 or 8 1/2. To me, there was no real comparison to being naturally good hitters and hitters that could either hit with a great deal of power or could spray the ball around and get on base and that kind of thing. There was a difference, and Ted could do it all. And that's what I think made the difference.

I would come out of my own clubhouse during batting practice between the two teams, go sit on the bench, and specifically watch him hit. There was something so unique about it and so much value in the way he approached hitting; it was just a joy to watch him.

As far as my being lucky against him, that's what it is. I mean, nobody actually outpitched [Ted]; he was just that good a hitter. I was just fortunate enough to be that lucky against him. You have the statistics here—which I did not know until I read this—that he only hit .156 against me. I did remember, though, that he never hit a home run and he only had one double.

As far as pitching against the other guys—[Mickey] Mantle, [Al] Rosen, and so on—those fellas were obviously good hitters, and Al Kaline was one of the better natural hitters that you'd ever want to watch. Mickey Mantle was just brutally strong and obviously a good hitter and could run like a deer, but Ted just was something out of the ordinary.

Jack Harshman

YEAR	DATE	RESULT
1954	June 2	Ground out
	July 25	Grounded into DP
		Single
		Walk
		Strikeout
	Aug. 3	Ground out
		Single
		Fly out
		Fly out
	Sept. 1	Fly out
1955	July 22	Fielder's choice
		Line out
1956	June 26	Strikeout
		Strikeout
		Ground out
		Ground out
	July 12	Foul out
		Walk
		Fly out
		Fly out
	Sept. 12	Foul out
		Single
		Fly out
		Double
1957	June 27	Walk
1958	May 10	Single
		Grounded into DP
		Strikeout
		Strikeout
	May 17	Strikeout
		Ground out
		Fielder's choice
		Strikeout
1959	May 30	Fly out
	Aug. 23	Ground out

Who was my toughest out? Well, it wouldn't be Ted, because he didn't work out to be my toughest out. He was probably the toughest hitter I ever faced; it just worked out to where he didn't do that well against me. My toughest out my first year or two was a catcher with the Washington Senators, Eddie Fitz Gerald, believe it or not.[58] That was just because he was able to hit the ball solidly in-between the outfielders.

But anyhow, as far as me and Ted talking when I was with the Red Sox, I did talk about how I would do this or do that against some of the better American League hitters, and my answers from his questions seemed to coincide with what he thought, so that made me feel pretty damn smart!

Of course, as a high-schooler, he was more interested in pitching than he was hitting. He really wanted to be a pitcher, and I think that's why he looked at hitting from that direction. Anyhow, it was interesting to do that with him and see that in most cases my theory of pitching against certain hitters kind of went along with the way he thought.

Then later on when he was a batting coach with the Red Sox and I was pitching for the Indians—I guess he was still playing, yeah, he was still with the Red Sox—but he and Herb Score both lived in Florida. When they flew to spring training, which were both being held in Arizona, Ted and Herb sat together, and of course, the conversation went to hitting, as it always did. And he said, you have a pitcher on your ballclub this year, and if you want to know how to pitch against the better hitters in the American League, all you have to do is ask him and he'll know. Of course, he was referring to me again. Herb told me that; it didn't come from Ted.

Anyway, it was a pleasure knowing him, and we seemed to have gotten along great as far as personal friendships were concerned, and he treated me just as well as you could [have] hoped that he would.

---

[58] Fitz Gerald was 18–66 (.273) lifetime vs. Harshman. But in 1955—Harshman's second full season—he was 5–12 (.417) with 4 walks.

He never really did pal around too much with the other players. He was friendly with them, but he sort of seemed like he was unto himself individually off the field, I think. One of his closest friends was the clubhouse boy at the time—of course, he wasn't a boy, he was a man—but they seemed to have gotten along very well. But as far as going out and buddying with him, Ted didn't do that much.

But in the clubhouse, that was a different thing. He was very, very congenial. He had stories written about how standoffish he was and how unfriendly he was with the media and the sportswriters, but I think he was a guy that didn't want to "yes" a man just because the guy wanted him to say it. He would say exactly what he thought, and sometimes it would be in complete contradiction to what the guy wanted him to say. And, of course, that made him standoffish and unfriendly, but that was just not Ted at all.

I had an opportunity one time to go to his home when he still had a house in Islamorada, Florida. Mickey McDermott and I went out to visit him and we spent a lovely day at his home. Like I said, he was just a real nice guy, and, of course, the best hitter that I ever saw.

As far as pitching against him, my strategy against Ted was just . . . I guess you could say, I just wanted to make a variety of pitches: Either a fastball or a slider or a screwball or whatever, not necessarily on any particular pitch count. You couldn't let him figure out what you were going to throw, because if he figured right and you threw a strike, he was going to hit it.

Something else about Ted that was outstanding was that I honestly [cannot] recall him *ever* taking an awkward swing. When he made his mind to swing, it was a fluid, good, solid, balanced swing. So many of the other hitters that were considered good very often would be totally fooled and would look awkward, but he never did. I never saw him do that. I think that could be attributed to his superior eyesight. I guess it's been pretty much documented that he had tremendous eyesight, and he said he could actually pick up the spin from the time it left the pitcher's hand. Well, that's something you can't believe, because you can't see that well, but he said he could and I'm not going to call him a liar—because he probably could!

He never swung at bad pitches. The day I struck out 16 in Boston,[59] I had him struck out a second time, but the umpire so often would give him the benefit of a close pitch. That particular pitch, it was on a 3–2 count, and I made a really good pitch on him. It was low and away on the strike zone. I mean, I know it was a strike. And I think—when he turned to throw the bat down and go to first base or turn and carry the bat back to the bench—he looked at it and the umpire said ball four, and he kind of gave me that little sly grin on his face. He was something else, he really was.

It says here that I struck him out seven times. I don't remember that I did that, but if it's there, it's probably true. Like I said, I had outstandingly good success against him; not necessarily because I was that good a pitcher, but it just worked out that way. There are other hitters that were not near as good as him that probably hit me much more consistently than Ted ever did, so it's just a matter as much of being lucky as it is being good.[60]

I think I probably considered myself a four-pitch pitcher who could throw those pitches at any count with some consistency. That made it easier for me to do things like that to Ted. Because if you're only a two-pitch pitcher—like so many in the big leagues were and are—it made it too easy for him to have a pretty good idea of what was going to come. That was just not going to happen too often with him; you were going to get it hit hard somewhere. But anyhow, I threw good pitches to him a lot, and I got him out pretty regularly, but it was more a matter of luck than me being that much better than him by any means.

---

[59] On July 16, 1954, in the first game of a doubleheader, Harshman struck out 16 at Boston in a 5–2 White Sox victory, breaking the club record of 15, set by Ed Walsh (twice in 1908 and 1910) and Jim Scott (1913). He struck out every starter at least once, including leadoff hitter Billy Consolo four times. Through the 2012 season, Harshman still is the White Sox record-holder for strikeouts in a game.

[60] Actually, the player with the highest batting average against Harshman (minimum 10 plate appearances) was Reno Bertoia, who went 9–17 with 1 home run, 4 RBI, and a .529 batting average. During his ten years in the big leagues, Bertoia had a .244 career batting average.

With me being left-handed, we didn't move that much to right field. We of course favored him to right field, but I don't think we put the second baseman out in short right field and the shortstop playing second. I don't think we did that. They would have shifted on a right-hand pitcher, but not with a left-hand pitcher. And that one double he got off of me was a double to left-center, believe it or not. He hit it hard, but it was to left-center, as opposed to pulling it down the line, or that sort of thing. [Ted] kind of felt like it was a battle between him and the other guys. He, by God, was going to prove that he could do it, and he did, what the hell.

I don't recall just sitting down with the other guys on the pitching staff and saying let's do this or let's try that or what do you do; I think that's kind of an overblown sort of conversation among pitchers. Now a pitcher has his abilities that he can do this or he can do that, which is sometimes quite different than another pitcher in that they deliver from a little bit different angle or they have a little bit different kind of fastball . . . so they have to pitch their own game. They go out there with the intention of using their best stuff at any one best count. So you can't really put a plan into action, so to speak. You can't say we're going to do this and that because it just doesn't work out that way. Pitchers are very independent and separate from one another in the way they pitch, even though it looks like there's a great deal of similarity, which there is because, let's face it, they have to throw pitches over the plate. In that respect, they're very similar, but in the manner in which they do it has a lot to do with how you will pitch against any one hitter.

I think [coming up as a first baseman] it did do me a lot of good, in that when I started pitching, I had a hitter's mentality. In other words, I looked at pitching from a hitter's viewpoint: What the hitter might be expecting or looking for or that sort of thing. So instead of me just thinking, "I'm going to throw a strike here or there," I would have a little bit more understanding about why. What would be their thought process as a hitter? And I did think—at least early on—when I first started to try to learn how to pitch. That's how my thought process was, as opposed to just try to throw it over the plate.

When we first met that day under the stands in Chicago, he didn't know me other than that I was from San Diego, and I did not know him other than he was from San Diego and was respected as an extremely good man, player-wise. When he spoke to me, we didn't have a whole lot of common subjects to speak about, but he did mention several names that were prominent in and around San Diego baseball—sandlots and so on—or coaches or what he thought I would know. So he brought their names up to me and some of them I had recognized but was maybe not acquainted with. He tried to be as friendly as he could with someone that he didn't know at all, and that's kind of an outstanding remembrance to me.

I have one more [memory] about him. After I had been out of baseball for about twenty years I guess, I was working for a company in San Diego that had been buying many season tickets in small packages, and they wanted me, because I had been in baseball, to go down and see if I could improve their location, which I did. I tried to go down there; I wasn't dressed in nice clothes at all, just in my work clothes. When I went near the general offices, I looked down the hall, and there was a group of guys standing around the doorway to one of the offices. So I got my nose stuck up there, I wanted to take a look myself to see what was going on, and when I got to this back of this group of guys, I could see over their heads into the room, and here's Ted Williams sitting on a desk in there, and he's carrying on a conversation about hitting. So what else, you know? Anyhow, I'm standing there for a matter of a few seconds, really, and I guess he saw me as I walked up, and it came to him, and he jumped down off that desk and came pushing out of there, and he put his arms around me and said, "How you doing, Lefty?"

And these guys around me, they looked at me like, "Who the hell is this guy?" But I thought it was a real tribute that he would have all those years remembered that's who I was. He came to say hello to me, and I thought that was real nice of him.

He used to come into San Diego on a rare occasion. I think that time he was there for the San Diego Hall of Fame presentations. He'd come in for that once in a while. He'd come in rarely other than that to maybe say hello to his mother. He didn't stay in San Diego for any longer than he had to. I think maybe it was because of his brother's reputation. He couldn't get along with his brother at all, and, consequently, didn't come in for more than a couple of days at a time.

I think he was the greatest hitter of all time. I've had this in mind. I've said it over and over again. If Ted Williams had not had to spend those two periods of time in the service and played his entire career in Detroit, he would have probably hit 1,000 home runs. I'm not joking. I'm serious.

Right field in Detroit was a *great* deal shorter than in Boston, and he was a high fly-ball hitter, and that's all you had to do in Detroit. And I'm serious now; he lost about five years when he was averaging close to 40 home runs a season. Well that's 200 home runs in Boston if he had played.

So I honestly believe that if he had played his entire career—uninterrupted in Detroit—he might very well have hit 1,000 home runs.

It was [the fences] shorter in New York then Boston, no question about it; *particularly* down the line in both fields. Both fields were short down the line, but it went down rapidly in both fields. New York was not quite as long in dead right field as Fenway Park. Ted hit a lot of home runs in the bullpen direction, which is kind of like dead right field but shading slightly toward center. In New York, that was still pretty short there. So he might very well have hit more home runs in New York than he did in Boston, and, of course, Yankee Stadium was a tough right-handed hitter's home run park. It was longer in dead left field than Boston is, obviously. Everywhere was shorter. He certainly would have hit a whole lot more had he not lost those years.

John James

Right-handed pitcher

1958, 1960–61:	New York Yankees
1961:	Los Angeles Angels
Career Statistics:	5–3, 2 saves, 4.76 ERA

Ted Williams vs. John James

0-for-0, 0 RBI, 1 walk, .000 batting average, 1.000 on-base percentage, .000 slugging percentage

John James

YEAR	DATE	RESULT
1960	July 10	Walk

I DON'T RECALL A clubhouse meeting to discuss how to pitch to Williams or any of the Bosox. I would like to think we had one and that I was in on it, but nothing comes to mind. Generally speaking, as I recall, Williams rarely swung at the first pitch, especially against pitchers he hadn't seen before. So [in my first appearance against him] I figured I could get a quick strike on him. My recollections of that at-bat are very clear as far as him being at the plate, however, I don't recall the inning or which team was ahead.[61]

I probably had the same thing going through my mind as any rookie pitcher who ever faced Williams for the first time. You are thrilled to be doing it, and you don't particularly care if you get him out. Take that with a grain of salt because you *do* want to get him out, but the

---

[61] James entered in the sixth inning with the Red Sox leading the Yankees, 7–5. He faced Williams with one on and one out. (Willie Tasby singled and Pete Runnels struck out.)

main thing is that you want to face him in Fenway Park so you can tell the story to all the guys you played ball with when you were younger, "How I pitched to Ted Williams in Fenway Park."

My undoing as far as walking him was the umpire behind the plate, Ed Hurley. He was known to be tough on rookies, and he [most certainly] was this day.

My side of the story is that I walked him on five strikes. I think he swung at one pitch for the only strike. I recall very vividly that Yogi [Berra] was going nuts behind the plate every time Hurley called a ball, which to the two of us appeared to be a strike. I also recall that Casey [Stengel] was on the top step yelling at the umpire in his distinctive voice. That may have been the only time he stuck up for me.

When I get questions about the toughest hitter I ever faced, I'm somewhat stumped for an answer. I wasn't up there long and pitched mostly in short relief, so I didn't face any hitter, let alone the Williams type, very many times. I will tell you he was the second most impressive hitter I ever faced.

I faced [Mickey] Mantle twice while pitching for the Angels after being traded in '61, and he was by far the most physically imposing person who ever walked up to the plate [that I faced]. I'm happy to report that I struck him out both times. He yelled at me after the second K that if I'd have pitched like that when I was there [with the Yankees], I would still be there.[62]

I'm sure you're aware that Williams' remains are in a facility where they are frozen in hopes that he can come back some day. That place is within a couple of miles of where I live and I go by it frequently. I always say, "Hi Ted" when we do, because he was my hero when I was a young boy wanting to be a ballplayer. My wife of course thinks I'm nuts and she's probably right. She usually is.

---

[62] On June 11, 1961, just over a month after being traded by the Yankees to the Angels, James struck out Mantle twice—caught looking in the fifth inning and swinging in the seventh.

Bob Kelly

Right-handed pitcher

1951–53: .... **Chicago Cubs**
1953, 1958: .... **Cincinnati Reds**
1958: .... **Cleveland Indians**
Career Statistics: .... **12–18, 2 saves, 4.50 ERA**

Ted Williams vs. Bob Kelly

2-for-3, 0 extra-base hits, 0 RBI, 2 walks, 0 strikeouts, .667 batting average, .800 on-base percentage, .667 slugging percentage

Bob Kelly

YEAR	DATE	RESULT
1958	May 4	Walk
		Single
		Single
	May 20	Fielder's choice
	June 3	Walk

EVERY ONCE IN a while around my town in Connecticut, they ask me to talk at baseball banquets and little leagues and so forth. And I've always taken great distress in watching kids on the bench during the ball games, eating everything from popsicles to talking to somebody else and not paying attention to what is going on in the field. So when speaking, I use an incident when I pitched against Ted as a prime example of that.

The first time I faced him was in Boston—it was the only time I faced him in Boston when I was with Cleveland[63] and I was pitching

---

[63] Kelly actually faced Williams twice in Boston: on May 4, 1958, which is the game he is referring to, and on June 3, 1958.

against a hitter—I'm not sure who the hitter was up in front of him[64]—and I was pitching against him, I noticed a presence watching me from the on-deck circle.

I got through that hitter and Ted Williams [came up to bat]. At that time, I had developed a palm ball, and it was a pitch that really benefited me getting back to the majors in 1958. I was very, very successful with it in Nashville the year before. I had won 23 games[65] down there with that thing, and I got called back up to the majors. It was a great changeup, and I think a predecessor to what they now call the split-finger. It was a pitch that you threw with all your might, and no matter how hard or what effort you put into it, it was a dead fish getting up there.

And sure enough, I got ahead of Ted and threw him this palm ball, and he was way out on his front foot and extended himself and just got the bat on the ball and hit it right on the plate and bounced over my head, dropping dead between the mound and second base, and he trotted to first with a single.

That was the first time I faced him. And sure enough—and this is what I tell the kids—the next time I faced him, he was in the batter's box and was just staring holes into me, trying to figure out what the pitch was, where I picked it up, and anything I did in my delivery I think to tell him what was coming.

And sure enough, the next time up I got ahead of him again and I come up with that palm ball. He just literally switched his feet waiting for that pitch to come up and dumped it into left field and trotted into second for a double.[66] It was one of the rare times I saw him do that, to hit to the opposite field. He just nonchalantly poked it out there.

---

[64] Williams actually led off in this at-bat, in the fourth. Kelly walked Williams in the first, after retiring Don Buddin and Pete Runnels.

[65] Actually 24; Kelly had been out of the majors since 1953.

[66] Retrosheet.org lists the hit as a single to left field.

And he picked up the pitch. He knew what I was throwing him before I threw it.

So I tell these kids that, if you spend time on the bench watching the game, no matter what position, you can learn something every minute.

You talk about going over him in the meetings beforehand and where to pitch him, sometimes you're better off walking him rather than getting in trouble with the ball going [out of] the ballpark.

Russ Kemmerer

Right-handed pitcher

1954–55, 1957 ....**Boston Red Sox**
1957–60: ....**Washington Senators**
1960–62: ....**Chicago White Sox**
1962–63: ....**Houston Colt .45s**
Career Statistics: ....**43–59, 8 saves, 4.46 ERA**

Ted Williams vs. Russ Kemmerer

4-for-15, 1 home run, 1 RBI, 6 walks (2 intentional), 1 strikeout, .250 batting average, .455 on-base percentage, .438 slugging percentage

Home Runs Allowed:

No. 496, June 10, 1960, at Boston

Russ Kemmerer

YEAR	DATE	RESULT			
1957	May 31	Single	1958	April 27	Fielder's choice
		Line out			Ground out
		Ground out			Intentional walk
		Intentional walk	1960	June 10	Walk
	July 2	Line out			Fly out
	Aug. 17	Walk			Home run (1 RBI)
		Single			Fly out
		Ground out		June 25	Strikeout
	Sept. 23	Walk			Single
	Sept. 25	Ground out		July 20	Walk
					Ground out
				July 28	Fly out

I WROTE A BOOK in 2002 titled *Hey Kid, Just Get It Over the Plate*, which was basically taken from when I was a high school senior. The Red Sox came into Pittsburgh, where I lived, to play a fundraising game with the Pirates. Since they had the brass along, they wanted to see me throw.

Anyway, I was pitching batting practice—of course I found out later that major-league ballplayers don't like to hit while high-schoolers pitch, but I was doing okay. I got through the reserve lineup pretty well and turned around to get some resin and there was Ted Williams. I think I described it in the book as my larynx was in full tilt. And he just pointed the bat out to the mound and said, "Hey kid, you're doing a good job, just get it over the plate."

I've had a lot of really, really great experiences with Ted. He took me in after the game—he came into the clubhouse as I was getting dressed—and he said, "You're going to play ball?" and I said, "That's all I've ever wanted to do." He said, "Well, I don't know what you have inside you, but from what I've seen tonight, you can play."

And he went on to encourage me to sign with the Red Sox. He said, "Who else is looking at you?" I said, "Pirates, of course, the Giants, Cincinnati, and Brooklyn." He said, "Well, all of those teams have about thirty farm clubs, and you can get lost down in those things." He said the Red Sox only had about eight and "if you can make it, and I think you might, you can move [up] much faster." Well, if he told me to sign with the Kokomo Brown Bears, I guess I would have.

But anyway, it was a little over two years later, and Ted came back from the service, and I had been called up to go to spring training with the team. I walked in and he said, "You're the kid from Pittsburgh, aren't you?" I said yeah, and he said, "I knew you'd make it." So that was my first meeting with Ted.

Every pitcher had an idea of how he could get Ted out. It was a combination of his best pitch, game situation, men on base, inning, and score of the game. In my case, my strategy was to stay away from him. My best pitch to a left-hand hitter was to keep the ball down and away. I had a good sinking fastball about 95 miles-per-hour. When I felt them moving closer to the plate, I tried to jam them with a hard slider in on their hands. I felt I did well, but remember few umpires called a knee-high fastball on the outside corner a strike on Ted. Ted was 4–16 against me; certainly not bad against *the greatest*.

Each pitcher has his best pitch against Ted. Game situations are always taken into consideration. The pregame advice was, "Ted's going to get his hits. With men on base, hope for a hard grounder at somebody. Outside of that, keep it in the ballpark." The White Sox and Senators moved the second baseman back on the grass and the shortstop closer to second. When Ted ripped it, unless it was right at the fielder, it got through.

[Mickey] Mantle, [Roger] Maris, and [Al] Kaline were all great hitters. The difference was that Ted had no apparent weakness. Mantle had a weakness: high and tight, provided you had a good fastball and you could keep it inside. If you got it high and away, he could lose it to left field. This was tough for me, because I was a low-ball pitcher. Maris was tough upstairs. The year he hit 61, he hit No. 15 and 39 against me. Kaline hit to all fields. He could handle the bat. He hit to the hole on the right side of the infield, bunt if the third baseman laid back, and drive the ball to left field if it was open, and seldom chased a bad pitch.

Any discussion with Ted always found its way to hitting and pitching. He remembered everything about pitchers because he studied them and would talk to other hitters about them. As a result, he had an idea once he faced them. We never discussed facing each other except the one homer he hit off me. Ted was the best hitter I ever faced. Willie Mays, [Hank] Aaron, Monte Irvin, Luke Easter, Hank Bauer, and [Roberto] Clemente were some of the greats I played against.

Unfortunately, from the standpoint to pitching against him, the Red Sox traded me to the Senators, and I didn't get to pitch against them very much, for no particular reason.[67] But when I was with the White Sox, I remember a particular game when we were in Fenway Park and were ahead 8–0.[68] One thing about Ted; I used to sit around and listen to him talk. Pitchers like myself, who were starting at that time, used to sit there and bone his bats. I always had Ted's bat to bone. I'd sit and listen to him talk so much that, if you ever threw a 2–2 slider for example, and got him out on it, next time or in that next series, don't ever throw him the same pitch again, because he was waiting for it. Just things like that. Listening to him talk about hitters and pitchers, what to do and what not to do. Anyway, in that particular ball game, I got him out—I don't remember, let's say a sinker and a slider—first two times he came to bat. He came to bat in the eighth inning and I was thinking about what I just told you. I'm thinking, okay, I got him out on this, I got him out on that, I'm going to throw him a slow breaking ball . . . and he hit that sucker about forty rows up in the seats.

If you've seen film of him running, [you'll notice that] he never really ran, he loped. He was going around first base and he was clapping. Of course the sportswriters don't know what he's saying; neither does the press or anybody else. But when he got to first base, he looked at me and said, "Hey bush, I got you in my book." He called everyone bush-leaguer. "You're in my book, I got you in my book, baby." He clapped all the way around. He was really laying it on me good. So the next day I was hitting fungos to left field, and I could hear him saying, "Hey, bush, you're in my book, baby." I turned around to him and said, "I haven't thrown a slow breaking ball to you in like two or three years, and you hit the damn thing like you knew it was coming." And he said,

---

[67] Kemmerer faced the Red Sox six times in 1957, but only once each in '58 and '59, which were his top two seasons in terms of innings pitched in his career.

[68] The game he refers to was one played June 10, 1960. It was the bottom of the sixth inning, and the White Sox were up 8–2 with one out.

"I did." Curious to find out how he knew, I asked him, "You want to tell me?" "Yeah, I'll tell you. When you got right to the top of your windup, you did a little something that you don't normally do, and I knew you were going to throw me an off-speed pitch."

He and Johnny Pesky became my mentors and [we] remained good friends. I was fortunate enough [to be invited] when they had the 60th anniversary of when Ted came into the league—the Mets were playing the Red Sox in the interleague games at Shea Stadium. He invited me, not just me, but Mel Parnell, Johnny Pesky, and Tommy Lasorda were there, because they were always close friends of Ted's. That was a magnificent evening.

Virgil Trucks and I had a talk about Williams one time, and he was kidding that he only hit one home run off him. I said I didn't play against him very much. I was with him the first years I was in the majors and didn't get to pitch against him too much after that.

In those days, Virgil said it was your best against his best. Virgil had a tremendous fastball, and he was going to throw his fastball. He said, well he hit 12 home runs off of me. I guess I wasn't ready to challenge him that much.

Marty Kutyna

Right-handed pitcher

1959–60: ....**Kansas City Athletics**
1961–62: ....**Washington Senators**
Career Statistics: ....**14–16, 8 saves, 3.88 ERA**

Ted Williams vs. Marty Kutyna

0-for-1, 3 walks, 0 strikeouts, .000 batting average, .750 on-base percentage, .000 slugging percentage

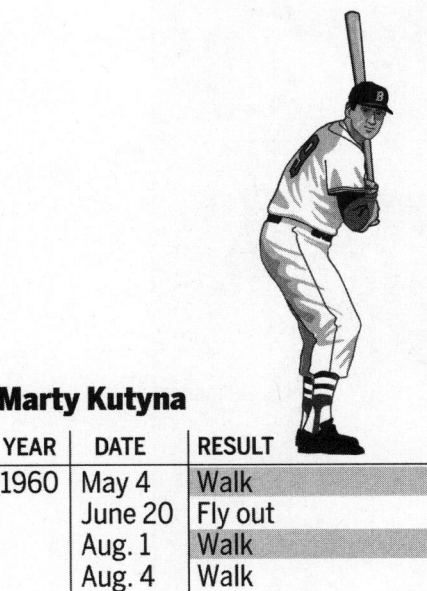

THE FIRST TIME I faced Ted Williams in 1960 was as a pinch-hitter on May 4. I came in relief with men on first and second and one out to face three left-handed hitters in the bottom of the eighth inning in Boston.

I got Vic Wertz on a fly ball. Then Ted Williams came up.[69] Harry Chiti was my catcher that day. He called for a slider, which I threw over the plate, and Ted had a good cut and fouled it off. Chiti came out to me and said, don't throw another one there, or he will hit it 400 feet. He told me to throw him inside. The next two pitches I did, and one of them was a strike, but umpire Nester Chylak called them [both] balls.

Marty Kutyna

YEAR	DATE	RESULT
1960	May 4	Walk
	June 20	Fly out
	Aug. 1	Walk
	Aug. 4	Walk

---

[69] With Boston trailing 5–3, Williams hit for Lou Clinton.

I took two steps forward and told the umpire they were strikes. The umpire came out to me and said next time you come toward me, you'll be out of the game. The next two fastballs I threw were again inside and called balls. I walked Ted.

I shook my head and looked at Williams at first. Ted looked at me from first base and shouted, "They were all strikes, rookie!"

The next hitter was Marty Keough, and I struck him out to end the inning.

Photo courtesy of Marty Kutyna

Don Larsen

Right-handed pitcher

1953:	St. Louis Browns
1954:	Baltimore Orioles
1955–59:	New York Yankees
1960–61:	Kansas City Athletics
1961:	Chicago White Sox
1962–64:	San Francisco Giants
1964–65:	Houston Colt .45s/Astros
1965:	Baltimore Orioles
1967:	Chicago Cubs
Career Statistics:	81–91, 23 saves, 3.78 ERA
World Series MVP:	1956

Ted Williams vs. Don Larsen

14-for-54, 3 home runs, 8 RBI, 18 walks (6 intentional), 4 strikeouts, 2 double plays, 1 sacrifice fly, .259 batting average, .438 on-base percentage, .426 slugging percentage

Home Runs Allowed:

No. 349, July 19, 1954 (game two), at Baltimore
No. 387, August 16, 1955, at New York
No. 449, August 14, 1957, at New York

I **THOUGHT HE WAS** the best hitter in the American League at the time I was playing. They say his eyesight was superb. The only thing I didn't like was no matter what you did, if you threw the ball down the middle of the plate and he didn't swing, it would be a ball. So he more or less umpired his own game and I didn't appreciate that. Being what a hitter he was and with the few breaks he got could be devastating.

Don Larsen

YEAR	DATE	RESULT
1954	July 19	Walk
		Intentional walk
		Home run (1 RBI)
	Aug. 8	Single
		Intentional walk
		Line out
		Ground out
	Aug. 28	Walk
		Fly out
		Walk
		Intentional walk
1955	Aug. 10	Ground out
		Walk
		Strikeout
		Fly out
		Fly out
		Intentional walk
	Aug. 16	Single
		Ground out
		Home run (2 RBI)
		Ground out
	Sept. 23	Strikeout
		Single
		Single

YEAR	DATE	RESULT
1956	April 22	Single (1 RBI)
	April 27	Fly out
	May 29	Fly out
	July 4	Walk
		Single
		Walk
		Ground out
	Aug. 7	Fly out into DP
		Ground out
		Fly out
		Walk
	Aug. 16	Line out
		Foul out
		Fly out
		Fly out
	Sept. 22	Foul out
		Fly out
		Walk
		Strikeout
	Sept. 28	Ground out
		Grounded into DP
		Grounded into DP

YEAR	DATE	RESULT
1957	April 20	Fly out
	April 28	Walk
	May 28	Pop out
		Walk
		Pop out
	July 4	Foul out
	Aug. 14	Home run (3 RBI)
		Ground out
		Single
1958	April 21	Strikeout
		Fielder's choice
		Single
	May 31	Fly out
		Line out
		Intentional walk
		Single
	July 6	Single
		Single
	Aug. 16	Sacrifice fly (1 RBI)
		Line out
		Pop out
		Fly out
1959	July 8	Walk
	July 13	Fly out
	Aug. 15	Fly out
		Walk
	Sept. 20	Intentional walk

I liked to pitch against him. I didn't care about him hitting the home runs; it was better than a walk. At least it keeps the ball in [the stadium] for someone to make a play on it. He hit a few home runs off me, but he never beat me in a game.

The years I played against him, he never had great luck in Yankee Stadium, which you think he would have, with right field that way. There was no park too small for him. I don't know why, but he never had good luck in Yankee Stadium.[70] Of course, we had a good staff,

---

70 In his career, Ted Williams hit .309/.484/.543 at Yankee Stadium. That slugging percentage is his third worst among stadiums he played in.

too. It was a good rivalry; I liked that. It was nice, good competition, and I enjoyed that very much.

It was a challenge, you know, and I'm glad I had a little luck against him. He was a little bit of a character in a way because everybody asked him about hitting and he always volunteered something. So he was a big asset to the players who came up during his time, too. I didn't think to [ask him about hitting], but maybe if I was playing regular I would [laughs].

He wasn't a small guy, either. He could tonk the ball out of any place. So it was a good time facing him, and you just tried to do the best you could in getting him out in certain occasions—or anytime. If he got a hit, so what? I didn't mind that a bit. Didn't want to walk him. Then you got no chance if you walk people. I did have some luck with him, and I appreciated that, too. I was happy when I got him out . . . very happy.

You had to be careful with any of the [great] hitters, it wasn't only him. You wanted to get those guys out when you really needed it. You didn't want them to beat you in a ball game, like in the eighth or ninth inning on a home run or something like that. I wasn't fond of walking him, but I did so a few times. But it's a challenge and we came up to it, and I enjoyed that competition with him.

I relied on Yogi [Berra] a lot, because I joined later, and Yogi faced these guys many, many times. Yogi knew *all* the hitters. Maybe they might change something, but he'd noticed that kind of stuff. Ted didn't change. He was a natural.

He wasn't a bad fielder in Boston, either, with that wall. He could play that wall pretty good. He wasn't noted for his fielding, but he did a good job for them.

I never played against [Stan] Musial, only one time, and that was in the National League. I spent most of my time in the American League. They had some good hitters in the National, too, like Musial. But Ted was the best I ever saw in the American League.

We may have used [the Williams shift], but I don't recall that part of it. I know a lot clubs did. Of course he'd challenge them anyway. He didn't care. He was going to go after it!

He would talk baseball to you all day long if you wanted to do that. He was very accommodating. Everyone looked up to him and tried to needle his brain. He and I became pretty friendly because he's from San Diego, where I grew up. I got to be with him at several functions in San Diego, and we had a nice relationship. More after, when we had more time to spend time leisurely. Not so much during our playing years. We weren't supposed to mingle too much, but we did anyway. That's much baloney, anyway. I liked him very much, the family and stuff. Of course, he never came back to San Diego. He spent most of the time in Florida; you know how he loved his fishing and stuff. He was the head honcho for Sears for quite a few years. He designed a few things, including making his own flies. I understand he was pretty damn good, top in the country in fly-fishing.

I saw him a little bit in San Diego when we were both retired. I didn't appreciate what happened *after* he passed away, but I don't think anyone liked that.

Bobby Locke

Right-handed pitcher

1959–61: .... **Cleveland Indians**
1962: .... **St. Louis Cardinals**
1962–64: .... **Philadelphia Phillies**
1965: .... **Cincinnati Reds**
1967–68: .... **California Angels**
Career Statistics: .... **16–15, 10 saves, 4.02 ERA**

Ted Williams vs. Bobby Locke

1-for-7, 0 extra-base hits, 0 RBI, 1 walk, 4 strikeouts, 1 hit by pitch, .143 batting average, .333 on-base percentage, .143 slugging percentage

HE WAS ALMOST out of baseball when I was pitching against him. He was still hitting a lot of home runs, though. I remember a guy I played with in Cleveland, Wynn Hawkins, I think he gave up the 513th home run.[71] So we was still hitting home runs in 1960.

Well, he was a great hitter, that's for sure. Anybody that faced him would tell me that. When I first faced him they said he's a great hitter. And he was. I just had some good success against him. Maybe it is because I hit him. You never know, right?

The best thing that I [heard] . . . Jimmy Piersall was my teammate. He came in and told me, he says "I had struck him out twice in one game, you know," he says "[Williams] very seldom ever strikes out twice in a game." So, also, that day I hit him,[72] Jimmy Piersall says, "Boy, he never gets hit by a pitch." He says, "What are you doing?"

He was glad I hit him, Jimmy Piersall was. He was a great ballplayer, a great teammate, and he didn't care for Ted Williams. They were

---

[71] Hawkins actually allowed Williams' 500th career home run; teammate Johnny Klippstein allowed No. 513.

[72] This happened in Locke's major-league debut on June 18, 1959.

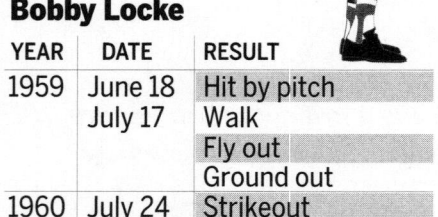

teammates at one time, but he always felt [Williams] got away with everything, he was like a prima donna.

That's probably why I struck him out so many times, I hit him once.

Well, I don't know, he was like any batter to me when I was pitching. What can I say? I was successful against him I guess. I threw him the same pitches I everybody else - fastball, slider, curveball.

I don't think we put the shift on him, I think we played him regular like everyone else. Not like baseball today. You see how they play three or four guys in the infield, they put them all in right, right-center. You got guys way out in right field almost.

Bobby Locke

YEAR	DATE	RESULT
1959	June 18	Hit by pitch
	July 17	Walk
		Fly out
		Ground out
1960	July 24	Strikeout
	Aug. 10	Strikeout
	Aug. 23	Single
		Strikeout
		Strikeout

The only thing I remember I got from him one time, I had a sore arm and I got sent to Indianapolis—Triple-A ball—and we were at the airport together and he told me, "Ah, don't worry about it, Bob, you'll be back in a short time." And I was. I was only there like a month or two and came back.

Oh, yeah, yeah, I talked to him. He made a good comment about me. He said I was the hardest pitcher for him to hit on the Indians staff in '59. That was a good comment. He said it to the sportswriter. Sportswriter put it in the paper, there was a good write up about it. So that was good.

As far as a person is concerned, I thought he was a great guy, you know. He'd talk to an Ordinary Joe, he'd talk to anybody. He was, as a player, respected by everybody. I know all the pitchers on our team respected him. They didn't want to see him come up to bat! Not with the bases loaded or something like that. Because he didn't strike out that often, you know, he had a good eye.

First time I ever pitched against him, I pitched against him in spring training in Mesa, Arizona, and I struck him out the first time. I got out of the service—I was in the service and got out in '59—and they told me, "You know who you struck out, Bob?" And I said no. "Ted Williams." I said, so? That's what I was supposed to do.

You know what, some of the best batters I ever faced, like Mickey Mantle and Roger Maris, I believe I got them easier out than I got some of them punch hitters. Really. Maybe I bared down on them more.

Ralph Lumenti

Left-handed pitcher

1957–59: ....**Washington Senators**
Career Statistics: ....**1–3, 0 saves, 7.29 ERA**

Ted Williams vs. Ralph Lumenti

1-for-4, 0 RBI, 1 walk, 0 strikeouts, .250 batting average, .400 on-base percentage, .250 slugging percentage

Ralph Lumenti

YEAR	DATE	RESULT
1957	Sept. 23	Single
		Walk
1958	May 14	Fly out
		Fly out
1959	Sept. 27	Pop out

IT WAS QUITE an experience to suddenly find yourself face-to-face with the guy you idolized growing up.

It wasn't nerve-racking, but it was a situation in which you were in awe. I faced him—it was the third game that I pitched in the major leagues, or at least participated in, not a full game. I started against the Red Sox, I think it was a season-ender in 1957. I believe I was out of the game by the third inning.[73] But the thing that stands out most in my mind was that I was caught in the streak where Ted Williams had gotten on base sixteen straight times in a season. I was a victim. That was my major contribution.[74]

---

[73] It was September 23, 1957, Lumenti's third appearance in the majors and his second start. He would last only 1 1/3 innings.

[74] Williams holds the modern major-league record by reaching base sixteen straight times, from September 17–23, 1957.

He singled to left field and I walked him in the other two times that I faced him when I was in there.

And subsequent to that, I think two years later in 1959, I pitched two innings of relief, I believe, against the Red Sox in Boston and faced him again. Got him out. I felt good about it because in the times I faced him, he wasn't able to pull the ball. I just don't think he could get around on me.[75]

I was wild. That was my problem in my time with the Senators. . . . And it was my undoing. Well, 1–4, if I had that as an average, it would have been great. I had a record for thirty-five years or so until Rob Dibble broke it—wildest pitcher![76] I had what amounted to a couple cups of coffee in the major leagues back then.

I talked to him kind of on a "hi" basis. When I got out of baseball, I was helping a friend coach a team in Johnstown, Pennsylvania, in the Johnstown tournament, and I ran across him down at the Norfolk prison in Massachusetts, and he remembered me. I of course remembered *him*. While he didn't mention specific at-bats, he did remember that I threw hard and said I had a good arm and he remembered batting against me. He was quite a guy.

Based on what he put up there for numbers, he was up at the top of the list. I think one of the toughest hitters I ever faced was [Carl] Yastrzemski. Another Boston hitter, left-handed, and I was a left-handed pitcher.[77]

Just determination, I guess, made him so good. Concentration. Very tough hitter.

---

[75] The detailed listing of Williams' at-bats vs. Lumenti on baseball-reference.com shows that every time Williams hit the ball against Lumenti—including his only hit—it went to the opposite field, with a single to left, two fly-outs to left, and a pop out to third.

[76] Lumenti walked 42 batters in 33 1/3 innings in his career, including 36 in 21 innings (15.4/9 IP) in 1958. Dibble walked 15.7/9 IP in 1995.

[77] Lumenti faced Yasztremski in the minors.

Morrie Martin

Left-handed pitcher

1949:	**Brooklyn Dodgers**
1951–54:	**Philadelphia Athletics**
1954–56:	**Chicago White Sox**
1956:	**Baltimore Orioles**
1957–58:	**St. Louis Cardinals**
1958:	**Cleveland Indians**
1959:	**Chicago Cubs**
Career Statistics:	**38–34, 15 saves, 4.29 ERA**

Ted Williams vs. Morrie Martin:

8-for-20, 2 home runs, 7 RBI, 2 walks, 0 strikeouts, 1 hit by pitch, .400 batting average, .478 on-base percentage, .700 slugging percentage

Home Runs Allowed:

No. 316, August 9, 1951 (game one), at Boston
No. 412, September 1, 1956, at Boston

YOU HATED TO get up there and face him, I know that. But I did my best and I had good luck against him. I had that luck because I pitched him right down the middle and up. Don't ever pitch him low because it's gone. I did that a couple of times. Once that I remember, I think that's the only home run that he hit off of me.

[He had the] best eyes I've ever seen in my life. He could take a pitch that was half an inch inside and wouldn't even bat an eye. He was great, and a good guy to go with it. I talked to him a lot of times.

The only time he hit a home run off of me was in Boston. I knew when I threw it; I said, "Uh-oh, too low," and it was gone.[78]

---

[78] Martin actually allowed two home runs to Williams and both were in Boston. The first occurred on August 9, 1951, in the first game of a doubleheader. Williams hit a solo home run in the first inning of an eventual 6–5 Philadelphia victory. On

Morrie Martin

YEAR	DATE	RESULT
1951	April 22	Ground out
	April 29	Walk
	June 27	Single
	July 4	Fielder's choice
	July 5	Fly out
	Aug. 9	Home run (1 RBI)
		Line out
		Ground out
	Sept. 7	Single
		Fly out
1954	May 25	Fielder's choice
	May 26	Fly out
	May 31	Ground out
		Hit by pitch
	July 25	Single
	Aug. 5	Fly out
	Sept. 1	Fly out
		Single
1955	Aug. 3	Walk
		Fly out
	June 27	Single
		Single
	Sept. 1	Home run (2 RBI)

Anyway, the next day he called me out into the outfield. I wondered what in the heck he wanted with me. So I go out there and talked to him, and he says, "Morris, it took me longer to hit a home run off you than any pitcher I've ever faced in my life." And he said that after the game was over, he'd leave something in my locker . . . and he left one of his rod and reels—that's when he was with Sears, you know—he left me one of his rod and reels engraved in gold. Unfortunately, I've since lost it and can't remember what I did with it.

It just said Ted Williams, home run, you know.

He told me that as soon as it [the ball] leaves your hand, he knew what it is going to be. I said, how the heck can you miss one then? And he said, well, you don't miss them—he didn't miss them either, very seldom—but he said it is just the idea of rotating the bat and getting the bat on it right.

September 1, 1956, Martin relieved for the Orioles in a 2–2 tie in the bottom of the eighth, after George Zuverink allowed a leadoff single to Billy Klaus. Williams followed with a two-run home run, and the Red Sox went on to win 4–2. It was the last time that Martin would face Williams.

He was a great hitter; one of the best I've ever seen in my life. Remember Gil McDougald of the Yankees? I could not get him out! But he was not a long-ball hitter, he was just a good hitter.[79] Stan Musial was another good one . . . one of the greatest.[80] I'll tell you, Williams had better eyes than Musial. You could actually fool Musial, but not very often. Not very often at all.

I knew I had to get it over the plate [against Williams]; I didn't want to walk him, you know. Oh yeah, I wanted to make him hit it. Always did, always did. Yup.

I had a fastball, curveball, slider, and changeup. I had different pitches, and he could read them all. The fastball was more effective. You couldn't throw him a slow breaking ball; he'd kill ya. You couldn't get him out very often. When I played against him, they put that shift on him, you know, and the second baseman would go out in the outfield and pick it up and throw him out. I had to [like it]. He was strictly a pull-hitter, and he defied you to hit it the other way. He wouldn't do it. He was that good a hitter. [We used the shift] all the time and he still got his hits, doggone right.

I talked to him all the time, great guy. He loved people. I'll tell you one thing—he didn't like sportswriters. I don't know why; I guess maybe they said something against him, I don't know what, but he just didn't like them. Didn't want to talk to them. He did most of the talking with his bat.

I remember once I intended to hit him—and really hit him—and I hit him right in the rear end, and he laughed. He said at least you hit me where it didn't hurt. I thought what the hell; I'm getting tired of him wearing me out.

He was the greatest hitter I ever faced. And a great guy with it.

---

[79] While some statistics are missing, of what is known, McDougal was 16–39 (.410) with 4 doubles and 1 home run off Martin.
[80] Martin played on the Cardinals with Musial from 1957–58.

Bill Oster

Left-handed pitcher

1954: .... **Philadelphia Athletics**
Career Statistics: .... **0–1, 0 saves, 6.32 ERA**

Ted Williams vs. Bill Oster

1-for-3, 1 home run, 2 RBI, 1 walk, 1 strikeout, .333 batting average, .500 on-base percentage, 1.333 slugging percentage

Home Runs Allowed:

No. 363, September 5, 1954 (game one), at Philadelphia

IT WAS THE biggest thrill of my life.

I came in relief in the fifth inning, and he was my first hitter.[81] To make a long story short, I struck him out on four pitches. That's the God's honest truth.

I tell a couple of people that, and they look it up, like this guy can't be telling the truth. And they look it up and say, you really did, didn't you?

I couldn't wait to pitch to him. I had a lot of confidence.

Bill Oster

YEAR	DATE	RESULT
1954	Sept. 5	Strikeout
		Fly out
		Home run (2 RBI)
	Sept. 20	Walk

---

[81] On September 5, 1954, in the first game of a doubleheader, Oster was brought in to begin the third inning. Williams would actually be the fourth batter he faced that inning.

I had nothing to lose. I'm a kid, twenty-one years old, and I could throw 96–97 miles-per-hour.

The first three were fastballs. I got two strikes on him immediately—he swung and missed. And then I shook off a curveball. You know, if I got him on the fastball, I wasn't going to fool him with the curveball [laughs]. The next pitch was high—just under his chin—and then he [the catcher] came back with the curveball again, so I threw the curveball and I guess I fooled him, because he missed it completely. It's in the record books, but that's my biggest claim to fame in baseball.

[I remember that] he commented on every pitch to the catcher. That ball was moving, blah, blah, blah, blah. When he came up a second time that game, he said, "He's starting to tire." And I was, because I gave it my all. And he hit a fly ball [out to center field].

Then the third time he got up, he said, "The kid's lost it" and hit a home run. So I went the route: from a strikeout to a home run.

He was the most respected ballplayer I've ever seen. He was just in his own class and a decent guy.

To be where I was, right out of college, that was a thrill in itself. But to face him, my first hitter, in Boston, I couldn't wait. I had a lot of confidence.

I watched him during batting practice shagging balls in the outfield, and he was all by himself. You'd see three guys together when they were shagging flies and stuff like that, but he was always by himself. He was a loner. I did observe that. I said like "hello" to him as I passed him.

I'll tell you another quick story. I just joined the team, and I'm sitting out in the bullpen with my pitching coach, Rollie Hemsley, and he says, "I want to go over these hitters with you. You have a good chance of getting in this game." Vern Stephens[82]—I can still remember all the things he said—you have to pitch him breaking stuff, low and away, blah, blah, blah. [Billy] Goodman got up and said you got to pitch to this guy. He said he gets a lot of walks, so he's not going

---

[82] Stephens actually was on the Baltimore Orioles in 1954.

to help you out. So Ted Williams gets up [laughs], and he didn't say anything. So I said, "So, Rollie, where do you pitch this guy?" He says, "Son, you just throw it and duck." That was his exact words [laughs]; you just throw it and duck.

About that same time when we played the Red Sox in Boston, we got there and we're dressing up for the game while the Red Sox were taking their batting practice. So the bat boy was hanging around and one of our players told the bat boy to let us know when Ted was taking his batting practice. So about ten minutes later, the kid came in and said he's taking his batting practice now. With that, the *whole* dressing room cleared out and went up on deck to watch him. That told me everything, you know. It was amazing.

The next trip we went into New York to play the Yankees. Mickey Mantle got up and maybe one guy went up to watch him. It tells you everything. Wow, what a respected guy.

Duane Pillette

Right-handed pitcher

1949–50: .... **New York Yankees**
1950–53: .... **St. Louis Browns**
1954–55: .... **Baltimore Orioles**
1956: .... **Philadelphia Phillies**
Career Statistics: .... **38–66, 2 saves, 4.40 ERA**

Ted Williams vs. Duane Pillette (data incomplete)

6-for-15, 2 home runs, 3 RBI, 12 walks (1 intentional), 0 strikeouts, .400 batting average, .667 on-base percentage, .800 slugging percentage

Home Runs Allowed:

No. 315, August 1, 1951, at Boston
No. 347, July 18, 1954 (game two), at Boston

WHEN I FIRST made the majors, it was with the Yankees. I never pitched against [Ted] while being with New York. I began my career as a long reliever and I wasn't very good at it. They sent me back to Newark—their farm team. In June of '50, I was traded to St. Louis [Browns]. I pitched a couple of years against him, but he hit me like he hit everybody. I thought he was the best hitter I ever saw. I'm not sure how well he did against me the two and a half years I was with the Browns. I only know that for me, St. Louis was tough on me.

You see, I'm a ground-ball pitcher, and St. Louis had both the Cardinals and the Browns playing on the surface—which seldom has grass—because the weather and the two teams using it constantly caused ground balls to go through much faster than the other parks. When the Browns played their last game ever in 1953, who lost that game? Me! We lost 2–1 in eleven innings. But then the Browns became the Orioles and I had another chance to have a better year.

Duane Pillette

YEAR	DATE	RESULT	YEAR	DATE	RESULT
1950	Sept. 15	Single	1954	July 18	Walk
1951	May 23	Walk			Home run (1 RBI)⚾⚾
		Walk (1 RBI)			Foul out
	Aug. 1	Home run (1 RBI)⚾⚾			Walk
		Fly out		Aug. 8	Walk
		Walk			Walk
		Walk			Fielder's choice
	Sept. 15	Walk			Single
		Intentional walk			Walk
		Single			Ground out
		Fly out	1955	July 8	Single
1953	Sept. 11	Ground out			Walk
		Fly out			
		Ground out			
		Ground out			

Getting back to Williams, it seemed as though I became a real pitcher—Ted will tell you so in the article a fan sent me. He actually said it himself.[83] Yes, then Ted was mine; he couldn't do anything good. Even went 0–4 once.

---

[83] An article Pillette sent along from the website Urban Shocker's Weblog reads: "Yankees manager Casey Stengel chose Pillette to throw batting practice for the American League All-Stars [in 1954], and the junior circuit's best went on the [sic] rack up a record (at the time) 17 hits in the contest. At the game, Red Sox great Ted Williams told Pillette he was the toughest pitcher he'd faced all year, and Al Rosen of the Indians—the reigning MVP—rated him one of the league's best fastball pitchers."

I also found out that Ted has said to umpires that he played with my father[84] on PCL San Diego when he was eighteen [in 1937]. He said my dad taught me how to cheat, but that's not true!

---

[84] Herman Pillette, who pitched in the majors in 1917, and from 1922–24.

Tom Qualters

Right-handed pitcher

1953, 1957–58: .... **Philadelphia Phillies**
1958: .... **Chicago White Sox**
Career Statistics: .... **0–0, 0 saves, 5.64 ERA**

Ted Williams vs. Tom Qualters

1-for-2, 0 extra-base hits, 0 RBI, 0 walks, 0 strikeouts, .500 batting average, .500 on-base percentage, .500 slugging percentage

Tom Qualters

YEAR	DATE	RESULT
1958	May 25	Fly out
	July 10	Single

I HAD JUST JOINED the ballclub[85] and didn't expect to be seeing any action. So they called down and I got hot, and I couldn't quite understand why they were using me. It was my lack of experience. I came in the game, and Al Lopez, who was just a great manager—you couldn't kid him on anything— I met him at the mound and he handed me the ball and said, "How you going to pitch this guy?" And of course that guy happened to be Ted Williams. I'm walking in there, and I'm thinking he's going to give me all kinds of advice on what to do and what not to do, but he just asks how you going to pitch this guy.

---

[85] Qualters was traded from the Phillies to the White Sox on April 30, 1958. He faced Williams for the first time on May 25, his fourth appearance for Chicago.

I threw a natural sinking fastball and I had a curveball that every-body raved and knew about. So I said to him that I was going to try to miss low and away on the outside and try to hope he goes for it . . . and if he doesn't, I'm going to go with breaking balls the rest of the way. He said okay and walked off the mound.

As I threw my warm-ups, Williams, he moves up close to get a good view of what you're doing. So I didn't throw the ball very hard. I just threw four-seam fastballs, which don't move at all, and just laid them up there at about three-quarter speed. I [also] threw some curveballs. I threw them all like changeup curveballs, off-speed curveballs, so he didn't have a chance to see what I threw.

So the first pitch I was lucky enough that I got the ball down and away. The thing is that the bases were loaded and there was a *huge* crowd. I don't know what the occasion was, but the place was packed.[86] I luckily made the pitch I was trying to make and he swung. He went after it and just hit a short pop fly to center field, so it worked out pretty well.

Some years earlier I was in a situation—I played half a year at B-ball and this new Triple-A club was going to be in Miami, Florida. I just wanted to make that club so bad and I never thought I could. But as spring training went through day after day, I was still on the team, but we still had too many players. Opening day comes and there were a lot of ex-major league players on the team, and we had a bunch of really great young pitchers who all went to the major leagues; but here it is, opening day, big crowd and I'm still there. All of a sudden—Bill Veeck was our general manager, and he was really a wild and crazy guy—here comes a helicopter over the stadium and it lands besides the pitcher's mound. And who gets out but Satchel Paige.

So maybe the first or second or third game, I don't know what, I enter in a pretty tough situation late in the game—men on base and all that—and I get out there, and from the time I was a little kid, as long

---

[86] It was a Sunday doubleheader in Chicago. According to ballparks.com, the atten-dance was 19,121. The Comiskey capacity in 1958 was 52,000.

as I had a baseball or a rock or anything in my pocket, I wasn't afraid of anything. So here I am, I get out there on the mound and I'm taking my warm-up pitches, and I get the shakes. I never had that in my life, I tell ya, I was shaking all over. Somehow or other I got them out, I don't know how the hell it happened.

I went home that night and I thought 'you can't bullshit another player.' Probably, in my mind, every player on that team knew I was gutless. I was trying to figure out what the hell to do. I was so fearful that these guys knew I didn't have the courage to play the game.

So I'm down in the bullpen the next night, I'm just sitting there and I guess I was pretty quiet. And Satch, as early in the season as it was, we had become close friends. He sat behind me, and he bumped me on the leg and said, "What's the matter son?" I didn't know what to do, so I told him what happened.

He just laughed and said, "I'm going to tell you something, son. Them sons a bitches can beat you, but they can't eat you." And damned if that same night I wasn't back in another close game. I went out there and got the shakes again. I just said to myself, "you sons a bitches, you can beat me, but you can't eat me," and I got over it and sailed through and from that day on, I could hardly wait to get out there in those situations.

The way you think of it—at least the way I do—when you come into that situation [against Williams], I was flabbergasted in the fact that I was even in that situation and he brought me in.

You look at it as an opportunity; you don't look at it negatively. You look at it as a positive, because here's the great Ted Williams. Well, hell, everybody knows he should hit me, so if I can get him out, then that's a plus for me. If he gets a base hit, that's Ted Williams.

So I learned early on because of Satchel Paige that you go out there and you do the best you can do. You win some, lose some, and some are rained out.

I knew it was Ted Williams, but to me it was just another hitter. I just think he was a special hitter, and if I get him out I get him out, and if he gets a base hit, it won't be his first one.

Hal Raether

Right-handed pitcher

1954:	.... **Philadelphia Athletics**
1957:	.... **Kansas City Athletics**
Career Statistics:	.... **0–0, 0 saves, 6.75 ERA**

Ted Williams vs. Hal Raether:

0-for-0, walk, .000 batting average, 1.000 on-base percentage, .000 slugging percentage

July 4, 1954, bottom of the eighth inning, led off with a walk.

Hal Raether

YEAR	DATE	RESULT
1954	July 4	Walk

THAT WAS MY first major-league game.[87] I had just graduated from the University of Wisconsin when they still had baseball. I completed my eligibility in June and signed that month with the Philadelphia Athletics. They kept me after I signed with them, which I felt was a little bit unusual. Of course, they were not very good, so I suppose they needed all the talent they could find.

What was probably the highlight of the whole thing was that I had a friend from high school who was stationed in Newport, Rhode Island, and when I got to Boston, I thought, gee, I ought to really give him a call and let him know I'm with the Athletics. So I did call him and got him a ticket, and he came to the game with his wife and little daughter.

---

[87] July 4, 1954

He and I have remained friends ever since, and for him to have seen me pitch in the big leagues in the first place, and then against Ted Williams, was kind of a unique thing for our friendship.

Well, anyway, I don't recall what inning I got in, but I know we were [laughs], well, behind in the game.[88] I can remember standing out on the mound and looking out at the crowd—obviously the biggest crowd I'd ever played in front of—and saying to myself, "Here you are, what are you going to do about it [laughs]?"

I think it was in the second inning that I pitched in which Williams came up—I don't think it was the first inning—and I'm trying to remember some of the other ballplayers that the Red Sox had. Jimmy Piersall might have been playing at that time. I think he might have been in center field.[89] Anyway, all of a sudden, gee, there's Ted Williams swinging a bat, getting ready to face me, and I'm saying to myself, for a guy from Lake Mills, Wisconsin, this is pretty big stuff. I had never seen him play in person before, and all of a sudden, I'm playing against him.

I'm trying to remember who was catching for us at the time. Possibly Billy Shantz? Joe Astroth probably would have been the catcher.[90] Anyway, I think I had him 3–2 if I'm not mistaken, and then on the [next] pitch, I walked him on what I thought was a pretty good pitch. I'm kind of reminded of the fact that most umpires probably realized Ted Williams had better eyes then them, so if he didn't swing, it had to have been a ball.

Well anyway, he gets on first base and I was as nervous, of course, as you can imagine. What I was doing was—I had my foot on the rubber and in my nervousness, I take the ball out of my glove and throw it

---

[88] Raether entered the game in the seventh inning with the A's trailing, 7–0.

[89] Raether faced Williams in his second inning of work. Piersall did play, but came in mid-game for Jackie Jensen and played right field.

[90] Shantz started at catcher, but was replaced by Astroth, who was behind the plate when Raether entered the game.

back into my glove. Take it out, throw it in. Take it out, throw it in. And in the definition of the rules, that's a balk.

I was warned by the umpire not to do that. In the meantime, Ted Williams, who was on first base after I walked him, asked Lou Limmer, who was our first baseman, to come over and tell me to relax and that things would be okay. So I thought that was rather noteworthy. I somehow or other ended up getting out of the inning. I think I gave up one run in the two innings, if I'm not mistaken.[91] But basically that was my experience facing Ted Williams.

What's really been neat about it is that I've been able to tell my grandchildren about it—and anybody else who wants to listen to me— that I pitched against Ted Williams. It was a very proud moment of my life.

The next spring—I had a big-league contract, so I took spring training with what was then the Kansas City Athletics—and if you recall, Eddie Joost was fired, and the team was sold, and they brought over Lou Boudreau, who had been the manager for Boston that previous year. And he brought over his pitching coach. I remember they were telling stories about Ted Williams—meaning the coaches— of his extreme, acute eyesight. One of the stories they told us was that when he got out of the service, he rejoined the Red Sox and he was taking batting practice. He said, you know, something is wrong with the pitching rubber. He said that the pitcher, when he throws to me, seems to be out of whack a little bit. The rubber must be wrong. They put a transit on it apparently, and found out that, I think, the rubber was like an inch off or something on one end. It wasn't square with the plate. So he had great eyesight.

Another story they told was that—you know, most ballplayers do go to a lot of movies because they have time on their hands. And they'd step out of the hotel they were staying at, and Ted would come out and they'd say, Ted, what's playing in that theater down there four blocks

---

[91] In two innings of work, Raether gave up 1 run on 1 hit with 4 walks.

down from the hotel? And apparently, he'd—according to what they said—he could tell not only what the movie was, but who was playing in it.

They also said that he'd—when they were on the road and in a hotel room—he'd spend a lot of time with his bats, swinging and looking at his swing while looking at the mirror. So apparently he worked very hard at what he did, or was good at. That's just another story, whether it is true or not, I don't know. Those are the things I heard.

Phil Regan

Right-handed pitcher

1960–65:	Detroit Tigers
1966–68:	Los Angeles Dodgers
1968–72:	Chicago Cubs
1972:	Chicago White Sox
Career Statistics:	96–81, 92 saves, 3.84 ERA
National League All-Star:	1966

Ted Williams vs. Phil Regan

0-for-0, 0 RBI, 1 walk, .000 batting average, 1.000 on-base percentage, .000 slugging percentage

I ONLY FACED WILLIAMS one time—threw six pitches down and away—he never swung at one.

The 3–2 pitch was good, down and away. Catcher[92] said to me, "Phil, that is a strike to everyone else—not to Ted Williams."

Phil Regan

YEAR	DATE	RESULT
1960	Aug. 6	Walk

---

[92] Regan's catcher was Harry Chiti.

Marv Rotblatt

Left-handed pitcher

1948, 1950–51: .... **Chicago White Sox**
Career Statistics: .... **4–3, 2 saves, 4.82 ERA**

Ted Williams vs. Marv Rotblatt:

2-for-7, 1 double, 0 home runs, 4 RBI, 0 walks, 0 strikeouts, 1 grounded into double play, .286 batting average, .286 on-base percentage, .429 slugging percentage

❙SIGNED WITH THE Sox in 1948, and they told me they were going to put me right in the majors, or else I would have signed with the Dodgers, which I would have anyway. But it worked out because I'm short-sighted. I'm thinking, "wow, they offered me a chance to play right in the majors. I have to do it. I might never have this opportunity again." So I took it.

I'm there about three days—it was in June of '48[93]—and they finally put me in a game against the Tigers on a Sunday. The guys on the bench are all telling each other "Hey, put Marv in the game," so I heard about it.

Marv Rotblatt

YEAR	DATE	RESULT
1948	July 23	Fly out
		Double (3 RBI)
1951	June 3	Fly out
		Grounded into DP
	June 22	Foul out
	June 24	Single
	July 12	Fly out

each other "Hey, put Marv in the game," so I heard about it.

---

[93] Rotblatt made his major-league debut on Sunday, July 4, 1948, in the first game of a doubleheader.

They bring me in the game in the eighth inning—two innings to go, we think. The first pitch I threw was up against the screen . . . I was a little nervous. So Mike Tresh, our catcher, comes out to me—this is true—he looks at me and says, "Marv, this is a ball. That's a glove. That's the mound. Now get the fucking ball over the plate." I believe he used the *f* word, but he might not have. He was a real gentleman. And I think I told you his son was Tom Tresh.

So I get all six guys out on ground balls. I don't know what I'm doing, but I get out of it. I can tell you an aside that happened. Bob Elson was our radio announcer, The Commander. He said he confronted Rogers Hornsby—a drunk and a boozer and a gambler who hangs out at the ballpark in the Bard's Room—that's where he drinks and eats. You know, the media room. So Elson went up to Hornbsy and says, "Rog, what did you think of that left-hander we brought up from the University of Illinois?" And he said [with a straight face], "Bob, if they turned the lights out in ballpark, I'd go 3–4 off of him." Which is a very funny remark for a guy like Rogers Hornsby to come up with.

The next game we're on the road in Fenway Park, bases loaded in the bottom of the eighth inning, and we're losing, 2–0. Bill Wight is pitching a very good game. They get the bases loaded with nobody out, and Ted Lyons brings me in. Wight was a lefty, why he was bringing me in—another lefty—I don't have the slightest idea. He wasn't exactly a genius manager, but Ted Lyons was a hell of a nice guy and a great pitcher. He was a competitor. You lose a game, a close game, he'd break down half the lockers. But on the surface was a real pleasant guy.

He brings me in the game, and again, I don't know what the hell I'm doing. I get Stan Spence, who led the league in hitting the year before for the Washington Senators.[94] The Red Sox got him, of course, to see if he could help them buy a pennant. I get him to 3–0—way

---

[94] Spence hit .279 for the Senators in 1947, which did not place him in the top ten of the leading hitters. Spence was 10th in hitting in the American League in 1946 (.292), 5th in 1944 (.316), and 3rd in 1942 (.323).

to get ahead of him, Marv. Fastball, 3–1, takes it. Fastball, 3–2, takes it. Three-and-two pitch, he hits a pop fly to the first baseman. I don't know what I'm doing, but I've got the out.

The next hitter is Vern Stephens. Good power hitter. I get him 3–0. I don't know how I'm getting the ball over the plate, but I am; I got guts. Then I get a strike, 3–1, then another one, 3–2, then he hits a pop fly to the shortstop for the second out.

I now have two outs and here comes Ted. I get him 3–0. I like to get ahead of these guys because I feel sorry for them—making a facetious remark, why didn't I. So the count is 3–0, and then I get a called strike, 3–1. Now, you tell me on God's earth, why Ted Williams, the greatest hitter of all time, is going to take a fastball off a little Jewish kid who is five-foot-six. With the count 3–1, he takes it right down the pike, 3–2. The next pitch ends up about four or five inches inside; I know that because I got it there. But he swings and pops it up to the second baseman for the third out, which if we count correctly, now means a one-two-three inning. And the crowd kind of gives me a nice standing ovation . . . and that was my first experience against Ted.

I came down from our dressing room to our ballpark and Joe Dobson, who pitched with us . . . I have a picture of us when we won twelve in a row on the road in 1951, which is damn hard to do *anywhere*. We won twelve in a row and I saved Dobson's game, as a matter of fact. He's holding me up in the picture.

Anyway, he said, "Hey, kid, how'd you throw that atom ball?"

"What do you mean?"

"Well, you throw it and they hit it at 'em."

It's a baseball joke. Never going to be funny anywhere.

So the next game he brings me in again. Think lightning can strike twice? Bases loaded, nobody out, and Ted Williams is the first guy I'm facing. First pitch, he's not taking a strike. He doubles off the monster; hit it hard. He just hit it out and got it up on the ball, no big deal. That was it for the time being. That was 1948. He [usually] pulls the ball, but he didn't pull it against me. My 110, 140 mile-an-hour fastball, he couldn't get around on it.[95]

The next time I faced him was 1951, and I faced him a couple of times. I got him out, but he beat me in a game in Fenway Park; it had to be in August. We were in first place at the time, barely, against the Yankees. He brings me in the game—but my fault though—first guy up, I walked. You don't do that in a tie ballgame, bottom of the ninth inning. My fault.

Next batter was bunting. Bob Dillinger comes in from [third] base, no one was covering third base. It was Dom DiMaggio, beats it out.

John Pesky comes up next, first and second, nobody out. And I'm a good fielder—I actually started a triple play.[96] So he bunts it down third, and I grab it right off the mound. After he bunted, I'm there, I'm ready, picking up the ball, ready to go to third base, and here's this schmuck, Bob Dillinger, standing next to me again. He was a good hitter, but a nitwit. A flake.

So now I have the bases loaded, nobody out, and of course I'll embellish the statement and say I looked into the dugout, and what are they doing? They're packing up their bags. They weren't really packing up the bags, but it's a good logical idea to get a head start.

So the first pitch to Ted, I throw him a fastball—extra fastball—I threw it by him, I know I did. So he turns and says something to Phil Masi, who after the game tells me he said, "What'd that kid do,

---

[95] Rotblatt pitched twice against the Red Sox in 1948, and they did come on back-to-back days—July 22 and 23. However, Williams did not play in the game on July 22. Rotblatt relieved Bill Wight on July 23, and pitched three innings, facing Williams twice in that game—flying out to left field in the fifth inning and doubling with the bases loaded in the seventh inning. Stan Spence played on July 22, but not on July 23. Also, Vern Stephens batted after Williams in the lineup on July 23, not before.

[96] On May 13, 1951, Rotblatt caught a pop bunt off the bat of Cleveland's Jim Hegan before it hit the ground, then threw to Chico Carrasquel to catch the runner off second, and Carrasquel threw to first to complete the triple play.

take something off that pitch?" I threw my best shot! I know damn well I threw it right by him—swing and a miss. Unless he just missed the ball, and Williams doesn't miss many fastballs down the middle.

The next pitch was a curveball—swing and a miss. I got him 0–2, and my changeup at that time was my best pitch. When I throw [my changeup] to right-handers, it tails away from the hitter. Mickey Mantle hit the ball off me three times—twice to the first baseman on spin jobs off the end of the bat. He was way out in front of it. It would tail in to the lefties, which was a little dangerous because you can get away with it; you can fool them and they can get wood on the ball if they're able to.

So sure enough, I got him 0–2, and we call a changeup. I tried to get it way outside, you know, try to get it on the outside corner and end up there. It went on the outside corner initially, and I fooled him on it, he was out in front. He hit a little ground ball, a dribbler past me, beats it out, ball game.

The next day I see him in the outfield. "Hitter my ass," I tell him.

"Marv, it looks like a line drive in the books." Can't argue with that![97]

The couple of times I met him—I'm selling insurance now. One time, I did a crazy thing. We were doing an insurance course in Boston. My home office was New England Life. It was actually the oldest charter company in America. We had a school there. So we go to school, and there's a buddy of mine who played a little pro ball, played in Class C, one of the agents. I said let's go out to the ballpark, I want to throw batting practice. Out of the clear blue! I'm going to throw fucking batting practice to the Red Sox—like I can get away with it!

So we go out there, and fortunately [for us] it rained, so they didn't have batting practice. We go to the dressing room. I'm trying to

---

[97] On June 24, 1951, Williams hit an RBI infield single off Rotblatt in the bottom of the seventh inning to give Boston a 6–5 lead in an eventual 8–6 Red Sox win, in which Rotblatt would suffer the loss.

remember the right-handed pitcher who played at Fenway Park the year before, when Pinky Higgins was the manager of Birmingham. He was now the manager of the Red Sox. Real nice guy, real nice guy.

We go into his dressing room—I can't think of the name of the guy; it wasn't Denny Galehouse; it wasn't Tex Hughson; it was a good right-handed pitcher with the Red Sox, and I'm sorry I can't think of his name.[98] Well, he recognizes me in street clothes!

He says, "Marv Rotblatt, what are you doing here?" Bah-ba-ba-dum. He says, "Come in and say hello to Pinky Higgins, he'd like to see you." Now why would Pinky Higgins like to see me? Rhetorical question.

So I go in there and the first thing he says is, "Hey, remember Marv Rotblatt?" And Pinky Higgins says to me, "Changeup my ass." That's what he says. First three words to me, because I had beaten Birmingham—when I won 22 in 1950. I was there at school in like 1957 or '58; I was out of baseball. He remembered. That year I was 6–0 against Birmingham.

So I see Ted and tell him that I'm in the insurance business. He says who you with? I say New England, and he says, "Oh, I have a policy with them. I got a policy with about ten companies." Probably can't say no to an offer. I didn't have the guts to say, 'Ted, let's make it eleven,' but he was friendly as hell.

I saw him two more times after that. I saw him when I was playing semi-pro ball and selling insurance in 1959. That was the year the [White] Sox won the pennant. I'm pitching batting practice with them; I'm also pitching with the Cubs because I'm playing semi-pro ball. I was 12–0 that year! They were riding the hell out of me. Get the old guy off the field, bah-bah-bah-dum. But I was tough and a good competitor.

---

[98] The player Rotblatt refers to likely was Frank Sullivan, who played for Higgins in Birmingham in 1950, and pitched for the Red Sox from 1953–60.

So after batting practice, I wanted to go get an autographed ball for one of my clients from Ted. The dressing rooms were next to each other in Chicago those days. I walked into the dressing room because I knew the clubhouse guy—it was a guy named Sharky Colledge. Ted is on the rubbing table and I go up to talk to him. He says, "Marv, I want to tell you a story about the ball game last night. I'm up, we're losing by a run, top of the ninth inning, and they bring in Gerry Staley." Staley was a relief pitcher that year and helped them win the pennant. "I'm in the batting box, and he throws *nine straight* knuckleballs warming up. What's his first pitch going to be, Marv?"

I said, "Fastball."

He says, "Right. I looked for the fastball, and I got the fastball, I was so anxious, I hit a one-bouncer back to him, I broke the fucking bat. I was so pissed because I was way in front of it and I guessed right."

See, you'd say the average guy would say, he threw nine knuckleballs warming up, he's going to throw a knuckleball, right? He was setting him up. I knew that because I would do the same thing, having pitching experience and so on.

Then in batting practice a couple of times, when I was still playing ball, I'd do my wind sprints and then come back down on the field and watch him hit because he was a pleasure to watch. He'd be behind the cage talking to Nellie Fox or Eddie Robinson about hitting and helping them. They had a second baseman named Bobby Doerr, who hit around .300, .310 with the Red Sox in those days. Ted once said of Bobby Doerr in an article, "I could have made him a .350 hitter if he'd have listened." That's the kind of rapport he had with ballplayers.

The last time I saw him—alive of course—was when he became the manager of the Washington Senators for a year after he retired from ball. He didn't exactly work at it very hard—you might say hardly working. I didn't have a lot of experiences with him, but enough to remember.

Nobody talks about this and it was a big happening. It was the last game of the year [in 1948], and they're [the Red Sox] playing us at Comiskey Park. And Cleveland, who they were tied with, had already lost, so they were half a game ahead going into the last game of the year. Williams is up and we're ahead by a run, first and third, two out. And they warned John Pesky, he was on first base. The coach at first base must have told Pesky to be aware of his [Bill Wight's] move, because he had the best move I'd ever seen in baseball, and I'm counting all the great moves like Warren Spahn, Whitey Ford, guys like that. He had a move that was dynamite. One split second and he'd already have the ball at first base.

So sure enough, on the first pitch, Williams has the bat on his shoulder, ready to hit, and Bill Wight picked him [Pesky] off. End of ball game. That's the way the ball game ended with the Red Sox, with Williams hanging with the bat in his hand. They walked off the field and I said, "They're beat." And the next day in the playoff game at Fenway Park, Boudreau hit two home runs, a double, a single, and drove in about five runs, and that was it. But they never talk about it. Imagine getting beat with a guy getting picked off first base and Ted Williams with a bat in his hand. They never talk about it. To me, it is a very important story about Ted Williams.[99]

There's an article from 1988 in *Sports Illustrated* called "Nemesis." That's a funny article. Army has Navy. Muhammad Ali has Joe Frazier.

---

[99] It is unclear which game Rotblatt is talking about, but the Red Sox actually ended the regular season with four straight wins over the Indians and Yankees. Boston lost eight games to the White Sox in 1948: A pair of 4–3 games to the White Sox in a May 23 doubleheader in Chicago; 5–3 at Fenway on June 12; 3–1 in Chicago on June 24; lost three of four in early August in Chicago (4–3 on August 6; 5–1 on August 7; 2–1 in game two of a doubleheader on August 8); and 17–10 in Chicago on September 15.

Oklahoma has Nebraska. Ted Williams has Marv Rotblatt, with a question mark. Great article. We don't know who started the rumor; it must have been by Rotblatt. That's how it ends, which is funny.

I had no idea. One of my son's buddies told him about it back in 1988: Hey, your dad is in *Sports Illustrated*. It's an honor to have gotten in there.

He was the best. I enjoyed watching him play. After a workout, we'd come downstairs and hang around the dugout by the batting cage just to watch him hit, because he had such great control of the bat.

Bob Shaw

Right-handed pitcher

1957–58: ....**Detroit Tigers**
1958–61: ....**Chicago White Sox**
1961: ....**Kansas City Athletics**
1962–63: ....**Milwaukee Braves**
1964-66: ....**San Francisco Giants**
1966–67: ....**New York Mets**
1967: .... **Chicago Cubs**
Career Statistics: .... **108–98, 32 saves, 3.52 ERA**
National League All-Star: **1962**

Ted Williams vs. Bob Shaw:

4-for-14, 2 doubles, 1 home run, 3 RBI, 3 walks (1 intentional), 0 strike-outs, 1 sacrifice fly, 1 double play, .286 batting average, .389 on-base percentage, .643 slugging percentage

Home Runs Allowed:

No. 509, July 27, 1960, at Boston

I THINK I WAS very fortunate against Ted Williams, but I consider him probably the best hitter that I ever faced. And then when I looked at the statistics, I realized that I did fairly well [against him]. I got a real swollen head.

In '59, he said in some article that I was the third-toughest right-hander for him to face. Well, woooo. That kind of blew my mind. But he was outstanding. The things that stick out in my mind are things that you've probably heard already.

If you were warming up in the bullpen, he would just watch every move you made. He studied you. I also did some lecturing, and I was on the dais with him, and he was very intelligent. If you were talking about fishing, he knew what he was talking about. If he was talking about baseball, he knew what he was talking about.

He believed in that four-degree upstroke. He was trying to get that ball out of the park. Now, you could argue—Joe Gordon used to teach hitting down on the ball, [Hank] Aaron, I think, hit down on the ball—but he really knew what he was talking about. He was a student of the game and a very impressive individual.

I do remember the home run. Bad news, yeah, I remember that. He hit it in Fenway Park way out there where that wall is. He hit it to right-center field. I can still see it going.

I had to keep the ball down, and that's the way I pitched. Now I'll tell you one thing, you didn't want to knock him down. There's a few guys in the league that you knew that if you knocked him down, he'd get pissed and be a better hitter. Because back in those days, you know, you'd loosen up some guys pretty good. But you didn't want to do that with Williams. We would talk about that, because he would just became a better hitter. Now that doesn't mean you don't pitch in, but you don't want to try to intentionally knock him down because the results were not going to be good.

Bob Shaw

YEAR	DATE	RESULT
1958	June 18	Sac fly (1 RBI)
	July 27	Intentional walk
1959	May 13	Fly out
		Fly out
		Single
		Ground out
	Sept. 13	Ground out
1960	May 12	Fielder's choice
	June 12	Walk
		Line out
		Double
	June 24	Line out
		Walk
		Double (1 RBI)
		Fly out
	July 27	Ground out
		Grounded into DP
		Home run (1 RBI)

When [I think about my] toughest out . . . if I had to name a couple guys, I'd mention Jackie Brandt, Tito Francona, Bob Lillis—a little shortstop for Houston. Now [Mickey] Mantle, he hit some gigantic home runs off of me, but I could still get him out.

I would have to say I was extremely fortunate [against Williams]. I mean, when I look at the stats—4–14, .286—hey, that's not too damn bad against him, someone I consider probably the best hitter I ever saw.

He would not swing at a bad ball. No matter what the score was, what the situation, he was not going to swing at a bad ball. But you still had to pitch to him carefully. Now when I look at it, I see where I did give him three walks. You had to be careful. He would not swing at a bad ball, which of course makes it more difficult. Some guys you can get them to go after a bad pitch, but not him.

I would pitch him low and away—because my ball sank—was probably my best bet. As I look back and reflect on it, I know that if I had to throw a strike, I had to throw it low and away to him. He was a very good breaking-ball hitter, so you had to be very, very careful about that. For me, my best shot would be low and away.

He'll hit the high ball, too. But my point is that I wasn't very effective high. Even if that's his strength, I had to go my strength against his strength because I was not effective up, as the ball would straighten out. I was not really overpowering, with a great fastball. The ball moved well; I had a good slider, a good sinker, but for me, reflecting back, if I gotta throw a strike, I still would rather throw the sinking fastball.

I don't know whether it was in Chicago [the last time I saw him], if it was a big clinic and I can't remember, Spokane or wherever it was, but he was there. They had him lecturing on hitting and they had me lecturing on pitching, and then for some reason or other, they got me and him and somebody else up there answering questions that the coaches might ask. But I got a chance to meet him personally, and he was a very dynamic person. If he walked into a room, he kind of electrified the room. He had quite a presence.

George Spencer

Right-handed pitcher

1950–55: ....New York Giants
1958, 1960: ....Detroit Tigers
Career Statistics: ....16–10, 9 saves, 4.05 ERA

Ted Williams vs. George Spencer

0-for-1
May 2, 1958, bottom of the eighth inning, led off by lining out.

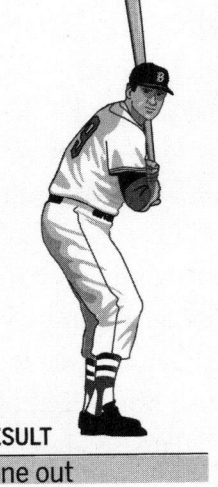

George Spencer

YEAR	DATE	RESULT
1958	May 2	Line out

WE WERE IN Boston and I was sitting out in the bullpen with my buddies. It was the first time I had ever been in the American League, and we were just talking naturally about Ted Williams, and they were good enough to tell me that if he hadn't seen or faced you before, he would not hit the first pitch. Well this is pretty good information for a pitcher to have, or at least you'd think.

Anyway, I get in the ball game—I think it was the eighth inning or so—and here's Ted Williams as the first hitter I'm going to face. I get my warm-up pitches in, and while I'm warming up, he's about halfway between the on-deck circle and home plate . . . and he's watching me like an eagle.

I finally finish up my warm-up pitches and I look up, and Dick Gernert was in the on-deck circle, and he hollered at Williams, and Ted walks back over to talk to Dick. Now I know exactly what Dick is telling Ted, because I had pitched against Dick in the American Association a couple of years [earlier].

Ted then comes back up to the plate and here we go. I was a sinkerball pitcher, and I knew Dick Gernert was telling him that he's a sinkerball pitcher, so watch for it low and away. But my buddies out there in the bullpen, they'd also told me that he won't hit the first pitch. Now I'm more inclined to go along with my own team.

I throw the first pitch, which was low and away. Good pitch. It was either a strike or just off of the plate. And he swings at it and hits a line drive to Ray Boone, who was playing first base. Boone thought the ball was going to carry and started to jump after it, and it was a sinker. Boonie caught it just about waist-high. If he hadn't jumped, he might have ended up in right field, the ball was hit that hard.

On how I came out of the experience on pitching to Williams . . . well thank God he didn't hit that ball back through the box! But that was my experience with Ted Williams. There's not much to it. I should have told Boonie to charge that ball, but it was quite an experience. It was one of the highlights, I think, of my career.

It was interesting to find about my teammates; those guys didn't do me any favors. Apparently they were giving me some good information, but I think the fact that Dick Gernert was in the on-deck circle and called Ted over and explained to him what he thought the kind of pitcher I was, gave Williams the edge. Because he was looking for a pitch and he got it. He didn't pop it up, I'll tell you that.

I can't remember what year it was, but I was in the Red Sox organization and went to spring training. I had hurt my arm in the winter time and was trying to rehab. You know, I can throw, and I'm starting to come around in the strengthening of the arm, and I'm doing halfway decent. The Red Sox go on the road, and they leave Rico Petrocelli.

Left him at home and Ted was one of the coaches who stayed at home. Anyway, I'm going to throw some batting practice to Rico. I get all warmed up and there we go, and I'm on the mound throwing batting practice. Now when I throw batting practice, I wasn't one of those guys who tried to lay the ball in and see how far the hitters could hit it. I'm trying to help the hitters; at least that's the way I felt. I won't say that I'm wide open, but I'm putting some pretty decent stuff on the ball. I threw two different fastballs—a cross-seam fastball and a sinking fastball. So we're in the process of taking the batting practice and Ted is behind the cage and I could hear him. I would throw a cross-seam fastball and hear him say, "Did you see it, did you?" Then I would throw the sinker, and he wouldn't say anything. I was mixing up the pitches, and I'm saying to myself—and I'm an older pitcher and I'm saying to myself, "What in the world am I doing that he can call every pitch that I'm throwing?" And I'm only throwing the two fastballs, I'm not throwing a breaking ball or anything. But, anyway, I didn't ask him what I was doing. I should have, but as smart as I am, I guess, why would you want to know what you're doing that he's reading? But that was another experience with Ted.

In that spring training, it was interesting to me—he had a voice that was absolutely explosive. We would be in the ballpark, and he was great with the fungo. He could lay that ball—where you're running the pitchers or something like that—he'd lay that ball out there, just off to where you couldn't quite catch it. Somebody would do something out there, teasing him or something like that, and you could hear him and his favorite thing to say was: *"Is that right?"* And it would just fill the ballpark. I don't think I've ever been around anybody who had a voice like he had in that ballpark. But he'd wear those pitchers out.

We were in the dressing room one day after the main part of the club had gone on the road. We were in the clubhouse and of course, when you're around Ted Williams, you have to be discussing baseball. So at one point, he looks over at me and said, "Spencer, you're an older guy, why does a baseball curve? When you throw a curveball, why does it curve?" I said, "Well, I think what happens is when you put the spin on the ball, there's some aerodynamics involved there that the spin of the ball causes the ball to curve."

And he didn't say too much, but he walked over to a trash can that was there, and he grabbed a big piece of cardboard that was in there and grabbed a marking pen. And he drew a wing, with, of course, the upper part of the wing was the curvature on it, and the lower part was flat. He had been in the Air Corps doing the war, and he went through the technicalities of why an airplane can fly. The fact that the air underneath goes straight, and the air up above has to go up above the wing. That was his explanation of why the curveball curves. And who am I to argue with him?

I always thought he was very interesting. It was a great experience being around him . . . one of the highlights of my career, and I'm glad I had the opportunity.

Dick Stigman

Left-handed pitcher

1960–61: .... Cleveland Indians
1962–65: .... Minnesota Twins
1966: ....Boston Red Sox
Career Statistics: .... 46–54, 16 saves, 4.03 ERA
American League All-Star: 1960

Ted Williams vs. Dick Stigman

0-for-2, 1 RBI, 1 walk, 1 strikeout, .000 batting average, .333 on-base percentage, .000 slugging percentage

SINCE WILLIAMS WAS at the end of his career, I can't really say my success against him was all that great. I just felt privileged to have pitched to him. My best memory is a game on May 20, in Cleveland, when I struck him out on three pitches, probably all perfect; he never swung the bat, but just whirled around and walked back to the dugout.

Al Kaline was the toughest out because I faced him more than Williams (no discredit to Williams, having only faced him three times).[100]

Dick Stigman

YEAR	DATE	RESULT
1960	May 20	Strikeout
	July 22	Fielder's choice
	Sept. 13	Walk (1 RBI)

Obviously pitching to someone so famous made your heart beat faster, and would bring your adrenaline to its peak.

---

[100] Kaline had 54 plate appearances against Stigman, going 9–43 with 9 hits, 2 home runs, 5 RBI, 10 walks, 6 strikeouts, and a .209 batting average.

Wes Stock

Right-handed pitcher

1959–64: .... **Baltimore Orioles**
1964–67: ....**Kansas City Athletics**
Career Statistics: .... **27–13, 22 saves, 3.60 ERA**

Ted Williams vs. Wes Stock

0-for-1, 1 strikeout
August 21, 1960, bottom of the ninth inning, led off by striking out swinging.

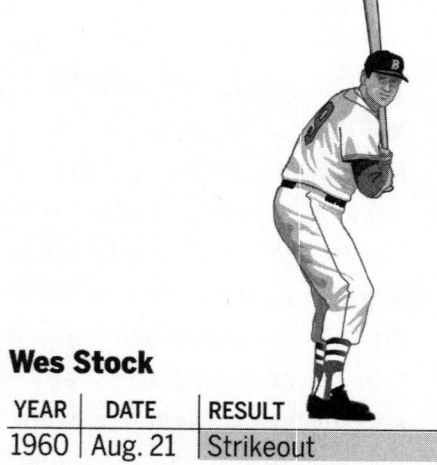

Wes Stock

YEAR	DATE	RESULT
1960	Aug. 21	Strikeout

TO START OFF, I only pitched against him one time. I saw his last home run when I was with Baltimore, and we played in Boston, and he hit a two-run homer[101] in the bottom of the eighth to go ahead.

Then, in the top of the ninth—I think Pinky Higgins was the manager—and when the inning was ready to start, he called time and sent Carroll Hardy in to exchange places with. And he [Williams] ran all the way hard, ran right into the dugout and down and up the runway, and for ten minutes they could not start the game because he would not come out and take a bow. Because he had announced that was his last game. So that's the only thing I know about Ted.

I was in bullpen [during the game]. He almost hit one in the at-bat before. When you're a kid coming up, you don't realize all the history to it, you know.

---

[101] It was actually a solo home run.

The slider was one of my best pitches. So I mean, coming up, I wanted to be successful, so I went with my best stuff. But I had very good control and I just struck him out on a slider [swinging]. I don't think he took too many pitches.

I did strike him out. He was forty-five and I was twenty-five, I think, and I struck him out on a slider. Paul Richards was the manager, and as soon as the inning was over, he said to me—and I don't know what day it was, but it might have been the day before. I wasn't in that ballgame [Williams' last]. Anyway, he said to me, "Hey son, you better get that baseball." And I didn't know what he was talking about. I think he was the last out of the inning for me; I struck him out on the slider, which I guess he didn't like. I heard later on that he didn't like the slider in baseball. I never knew what Paul Richards was talking about. Of course, now, after I realize it and everything . . . because he would have signed it. Ted was that kind of a guy.

I can remember when he was managing the Washington Senators and being in Baltimore . . . what was the last year of his home run, his last year playing? 1960? See, I had just come up. We had to come over earlier, because we just took a bus over there, and the guys got out, and he had both clubs down there and was teaching them how to hit! And the umpires came out there and said, "Ted, the gates are about ready to go open, you can't do this!" He said, "These guys want to learn something about hitting, I'm going to teach 'em." Both clubs. He didn't care. That's just the way Ted was.[102]

---

[102] Williams managed the Senators from 1969–71. Stock's final year in Baltimore was 1964, and his last year in the majors was 1967. However, Stock was the pitching coach for the Milwaukee Brewers from 1970–71, so this is likely when the incident took place.

I met him, talked to him a couple of times after his career was over, and he was a big fly fisherman and stuff like that. You'd mention your name and he'd say, "Oh, yeah, I know who you are." Whether he did that on purpose or not I don't know, but he'd sit and talk to you. But he didn't like the press; he wouldn't talk to the press.

I think the next year [after he retired], we happened to be up there [in Boston], and they had a day to honor him the next year, and we were there for that, but I can't remember much from that day. But he would not come out and take a bow for that [his last] game. No way. I don't know what it was. But of course, I didn't see him in his real great career. I saw [Mickey] Mantle and, to me, he was the greatest player I ever saw.

At that age—1960, it was—I had just been called up in June or July, and I'm just up there wanting to make the big leagues. I came up for about a month and had to go back down, and then I got called back up in June or July. It must have been July, because my son was born the night before I won by first ball game. No, he was born the next day; I won my first ball game on July 31, 1960, and my first son was born on August 1.

When you just come up to the big leagues in those days, you were just in awe of every player, so it didn't make any difference. I can remember Jimmy Piersall in one of my first games. He talked up there while he was hitting. Things like that you remember. I became more in awe of him as I got older in the game and realized what he [Ted] did and what people talked about the things he had done.

I did get an autographed ball from him; I was smart enough to do that. I can't remember when I got it, because he came to a big clinic out here in Washington [that] I was involved in. I probably got it then, but I can't remember exactly. You know, when you're in the big leagues your first year, and you're a big country boy, any of the ballplayers . . . was in awe of them all.

Now that I think about it, as a young guy, I wish I observed more of those guys. But Ted, the only time I pitched against him; at least I got to pitch against him and I was lucky to strike him out. But again, he was forty-five and I was twenty-five. He was over the hill [laughs].

Virgil Trucks

Right-handed pitcher

1941–43, 1945–52: ....Detroit Tigers
1953: ....St. Louis Browns
1953–55: .... Chicago White Sox
1956: ....Detroit Tigers
1957–58: ....Kansas City Athletics
1958: ....New York Yankees
Career Statistics: .... 177–135, 30 saves, 3.39 ERA
American League All-Star: 1949, 1954

Ted Williams vs. Virgil Trucks (data incomplete)

32-for-92, 6 doubles, 1 triple, 9 home runs,[103] 17 RBI,[104] 20 walks (2 intentional), 9 strikeouts, 1 hit by pitch, .348 batting average, .469 on-base percentage, .728 slugging percentage

Home Runs Allowed:

No. 108, June 24, 1942, at Detroit
No. 115, August 2, 1942 (game two), at Detroit
No. 146, April 26, 1946 (game two), at Detroit
No. 174, May 19, 1947 (game two), at Boston
No. 189, August 2, 1947, at Boston
No. 226, May 4, 1949, at Detroit
No. 236, June 5, 1949, (game one) at Detroit
No. 243, July 16, 1949, at Detroit
No. 320, August 29, 1951, at Detroit

---

[103] Of the known available box scores, Williams hit 9 home runs off Trucks. But the data is available for all of Williams' 521 career home runs, and he ended up with 12 off Trucks, the most he hit off any pitcher.

[104] Retrosheet.org has more data of Williams vs. Trucks, but does not include RBI. Baseball-reference.com lists Williams with 17 RBI in 74 at-bats (93 plate appearances) vs. Trucks.

No. 342, June 3, 1954, at Boston
No. 437, June 23, 1957 (game two), at Boston
No. 444, July 16, 1957, at Kansas City

Virgil Trucks (data incomplete; missing 1946-47)

YEAR	DATE	RESULT	YEAR	DATE	RESULT	YEAR	DATE	RESULT
1948	May 5	Ground out	1950	May 9	Fly out	1955	June 2	Walk
		Strikeout			Fly out			Walk
		Fly out			Fly out			Fly out
		Single	1951	May 3	Walk		July 23	Single
	May 18	Grounded into DP		July 21	Ground out			Strikeout
		Strikeout			Walk		Aug. 3	Fly out
		Double (RBI)			Reached on error			Intentional walk
	July 29	Fly out		Aug. 5	Single		Aug. 30	Single
		Pop out			Walk			Walk (1 RBI)
		Ground out			Fly out	1956	June 5	Fly out
		Ground out		Aug. 29	Strikeout			Pop out
	Sept. 1	Fly out			Home run (3 RBI)			Ground out
		Strikeout			Walk		July 20	Ground out
		Double			Single			Line out
1949	May 4	Ground out	1952	April 30	Single		July 30	Walk
		Strikeout			Strikeout			Fly out
		Home run (1 RBI)	1953	Aug. 27	Single			Ground out
		Single			Ground out			Walk
	May 22	Walk			Ground out			Ground out
		Fly out			Fly out	1957	May 1	Ground out
		Double		Sept. 13	Ground out			Fly out
		Ground out	1954	June 3	Strikeout			Walk
		Ground out			Fly out		May 18	Double (1 RBI)
		Grounded into DP			Walk			Walk
	June 5	Home run (2 RBI)			Home run (3 RBI)		June 23	Home run (1 RBI)
		Hit by pitch			Fly out		July 16	Walk
		Walk		June 27	Strikeout			Walk
		Walk			Ground out			Ground out
	July 16	Home run (2 RBI)			Single (1 RBI)			Home run (1 RBI)
		Fly out			Fly out		July 23	Walk
	Aug. 8	Triple		July 23	Fly out			Fly out
		Single						Out (unknown)
		Fly out						

THERE'S NO ONE today better than him. He's the best hitter I ever saw or ever will see. He just had that great hand-eye coordination; you couldn't fool him on pitches. I never even tried to fool him, because it would just be wasting a pitch anyway. So I just pitched him power against power. He liked that because he knew he had the over power. He could hit anybody, I don't care who they were.

He [Ted] always wanted to play in Detroit, but really, the right-field fence in Boston was not bad as it went out, but down the line it was only 300 feet or something . . . less than 300. That was the smallest ballpark in the major leagues when I played. I would have rather faced him in Detroit any time. Oh yeah, he could pull the ball. He'd pull the ball all the time, just like I said, the second baseman—when you're talking about the shift—he'd hit balls between the first baseman and second baseman, and they could almost shake hands. He'd hit a line drive right past him. I never ever saw him hit a ball to the left of second base. Never. It didn't work. You could put the whole infield over there, and it wouldn't work. And you know [how] they talk about always wanting him to try to go to left field? He said no, I'm not going into my batting stance to try to go to left field. They pitch me out there; I'll pull the ball anyway. And he could. He could pull it off anybody on the outside corner. So he didn't worry about them putting [on the shift]. He wasn't going to change his batting style.

I tried to throw him some sliders inside and he'd just lay off those because they were balls. If I threw the fastball and it was over the plate, it was a goner. He was just phenomenal, that's all. His hand-eye coordination was terrific and he would always figure out a pitcher. Facing him two or three times, he'd know ten times later if that same pitcher pitched against him, he knew everything he threw. And he knew *the way* he threw it, too.

You'd try to hide the ball from him, and he would still pick it up. He'd see that ball and he could see those seams and he knew what you were throwing. If you showed him that ball at all—just up here before you release it—he could pick it up right there. He could see a gnat on a gnat's nest from 100 yards.

He was absolutely terrific and was a good friend. He was good to me and I was nice to him. I think I was too nice to him on the mound.

I faced him for fourteen or fifteen years. That's still not one [home run] a year. I know one time in Detroit I was going into the game, and it was 0–0 in the seventh, and he hit a home run off me, and they won the ball game, 1–0—because we didn't score any runs![105] It seemed that way every time I pitched, we didn't get any.

He just liked me, I guess, and he put me and Gaylord Perry in there [to his Hitters Hall of Fame] as the last two guys to go in [before his death], and we were both pitchers. He thought we were great enough to go in as pitchers. He had several pitchers, I don't know how many were in there, but there were quite a few. We were just the last ones.

He told me when he came back from the service [in Korea] and we were in Boston—it was the first time I had seen him since he got out of the service—and I went over and told him that I was glad to see him back and wished him luck. And he told me later that I was the only player from the opposition that ever mentioned that to him. And that's a true story, because I know I was there when he told me.

I know if he had not gone into the service, he'd probably be leading the home run circle. I think he would have had 800 or 1,000. If you look at the amount of at-bats he missed, I guarantee if you figured it out, you'd see he'd hit at least 800 home runs or more.

There was no way that they [other good hitters of that era] could touch him. Of course, [Mickey] Mantle was a great hitter. After all, he was a switch-hitter, and the first real good switch-hitter that came up. Another good switch-hitter nobody knew about was Roy Cullenbine. Now Cullenbine was the best switch-hitter before Mantle. I've not seen one since who has been better than Mantle. I don't know how great Williams would have been if he were a switch-hitter. If he could hit like he did left-handed—jiminy—it would have been something awesome.

He was great. There's just none greater, and I'm glad I got to know him personally and been able to pitch against him. I got to know him

---

[105] On June 24, 1942, Williams homered off Trucks in the top of the seventh inning of a 1–0 game. It was Williams' 108th career home run and his first off Trucks.

[well], oh, the last ten years he lived. I would talk to him at least once or twice, maybe more, a month. I lived only about 200 miles from him. I would go up to see him and he had a golf tournament every year that I played in. And his museum was there, too. I got to know him, I guess, as well as anybody. We would sit and talk when I would visit. I would to go his house . . . he had an electronic gate on his yard where you couldn't get in, and the gate was probably 100 yards from the house; they had to let you in and out. I went in his house, had pictures taken with him in his kitchen, and spent quite a bit of time with him. We talked about everything. We talked about our days of playing, players, he would talk about pitchers he hit against, and he had me there to back up everything he said.

Oh, he loved to face me. He [looked forward] to hit against me. He loved to hit against the Detroit staff, Newhouser and Trout; mainly because we all threw hard, and of course, Newhouser had a pretty good curveball, and he would throw that to him. But he hit Newhouser right on. I bet you Newhouser didn't strike him out much. I only remember one time that he did.[106] I can only recall one time striking him out myself. And that upset him. He turned and walked away, and on the way back to the bench, he hit the bat on the ground with the little knob—and his handle wasn't bigger than a finger—and it just snapped in two. I said, I hope he doesn't have any more. I hope he had to use somebody else's bat. I don't know what would happen if he were playing today with all those bats breaking up like they do. Jiminy. I didn't want to agitate him in any way. He hit me well enough. If I had agitated him, there's no telling. I probably never would have gotten him out.

He was just a great guy and a great hitter and not appreciated as much as he should have been in Boston. But of course, he wasn't very good to the fans there. In that field, they booed him all the time, espe-

---

[106] Retrosheet.com has incomplete data of Williams vs. Newhouser, but lists 6 strikeouts in 64 at-bats.

cially the fans sitting out in left field right near him. I'll never forget one day we were playing them and I wasn't pitching, but the ball was hit to left field. It was a ground ball between third and short, and it went between his legs. He turned around to go back to the fence to get it—he didn't have a long ways to go—but he went back and then he made a bad throw and the fans booed him . . . especially the ones in left field. Then he came up to bat in that half of the inning, and they booed him when he came to bat. And he just politely hit a home run. As he rounded the bases, when he got to first, he gave [the fans in right field] them the middle finger; then he got to second and gave it to the [fans in the] bleachers in center field; then he got to third and gave it to those bunch around the third-base line. And when he got to home plate, he gave it to the press box.

They fined him $5,000 for that. What happened was, the fans took up the $5,000 to pay the fine, but that wasn't permissible. You had to pay your own fine if you were fined. So he took that money and he couldn't keep it, so he gave it to the Jimmy Fund. That was his big organization. He originated that.

Another time we were playing Boston and [Joe] Ginsberg was catching and Williams came up and [walked on] four straight pitches, and Joe's questioning the umpire about it. On the last one, he said, "Bill"—Bill Summers was the umpire. He said, "Bill, don't you think that ball was a strike?" And Bill said to Joe, "Mr. Ginsberg, Mr. Williams will let you know when it is a strike." And that's about the sum of it. He could umpire his own ball game. I never, ever saw a bad pitch called on him, but I never saw him *swing* at a bad pitch, either. If it wasn't a strike, he'd just put the bat on his shoulder and let it go by. But he was always set to swing if it happened to be over that plate, and especially to his liking. You see, pitchers knew that they couldn't just throw balls. If they did, he was going to walk every time. They knew they wanted to get him out. All of them wanted to pitch against him, naturally, or they wouldn't have anything to talk about the rest of their life if they didn't.

It's really amazing and too bad that everybody couldn't have seen him play. The same way with me; I would have loved to have seen [Ty] Cobb and those guys play. They were great, too. I'm not taking away from them. The players today think they invented the game. They don't even know who [Abner] Doubleday was. Some of them don't know who Ted Williams was. If they don't, they don't care about baseball, because I always cared about Cobb and [Babe] Ruth and [Lou] Gehrig and all those guys. They set the stage for us. We tried to set the stage for these guys. We did for 'em to make more money.

His swing was as fluid as you can get; that's why he was such a great hitter—his timing, his swinging. I never saw him hold on a pitch, like some hitters will part-swing. Not once. Of course, I didn't see him every game, but I saw quite a few. I never saw him do anything close to that.

Pitching him low and behind would hold him to a double. That's about the sum of it, too. I'll tell ya, the infield didn't play close up. The second baseman was almost out there with the right-fielder. The shortstop was on that side of second base, and the third baseman was right back of second base. There was nothing on the third-base side. Even the outfielders were shifted, but not as much as the other players, the infield. But the outfield shifted as well. When you got a hitter like him, you have to try to play some shift or something to try to get him out, and that wasn't easy.

Oh, I got him out a few times, and I felt good about it, being able to get him out at all.

Ozzie Van Brabant

Right-handed pitcher

1954: .... **Philadelphia Athletics**
1955: ....**Kansas City Athletics**
Career Statistics: .... **0–2, 0 saves, 7.85 ERA**

Ted Williams vs. Ozzie Van Brabant

1-for-4, 0 RBI, 1 walk, 0 strikeouts, .250 batting average, .400 on-base percentage, .250 slugging percentage

HE WAS AN incredible hitter. He knew the strike zone as well as anybody and, you know, he had a heck of a lot of base on balls. A lot of people didn't want to give him anything good.

[I remember when] I pitched against him that he hit one dead center. I thought it was gone, but luckily it wasn't. The ball was against the center-field fence, you know, the flat fence in dead center field [in Fenway]. The guy was right to the track. It wouldn't have gone over, but that's the kind of hitter he was.

Ossie Van Brabant

YEAR	DATE	RESULT
1954	May 31	Single
		Ground out
		Fly out
	Sept. 21	Walk
		Pop out

I faced him maybe three or four times, but he always hit the ball well. The thing is, I started too late and ran out of gas too soon. No excuse about it.

Well, they gave him a lot of wrongs, I tell you, because he was a nice person. They [the media] always had something [negative] to say about him. I'd seen him one time going around third base, looked up at the press box, and spat at them. That's how bad it was. They just hounded him continuously.

Vito Valentinetti

Right-handed pitcher

1954:	**Chicago White Sox**
1956–57:	**Chicago Cubs**
1957:	**Cleveland Indians**
1958:	**Detroit Tigers**
1958–59:	**Washington Senators**
Career Statistics:	**13–14, 3 saves, 4.73 ERA**

Ted Williams vs. Vito Valentinetti

3-for-10, 1 triple, 1 home run, 3 RBI, 3 walks, 1 strikeout, .300 batting average, .462 on-base percentage, .800 slugging percentage

Home Runs Allowed:

No. 480, September 26, 1958 (game one), at Washington

YOU'D LOVE TO face these guys, because if they hit a ball out of the park, well, that was their job. They're good and they're known for that; like [Mickey] Mantle, [Willie] Mays, and the rest of them.

I had pretty good luck against Ted. I just see that he had one home run off me. Of course, I didn't pitch against him that much. I was in the American League and the National League. In the American League, I was with Detroit, Cleveland, and the old Washington Senators. When I was with Washington, I was a reliever and a starter.

I remember one game up in Boston against Ted and his buddies when I pitched a two-hitter, although I lost the ballgame, 2–0. [I remember that] I had two hits [in that game]. I hit one off the Green Monster, but Ted held me to a single, which was fine, as I didn't run that fast anyway. I had two hits and the rest of the team only had one. Our old catcher, Clint Courtney, pinch-hit for our second baseman, John Schaive, and he got a base hit.[107]

But it was fun pitching to Williams. Here's a guy, he's supposed to beat your brains in, you know? So after that game—it was a Saturday or Sunday— the next day we're standing on the sidelines and I start talking with him. Because he hit a ball I thought was going out in center field. He says, "Nah." Our center fielder caught it in front of the monument.

Then he said, "I'm 3–13 off of you, Vito." So he counted those three walks as times at-bat. He was probably 3–13 because he wanted to hit the ball four. But anyway, that's what he said to me.

Vito Valentinetti

YEAR	DATE	RESULT
1958	June 9	Ground out
		Walk
	June 12	Lined into DP
	Aug. 6	Triple (1 RBI)
	Aug. 7	Ground out
	Aug. 11	Strikeout
	Sept. 20	Fly out
		Walk
		Fly out
		Ground out
	Sept. 26	Single
		Walk
		Home run (2 RBI)

He walked a lot and had one home run off me. It's like I say, pitching to those guys was like . . . what are you going to be nervous about? It's the .220 hitter that you got to worry about if he gets a base hit or a home run. The other guys—[Mickey] Mantle and Williams—that's what they're supposed to do!

---

[107] The game was September 20, 1958, and the Senators actually had four hits, as Bob Allison had the other. The Red Sox only had three hits, but one of them was Jackie Jensen's two-out, two-run single in the bottom of the eighth. Ted Williams was 0–3 with a walk.

He had a great batting eye. I remember striking him out once in Washington. He had a bad wrist, his wrist was taped up and he just took the pitch, you know. Got a called third strike on him.[108] It was just a fastball, but the lights weren't that great in the old Washington stadium; maybe that had something to do with it. Normally when he took [a pitch], the umpire called it a ball. He had great eyes, being a pilot and all. He probably would have broken all kinds of records [had he not gone off to war]. The guy didn't have any weaknesses. I mean, your best bet was maybe a changeup and to just mix it up [against him].

I don't [remember the home run], I really don't. I don't know if it was in Washington or Cleveland. I'd like to know what ballpark it was in, because that Washington ballpark was a big park. In the old days, it was pretty big, and then they shortened center field.[109]

Was he the best? I think he was the best power hitter, but I think [Stan] Musial . . . well, I was a right-handed pitcher and Musial was left-handed, and so was Williams. But Musial, one day pitching to him—that son-of-a-gun—I could see him switch his feet like he was going to hit the ball over the third-baseman's head . . . and he did. I pitched him outside and he hit the ball over the third-baseman's head. So he was a pretty good hitter, a cagey hitter. Well, the records show, right?[110]

I mean you're going to get them out once, maybe, once out of four, twice out of four? But you're not going to get them 0–3 or 0–4, not those guys. But they're going to hit the ball hard someplace.

I'd hardly see him hit the ball to left field. He was going for the home run; he was going for the downs on every pitch he could pull. I

---

[108] The strikeout occurred in the seventh inning of a 6–3 Senators win on August 11, 1958, at Griffith Stadium in Washington.

[109] The home run occurred in the fifth inning of Boston's 6–4 win on September 26, 1958, at Griffith Stadium in Washington. It would be the last time Valentinetti would face Williams.

[110] In seven plate appearances against Valentinetti, Musial went 4–6 with 4 hits, 1 home run, 2 RBI, 1 walk, 0 strikeouts, and a .667 batting average.

think he was, yeah. He was a power hitter. What else could you expect from a power hitter? Hit one out of the park, hit one off the Green Monster, or hit one to deep center field? He enjoyed that, I guess, hitting home runs off of people.

The coaches did that [watch Williams during batting practice] a lot. Sometimes a pitcher was pitching that day and would sit down with the coach on the bench. This guy likes this ball here and that ball there. Then they'd have meetings in the clubhouse. And half the time [laughs] they'd tell you to pitch one way and the ball don't always go where you want it to. You don't have that kind of stuff. I didn't have a good curveball, but I had a good slider, a good changeup, and a pretty good fastball and sinker. They tell you to pitch him one way, and if you can, fine.

[From what I remember], he was kind of a loner. You never saw him outside the ballpark. I knew where he would stay, but you never saw him around a restaurant or a bar. He was a good boy.

Jerry Walker

Right-handed pitcher

1957–61: .... **Baltimore Orioles**
1961–62: .... **Kansas City Athletics**
1963–64: .... **Cleveland Indians**
Career Statistics: .... **37–44 13 saves, 4.36 ERA**
American League All-Star: **1959**

Ted Williams vs. Jerry Walker

4-for-6, 1 home run, 3 RBI, 1 walk 0 strikeouts, 1 double play, .667 batting average, .714 on-base percentage, 1.167 slugging percentage

Home Runs Allowed:

No. 483, May 30, 1959 (game two), at Boston

IREALLY DON'T REMEMBER the first time I faced him, but I remember the first game I was ever in where he was supposed to be the first hitter. It ended up being a lopsided game, and they pinch-hit for him. I know it was his spot in the order and he would have been the first guy that I faced.[111]

I remember the first game that I lost; he hit a home run in that game. It was my first major-league loss.[112] It wasn't the first home run I had ever given up, but it was the first game I lost [in the majors]. It was a game in Boston, and he hit it right down the right-field line. A lot of 'em hit home runs off me.

---

[111] Jerry Walker made his major-league debut at eighteen years old on July 6, 1957, for the Orioles at Boston. Walker began the seventh inning; Williams had been the final out in the sixth.

[112] Williams hit a two-run homer off Walker in the seventh inning to give the Red Sox a 4–3 lead in an eventual 8–3 win over the Orioles in the second game of a doubleheader on May 30, 1959. Walker had been 1–0 in thirteen appearances in 1957, and had no decisions in six games in 1958.

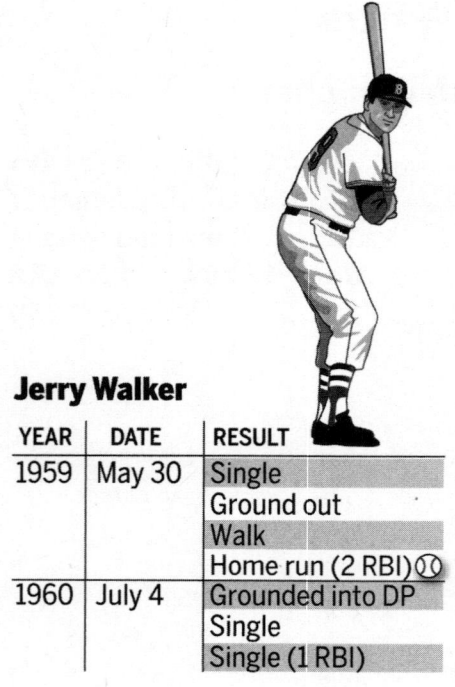

Jerry Walker

YEAR	DATE	RESULT
1959	May 30	Single
		Ground out
		Walk
		Home run (2 RBI)
1960	July 4	Grounded into DP
		Single
		Single (1 RBI)

You just had to make the pitches that would be the safest ones to throw him. You know, obviously the charts that told how much he hit at different places, you tried to pick out one of 'em where he hit in the .200s and .300s. And that didn't mean he wasn't going to get hits off of you, it just meant you had a little better chance of getting by without him hurting you too bad.

I never really talked with him. Pretty much in those days, hitters and pitchers didn't do a lot of talking. To some extent, you didn't spend a lot of time dealing with some hitters on your own club.

Looking at what he had done in the past and what he did in his last couple of years, you could certainly see that there wouldn't be too many hitters better than him. In fact, I was in the park the day he hit his last home run. Baltimore, Jack Fisher. It was late in the season and the rumor was if he hit a home run, he wasn't going to go to New York. He did not want to go to New York and have to hit a home run and have to walk off the field from that. So—I think it was the last home game; I think they were going on the road the next day[113]—the wind was blowing in from right field about 15–20 miles-per-hour, and he went up there and he, you know, he was trying to hit a home run every

---

[113] It was September 28, 1960, and Boston's final home game of the season. The Red Sox finished up the season with three games in New York against the Yankees from September 30–October 2.

time. He hit some balls in the air that got up and just didn't . . . he didn't hit them solid enough to get them past the wind.[114] But that last one, there was no doubt about it. He ran the bases, kept his head down, and ran right into the dugout and right down the runway to the clubhouse. And the manager made him go back to left field to start the next inning, and then he sent a replacement out for him.

That's just a part of the game. You pitch against a guy . . . my understanding is at some point he contacted Jack and thanked him for challenging him and not walking him, but that's just part of the game. Those kinds of hitters are going to get hits off you. You feel worse about a guy who hits one a year hitting a home run off you than someone like Williams. You don't think anything about it at the time. Looking back several years later, and even just a few years later, you realize the significance of the player and what happened. You were kind of glad you were there and saw it happen, just like a no-hitter, perfect game, or someone hitting for the cycle; you remember those things, and you especially remember them if it's a guy of the caliber of Ted Williams. I think he probably was [the greatest hitter], you know, because of his ability to hit for an average, he didn't strike out a lot . . . he was just a good hitter.

---

[114] Williams had flied out in his two previous at-bats. He also walked in the first inning.

George Zuverink

Right-handed pitcher

1951–52: .... Cleveland Indians
1954: .... Cincinnati Reds
1954–55: .... Detroit Tigers
1955–59: .... Baltimore Orioles
Career Statistics: .... 32–36, 40 saves, 3.54 ERA

Ted Williams vs. George Zuverink

2-for-20, 1 home run, 3 RBI, 2 walks (2 intentional), 3 strikeouts, 1 hit by pitch, 2 double plays, .100 batting average, .217 on-base percentage, .250 slugging percentage

Home Runs Allowed:

No. 305, June 10, 1951 (game two), at Cleveland

George Zuverink

YEAR	DATE	RESULT	YEAR	DATE	RESULT	YEAR	DATE	RESULT
1951	June 10	Home run (3 RBI)	1955	June 22	Fly out	1957	April 22	Strikeout
1954	June 5	Grounded into DP		Sept. 2	Grounded into DP		May 30	Ground out
		Pop out			Hit by pitch			Grounded into DP
		Pop out		Sept. 4	Fly out	1958	April 23	Strikeout
		Fly out	1956	June 29	Intentional walk		July 3	Fly out
	July 15	Foul out		July 8	Reached on error			
		Ground out			Fly out			
		Intentional walk		Aug. 8	Single			
		Strikeout		Sept. 2	Ground out			

THE FIRST TIME I faced him was in Cleveland in 1951. He welcomed me to the major leagues by hitting the ball over the center field fence!

He was a terrific hitter. Before each game against Boston, as he took batting practice, we would all stop playing catch and admire this star.

His next hit against me was in 1956, and he hit a single to right field. I had good luck against him; most of the time was while I was a reliever. I changed speeds so that no pitch was alike.

In 1961, when the Red Sox had spring training up in Scottsdale, Arizona, and I was retired, I went to the ballpark and introduced myself to him. He said, "George, I think you could still get me out!"

What a compliment!

INTERVIEWS

Chuck Churn

Right-handed pitcher

1957: ....**Pittsburgh Pirates**
1958: ....**Cleveland Indians**
1959: ....**Los Angeles Dodgers**
Career Statistics: ....**3–2, 1 save, 5.10 ERA**

Ted Williams vs. Chuck Churn:

0-for-1, .000 batting average, 1.000 on-base percentage, .000 slugging percentage

May 5, 1958, bottom of the eighth inning, led off by grounding out to shortstop with the Williams shift in effect.

Chuck Churn

YEAR	DATE	RESULT
1958	May 5	Ground out

Q. What was your strategy against Williams, and how do you think you fared?

A. Only faced him one time! Pitched him [on the] low outside part of the plate.

Q. Did your teams use the "Williams shift," and if so, did you like that and how did it fare? If not, do you wish they did?

A. I liked the shift!

Q. Was he the toughest hitter you faced?

A. For me, Gil Hodges was tough to pitch to!

Jerry Davie

Right-handed pitcher

1959: ....Detroit Tigers
Career Statistics: .... 2–2, 0 saves, 4.17 ERA

Ted Williams vs. Jerry Davie

0-for-0, 1 RBI, 2 walks, 0 strikeouts, 1 sacrifice fly, .000 batting average, .667 on-base percentage, .000 slugging percentage

Q. What was your strategy against Williams, and how do you think you fared?

A. Move the ball around, in–out.

Q. Recollections of any specific at-bats vs. Williams.

A. 3–2, threw the ball, and I knew it went down the middle, belt high. He took the pitch, and I thought I had a strikeout, but the ump called it ball four.

Jerry Davie

YEAR	DATE	RESULT
1959	May 17	Walk
		Walk
	June 9	Sac fly (1 RBI)

Q. What was the talk among other pitchers, pitching coach and/or catchers on how to face Williams in pregame meetings or just in general?

A. Just hope he screwed up.

Q. Did your teams use the "Williams shift," and if so, did you like that and how did it fare? If not, do you wish they did?

A. Yes we did.

Q. Was he the toughest "out" you faced?

A. Him and Minnie Minoso.[1]

---

[1] Minoso was 3–6 with a double, home run, and walk vs. Davie.

Sonny Dixon

Right-handed pitcher

1953–54:	....Washington Senators
1954:	.... Philadelphia Athletics
1955:	....Kansas City Athletics
1956:	....New York Yankees
Career Statistics:	.... 11–18, 9 saves, 4.18 ERA

Ted Williams vs. Sonny Dixon

5-for-10, 2 doubles, 1 home run, 3 RBI, 1 walk, 0 strikeouts, 1 double play, .500 batting average, .545 on-base percentage, 1.000 slugging percentage

Home Runs Allowed:

No. 329, August 23, 1953, at Washington

Q. What was your strategy against Williams, and how do you think you fared?

A. Keep the ball away from him. The first pitch to him he hit for a home run.

Q. Recollections of any specific at-bats vs. Williams.

A. Ted hit a double down the left-field line. I went to second base mad, because he got a double. Ted said, "Sonny, you threw the ball by me." I told him that was all I wanted to know.[2]

---

[2] On July 10, 1954, Williams doubled to left field off Dixon in the top of the tenth inning to score Jimmy Piersall and break a 2–2 tie in an eventual 5–3 Red Sox win in eleven innings.

Q. What was the talk among other pitchers, pitching coach and/or catchers on how to face Williams in pregame meetings or just in general?

A. Was not too much chatter.

Q. Did your teams use the "Williams shift," and if so, did you like that and how did it fare? If not, do you wish they did?

A. Yes. Most of the time it worked.

Q. Was he the toughest "out" you faced?

A. No, Nellie Fox.[3] He was tougher; I never got him out.

Q. Can you compare how it was to face Williams vs. hitters like Al Kaline, Larry Doby, and Harvey Kuenn.

A. I was lucky with Ted. He always was kidding me that I was his "out man." He signed a picture for me and put, "Your out man."[4]

Sonny Dixon

YEAR	DATE	RESULT
1953	Aug. 23	Home run (1 RBI)
1954	July 4	Fielder's choice
		Single
	July 10	Double (1 RBI)
	Sept. 5	Double
		Grounded into DP
		Fly out
		Ground out
	Sept. 21	Single (1 RBI)
		Walk
1956	Sept. 29	Single

---

[3] In 11 at-bats, Fox went 4–11 with 2 RBI, 1 strikeout, and a .364 batting average against Dixon.

[4] It might seem strange that Williams would say Dixon was his "out man," but Dixon allowed just one single and one walk to Williams in the last six times he faced him.

Bubba Harris

Right-handed pitcher

1948–49, 1951: .... **Philadelphia Athletics**
1951: .... **Cleveland Indians**
Career Statistics: .... **6–3, 8 saves, 4.84 ERA**

Ted Williams vs. Bubba Harris (data incomplete)

2-for-8, 1 home run, 2 RBI, 4 walks, 0 strikeouts, .250 batting average, .500 on-base percentage, .625 slugging percentage

Home Runs Allowed:

No. 259, September 3, 1949, at Boston

Q. What was your strategy against Williams, and how do you think you fared?

A. Don't throw strikes. Pitch low and behind.

Q. Did your teams use the "Williams shift?"

A. Yes

Q. Was he the toughest hitter you faced?

A. Yes

Bubba Harris

YEAR	DATE	RESULT
1948	May 31	Fly out
	Aug. 18	Single
1949	April 27	Walk
	May 30	Fly out into DP
	July 8	Ground out (1 RBI)
	July 9	Walk
	Sept. 2	Fly out
		Walk
	Sept. 3	Home run (1 RBI)
	Sept. 10	Foul out
1951	April 21	Walk
	April 29	Ground out

Don Johnson

Right-handed pitcher

1947, 1950: ....New York Yankees
1950–51:..St. Louis Browns
1951–52:...Washington Senators
1954: .... Chicago White Sox
1955: .... Baltimore Orioles
1958: ....San Francisco Giants
Career Statistics: .... 27–38, 12 saves, 4.78 ERA

Ted Williams vs. Don Johnson (data incomplete)

4-for-16, 1 triple, 1 home run, 6 RBI, 3 walks, 0 strikeouts, .429 batting average, .529 on-base percentage, .786 slugging percentage

Home Runs Allowed:

No. 291, September 15, 1950, at St. Louis

Q. What was your strategy against Williams, and how do you think you fared?

A. Good

Q. Recollections of any specific at-bats vs. Williams.

A. None

Q. What was the talk among other pitchers, pitching coach and/or catchers on how to face Williams in pregame meetings or just in general?

A. Throw it down the middle and poof.

Q. Did your teams use the "Williams shift," and if so, did you like that and how did it fare? If not, do you wish they did?

A. No shift

Q. Was he the toughest "out" you faced?

A. Yes

Don Johnson (data incomplete; missing 1947)

YEAR	DATE	RESULT
1950	April 18	Walk
	Sept. 15	Ground out
		Single
		Fly out
		Home run (3 RBI)
1951	May 23	Walk
	Aug. 12	Ground out
		Reached on error
		Single
		Single
	Aug. 18	Triple (2 RBI)
1954	June 26	Single (1 RBI)
		Ground out
		Ground out
	July 25	Ground out
		Fly out
		Walk

Don Lee

Right-handed pitcher

1957-58: .... Detroit Tigers
1960: .... Washington Senators
1961-62: .... Minnesota Twins
1962-65: .... Los Angeles/California Angels
1965-66: .... Houston Astros
1966: .... Chicago Cubs
Career Statistics: .... 40–44, 11 saves, 3.61 ERA

Ted Williams vs. Don Lee

2-for-7, 1 home run, 1 RBI, 2 walks, 0 strikeouts, .286 batting average, .444 on-base percentage, .714 slugging percentage

Home Runs Allowed:

No. 517, September 2, 1960 (game one), at Boston[5]

Q: What was your strategy against Williams, and how do you think you fared?

A: Change speeds—yes

Q. Recollections of any specific at-bats vs. Williams.

A. Ted Williams hit a home run off my father and one off me (it's a trivia question)—the only player to hit a home run off of a father and son. My father was Thornton Lee, who pitched for Cleveland and the Chicago White Sox from 1933 to 1946. Ted Williams has called my father one of the toughest left-hand pitchers he ever faced.[6]

---

[5] In the listing with his statistics, Lee wrote in under the one home run that it was No. 518 (it was actually Williams' 517th career home run).

[6] In four at-bats against Thornton Lee, Williams only had one hit and struck out once.

Q. What was the talk among other pitchers, pitching coach and/or catchers on how to face Williams in pregame meetings or just in general?

A. Pitch around him—don't give him anything good to hit.

Q. Did your teams use the "Williams shift," and if so, did you like that and how did it fare? If not, do you wish they did?

A. Yes, and we fared well.

Q. Was he the toughest "out" you faced?

A. Yes, even though I only faced him one season.

Don Lee

YEAR	DATE	RESULT
1960	June 2	Walk
	Sept. 2	Ground out
		Fly out
		Pop out
		Home run (1 RBI)
	Sept. 18	Ground out
		Single
		Walk
		Line out

Q. Can you compare how it was to face Williams vs. hitters like Mickey Mantle, Roger Maris, and Carl Yastrzemski?

A. Mantle and Maris were no real problem for me. Yaz was somewhat a problem. Williams was feared more.

Bob Savage

Right-handed pitcher

1942, 1946–49: ....Philadelphia A's
1949: ....St. Louis Browns
Career Statistics: .... 16–27, 9 saves, 4.32 ERA

Ted Williams vs. Bob Savage (data incomplete)

6-for-15, 3 doubles, 2 home runs, 5 walks, 2 strikeouts, .313 batting average, .476 on-base percentage, .875 slugging percentage

Home Runs Allowed:

No. 166, April 18, 1947, at Philadelphia
No. 178, June 29, 1947 (game two), at Philadelphia

Q. What was your strategy against Williams, and how do you think you fared?

A. No particular strategy

Q. Recollections of specific at-bats vs. Williams.

A. I remember one game I had three strikeouts the first three at-bats. Homer and double the last two at-bats.[7]

Q. What was the talk among other pitchers, pitching coach and/ or catchers on how to face Williams in pregame meetings or just in general?

A. No discussion

---

[7] Savage allowed 2 home runs to Williams: April 18, 1947, in which Williams went 1–3, and June 29, 1947 (game two), with Williams again going 1–3.

Bob Savage (data incomplete; 1942, 1946-'47)

YEAR	DATE	RESULT
1948	April 22	Ground out
	April 29	Walk
	July 9	Fly out
		Walk
	Aug. 18	Ground out (1 RBI)
		Fly out

Q. Did your teams use the "Williams shift," and if so, did you like that and how did it fare? If not, do you wish they did?

A. No

Q. Was he the toughest hitter you faced?

A. Joe DiMaggio

Carl Scheib

Right-handed pitcher

1943–45, 1947–54: .... **Philadelphia Athletics**
1954: .... **St. Louis Cardinals**
Career Statistics: .... **45–65, 17 saves, 4.88 ERA**

Ted Williams vs. Carl Scheib (data incomplete)

6-for-30, 1 home run,[8] 2 RBI, 9 walks, 2 strikeouts, .200 batting average, .385 on-base percentage, .300 slugging percentage[9]

Home Runs Allowed:

No. 179, July 2, 1947, at Boston
No. 192, August 31, 1947, at Boston
No. 234, May 30, 1949 (game two), at Boston

Q. What was your strategy against Williams, and how do you think you fared?

A. Pitching to Williams, I tried to pitch him low and inside, maybe on curveballs. I think I fared pretty well against him.

Q. Recollections of specific at-bats vs. Williams.

A. Specific game against Williams, I pitched him curveballs low and inside and got him out three times at-bat. A story later was that he told

---

[8] Of the known available box scores, Williams hit 1 home run off Scheib. But the data is available for all of Williams' 521 career home runs, and he ended up with 3 off Scheib.

[9] Retrosheet.org has more data of Williams vs. Scheib, but does not include RBI. Baseball-reference.com lists Williams with 2 RBI in 25 at-bats (31 plate appearances) vs. Scheib.

Carl Scheib (data incomplete; missing 1947)

YEAR	DATE	RESULT	YEAR	DATE	RESULT
1948	Aug. 18	Single	1950	April 30	Pop out
		Single			Grounded into DP
	Sept. 3	Strikeout		June 29	Fly out
		Fly out	1951	April 22	Walk
		Walk			Fly out
		Fly out		June 27	Ground out
1949	April 27	Fly out			Single
		Walk			Fly out
		Walk		July 4	Ground out
	May 30	Ground out			Walk
		Ground out			Fielder's choice
		Ground out		Aug. 14	Single
		Home run (2 RBI) 		Sept. 9	Foul out
	July 8	Strikeout			
	Sept. 11	Fly out			
		Fly out			
		Walk			
		Fly out			

the guys on the bench, if I started him again on curveballs, he would hit a home run . . . and he did. It beat me in the ball game.[10]

---

[10] Scheib likely is talking about the second game of a doubleheader between the Red Sox and A's on May 30, 1949, in which Williams hit career home run No. 234 in the bottom of the eighth inning of a 4–3 Boston win, a two-run home run that provided the final score. Williams had been hitless in his previous three at-bats in that game.

Something you learn, not to start a good hitter four times the same way in a game.

Q. What was the talk among other pitchers, pitching coach and/or catchers on how to face Williams in pregame meetings or just in general?

A. First of all we were a second-division club[11] and therefore not many pregame meetings were held. You pitched Williams the way you thought was best for you.

Q. Did your teams use the "Williams shift," and if so, did you like that and how did it fare? If not, do you wish they did?

A. We did not use the shift.

Q. Was he the toughest hitter you faced?

A. Each pitcher has a few hitters which were tough for him, not saying they were better hitters. Williams was probably one of the toughest hitters to face, but some other hitters gave me more trouble. But overall, I would vote Williams as the best hitter ever.

---

[11] In Scheib's ten seasons with the A's, Philadelphia finished in the second division eight times and in fourth place the other two occasions.

Bobby Shantz

Left-handed pitcher

1949–54: .... Philadelphia Athletics
1955–56: .... Kansas City Athletics
1957–60: ....New York Yankees
1961: ....Pittsburgh Pirates
1962: .... Houston Colt .45's
1962–64: .... St. Louis Cardinals
1964: .... Chicago Cubs
1964: .... Philadelphia Phillies
Career Statistics: .... 119–99, 48 saves, 3.38 ERA
American League All-Star: 1951, 1952, 1957
American League MVP: 1952

Ted Williams vs. Bobby Shantz (data incomplete)

15-for-49, 4 doubles, 2 home runs, 8 RBI, 13 walks (2 intentional), 9 strikeouts, .306 batting average, .452 on-base percentage, .510 slugging percentage

Home Runs Allowed:

No. 287, June 27, 1950, at Philadelphia
No. 403, July 26, 1956, at Kansas City

Q. What was your strategy against Williams, and how do you think you fared?

A. My strategy was to make him hit breaking balls and try to keep the ball in the ballpark.

Q. Recollections of any specific at-bats vs. Williams.

A. All of his at-bats were tough because he made me throw strikes and had a great eye.

Bobby Shantz

YEAR	DATE	RESULT
1949	May 30	Grounded into DP
		Walk
		Ground out
		Walk
	July 10	Walk
	Sept. 2	Strikeout
		Ground out
1950	April 30	Walk
		Fielder's choice
		Pop out
	June 27	Double
		Home run (2 RBI)
		Double
		Walk
		Foul out
1951	Aug. 9	Strikeout
	Aug. 16	Ground out
		Line out
		Single
		Fly out
	Sept. 9	Ground out
		Fly out
		Single (1 RBI)
		Ground out
1955	June 3	Single
		Ground out
		Ground out
	July 21	Single
		Walk
		Ground out
		Ground out

YEAR	DATE	RESULT
	Sept. 13	Ground out
		Ground out
1956	June 2	Line out
	June 23	Strikeout
		Single
	July 17	Walk
	July 25	Strikeout
	July 26	Home run (2 RBI)
	Aug. 26	Strikeout
1957	April 20	Single
		Strikeout
	April 27	Single (RBI)
		Walk
		Fly out
		Ground out
	July 4	Strikeout
		Ground out
		Ground out
		Walk
1958	July 6	Walk
	Aug. 17	Double (1 RBI)
		Single
1959	July 8	Ground out
		Single
		Strikeout
	Aug. 11	Double (1 RBI)
	Aug. 14	Walk
1960	June 3	Fly out
	June 5	Intentional walk
	Sept. 5	Intentional walk
	Sept. 23	Strikeout

Q. What was the talk among other pitchers, pitching coach and/or catchers on how to face Williams in pregame meetings or just in general?

A. We never talked that much about him to get him out because he was that good.

Q. Did your teams use the "Williams shift," and if so, did you like that and how did it fare? If not, do you wish they did?

A. Yes, we used the shift, but it didn't do much good. He could have gotten a hit every time up if he wanted to push the ball down the third-base line. Of course, he didn't do that!

Q. Was he the toughest "out" you faced?

A. Yes, he was the toughest hitter I ever faced.

Q. Can you compare how it was to face Williams vs. hitters like Al Kaline, Rocky Colavito, and Minnie Minoso.

A. I would rather face Minoso, Kaline, and Colavito before Williams anytime!

Dave Sisler

Right-handed pitcher

1956–59: ....**Boston Red Sox**
1959–60: ....**Detroit Tigers**
1961: ....**Washington Senators**
1962: ....**Cincinnati Reds**
Career Statistics: .... **38–44, 29 saves, 4.33 ERA**

Ted Williams vs. Dave Sisler

1-for-3, 1 home run, 1 RBI, 0 walks, 0 strikeouts, .333 batting average, .333 on-base percentage, 1.333 slugging percentage

Home Runs Allowed:

No. 485, June 23, 1959, at Detroit

Q. What was your strategy against Williams?

A. No pattern

Q. How do you think you fared?

A. Bad

Q. Recollections of any specific at-bats vs. Williams.

A. He hit a home run on a day I shouldn't have been pitching.

Dave Sisler

YEAR	DATE	RESULT
1959	May 17	Fly out
	June 10	Fielder's choice
	June 23	Home run (1 RBI)

Q. What was the talk among other pitchers, pitching coach and/ or catchers on how to face Williams in pregame meetings or just in general?

A. Everyone said he was the best.

Q. Did your teams use the "Williams shift?"

A. Yes

Q. Did you like that and how did it fare? If not, do you wish they did?

A. Didn't face him enough

Q. Was he the toughest "out" you faced?

A. Among the best

Q. You played with Williams from 1956–59. Did you ever discuss your matchups with him and/or his theories of hitting?

A. No

Q. Did playing with him help you in preparing to face him in later years?

A. Yes, but not enough

Q. What was it like watching him hit every day?

A. Priceless—the best hitter I ever saw, though not the best player or teammate.

Section Two: Catchers

Del Crandall

Catcher

1949–50: ....Boston Braves
1953–63: .... Milwaukee Braves
1964: ....San Francisco Giants
1965: ....Pittsburgh Pirates
1966: .... Cleveland Indians
Career Statistics: .... 1,573 games, 179 home runs,
.254 batting average
National League All-Star: 1953–1956, 1958–1960, 1962

MY INTERACTION WITH Williams was very limited, since he was in the American League.

When I first went to the Braves in 1949, the Braves and Sox always played a Jimmy Fund charity game. I was nineteen at the time. Anyway, some of our veterans didn't want to take part in the home-run hitting contest before the game. Ted was in it, and the Braves asked me to be in it. As it turned out, Ted and I wound up in the finals and hit the same number in the playoff. Now that was a tremendous thrill for me, not Ted!

In the early '50s, we played the Red Sox in the Hall of Fame Game, and it was great to listen to him talk about hitting. He was very generous with his time and enjoyed talking hitting. I was part of the limited group that was talking with him. He was more than willing to share, and he just loved talking to ballplayers—I'm not sure about other people—but he was just a great guy as far as other players were concerned. And he spent as much time talking baseball as he could. I'm talking half-an-hour, forty-five minutes, maybe even an hour. I was twenty-four at the time and hadn't made much of a name for myself, so I was a listener. There's no way I can remember [exactly] what he said. We were talking about swings and that sort of thing, but no, I didn't come away with anything that was seared in my brain that I used over and over again.

Whenever I was around him, I tried to watch what he did when he was hitting. He was just one of those magical players that you just couldn't take your eyes off of. I wasn't around Joe DiMaggio much, but it was the same way [with him]. I was just there with him in spring training when he had that heel problem, I think, but whenever he was on the field, I couldn't take my eyes off of him, either.

Del Crandall was an eight-time All-Star in the National League.

There wasn't [an aura around Williams] because we didn't get to see him. We got to see [Stan] Musial, and we knew how great he was, but Williams had that mystique about him that he was better than the best we had in our league—although I think Musial has been *totally* under-rated over the years. But we couldn't really identify with Williams because of the fact that we really didn't see him a lot. And not during his prime, either. So we had our own stars, you know. Musial, [Willie] Mays, [Hank] Aaron, and whoever else I've forgotten.

I was so young [when I played in Boston for the Braves], I'm not sure I got much of an impression from all this. What I got was from the newspapers mostly, reading about his trials. But he was just a hero. He was just a guy who was the best. Once again, I had to read about him mostly and hear what people had to say because not being in his league, it was difficult to form any real opinion.

You got the sense that he was kind of a laid-back manager. I can't remember him being real aggressive in the field, I can't remember him . . . I'm sure that hitting was really his big thing. I know it was probably intimidating for hitters to go up there and do their measly little thing when you had the greatest hitter in the history of baseball—possibly—sitting over there on the bench. So I'm sure it was hard to play for him.

When I managed the Brewers, Ted was the manager with Texas. George Scott was on my club and he gave the fans the finger when they booed him when he was having a tough time at the plate. Scott was fined and went into a pout. I remember Ted also had an incident with the fans and was fined for his "obscene gesture." I asked Ted if he would talk to Scott and he did willingly. He just never hesitated [when asked to help out in the Scott incident]. He went right out and went to center field and talked to him. Scott came [into the locker room after that] and apologized and went on to have a great year with Milwaukee.

I liked him. He was a real baseball man and always had time for people in uniform.

Jim French

Catcher

1965–71: ....Washington Senators
Career Statistics:............................. 234 games, 5 home runs,
.196 batting average

Note: French did not play against Ted Williams, but was managed by him in 1969 with the Senators.

THERE WAS AN awe factor to start with. I would say that he's was the most charismatic man that I ever knew personally. To give you an example, a number of years ago we had a reunion in Washington, DC, and he was in a wheelchair. And, I don't know, there had to be 600 people in there eating dinner and he came wheeling into the crowd and the whole place went silent. Just totally silent. But he was like that.

He was very charismatic. A very likeable guy at the same time a pretty nasty son of a bitch when he wanted to be. Which was quite often. Mercurial I guess would be the right word, I don't know.

Gosh, you know, you remember little things. His favorite term was bush. If you had a shirt on that was out of style or something, you were bush. This is off the field. On the field, he was not the greatest tactical manager. I don't think he had the patience to be what I would call a great manager. He certainly was a hell of a lot better hitter than he was a manager, just like I'm a hell of a lot better lawyer than I was a catcher—so that's not saying much.

He and I got along very well. We used to argue all the time about pitchers. With pitchers, he thought pitchers were stupid. And I guess because he hit .400 and a bunch of home runs he would.

We worked together pretty well. I was like a second-stringer . . . you know, back then, we called the pitches, the catchers. And he loved the slider. Loved the slider. Even if the pitcher had a shitty slider, he loved it.

It was a strange relationship that he had with all the players. Some players, I mean, *vehemently* disliked him. Vehemently. Bernie Allen was one that I can recall. And I can't remember why. I talked to Bernie about it and he did something, whatever. But I guess he was that kind of a guy, you know.

He would, I guess when I said patience, he would talk to pitchers about how to pitch and they'd they go out and get beat up, get him and then he would drop it. He didn't stay with somebody long enough to . . . he didn't know how to throw sliders, he didn't know to pitch other than strategy pitching. In other words what pitch, when, where, whatever. Hell, I was just as good as he was at that or better because I knew the pitchers. And I knew the hitters better. If I was good at anything that's what I was good at.

He thought that, I think, that pitchers should pitch to everyone like pitchers should have pitched to him. But you know in retrospect, it was a great experience to play under him. I mean, one day he'd come in and make you feel like a million dollars and the next day not speak to you and you'd wonder what the fuck you did wrong. Pardon my language, I don't talk like this when I'm a lawyer but when I get to talking baseball I regress.

Here's his biggest problem as I look back. He had a bench coach, Joe Camacho. And Joe's credentials—don't get me wrong, nice guy, really nice guy—his credentials were that he played some minor-league ball and then ran Ted's baseball camp. And Joe didn't have the respect that someone that had some experience or whatever would have had. Wayne Terwilliger, good friend of mine, Nellie Fox, God bless him good friend of mine, Sid Hudson, another coach and a good friend of mine, George Susce, I don't know how a good friend—I used to tease George too much and when I look back I say, why did I do that?—in my opinion was not the greatest coaching staff in the world.

Twig, good third-base coach, worked hard with the infielders. I don't think any of his coaches—and I may be wrong, because I didn't sit in any of the meetings—would stand up to him, and say this is stupid, you're doing this wrong or whatever. That's the impression I got. Obviously I wasn't in the meetings.

I also played under Gil Hodges and Hodges had a hell of a staff, ok. Plus, Hodges was a much, much smarter manager and handler of guys even though he . . . I guess we all have our drawbacks. And Ted lost interest at the end, no question. No question. He just lost interest. And you can't do anything, write your books, go into a case, if you don't have interest in it. You go through the motions. Plus, I guess his personal relationships were not the greatest. Who knows, who knows.

You know even though I was a college grad—I signed after I got out of college and went to grad school in the offseason—I was relatively older than most of the guys and, I won't say worldly, but educated, if that's the right word, and I was still—I don't know if awe is the right word—I was a little bit afraid of Hodges.

You have to understand I was far from a star, a pretty good ballplayer but if I screwed up enough I was gone. That's just the way it was. But I would say I was on the fringe, let's put it that way. So I was concerned, because I came up under Hodges. Hodges was a very aloof guy, very aloof. Even if you screwed up, he very seldom would say anything. He'd have Joe Pignatano tell you. And that bothered me.

Whereas Williams, I was never afraid of him like I was Hodges. Apprehensive is the better word with Hodges. And that was never the case with Williams.

I was more of what you'd call a banjo hitter when compared to him. If the fences were in 10 feet closer I would have had 150 home runs instead of four. So I can remember the first or second year of spring training, he came down in the batting cage to work with my hitting. And after about twenty minutes he gave up. Because I hit different. He had he classic turn the hips good, slightly uppercut swing. Well, shit, if I hit the slightly uppercut I had a 150, 200 fly balls on the warning track. Where I should have been hitting line drives.

He could not, in my opinion, teach somebody to hit except the way he hit. And so if you weren't like him, alright, that type of swing, that type of power . . . two differences between he and I, besides size, was that his eyesight was better than mine—because I wore contacts—and he could open up his hips at the last moment and really get around on the ball, which I could not do.

I got along really good personally with Williams. Except you'd argue long enough with Williams and he'd call you a bush dumbass and walk away. You know, because you were winning the argument. Or at least you thought you were. In his mind I don't think he ever lost an argument. He was a *very, very* strong personality and at times not a very nice guy.

I spoke to him a couple times at reunions or old-timers game, and my God, he greeted me like his long-lost brother every time.

Hal Keller

Catcher

1949, 1950, 1952: ....**Washington Senators**
Career Statistics: ....**25 games, 1 home run,
.204 batting average**

AS YOU KNOW if you looked it up, I had a very abbreviated major-league career. As I recall, I didn't play more than one or two series, and I only caught one game I'm sure of that Ted hit in.

I hit my one and only home run in Boston in the left-field bullpen, and Ted walked up and said, "Did it feel good?" And of course I said yes.

Ted was a unique individual, really, but he was a very kind person. Very intense in his opinions. I don't think [he] really appreciated the fine points of baseball, but he was consumed by the battle between the pitcher and the hitter. I doubt if he ever would attempt to instruct a middle infielder on how to make a double play, that sort of thing. His all-consuming passion was hitting.

He didn't have the best product to work with, of course, but you know, I think hitting—I've never had much faith in hitting coaches. The best they can do, I think, is help your mental approach. You can either hit a baseball or you can't, it's that simple. Whoever made George Brett into a .350 hitter did nothing for Frank White.[1]

The best hitting coach I ever worked with was an old player named Deron Johnson, who just emphasized mental approach . . . did very little with swing.

---

[1] A career .255 hitter.

I never saw Ted—the years I worked with him[2]—screw with a hitter's swing. He always emphasized two things: Get a pitch you can hit and pop your ass and turn your hips, so your body releases all this power into it. You probably read his book with the average zones; he stressed that.

---

[2] Williams and Keller worked together when Keller was the farm director for the Washington Senators, from 1969–1972.

Hal Naragon

Catcher

1951, 1954–59: .... Cleveland Indians
1959–60: .... Washington Senators
1961–62: .... Minnesota Twins
Career Statistics: .... 424 games, 6 home runs,
.266 batting average

IT WAS ALWAYS very interesting [facing Ted], because he was a great hitter. Of course at the time I caught behind Williams I was with Cleveland, and we had a great pitching staff, so it was always a real battle. I'm not sure how well he did against us at that time. But I was a Ted Williams fan, I can tell you that. I told this story and my wife didn't really believe it, but when he would swing and miss the ball, you could kind of smell burning a little bit. I always remembered that. And it wasn't too long ago, I was listening to an interview on one of those stations—I can't remember who said it—and they said the same thing! So I guess I really wasn't dreaming. It really happened [laughs].

I remember we had a situation once in Cleveland on a Thursday afternoon. Back in those days, the way the stadium was situated late in the day the shade would come in and the pitcher would be in the sun, and the batter would be in the shade, and the shadow would be about halfway between the pitching mound and home plate. It's kind of difficult picking up the ball. Mike Garcia was pitching, and he threw his sinker. The ball was about halfway up to the plate and Williams says, "There is something on that ball." I didn't say anything; I just caught the ball. It was a strike, but the umpire called it a ball; it was one of those close pitches. Nobody argued, and I flipped the ball back to Mike. Hank Soar was the umpire, and he walked around and said, "Mike, I'd like to have the ball." So Mike rolled the ball into him. Williams then said to me, "What was that pitch?" I said, "a sinker," and that's all that was said [laughs]. They always said he had good eyes.

I always found Ted to be very friendly towards baseball players. If you had a uniform on, he knew your name and a little bit about you; that was my opinion. He'd speak to you; if you said something, he'd talk to you. But I know this—I remember when being a rookie, my first full year in the major leagues—Kenmore Hotel was the one we stayed at in Boston. Well, we used to walk to the ballpark because it was that close, which was nice. We'd always go out early—get dressed and go out—because we always wanted to watch Ted Williams take batting practice. When Ted Williams came to bat up in Boston, I think everything stopped [laughs]. And I wasn't alone either. Half the team was out there. And we had some good hitters on that team that year, too [in 1954]. We won 111 games that year.

But what I really remember most, other than his great hitting, was—I think it was my second year in the major leagues, I'm not quite sure—I asked Ted Williams for an autographed picture. We were in Cleveland then, and he said to me, "Well, when you get to Boston, you tell the clubhouse gentleman"—his name was Vince—"and I'll make sure you get the picture." So I go to Boston and I go out to the ballpark early with other ballplayers to watch Williams, and we're just leaning against the fence there, just outside the dugout. And the truth is, I kind of forgot about the picture. But after he got through hitting, he came over and told me, "I sent that picture over to you." So I thought that was pretty good. And I still have it.

You know he served his country twice. He was in the Air Force. He did this *twice*. I wonder what his record would have been if he only had one military service instead of two. Same way with Bob Feller. Well, there were a lot of guys back then who did that playing major league baseball.

[I'm not sure if he had the benefit of the umpires]; that's probably stressing it a little. But he did have a great eye at the plate. I mean, he didn't offer at bad pitches. And I would think maybe, you know, you get a reputation of swinging at anything, and the umpire might widen your strike zone a little bit. But Williams was the other way around.

You had to throw the ball over the plate, or at least hit some part of the plate, for him to go for it. He was a disciplined hitter. That's the reason he was such a great hitter.

We had Bob Lemon, who was a good sinkerball pitcher. I read where Williams said that he thought Lemon was a tough pitcher to hit, because he had great movement on his pitches. I can't tell you exactly which one that you would throw Williams if you're Lemon. He had great pitches, so you couldn't go wrong calling any of them.

I don't remember so much about the discussion on how to pitch Ted Williams. I think it would just be a waste of time [laughs]. I think our manager, Al Lopez, who would never hold any group meetings, as far as going over hitters was concerned. He left it up to the pitcher and the catcher that day. I thought that was the way to go—I still think that's the way to go, because when you get into a group meeting, you may come out with four or five suggestions that need not be said. Where the pitcher and catcher, they're on the team within themselves. They can work it out much better and very effectively. I thought with Al Lopez, that was a great way to go.

We won 111 games [in 1954], and I think they [the entire starting staff] completed like 73 of them. I think Lemon, and Early Wynn, and Mike Garcia, I think those three—or at least two of them—completed over 20 games. That's unusual today.

We did shade him to right field. Williams, you know, he's going to hit the ball over your head and over the fence. He didn't hit to left field much. I don't know if he bunted once just for fun.

He was one of my favorite players even before he got there, and then to catch behind him and *talk* to him—it was a real thrill. He liked to talk about baseball. He would help you. If you went over there and ask him or get into a conversation about hitting, he would give his thoughts. He wouldn't back away about that. But he was a great hitter; probably the best I've ever caught behind.

Nobody hit like Ted Williams—I didn't—but he did tell me once that he liked my idea of hitting. I wasn't a power hitter at all, but he told me he thought I had a good stroke for what I was doing, which will give you a little confidence.

He seemed to be a very friendly guy in uniform, and I've talked to some of his former teammates, and they thought he was a really good teammate and very helpful when you wanted to talk to him. The players seemed to really like him.

I don't remember them [booing him in Boston]. There could have been, but I don't remember. I don't know how you could boo Ted Williams [laughs]. If they did, I don't know how long they stayed in the ballpark.

I have two pictures of Ted Williams at my home; I have the one he gave to me and then a picture of us talking when we were in Cooperstown playing the Red Sox. That's probably the time we talked more than when he would come to bat. I was probably too flustered to really talk to him [laughs].

There was a writer that was here, he was from Canton, Ohio, and I remember him telling me that he asked Ted Williams if he could have an interview. He said he was kind of timid about doing it, and Ted said, "Yeah, let's go in the dugout." He said it was just like that. He said, "We went out there and had a nice chat." He told me this a few years ago, and I said you are probably the only one [laughs]. Oh, I think he treated the press better than what they'd like you to believe.

When you have your team, like Dale Mitchell, who hit .315 lifetime,[3] and you had people like Al Rosen, Vic Wertz, and Larry Doby—we had a good team, I hate to mention names because I know I'm going to forget some—but they would go out and before the game, go early

---

[3] Mitchell's lifetime batting average was .312.

to the ballpark and watch Williams hit! Well, that's quite an honor, I think.

I remember he would hit balls to the opposite field if he wanted to [in batting practice]. But he was hitting them over the fence in right field, too [laughs]. But he was definitely the best hitter I ever caught behind, and I'm sure there are a lot of other catchers who would say the same thing.

He was a great hitter. I remember him once saying during an interview, he asked the press when they were going to have a good year!

Neal Watlington

Catcher

1953: .... **Philadelphia Athletics**
Career Statistics: .... **21 games, 0 home runs,**
.159 batting average

IT IS WITH great pleasure that I can relate what I remember about the days I played against the great Ted Williams.

As a catcher, it was very hard to call pitches when he was hitting. I think the umpires favored him because of his great eyesight. If he did not swing, they thought it had to be a ball.

Some said to call the fastball down the middle and surprise him. We, the Philadelphia A's, had a pitcher named Harry Byrd, who proclaimed that he was going to see how Ted hit laying flat on his back. He found out—the first time Byrd faced him, he knocked him down—Ted got up, brushed himself off, and proceeded to hit the next pitch nine miles out of the park.

I broke into the majors at Fenway Park in 1953,[4] and Ted was just back from the Armed Services and the Korean War. I remember that day well, too. When I came up in the latter part of the game, I hit a ball to the 380-foot marker in right field, and Jim Piersall jumped up and speared it. Ted came up in the eighth and hit a prolific blast to right that beat us.[5]

That year, when Boston came to Connie Mack Stadium, Ted and Gus Zernial staged a home run contest . . . this being the only game the stadium was filled. I was kind of thrilled to be designated to catch

---

[4] Watlington's debut was July 12, 1953, for the A's in Boston.
[5] Williams returned to action on August 6, 1953, against the St. Louis Browns. He played against the A's four times: August 11 (game two of a doubleheader), August 13, August 18, and August 19. Williams' home run in the seventh inning on August 19 at Fenway put the Red Sox ahead, 5–4, in a 6–4 win.

the contest. They were to have ten swings each. I think everyone was surprised when Gus out-hit him 4 home runs to 3.

The only conversation I ever had with him was briefly while catching the home run contest, but I did hear him talking to other ballplayers around pregame batting practice. He was eager to help players with advice and was well liked by all ballplayers.

There is one thing that stands out in my mind, and that is every time we saw him hit in pregame batting practice, everything got so quiet and [the stadium] came to a standstill. All activity stopped on the ball field and in the stands. I am privileged to say without a doubt that Ted Williams was the most pure hitter that I have ever seen.

INTERVIEWS

Bob Oldis

Catcher

1953–55: ....Washington Senators
1960–61: ....Pittsburgh Pirates
1962–63: .... Philadelphia Phillies
Career Statistics: ....135 games, 1 home run,
.237 batting average

Q. Being a catcher, you had an interesting vantage point. What was your defensive/pitch selection strategy against Williams, and how do you think you fared?

A. High and tight, low and away

Q. Do you think Williams got the benefit of the umpires' calls and, if so, why?

A. No

Q. Recollections of any specific at-bats and/or plays vs. Williams.

A. Connie Marrero, a knuckleball pitcher for us in Washington was pitching, and Ted hit two home runs on knuckleballs. In the dugout, he said, next time he hits, we are going to give him four fastball pitchouts.[1]

Q. Was he the hitter you feared the most in the field?

A. He was just a good hitter—knew strike zone.

---

[1] On August 11, 1954, in the first game of a doubleheader at Boston, Williams homered off Marrero in the first and third innings. Marrero was lifted for a pinch-hitter in the fifth inning and wouldn't face Williams again that day.

Q. Did you ever have occasion to interact with Williams either when he was up at bat or off the field? If so, what kind of guy was he like?

A. In 1953, both teams came out of the Red Sox dugout, and the visitors had to walk across the field to the third-base dugout. The Red Sox were taking batting practice, and Ted stopped me and [my first time in Boston] wished me good luck and hoped [that I had a] successful career in the big leagues. After a little bit, he asked me about a rookie pitcher we had by the name of Pedro Ramos. I told him that he had a good fastball, hard curve (now slider), and good control— and when I went to our dugout, Mickey Vernon and Eddie Yost, my teammates, asked me, what did that big donkey want? He wished me good luck and congratulated me for getting to the big leagues and then asked me about Ramos, I told them. Mickey said to Eddie Yost, see, he already got a scouting report on Ramos.[2]

---

[2] In his career, Williams would end up hitting .365 with 6 home runs and a .730 slugging percentage against Ramos.

Red Wilson

Catcher

1951–54: .... Chicago White Sox
1954–60: .... Detroit Tigers
1960: .... Cleveland Indians
Career Statistics: .... 2,037 games, 24 home runs,
.258 batting average

Q. Being a catcher, you had an interesting vantage point. What was your defensive/pitch selection strategy against Williams, and how do you think you fared?

A. Pitch selection: Throw strikes or walk him—he didn't swing at "balls." We did okay.

Q. Do you think Williams got the benefit of the umpires' calls and, if so, why?

A. He got little if any favoritism from umpires.

Q. What was the talk among other players on how to face Williams in pregame meetings or just in general?

A. Ted Williams was respected as a player and an individual. Our effort was to concentrate on keeping his teammates off the bases, so he couldn't hurt you as much with his bat when hitting with the bases empty.

Q. Was he the hitter you feared the most in the field?

A. Yes

Q. Did you ever have occasion to interact with Williams either when he was up at bat or off the field? If so, what kind of guy was he like?

A. No contact off the field. Brief conversations about fishing in Wisconsin. He was a man of few words.

Section Three: Infielders

Dr. Bobby Brown

Third base / Shortstop

1946–52, 1954:...New York Yankees
1984–94:...President, American League
Career Statistics: ....548 games, 22 home runs,
.279 batting average

WHEN I WAS playing shortstop, that shift wasn't in vogue. I think Lou Boudreau started that thing. I believe what we did is the third baseman would move over to shortstop, and then of course the shortstop went over behind second base, and the second baseman moved more towards first and a little deeper. I don't think they moved into the outfield like they do now.

I do remember that if they had a man at first base and he came up—usually [Johnny] Pesky hit second and Dom DiMaggio hit first—and if either one of them was on first, and second base wasn't occupied, the first thing Joe Collins would do is signal to the bench that he'd like to get halfway. He didn't want to be that close [laughs] when he was hitting. And he'd look over there with this look on his face, like, you've got to let me get back a little bit.

I read somewhere not too long ago that the shift never really bugged Ted too much. He'd either just hit over it or through it or whatnot, and he just whaled away [as usual]. They said that someone tried to teach him—well not teach him—but try to get him to hit to left field and [he] tried it but gave up on that. He just popped away in his usual way.

He was a swell guy. He was *extremely* popular with not only his own teammates, but with all of the opposing players, too. He'd talk to everybody if they wanted to talk. He was very, very helpful and always wanted to talk about hitting and whatnot.

One year I guess he broke his collarbone and they went in and tried to reattach the fragments. They used screws and whatnot, hoping that he'd be able to get back sooner. I remember visiting and asking him how it went and so forth, and he said, well, he was just getting his swing back. I saw him swing a few times and he knocked all the air out of the place where he was swinging, and I said, "Well, I think you're doing okay, Ted." He was very much interested in surgery. When he was in the hospital, he told me that what he did . . . I think he broke his clavicle, and then he also broke his radius in the All-Star Game.[1] He injured the head of the radius, which is a bad break, and they were very worried whether they'd be able to get a good result, but they did. But he told me that he would show up in the operating room at about six o'clock in the morning before anybody got there and they'd let him scrub in, and he'd stay in the operating room all day, watching operations. He really enjoyed that. I said, "What did you like the most?" He said, "I like the eye operations the best." So I do remember that.

Outside of the ball field, I didn't see much of him. As I said, I did see him when he was getting over those injuries, because I was a doctor or I was in medical school. I was in med school when I was playing and graduated in 1950. I was just curious of how he was getting along. Usually he was rehabbing when I'd see him.

He was done managing by the time I started in the American League [as President], but I was in Texas when he came down for his first year; he came down with the Senators. He was just here one year. I had little chance to talk with him. I might have said hello a few times, but as I recall, there was no lengthy conversations or anything.

He loved to fish. He loved to hunt, but he *really* loved to fish. As you know, he gave those exhibitions of fly casting at Madison Square

---

[1] In the 1950 All-Star Game at Comiskey Park, Williams crashed into the wall catching a Ralph Kiner fly ball, injuring his elbow.

Garden when they had the big hunt and fish show up there. He'd put [on] demonstrations of fly casting. I guess he was one of the best in the world at that. For a long time, he was the top expert at Sears in testing new equipment: camping equipment, fishing rods, guns, and so on and so forth. He was excellent at that.

We were all friendly with the Red Sox, but it was a war on the field. But they all had good guys; there was no viciousness to it. It was just guys that *really* played hard because they knew it was two tough teams that would hook up. But they were all good guys.

Ted got along with everybody. He had his deals with the press and the fans, but with the ballplayers, he was always first-rate. He missed, what, five seasons with Korea and World War II?

He was ultimately dangerous wherever he was. It didn't make any difference what ballpark he was in. There was no such thing as he'd hit better in the short fields. No, he made all fields just . . . they were all very good for him. He could just flat hit, as you know.

Joe [DiMaggio] was a more complete player. He's a guy who could run and throw and field and hit, but Ted as a hitter was probably the best hitter of that era. He and [Stan] Musial and Joe were all three right in there together. There were a couple of others that were close, like Johnny Mize and some of the others. And then Hank Aaron came on a little after I left. I think he came on the first year that I retired, and he was in the National League, so I didn't see him. But Ted was certainly the best hitter of his era.

They talked about that [the supposed DiMaggio-for-Williams trade], but Joe would have hit . . . if Joe didn't have to go into the service and played in Fenway Park, he would have hit 700 home runs. He would have! And Ted would have hit more home runs, too. But both of them would have hit better if Ted hit in Yankee Stadium and Joe hit in Fenway. Joe—I think one series up there, maybe in '49—I think he hit five home runs in three games.

That's a lot of baloney [that if Williams didn't swing the umpire would call it a ball]. That's just a lot of baloney. Obviously he was a good hitter, and good hitters have good eyesight. You watched everybody at batting practice, but you always watched him, too, because he was fun to watch.

You have to remember, in those days, they must have had maybe five dailies in Boston, and, of course, they had other New England papers, so they were always looking for angles. That put a real strain on the ballplayer because they were always trying to find some gimmick that they could write about. And the same thing happened in New York. We had, I think, maybe seven daily papers in New York at the time. They had big press corps that really tried to write about things. Of course in those days, they had to write a lot more about the ball game itself. Nowadays, they don't have to write the exact account because it's on TV. But before TV became commonplace, they had to write about the ball game. That was a good bit of their writing, but they were always looking for an angle somewhere. Especially in Boston.

He would speak his peace. Sometimes in Boston that wasn't exactly beneficial. They were irate fans—just like they are now. They lived and died with the Red Sox, and anyone else that came in there was the enemy. So you expected that. They would get on Ted, sure. One of the columnists was really hard on him—Egan, the old Colonel, I think his name was—he was always on Ted with bad write-ups and so forth. But it couldn't be too bad; the guy hit .350 every damn year.

There wasn't a big contingent of fans that were against him. They loved the guy up there, but he did some things and whatnot, and they'd get mad at him. Just like in New York; they'd get mad at DiMaggio. They'd want a perfect game every day, and of course, that's not going to happen.

Tom Carroll

Shortstop / Third base

1955–56: ....New York Yankees
1959: ....Kansas City Athletics
Career Statistics: .... 64 games, 0 home runs,
.300 batting average

WELL, I WAS a rookie bonus player in 1955, and I pinch-ran in several games, played in the field a couple of innings, and didn't even get an at-bat until the last day of the season. We were in Boston and had clinched the pennant in '55 that day, and there was a doubleheader to end the season. So I played both games of the doubleheader the next day at shortstop.[2]

I had never played on the second-base side—in Little League or anytime else. So when Williams came up, you know, we put the shift on. I'm on the second-base side on the outfield grass, and I'm very uncomfortable. I'm not so uncomfortable just because it's *him*, but because I'm on the wrong side of second base [laughs]. But as I said, I'm on the outfield grass, so one thing I could do is really throw the ball.

Anyway, I don't remember what at-bat it was of his—it was either his first or second at-bat[3]—and he hit a line drive at me. And you instinctively know whether, you know, it's in range or not. It was definitely in range. It was about a foot or two to my left. A really well-hit line drive is *dead* at you, and maybe a little bit rising. Occasionally, you get a line drive that *knuckleballs* at you.

---

[2] Carroll pinch-ran, played shortstop, and batted twice in the first game of a doubleheader on September 25, 1955, and started and led off in game two.

[3] It was his first at-bat. Williams walked his second time up and was replaced by a pinch runner.

This didn't do any of those things [laughs]. And I stuck out my arm, you know, I've got the ball, I've got the ball. And it was *by* me! And that line drive came at me not on the dead level, not rising, and not a knuckleball. It came at me like a golf shot. Terrific overspin on the ball. I mean sort of [like]—what was the great Swedish tennis player? [Bjorn] Borg. That used to get this tremendous undercut topspin, only more so on me [laughs]. It was just amazing. I never—I mean, I did play six years of ball in Triple-A and the majors—but I never saw that. I never saw a ball come at me like that.

The most amazing thing that I saw in baseball involved Ted Williams. He was, in my opinion, the greatest hitter I ever saw—and I played with [Mickey] Mantle and [Roger] Maris. I played with Maris in Kansas City and Mantle in '55, '56, and again briefly in '59. In '59, I played two years—'57 and '58—in Triple-A, but knew I wasn't going to make the team. I was in the army that winter and got to spring training late. But to make a long story short, I went north with the team because my options were up. So I was sitting on the bench when the season began, and we began it against the Red Sox in New York.

Williams had apparently been hurt and missed most of or part of the end of the season in '58. And how old was he in '59? I think he was thirty-nine or something like that. He was born in 1918? So he was forty-one . . . forty to start the season. I don't know what kind of year he had in '58, but I understood that he banged into a wall or hurt an arm and had missed a month or two at the end of the season.

It was the first series of 1959, and Bob Turley was pitching. He was not only the Yankee player representative, but he was one of the hardest throwers in the league. A power pitcher. He first faced Williams in the top of the first. Turley was throwing him fastballs. Williams didn't get around on the ball and hit a lazy fly ball to left-center, which, because Mantle was playing [him] as a strict pull-hitter as he should have been, played him in right-center and didn't get to the ball, and Williams had a loafing double.

So, the second time he was up—and Turley was still on, throwing really hard—Jim Turner was our pitching coach. He was very aggressive . . . we used to call him Colonel Jim. He took a lot of things on himself, and Stengel gave him free reign with setting up the pitching rotation; but occasionally, Turner exceeded his brief. But he's decided that Williams, who was injured in '58, and was fairly old at this time, can't get around on Turley.

So he tells [Frank] Crosetti, who was the infield coach, to get Mantle over in center field from right-center. And Crosetti jumps up on the dugout steps in the stadium and starts whistling in this very piercing whistle at Mantle to move, waving him over. And Mantle doesn't see him for a while, so the whole game is stopped. And I don't know if you know, but Williams was famous for having rabbit ears: always looking in the other dugout, always wanted to see what was going on. He's watching all this by the way. And in fact, they used to do things when he was at-bat to try and distract him by whistling and doing all kinds of things . . . not very successfully.

So, Mantle didn't see him for the longest time. When he finally saw Crosetti waving him over, he just refused [laughs] . . . he refused to believe it or act on it, so he's sort of stuck in right-center. The game is totally stopped, but Crosetti keeps waving at him, and finally Mantle kind of stomps toward dead straight-away center field.

As I said, Williams is watching all of this. So Mantle gets positioned in dead center field, and I don't know if it was the next pitch or the second pitch thereafter, but Turley threw a fastball in on Williams' hands, and he hit into the third deck of Yankee Stadium about five feet fair. And that was the most amazing thing that I've ever seen.[4]

And you know, he was well-respected by his teammates and by his opponents. Everybody thought he was a great hitter. His being a bad guy or not a team player—that was all started by the newspaper situation in Boston and by this guy Colonel Egan, Dave Egan, who was a *drunk*. Early in Williams' career—I think Williams came up in '39, is that what it was? And you know he had terrific years right from the get-go. But he was sort of invited or commanded to an interview with Egan, who wrote for the *Boston Eagle* or something,[5] I don't remember which particular paper. And one of the problems in Boston is that they [have] six or seven papers that were all competing with each other. And Egan, who was a lush, had Williams come in for this interview. I think it was in a hotel room. And Egan was drunk, just so you know, and Williams walked out on him. So they were enemies from then on. So Egan did his level best to defame Williams. And then there were pro- and anti-Williams factions on the newspapers and stuff. But he loved to talk hitting, and he'd talk hitting with everybody, including with people on the other team. He was very supportive of me. We only had one conversation, but he was very encouraging.

He hated lousy hitters, bad hitting. Sammy White was a great defensive catcher for the Red Sox for years. He was a tall, rangy guy, and he did everything wrong at the plate. And [I believe] he was a .220 hitter for his career.[6] So much so that Williams, when White would be in batting practice, would get so upset with White not changing and

---

[4] The game Carroll is likely talking about occurred in July 4, 1955. In that game, Williams doubled off Turley in the first inning and homered in the fifth. The Yankees did open with the Red Sox in 1959, but Williams didn't make his season debut until May 12. Carroll was traded from the Yankees to Kansas City on April 12. Williams hit four other homers off Turley, but Carroll was not with a major-league team during any of those times.

[5] The paper was the *Boston Record*.

[6] White's career batting average was .262, but it was .261 and .245 in the years that Carroll was with the Yankees.

improving and doing some things fundamentally different, that he'd turn his back. He couldn't bear to watch White swing the bat [laughs]!

His book, *The Science of Hitting*, is absolutely interesting. He divides the strike zone into probably twelve squares in that book. And he shows as you wander away from the fat part of the strike zone . . . what his projected batting average would be. As you got out on the corners, his average dropped. He was a .250 hitter in some of these places, which is very interesting, and I think very accurate description of the facts of hitting.

He would do one thing very unusual; he didn't have a narrow stance with his feet. He had an average or I'd say a little longer than average stance, but as he hit in a game—I mean, for real—he'd stride forward, oh, six inches or more, which is very normal.

I saw him take batting practice a lot, and he'd spread out his feet to where his foot would be after the stride in a game and hit that way. I guess it would force his arms and his hands to be quicker, because he wasn't getting the impetus from the weight moving forward. I never talked to him or got an explanation from him, but I suspect that's what it was.

Jerry Coleman

Second base / Shortstop / Third base

1949–57:	New York Yankees
American League All-Star:	1950
Career Statistics:	723 games, 16 home runs, .263 batting average

HE WAS THE best hitter in baseball, maybe one of the greatest hitters of all time. He doesn't have as many hits as [Ty] Cobb—he hit .344 and Cobb hit .367—but Cobb was a running guy and a bunting guy, and Williams . . . you know, if he had done early in his career what he did the last year he led the league in hitting—bounce the ball off the left-field wall—he'd have hit .900. But he was a power guy and in Fenway Park, the toughest part of the ballpark was to right-center field, and that's where most of his balls went.

Of course [Yankees manager Casey] Stengel pulled me in [for the shift]. I forget when it was . . . I think [Cardinals manager] Eddie Dyer was the first guy to use that shift in the World Series. They played the Cardinals in '46, and I think Dyer was the first one to have the swing-around—and of course they do it all the time now.[7] Anyway, Stengel sent me to short right field—and this is a true story. I'm out there [thinking], I've been out here for a couple years and he's never hit a line drive to me since I've been out there. So he says to me come on in. And I'm going to tell you this is the God's honest truth. The first game, a sinking line drive right over my head right where I would have been standing, but I wasn't. It was amazing. I stayed in [from then on]. See, the problem is, anytime there's a runner at first base, you have to come in for a possible double play. And so I'm trying to think, [Al] Zarilla was the number two hitter or Billy Goodman, and Dominic

---

[7] Dyer had the Cardinals play a form of the shift in the 1946 World Series, but Cleveland manager Lou Boudreau used the Williams shift earlier that season.

[DiMaggio] started it off, but there was always someone at first base [and] I had to come in. But there were probably, because of that ball-club and their hitting skills and their 1-2 hitters, I didn't get to play out there as much as I did out there normally if they had bad 1-2 hitters.

He was such a great hitter and [received] the greatest animosity of any ballplayer in history. You know, the sportswriters hated him there. The highlight of my career (and his) was when he came around and hit a home run and jumped up at home plate and spit at them at Fenway Park [laughs]. I just thought that was outstanding!

[Albert] Pujols is a good player, but Williams was a *nationally* good player, as were [Joe] DiMaggio, [Mickey] Mantle, and [Willie] Mays. These were guys that covered the entire United States. Pujols was great with the Cardinals, but not to the extent that these guys were—not from a press standpoint. There's more things going on in baseball *and* in sports these days.

But he was not a great defensive player. In fact, the reason we beat the Red Sox in one of those final two games was that he butchered a line drive that went by him. Should have been a double and it became a triple. [Phil] Rizzuto hit it. Then [Tommy] Henrich hit a 27-hopper ground ball to Bobby Doerr, and we stayed ahead in the game. That might have been the final game, I'm not sure.[8] That play Williams *didn't* make might have cost the Red Sox a pennant. It's a true story. The triple was really a double that he botched.

He wasn't bad in left field. He knew how to play that left-field wall very well, even when the ball was going to hit the wall and he couldn't get it. And he could run. You know, if you played too deep on him . . . I got a couple of ground balls back in right field and he'd beat

---

[8] On the final day of the season in 1949—October 2—the Red Sox and Yankees were tied for first place. Phil Rizzuto led off the bottom of the first with a triple, and the next batter, Tommy Henrich, drove him in. The Yankees would never trail in the game, which they would go on to win, 5–3.

them out. It was amazing. He could run quite well, I thought, for a big man. He was a thin guy, of course, but this was at the end of his career.

He basically, I think, was the greatest hitter I ever saw. He had *one* great day against us and Vic Raschi, hitting two home runs at Yankee Stadium in the upper deck. And I'll tell you, we pretty much stopped them. Now, you have to look these things up. My memory bank is dead. Now, you're talking a couple of years ago. More than a week or two [laughs]![9] Tommy Byrne struck him out twice in one game and he walked. But I do know this—Ted was a *very* sharp person. He used to stroke the umpires all the time. Sit with them and talk with them and this and that. Well, you know, umpires are human. I'm not saying they gave him the benefit of the doubt all the time, but I do think when you have that situation, you have this guy Williams, you are prone to not strike him out, if it's a marginal thing, you see. So you give him the benefit of the doubt. That might have happened, and I personally think it did happen. I know Tommy Byrne, our left-handed guy, had a fastball and a breaking ball that exploded; the trouble was that he walked 27 men a game. That's why they traded him; he walked too many people. But I know he struck him out twice and he got ball four.[10]

I roomed with Mickey [Mantle] for two years, and he was one of the finest human beings on this earth. He was a follower. When somebody said, let's go have a cocktail, he'd go with them. If they said, let's go to a movie, he'd go to a movie. Had Mickey been a guy that didn't drink, didn't smoke, didn't do all these things, he would have lived another

---

[9] On September 24, 1950, Williams hit two solo home runs off Vic Raschi in a 9–5 New York win at Yankee Stadium.

[10] On April 30, 1949, Tommy Byrne struck out Williams the first two times he faced him, then walked him the third time.

ten years. Now, Williams, he took good care of himself. Of course, for him, his goal was to be the greatest hitter that ever lived. And he might have been, if you consider average and power.

A lot of those other guys were doubles hitters or single hitters, Cobb was a bunter and runner and so forth, and even [Tony] Gwynn at .338 doesn't touch Williams' .344. But I do think this—I think it is harder to hit now than when Williams played. The pitchers are better; the bullpen has changed the game. If the guy hiccups in the fourth inning, he's gone, and you bring in a 100 mile-per-hour fastball or 98 or something like that, then two more guys just like him. And pitching is tough to hit now, that's what I think.

Photo courtesy of the United States Navy

Jerry Coleman played against Ted Williams, took his military physical in the same place as Williams, and, in his post-baseball career, saw Williams when he visited.

He lived in San Diego. The man who ran sports things in San Diego at the park—Williams was his god. And he's got Williams' bat that he hit .400 with and those kind of things. If he ever wanted to sell it— well, he's dead now—but he's got a fortune in his office somewhere. But Ted used to come all the time and we'd entertain him at our dinners. I was there the day they named the boulevard after him. In fact, I got up and made a speech and told everybody how much I hated him—no, I didn't [laughs]. I use that phrase—I didn't like Ted—because he was on the other team, that's all.

He didn't talk to banjo hitters [laughs]. The last time we met to hold hands was when we went overseas down in El Toro,[11] and they were taking pictures of these two great ballplayers going to win the war. Of course we did win the war single-handedly.

We took our physicals together in Jacksonville. And [laughs] Ted had broken his elbow or something in Chicago the year before—I don't know what happened, he ran into the fence—and the guy patted it twice and said, "You're fine." He had no chance of missing that physical, I tell you. But he went to a different place for preparation, somewhere in the East; I was on the West Coast. But we had the same gathering together when we went overseas to Korea. He went to k-3 and I went to k-6.

The only time I ever heard about Williams overseas after departing— when we went to our various squadrons—was when the Marines went on a big mission once in North Korea somewhere. And all of a sudden, "I'm hit, I'm hit! I've got a mayday, I've got a mayday!" We're listening to this. Now *that* becomes your brother, because you know it is one of your guys. And we're listening and finally someone says, "I got ya, I got ya. We'll go to 55, follow me." And the next thing I know, they get to 55, and there's no more conversation on the air. The next day I find out it was Ted Williams. He landed at k-55, I believe it was no wheels, no flaps, going about 80 knots faster than he should—you land at 150, and he was going about 220 or something. Why he didn't blow I'll never know. Usually you blow up when you get like that. When he got out of that, it was really a miracle that he survived.

What happened [laughs] . . . Ted started castigating the Marine Corps for getting him there, and they took him out of there because they didn't want the bad publicity. He did a great job over there, but he was such a prominent figure that if he said, "I didn't like this," it went all over the United States.

---

[11] El Toro is a Marine Corps air station in San Diego.

The trouble is, if you said, "Ted, what about this slider?" Thirty minutes later, he was done. One of the great things . . . he came out here to one of our dinners, and Gwynn at one time had four batting titles and missed the last one. And they're chatting and chatting and chatting. And Gwynn—what he got from Williams in that one meeting—led the league in hitting the next four years. You could look it up.[12] Late in his career as well, and Williams led the league in hitting when he was thirty-nine, I believe.[13]

He wasn't a great defensive player or a great runner or stuff like that, but his bat and knowledge of the game was unsurpassed. The more I think about it—what he did and how he did it—just incredible. We used to stack all the time against him, and we had great pitching, too. The only game where I recall where we really got nailed by Ted was when he hit the two home runs off Raschi, off hanging curveballs or something.

I'll never forget; we were in spring training in '52, and we both had our [military] call-up coming up, and they gave us a physical in Jacksonville in some hotel. So when it's over, we go into the elevator down to the bottom. The way it worked was that the garage let out onto two different streets. It went right into a through street and into the next one and then right into another one. And some little midget of a writer came up about the time we got there, and looked up [laughs] at Ted from the street, and then he [Williams] said, "You little son of

---

[12] Gwynn won three straight batting titles from 1987–89, then went four years without winning one, although he finished second in the National League in 1993. From 1994–97, Gwynn, from the ages of thirty-four to thirty-seven, won four straight batting titles with averages of .394, .368, .353, and .372. He had hit higher than .353 just twice in his first twelve seasons.

[13] Williams won his final batting title in 1958 at the age of thirty-nine, with a .328 average.

a bitch, get the hell away," and started running in the other direction [laughs]. He tried to track him.

Apparently the writers were really maliciously difficult on him . . . and because he was the one to write about. He was *the* guy. Like DiMaggio in New York, he was *the* guy. They weren't bad on Joe, but I think they burned him [Williams] pretty bad in Boston, and I think he resented it deeply over the years.

Billy DeMars

Shortstop / Third base / Second base

1948: .... Philadelphia Athletics
1950–51: .... St. Louis Browns
Career Statistics: .... 80 games, 0 home runs,
.237 batting average

IN THE MAJOR leagues we used the Williams shift. It was the best way to play him, but he still managed to get his base hits.

We all knew that he was the best hitter in the game. During batting practice before the game, we would all stop and watch him hit.

I played with him in 1945 at Jacksonville Naval Air Station, where we were 45–6. He didn't have much to do with the minor league players. We had Charles Gehringer and Bob Kennedy, and he spent most of his time with them.

Gail Harris

First base

1955–57: .... New York Giants
1958–60: .... Detroit Tigers
Career Statistics: .... 437 games, 51 home runs, .240 batting average

PLAYED IN BOTH leagues, and Williams was the greatest pull-hitter of all-time. His ground balls and line drives would eat you up. I played on the outfield grass with nobody on base. We used the shift to no avail, as he was able to just hit balls through the shift.

On July 20, 1958, we played the Red Sox in Fenway. It was Vermont Day, and they were giving maple candy for base hits, extra-base hits, home runs, etc. [Jim] Bunning had retired 26 batters in a row. The last hitter was Williams for his no-hitter. I walked over to the mound, and Bunning said to me, "I could pitch around Williams and pitch to Jackie Jensen, who has never hit me. I'm going to give that big sucker all I have left. If he hits it, he hits it." Williams fouled off two fastballs. With the count 2–2, he hit a monstrous fly ball that [Al] Kaline caught for the final out. I thanked the Lord for keeping the ball away from me.[14]

He was a perfectionist. A great baseball player, a marine pilot, and an expert fly fisherman. His vision was unbelievable. Only two players said they were able to know the type of pitch that was coming to the plate—Williams and [Stan] Musial.

The greatest scene I ever saw was the reaction of the major league players when Williams came out in the golf cart at the All-Star Game.[15]

---

[14] Bunning pitched a no-hitter against the Red Sox on July 20, 1958, walking two and striking out 12. Williams went 0–4 and flied out to right field to end the game. Frank Malzone batted behind Williams, with Jensen after Malzone. In his career, Williams hit .377 with a .500 on-base percentage and .852 slugging percentage off Bunning. Malzone was .250/.293/.326 vs. Bunning, and Jensen was .165/.242/.259.
[15] At the 1999 All-Star Game in Fenway Park.

Grady Hatton

Third base / Second base

1946–54:	Cincinnati Reds
1954:	Chicago White Sox
1954–56:	Boston Red Sox
1956:	St. Louis Cardinals
1956:	Baltimore Orioles
1960:	Chicago Cubs
Career Statistics:	1,312 games, 91 home runs, .254 batting average
National League All-Star:	1952

I NEVER PLAYED AGAINST Ted and only played two years with him. Players who did play against him played short right field. Ted had no speed and infielders could play deep.

When I played with him, he liked to talk hitting with all.

Ted was a fine man and was fun on the club. He was good to young kids and signed autographs.

Randy Jackson

Third base

1950–55: .... Chicago Cubs
1956–57: ....Brooklyn Dodgers
1958: ....Los Angeles Dodgers
1958-59: .... Cleveland Indians
1959: .... Chicago Cubs
Career Statistics: .... 955 games, 103 home runs,
.261 batting average
National League All-Star: 1954, 1955

IWAS JUST TRADED to Cleveland from the Dodgers, and my first time up in Cleveland, I hit a triple and pulled a muscle between second and third, so I'm out again.[16]

[After I] recovered, we came into Fenway to play a weekend series. Friday night, the manager let me pinch-hit, and I hit a ball over the wall in left field. So he said, "Okay, you're playing tomorrow."[17]

So I went out there and Williams came up in the first inning. They, of course had the shift; they moved over, and I moved over from third to shortstop. And I was just standing there. This was maybe about my fourth week in the major leagues [that season], and I had only played one game because of my injuries. And I was standing there saying, you know, god almighty, this is the first time I've seen Fenway Park—I had spent all of my career in the National League—and I was just standing there saying, god almighty, here's Ted Williams [coming] up. I came out and watched batting practice just to see him hit and there he is,

---

[16] Jackson was purchased by Cleveland from the Dodgers on August 4, 1958. In his first game with the Indians, game one of an August 10 doubleheader, he tripled to lead off the bottom of the sixth, and then was replaced by a pinch runner.

[17] Jackson first returned on August 17 and struck out as a pinch hitter. On August 20, he entered in the ninth inning at third base and did not bat. On August 21 at Fenway, he hit a pinch-hit home run.

he's up at the plate and he doesn't ever hit it this way, so I can just stand here and watch him . . . and he hit a one-hopper off my shins and I didn't even have a chance to move. You talk about a big knot on your leg the next day. My leg stopped it. I can't remember if they gave him a hit or not—I'm sure they gave him a hit.[18] I don't know how long the American League insignia was on my leg, but it was there for a while.

Randy Jackson took home a "souvenir" the only time he played against Ted Williams.

But that was my first and only experience playing against Ted Williams and the only time I've ever seen him play, except on TV or something.

There wasn't much reason to talk about him in the National League because you never saw him. Pitchers weren't going to get together and say how we going to pitch Ted Williams. They're in the National League; they're not going to be pitching against him.

He just was an idol— not an idol—but had the utmost respect. Because you knew what kind of person he was

---

[18] Williams was credited with a single.

and what kind of record he had. Even though he may be in another league, you had respect for him.

I never met him. I was never around him other than that one three-game series. But you just read about him and listen to commentators. I don't think I ever asked any ballplayer who came over from the American League, "What you think of Ted Williams?" The only thing I knew is that he and Mickey Mantle were the highest-paid players in the league one year, and they made $100,000, and $100,000 was like way out of there.

You hear about people, about other ballplayers, and you've never seen them, and they're the best that there is, so why not go out there and sit in the dugout and watch Ted Williams hit batting practice? I mean, that was a thrill to me, just to see that. I don't remember if there were other guys—I didn't really care, I just wanted to do it for myself because I knew I probably wouldn't get to do it again. I don't think any ballplayers lost any sleep out of going out and coming out to watch me hit.

I had a very interesting experience [with Ted Williams] and got a sore leg out of it.

Bob Johnson

Second base / third base / shortstop

1960:..Kansas City Athletics
1961–62:..Washington Senators
1963–67:..Baltimore Orioles
1967:..New York Mets
1968:..Cincinnati Reds
1969:..St. Louis Cardinals
1969–70:..Oakland Athletics
Career Statistics:...........................874 games, 44 home runs,
.272 batting average

HIS LAST YEAR was 1960, which was my first year. The story that you hear the most is his last time up in Boston and he hits the home run and goes right to the clubhouse, never tipped his hat, decided this is it, see you guys later. And I think if I'm not mistaken, that's what happened on the last play of his career.

I got to know him a little bit. He had a good friend who was in charge of the scoreboard at Metropolitan Stadium. That fellow's name was Charlie Wilcox. Charlie was a little older, but somehow he and Ted became good friends. Charlie worked the scoreboard at the ballpark out in Bloomington. And Charlie, he'd come in and sit in the dugout and they'd talk. I think Charlie was probably one of Ted's favorite people in the major leagues. Ted wasn't going to overwhelm you with his desire to talk, but he really just made friends with Charlie. And I knew him [Charlie] quite well. Our daughter, he always took a liking to our daughter, and we used to go out for dinner a lot of the times and the conversation always seemed to come back to Ted Williams. And what a neat guy he was.

I recall one incident where Williams and Charlie decided to—he had to catch a train, I think, to go somewhere, Williams did. They had played what might have been an afternoon game. So they went to a movie and Williams had to leave to catch a train to go to Chicago, and he said, "Charlie what I want you do to is, this is a pretty good movie and it will take us a while to get down there, so as soon as this movie is over call me at the hotel and let me know how it comes out."

He had his own individuals that he talked to more than somebody else. I'm not sure where they fit in with the sportswriters, some he preferred more than others. But this Charlie Wilcox that I mentioned, he became like a brother to Charlie.

And to go back when he was playing with the Minneapolis Millers way back, and how he broke the water cooler over a called strike that wasn't a strike, as far as he was concerned. He took out his frustration on the water cooler when he went back to the dugout.

But Williams, his reputation always seemed to precede him, but he had the great eye. Joe Mauer has that kind of an eye, where if he doesn't swing at it, the umpire doesn't call it a strike. But Williams, he had that bat in his hand he was just like squeezing it and moving it, and somehow whether you're an infielder or an outfielder you need to have some kind of a way of being able to relax, and that's how Ted used to do it.

I used to go out and watch him take batting practice before the game started. I picked up his bat one time and looked, I was trying to determine where he hit the ball and it was right on the sweet spot every time. Everything else was smooth, there wasn't any detail or anything. Where he hit the ball on the sweet spot, right below the lettering, he hit it there every time. You pick my bat up and it's all over the bat! His was strictly the sweet spot and mine was whatever spot I swung at.

You know he'd be right at the top where great hitters are concerned. I think he had to learn how to play the outfield but that gave him more time to . . . he knew he'd always be able to hit, so that gave him more time to put in to be a better outfielder, too. He learned how to play left field pretty well, too, there in Boston with the Green Monster. But he was quite a guy . . . heh, heh . . . the Thumper.

What I enjoyed doing was going out and watching him hit and take batting practice. He provided a lot of thrill to watch him go out there and look for a pitch. It seemed like he never swung unless it was to his liking—not to the pitcher's liking. You get somebody like that . . . and I don't know how many walks he had, but to measure a good hitter and a guy with a great eye, he usually has more walks than strikeouts. And that would have been Ted.[19] And as probably as many or more walks that they put him on purposely.

It was a thrill to just be sitting out on the bench and hear him talking and see him play. A lot of guys didn't get a chance to see him play because his career was over in 1960.

There's some that can talk a good game but they maybe don't play it. He played it, talked it, and did everything necessary to be a great player but also somebody where you'd want to pick up the paper and see how'd he do last night.

He was a little kind of red-ass, but that was okay. I think that in his case that's just the way he was and he got by with it. But boy, when it came time to go up there and hit that ball, he just attacked it. When you have a great eye, you can wait for your pitch and you can get to a point where you'll take two pitches if you're looking for a certain pitch and aren't going to get it until the third pitch, he's probably going to get it and still hit it hard.

I had a friend that said one time, I think he kind of put it wisely, he said how'd you like to go to the ballpark every day and hit the ball three out of four times right on the sweet spot. He was referring to Williams.

It would have been nice to know him a little more, but you need those kind of guys to show you how to *play* the game. They know how to play the game, they know what it takes to be a winner and that was Williams.

---

[19] For his career, Williams never struck out more than he walked, and his season-high was 64 Ks, which was in 1939, his first year in pro ball.

Charlie Kress

First base

1947, 1949: .... Cincinnati Reds
1949–50: .... Chicago White Sox
1954: .... Detroit Tigers
1954: .... Brooklyn Dodgers
Career Statistics: .... 175 games, 1 home run,
.249 batting average

HE HIT BULLETS. He was the greatest hitter that I ever saw. He hit line drives, I mean, you had to have your glove up. At first base, I got out as far back in right field as I could get and still get back to the bag. I would be back on the grass quite a bit.

Photo courtesy of Charlie Kress

Charlie Kress played against Ted Williams both in the American League and the military service.

When you had to hold a man on first base . . . to give you an illustration, we were playing up in Fenway Park, and Dom DiMaggio was on first base, and I was holding him on. When I held him on, I would just pivot around real quick and put the glove up in front of my face. I mean, I didn't run out, didn't take a step or anything. Anyway, he hit a bullet over my head, and Dom DiMaggio never moved. I turned and looked, and the ball was already bouncing in the right-field seats in Fenway Park. That's how quick it got out there. Oh, he was uncanny.

We used to pick up the bat when he took batting practice and there'd be one spot, one area, which had grass stains on it from the ball. Not on the handle, not down the barrel, not down the end of the bat, not on the underside—just one spot, like he painted it there. Oh, he was unbelievable, really.

I played against him in the service, too. I was lucky to play against him quite a few times. A real nice guy, too, I really enjoyed talking with him. When I played against him in the service, we had a pitcher by the name of Homer Spragins, who pitched for the Phillies, and could throw about 95–96 miles-an-hour. One day in the gym after we played a ball game, Williams and I we were having sandwiches and stuff, and he asked me, "Would you call that fellow over that pitched today?" So I called Spragins over, and I said, "Ted wants to talk to you." So we stood there and he [Williams] said, "Now, son, I don't want you to think I'm getting cocky or anything, but, when you hold your fastball, you hold it with the seams, don't you?" And Spragins said, "Yeah, why?" And Ted said, "Well, when you hold it with the seams, I can see the rotation of the ball. If you hold it across the seams, it makes it a little tougher for me to follow." Can you imagine that?

He's the one guy—and this has been documented—that [said] when the ball hits the bat, the bat actually bends a little and the ball flattens a little bit. And they said you can't actually see that. So they took slow-motion pictures and the bat *does* bend a little bit and the ball *does* flatten. So that will tell you what kind of eyesight he had.

[While we were in the military], he was over near Pensacola, and I was at Eglin Field in Florida. They had a catcher—we were playing Tyndall Field one day, another air force base nearby—and this catcher says, "Charlie you want to look at this." He had an 8 x 12 photograph—and he wouldn't sell it to me and told me he wasn't going to make any copies because it was the only one—and it showed Ted Williams in the batter's box, and his eye was focused right on the ball, like he's going to drill a hole in it. And it's in the picture. And he hadn't moved a muscle, and the catcher said I could field the ball. We had him!

And he hit that ball over a hangar in right field about 500 feet from home plate. That's how quick he exploded. He was just uncanny.

I talked to him about everything. Herb Score was a great left-handed pitcher. Gil McDougald put him out of baseball; hit him with a baseball right in the face. But Herb Score was a terrific left-hander, real hard to hit. When we played the Red Sox, he [Williams] came over to me and said, "Have you faced Herb Score yet?" And I said, no [laughs], they don't play me against guys that good. I play against the right-handers. And he said, "What do you think he throws in the clutch?" And I said, "*Well*, he's got a hell of a fastball and he probably can get that over a little better than his curveball." And I remember Ted saying, "Well, I'll see what I can do with him." I watched the box scores and the first time he faced him, he hit one up in the seats in left-center field.[20] He made a study of hitting. He just knew what it was all about.

We had a ceremony up in Fenway Park, and they had a Ted Williams Day, and we're all lined up at home plate. Our team was on one side, on the third-base side towards home plate lined up, and the Boston Red Sox were lined up on the right side. And the microphone with Ted and the emcee was right there at home plate. And they gave him—and right next to me, I was the second guy in line [was] Joe Tipton, [who] was our catcher.[21] He was right next to Ted, and I was next to Tipton, and they gave Ted all this fishing equipment: fly rods, reels, all kinds of lures and flies, I mean, a whole bunch of stuff. And Tipton leaned over to Ted and [whispered], "Ted, if you don't need this stuff, I can use it [laughs]." And Ted just grinned at him.

---

[20] Williams first faced Score on June 7, 1955, and doubled his first time up against him. The second time Williams faced Score was June 19, 1955, and he homered off him in the fifth inning.

[21] Kress and Tipton were teammates with the White Sox in 1949.

So we're in the clubhouse after the game, and here comes the clubhouse fellow and he gave all that stuff to Tipton. The whole works. I don't know the value of that stuff, but it had to be a lot of money. And I thought, "Charlie, why in the hell didn't you say something?" But I wasn't a fly fisherman. I love to fish, and that's how Ted and I got to talk a little more because of fishing. I could talk his language, although not the kind of fishing he did all the time.

I've got pictures with him at a reunion we had down in Florida, and I remember we were all standing around waiting, and someone [whispered], "Here comes Ted, here comes Ted." And sure I saw all these guys came around. And what amazed me, the players he played with—like Walt Dropo and Mel Parnell—they all stood in line to shake hands with Ted. He just sat there on the sofa. Fortunately, I got to sit next to him and have my picture taken with him. But, yeah, I thought, here's a guy they played with all year and they're still standing in line to shake hands with him. That's respect.

He's the only player that I saw—and I played against [Joe] DiMaggio and Stan Musial and guys like that—and he's the only guy that stopped everything on the ball field when he stepped into the batting cage. Guys running in the outfield, guys playing pepper in back of the cage, guys just playing catch, talking around—when he walked in there, it was just like a curtain dropped down that field. Everything stopped. And he hit until he had enough. But he was fantastic. The ability that man had. If he hadn't put in those four years in the marines, there'd be records out there that no one would catch. Normally you'd go up there and bunt one and hit five, but he just walked in there and he hit until he was ready.

Yeah, he was a quite a hitter . . . and a good outfielder, too. I remember I hit a couple of balls off that Green Monster in Fenway Park in left field, and he held me to a single. Most of the time you can get a double out of it, but not with him. He played that wall like he knew where it was going to bounce.

I think they stole the player of the year award away from him when DiMaggio hit in those consecutive games and Williams hit .406.

I mean, who in the hell's going to hit .406? Of course, like they say, who in the hell is going to hit in 56 consecutive games? And you know the story was—and Joe Cronin was the manager—they were playing in Philadelphia, playing the Athletics in a doubleheader. And after the first game in the clubhouse, Cronin said to Ted, you're hitting .39999 or something. He said, they'll give you .400 on that, I think I'll sit you out the second game. And Ted said, no, if I hit .400, I'm going to hit .400. And he played that second game and I think went 4–6 or something like that to get him up to .406. Isn't that something? Now that's guts.

He said he did [remember me]. I'm not sure though, because I was just a humpty-dumpty. I wasn't a big-name player. But, well, he must have remembered me, because he used to go duck hunting and stuff in a little game reserve right outside St. Joe, Missouri. He used to go there all the time, and when I heard about it, I wrote him a letter and said he'd be welcome to stay with me and I'd supply my car if he wanted to go up there and do hunting and stuff. And he wrote me back! And he said, I'll take you up on that. He never did, but I still have the letter—my son has the letter—but I guess he did remember something then.

He knew baseball, he knew how to hit, no question about it. I think he was the best ever, in my book. I told him that at that reunion. I told him, "Ted, you're going to hear this a lot, but I'm going to tell you because I played against you—I think you're the greatest hitter I ever saw." And he just beamed; of course, that's what he wanted to hear. And he was.

He wanted to take me for a ride one day. He used to fly his plane over to our field when we had a ball game. And he said, "Charlie, I'll take you up for a ride someday." And some of the other guys came over and said, don't do it, he's nuts. And I said, what do you mean he's nuts? And they said, well, you know, he comes over here and you know all those bayous we have all around the field here in Florida? He said there's one bridge under there, and someone said, "Ted, you think you can fly under that?" And he said, oh hell yes. And it would be like maybe only 6, 8 inches, maybe a foot on either side of the wingtips. And he flew under it. And I said, "Ohhh, no way! No thanks." I didn't put it that way to him. I said maybe sometime, Ted. But there's a million stories about him.

They're [the Red Sox] coming up, and they played in Birmingham. Coming north, you know, at the end of spring training [on their way up to Boston]. And he walked out on the field, and he said their pitching mound was off-center to second base, the rubber. The groundskeeper was there and he said, "Well, Ted, I'm the groundskeeper here, and I hate to tell you, but you're wrong." And Ted says, "Ehhh, it's off-center; it's not lined up properly with second base and home plate." And they remeasured it and sure enough, he was right. The grounds-keeper couldn't believe it.

There's so many stories. This guy was a phenom. One-in-a-million. And all the guys liked him.

The fans up in left field used to gamble on whether he'd swing at the next pitch, whether he'd hit it, and where he'd hit it. And if he didn't hit it or he took the pitch or took a strike, they'd get mad and boo him. They were all gamblers and they'd give him the old finger. But everyone else liked him, and he did a lot of good, too. That Jimmy Fund he founded. You didn't hear much about it, but he did a lot of good.

Don Leppert

Second base

1955: .... **Baltimore Orioles**
Career Statistics: .... **40 games, 0 home runs,**
.114 batting average

WELL, PLAYING SECOND base, of course, the first baseman played right on the right-field grass, and I played about ten steps to his right, the shortstop played normal second base, the third baseman played right over the second-base bag . . . and he never tried to hit to left field. I think if I'm not mistaken in that year, 1955, he still hit over .400.[22] You didn't have to fear him where we played him because if he hit the ball on the ground, he missed it. He just didn't hit it . . . when he hit line drives, he hit line drives and they were by you. But a ground ball for him—and he wasn't the fastest guy on the field—so you didn't have any trouble throwing him out even playing as far deep as we did.

If he hit it right to you—without a line drive being too high or a ground ball—you could throw him out. It just wasn't like him to hit a soft . . . he could hit a hard ground ball, but it wasn't so bad because we were playing so far back.

Photo courtesy of Don Leppert

Don Leppert only played 40 games in the major leagues, but he considered it an honor to play against Ted Williams.

---

[22] Williams hit .356 in 1955.

As far as the toughest—who was the most-feared hitter we had to face—I'm going to say Mickey Mantle was, because you had to play him on the very front of the infield grass, [as] he was so fast. If he hit a ground ball, you better get it as quick as you can and get it to first base, because he could beat you. I think they timed him once at 3.2 seconds going down to first base batting left-handed. You had to play him way up there on the infield grass, almost to the front of the infield grass.

I think Williams was a better hitter. Gosh, he hit more line drives . . . more home runs on a line, whereas Mantle just hit those towering home runs. Like I said, you had to play Mantle up close, and when he batted left-handed, it was almost frightening to play him up close. He hit a ball over my head, I'm going tell you what, I was playing him up close and he hit a low ball left-handed, and I jumped up and I just barely missed it going over my glove and it went out of the ballpark. When I came down, I said a little silent prayer, thanking the Lord that I didn't get my glove on it.

As far as Williams and balls and strikes, if he didn't swing at it, it wasn't a strike. He probably had the greatest feel of the strike zone of anybody that I've ever seen. That was his batting eye, really. If he didn't swing at it, it was probably a ball. He was that good.

You always watched when they were taking batting practice. Everything he hit was right on the nose. If he hit a ground ball, you knew he didn't get it good. If he hit a *hard* line drive—it might have been low—but it was by you before you had a chance to get it.

When he got on first base, he'd hardly talk to you. He wasn't that friendly a guy. He was jittery; he had all sort of little tics. And when he got on first base, I guess he was just so focused, he was thinking more about the ball game and he didn't really converse with you. But I didn't hold that against him. Hell, I'm just a rookie and this guy's a hall of famer.

[When we spoke], he didn't carry on a long conversation. You could ask him questions and he'd answer them in very short sentences. Like I said, he was always kind of jittery. But you didn't take anything personal, because that's just the way he was. But no matter what, he was a good guy. Nobody ever said anything bad against him. I mean, you had to admire him. He served two terms in the Air Force, and they said, he could identify planes—if they showed him foreign planes: Japanese planes, German planes, or whatever—that he could identify them probably five times quicker than anyone else could. His eyes were that quick.

As far as Ted Williams goes, he's got my vote. My time was short in the big leagues, but just to be on the field with that guy was an honor I'll never forget.

Al Naples

Shortstop

1949: ....St. Louis Browns
Career Statistics: ....2 games, 0 home runs,
.143 batting average

THE ONE THING that stands out in my mind regarding Ted Williams was that he always had batting practice first. It seemed like the rest of the team just followed him. I remember the outfield (never left field) and chasing his hit balls along with a bat boy and whoever was around. The Sox would then come on the field and have their batting practice. He would then head down the dugout alleyway, and it seemed no one could enter the clubhouse. I'm not sure about sportswriters.

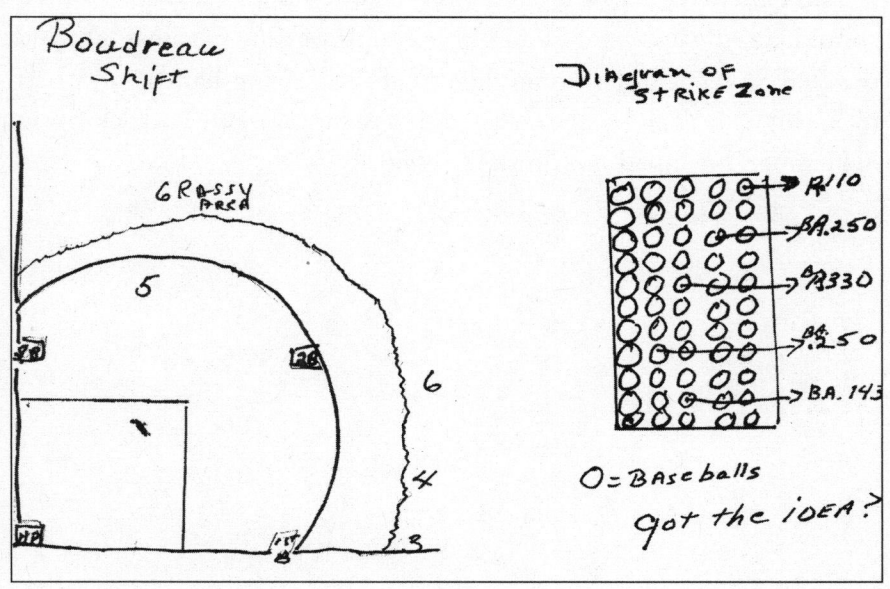

Al Naples drew his version of the Williams shift, as well as Williams' strike zone chart.

The Browns used the Boudreau shift. As you know, the first baseman played the right-field line and on the grass. The second baseman played on the grass and about 25 feet from the line of the first baseman. The shortstop was as deep as the second baseman and about 25 feet or so from second base. In other words, there were three men on the right-field side of the infield. The third baseman had the left side of the infield to himself. I imagine he could have lifted his batting average thirty points or so if he took advantage of this opportunity; I know I would have.

I know that another thing he developed was the strike zone chart. It was covered with circles representing baseballs. Each circle had batting averages in it for your chances of getting a base hit in that part of the strike zone. I thought it was very clever; show you how he approached hitting from a scientific point of view. He was an extremely disciplined hitter!

I do remember throwing him out on a one-hopper at first . . . it felt good! I had the opportunity to play a couple of games against him and the Red Sox.[23] I broke my middle finger [throwing hands], was sent to Springfield [Triple-I League], and was supposed to go back up in September, but I had not finished college.[24]

---

[23] Naples played in two major league games, and both were against the Red Sox, June 25–26, 1949.

[24] Naples never played professional baseball again.

Herb Plews

Second base / Third base

1956–59: ....**Washington Senators**
1959: ....**Boston Red Sox**
Career Statistics: .... **346 games, 4 home runs,
.262 batting average**

IWAS ALWAYS GLAD to watch him [Ted Williams] perform. Never saw him swing at a pitch and miss it completely. His hits were mainly line drives with plenty of topspin. They would sail over the infield and then sink in front of an outfielder.

At the close of the '56 season, he and Pete Runnels were almost at a dead heat for the batting championship.[25] There were three games remaining to be played in DC, and [Manager Chuck] Dressen[26] told our pitchers to pitch to Williams and not walk him. Anyway, Williams put on the greatest hitting clinic you could ever imagine. Line drives flying everywhere. Runnels was also hitting well, but all his hits were right at someone. As a result, Williams beat out Runnels for the AL batting championship by a few points.[27]

I never saw any one player hit the ball with so much authority like Williams. It's something I'll never forget. This proved to all of us why he was the greatest hitter; he really was.

---

[25] Plews is actually speaking of the 1958 season.

[26] Dressen was the manager for Washington in 1956, but Cookie Lavagetto was the manager in 1958, when Williams and Runnels entered DC, battling for the batting crown.

[27] Boston closed the season with a four-game series in Washington. Williams entered the series hitting .320, Runnels .324. Runnels played in all four games and went 5–19 to finish at .322. Williams played in three of those games, sitting out the second game of a doubleheader in the series opener, and went 7–14—with a home run in each game—to finish at .328 and lead the league, with Runnels finishing second. It was Williams' sixth and final batting title.

When in the field, we would put on some modified shift, but he seldom hit grounders to any of the infielders. Third baseman between third and second, shortstop just left of second, and second baseman in shallow right field. He could find the holes no matter what.

I wasn't with Boston long enough to ever converse with him one-on-one.[28] However, if you had a question, he would be glad to answer it. He did pretty much everything by himself. Just being around him for a short time was very special for me.

---

[28] Plews was traded to Boston on June 11, 1959, and played his final major league game on July 26, 1959.

J. W. Porter

Catcher / Outfield / First base / Third base

1952: ....St. Louis Browns
1955–57: ....Detroit Tigers
1958: ....Cleveland Indians
1959: ....Washington Senators
1959: .... St. Louis Cardinals
Career Statistics: .... 229 games, 8 home runs,
.228 batting average

WILLIAMS WAS SUCH a great hitter and so revered that he was almost passed over in meetings when you were going over Boston hitters. "Try to keep Dom DiMaggio and Johnny Pesky off the bases, try to keep Ted in the ballpark. We will have seven guys on the right side of the diamond, and Jackie Jensen hits into a lot of double plays." You never heard about what type of pitch to throw him or what location to try to throw the pitch; it was like it wouldn't matter. Throw and duck seemed to be our strategy.

Two games [against Ted] stand out in my mind. They [the Red Sox] came into Detroit, which was always Ted's favorite park to hit in. I would think he'd have averaged well over .400 against Detroit; he loved to hit in Briggs [Tiger] Stadium.

Future Hall-of-Famer Jim Bunning is pitching for us, and Ted hits singleton homers, but we are holding on to a 3–2 lead. Ted comes to bat with one out and nobody on. Our manager, Jack Tighe, yells out to walk him. We can't believe it, but we purposely put him on. Jackie Jensen then grounds into a double play.

The top of the ninth rolls around—same exact situation—and Tighe yells out for us to walk him again. Ted went nuts, threw his bat away, and cursed his way to first base. Jensen grounded into another double play, and we win, 3–2.[29]

The other game that stands out is one where I was playing first base and was holding a runner on. He hit a laser headed right for my nose. By the grace of God, I managed to get my glove up and slightly deflect the ball. I then heard some noises I don't ever want to hear again. The ball had hit the umpire right in the pit of his stomach and came to rest within a foot of the first-base bag. I can hear the umpire in front of me wanting to die and Williams behind me wanting to kill.

Great hitters like Williams and [Stan] Musial had such great eyes and I never saw either of them argue on a pitch. They would tell an umpire with a glance. Knowing this, I think they [the umpires] simply bore down more when those kinds of hitters came to bat. They didn't mind missing a pitch on me, but certainly didn't want to miss one on the great ones.

Williams and [Mickey] Mantle were the most feared hitters I ever played against. When they came to bat—even in batting practice—all other activities ceased. You wanted to see Ted's perfect swings and the line drives it produced and how many balls Mickey put in the seats and how far they went. In 1956, Mickey's Triple Crown year, he turned Briggs Stadium into a little league park.

I finished a season in Atlanta, and Ted was instrumental in getting me and many other players winter employment at Sears. I had lunch with

---

[29] I cannot locate the game Porter is referring to. However, Williams did hit two home runs off Bunning on July 12, 1957, in Detroit in a 5–3, Tigers win. Porter did not play in that game, however, and one of Williams' homers was a two-run shot. Also, Bunning walked Williams intentionally once, but it was with two out in the fifth, and Mickey Vernon followed with a pop out.

him a few times. He and I, Bobby Richardson and others, were asked to help open an American Legion national tournament in Memphis one September. He, along with Satchel Paige, was the most intriguing person I ever met.

Bobby Richardson

Second base

1955–66: ....New York Yankees
Career Statistics: .... 1,412 games, 34 home runs,
.266 batting average
American League All-Star: 1957, 1959, 1962–1966

I WAS A FRIEND [of Williams'] because of [our love of] the outdoors. He would slide into second [base] and say, "How are your bird dogs? Still shooting the Browning 28 gauge over and under?"

Ted Williams and Red Sox owner Tom Yawkey.

We spent an entire flight from California to New York after an All-Star Game talking about hunting and fishing and about Mr. Yawkey [the Red Sox owner], who had a big plantation in South Carolina. When he passed away, he gave it to the state of South Carolina.

Art "Dutch" Schult

First base / Outfield

1953:	**New York Yankees**
1956–57:	**Cincinnati Reds**
1957:	**Washington Senators**
1959–60:	**Chicago Cubs**
Career Statistics:	**164 games, 6 home runs, .264 batting average**

I CONSIDERED HIM [TED] a good friend of mine. The funny thing is, most people think that, because I was playing with the Yankees, we were rivals at that time. But I had just come back from overseas when I joined the Yankees, and they in turn were trying to cut my salary and send me where I could play. I had a wife and kid to support, and they called me a clubhouse lawyer because I used the G.I. Bill of Rights. I hung around until they got eleven games in front of the league and then I got part of the World Series [money, laughs], so they sold me to Cincinnati to get me out of the league because I had a real good spring training and their club was reasonably set at that time—they had won three straight World Series.

So when they sold me to Cincinnati, I went over there and played a little bit and they sold me to Washington. And it was at Washington I was playing a little first base and I had a couple of good games against Boston in Washington. I can recall that I got four hits against Boston, and every time I'd trot by Williams, he would call me a sonuvabitch [laughs]. And I got to talking to him.

[After that series], we went on a road trip to Chicago and played against Early Wynn. I think I got a double the first time up and I never got a hit against them the rest of the series. At the end of that road trip, I was having a tough time. We went back to Boston before to finish up the road trip.

I got out to the ballpark early in Boston to get some extra batting practice. I wanted to find out what the hell I was doing wrong; why I was having such a tough time. So I stuck my head out of the dugout and I hear this "Crack! Crack!" and it was Williams. He was hitting in the cage, also taking extra batting. So he looked over and saw me and said, "Hey, Dutch, come over here. You're 0–for one week, what the hell did you do?" I said, "Well, I faced that goddamn Early Wynn first." And he said, "Yeah, he can do that to you. Get in here and take a couple of swings." I said, "No, no, you finish up what you're out here working for. I got a guy who is going to pitch to me. He's in the dugout." He said, "No, no, get in here. I want to see what you're doing."

And when I stepped into the cage—before I even took the first swing, he says, "Woah! Stop!" He then went on to say, "Your hands are four-to-five inches lower then when you got those four hits against us. Move them up to where they were." I was shocked, "No kidding?" I took a couple of swings and got four hits that night,[30] and Ted called me a sonuvabitch again! He was that kind of guy. He didn't want to play against anybody that wasn't up to snuff, either. He enjoyed the competition.

But the tough part about Ted was when we had a man on first and third, and I was holding the man on first and he was the hitter [laughs], because I couldn't move! I had to play 90 feet from him.

I'd kid around with him because I really liked him. With the guys, he was always 100 percent, but he didn't particularly care for sportswriters or authorities, and he'd let them know it. But we both got [drafted]—I got drafted into the service in Korea, too, so we had some other things in common. But I really liked him.

I remember one point towards the end of the season in 1957—I think he ended up hitting .390 or something[31]—so he was spending

---

[30] Schult had four hits against the Red Sox twice in 1957: On August 9 in Boston, and on August 17 in Washington.

[31] Ted hit .388 in 1957.

part of the time on the bench. [Rather than just hanging out], he'd take a pretty close look at what everybody was doing. He was a student of anybody with a bat. If there was something that he didn't know, he'd find out.

When you picked up his bat, the distance between your forefinger and your thumb was the only part that had any black resin marks on it [laughs]. The rest of the bat was like new.

[When it came to the shift], the Senators used to play Pete Runnels on *just* to the right side of second base, and the second baseman, [Milt] Bolling, was almost where he could touch me [laughs]. So we did have a shift. And then the center fielder was over in right-center. If he got his pitch, it didn't matter where they were playing. We thought the best way to pitch him was low and behind [laughs].

If he and [Joe] DiMaggio had ever switched ballparks, they both would have broke every record there was. At one time they were talking about that trade. If DiMaggio had played with that short left-field porch, he would have left so many dents out there, it would have looked like a golf ball. And Ted in Yankee Stadium? With that short right-field fence? There's no question how many he would have hit. To me, he was the ultimate as far as left-hand hitters goes; he was the best I ever saw. He also had phenomenal eyesight. And his reactions—he was so quick with his hands. His depth perception must have just been amazing.

But right now, his daughter is frequenting the same restaurant that I go to down here all the time. The owner of the restaurant is a friend of mine and he's got my picture on the wall. She always says, jokingly, "Why do you have that picture up there of those damn Yankees . . . [laughs]." So it's a small world.

And he was living not too far from me in Ocala, where his museum was is only like 8–10 miles away. I did stop over there one time to see him, but he was not that well, I guess, or he was out fishing or doing something.

Jerry Snyder

Second base / Shortstop

1952–58: ....Washington Senators
Career Statistics: .... 266 games, 3 home runs,
.230 batting average

I'M SITTING HERE right next to a picture of Ted Williams, Mickey Mantle, and Joe DiMaggio. Williams was one of my favorite players. He knew I played against him and [I also] knew Mantle pretty well. I'm from Oklahoma, like Mantle. I also have fond memories of Joe DiMaggio; he was kind of my hero, too. He was the only one that greeted me when I broke in at nineteen years old with the Yankees in spring training. The other guys kind of ignored me, but he came out and introduced himself. So I always thought of that when I think of Joe. He quit the year I was with the Yankees after that.

I played several games against Williams, mainly second base. Strangely enough, my record against Boston was the best I ever had against any other team. They never did have much pitching when I played against them. They had a good offensive club, but not much pitching. I had one of my best nights against them. I had 4 hits, 6 RBI—well, I never drove in any runs [laughs]. I even had an inside-the-park home run in that game.[32] That was by far my best game—very unusual for me.

But I did play second base and I did play, oh, I'd say 3 or 4 feet back of the infield grass . . . and Boston had a deep grass. Some of the infields were cut a little shallower than the grass angle. And he never hit me many balls. He hit the ball in the air *a lot.*

I do remember one shot he hit at Mickey Vernon. He hit it so hard—have you ever seen one that it takes off like a bullet, and it bends in

---

[32] On May 12, 1952, Snyder went 3–5, with 3 runs, 5 RBI, 1 double, 1 triple, and 1 home run, in a 12–9 win over the Red Sox in Washington.

the middle? You kind of top it, and it sinks suddenly. Mickey kind of half-jumped [laughs] and ended up catching it around his waist. It was interesting, because he was a hell of a first baseman. He did catch it, but it was one of those hard balls that . . . he just hit it with a lot of topspin on the ball. He hit a lot of balls in the air and I don't remember him hitting many my way.

But there's one play in particular that I do remember. The bases were loaded—it was towards the end of his career. I'm going from memory here, but I think it was one of his last few games. Bases were loaded and he hits this *tremendous* pop-up. I had time to think about it, you know? I probably didn't drop a pop-up but one time in my career, but I got to thinking. I thought, "God, if I drop this ball [laughs]." I did catch it, but it was funny because I still remember that play all this time. He could hit some pop-ups that were out of this world in terms of height. That's one play I do remember. It would have been horrible [if I dropped it].

[When we played the shift], the shortstop usually played, as I remember, back in second base, like an ordinary real pull-hitter. Of course, I played over toward the line, but I played real deep. It wasn't like a dead pull-hitter, a guy that will never hit to left field much. Third base would shift way over, but not tremendously. If he wanted to bunt, they'd give it to him. He could have had some [hits] easily, if he could, you know, eliminate the pitcher. Bunt it hard enough. But I never saw him try it. I did see . . . he used to, he'd run up on the ball. Did you know that? Okay, he actually would run up on a ball to try to hit it to left field. Very occasionally, but he would do it. He'd intentionally try to hit it to left field. I never saw him get a hit with that run upfield, but he would kind of fake it to try and get 'em, I guess, to keep them from doing that shift.

He'd never bunt. Never heard of him trying to bunt. He may have against somebody, but I never heard of him doing that. Mickey Mantle would bunt. He would try to pull a bunt, which is the hardest thing in the world to do and beat out. Because everybody's playing deep—now this is Mantle; Ted Williams would never do that. [Williams] would take a couple of steps and just kind of obviously try to hit it over there. I used to kind of do it too. I was a bunter. I got parts of about six years in the majors, but I was on the bench half of the time, so I wasn't a great player. But I was there long enough to get a pension and things like that.

He'd beat you a lot of times with his bat, but he'd really hurt you in the field. He wasn't a good fielder. Of course, he had that short left-field fence—he played left field—so he didn't have to do too much defense. But he and [Jackie] Jensen, when I hit that inside-the-park home run, they were playing me real short, especially Jensen. So I hit it kind of to dead center field, and that's about 450 feet in center field in Washington. Ted just loped after the ball and Jensen—I always hit to right field—they both just kind of loped after the ball. So I noticed that. I thought, "God, they're actually loafing." And they could do that, especially Ted. Anyway, I thought hell, I might get an inside-the-park home run—and I did. One of the few I've actually seen in the big leagues. You don't get those too often.

What a hitter. We had a wild left-hander, Mickey McDermott, who also played with Boston.[33] I thought to myself, this is going to be fun to watch, because Mickey was so damn wild. And he had Ted jumping around. It didn't bother him, though. He'd just take his walk. But McDermott, he got a couple of hits off of him when he got one in there. It didn't bother him one bit.[34]

He wasn't bothered by left-handers like a lot of left-handed hitters are. It's true. A lot of left-handed hitters have trouble against left-handed pitchers. I think [Williams was the best hitter I ever saw] because [he] had such a good eye. He hardly ever swung at bad balls. Another thing

---

[33] McDermott played for the Red Sox from 1948–53, and was a teammate of Snyder's on the Senators from 1954–55.

[34] Williams was just 2–14 against McDemott, with 3 walks and a hit by pitch. Both of his hits were singles.

about Williams was that if he took a strike, it was a ball to an umpire. I guess you've heard that before. Oh yeah, it was bad. Of any player I've ever seen, it was the worst, [more so than with] DiMaggio or anybody else. And he didn't get rattled by left-handers like a lot of them do nowadays. Those big sluggers. And he was a skinny guy. He was tall, but he wasn't strong looking. He had those terrific wrists and had a pretty big swing to go with such a good eye. A lot of those players that have good eyes, they don't have a big swing. But he had a big, loose swing.

He'd have 30 [home runs a season]. I don't know if he ever had 40, but 30 is good. Without the steroid[s]. I'm wondering if some of them don't—like [Albert] Pujols. He hits the ball so hard. Used to [wonder if he took steroids] when I watched [Barry] Bonds. Like, God, is it possible to hit the ball that far? And sure enough. . .

He'd talk to you about your swing. I didn't know him well, but a guy who was like a star on the club, like Vernon or [Pete] Runnels, I guess. We didn't have many stars. Anyway, he'd talk to them or even linger while we were batting at times. He was a good guy; guys liked him, but fans would boo him. In fact, I think we were there at his final three games.[35] He was being honored for something, and he finished it up off-camera, saying, "Well, you New England sonuvabitches." They were on him so much. Somebody told me he said that. They'd boo him, they'd get on him. One time—I think I read this—he was running up on that ball and hitting it in the stands in left field. I read it somewhere, but it wasn't with us.

---

[35] Snyder's last season in the majors was 1958; Williams' last season was 1960.

Chuck Stevens

First base

1941, 1946, 1948: ....St. Louis Browns
Career Statistics: .... 211 games, 3 home runs,
.251 batting average

I WILL OPEN IT up by saying that I always called him, "The Thump." That goes back to high school days.

Even as a high school outfielder—he played at Hoover High in San Diego—we played in a couple of tournaments against each other, and every time he struck a ball, it sounded like you were hitting a bass drum. You knew the ball was solidly struck; that he got it right on the meat part of the bat. He did that the rest of his life; so we go back a long ways.

I'll tell you an amusing story. When we were in high school . . . there was a club at one time called the 20-30 club, and that meant between the ages of twenty and thirty, you joined this club—I don't know if you are familiar with it, or if it was a West Coast movement; I really don't know or don't remember—they taught you how to do public speaking and that kind of thing. It was kind of a constructive thing for guys that age. They [the 20-30 club of Southern California] sponsored a baseball tournament in Pomona, California, during the Easter break. Pomona High School had a massive football field and they had two diamonds at each end and had ball games going on at the same time. It was so large that the outfielders were not in conflict of any kind.

We're playing a Pasadena ballclub, their second baseman or shortstop, I don't remember what he played, was a guy named Jackie Robinson. During the ball game, I remember we were in the infield. We had the best ballclub and won the tournament, and we *knew it* going in. The umpire began screaming, "time, time, time," everybody looked around, and a ball came through our infield on the ground. We looked down at the other end of the field, and Thump's galloping around the bases. He touched one off; must have hit it 400 feet, and it rolled another 200. So that's when it dawned on us that this guy had awesome power. Not just power, but awesome power.

When we were in high school, we played against Jackie Robinson, Bob Lemon, Jack Graham, [Bobby] Doerr . . . you know, there were just all kinds of guys out here that were superior ballplayers. On our ballclub in high school, Vern Stephens was the backup second baseman. I was the first baseman, and Vern played a little second. Bob Sturgeon with the Cubs played third, Bob Garbo—I think he got a shot with Brooklyn—and the best ballplayer of all was a guy named Dick Lang, who was a center fielder and he was wounded during the war, which halted his career, but he was a great ballplayer.

Anyway, getting back to Williams. Yes, we played deep . . . as deep as you could get. I used to tell him it wasn't deep enough because I was married then. He thought that was funny. I didn't, because when he hit screamers at you, they were hit hard.

[I remember] we were playing in Boston one afternoon, and he hit a screamer down the right-field line. I dove, got my glove on the ball, and it took the glove off of my hand. I picked the ball out of the glove, threw him out at first base, and he came galloping by and said to me, "Thanks a lot, asshole."

Bob Lemon and I were like brothers, as we grew up together. Lem made his first appearance as a relief pitcher against the Browns. I think the only base hit I got off him was a double to right-center. As I slide in [to second]—[Lou] Boudreau was covering—I beat the throw. But there are three of us there and I look up and Lem is bent over me, and says, "Thanks a lot, asshole." So I began to realize I must have been [an asshole], but I thought that was kind of funny coming from two of those guys who had accomplished so much in their careers.

[I remember] we had a guy [named] Ellis Kinder, who was a reliever. Williams *hated* him. Frankly, Williams couldn't hit him with a two-by-four, if you can believe that.[36] And Kinder was a free spirit. He would relieve against Williams—and you remember how Ted would scrape that right foot to kind of dig a hole? And held everybody up until he got that hole dug up, scratching around with his spikes, getting real comfortable. Kinder would patiently stand up there on the mound. The first pitch he threw at Williams would be at his right foot. And Williams, it'd just upset him. So the next thing we know, Mr. Yawkey [the Red Sox owner] had bought Kinder, and he ended up with the Red Sox. I know that he bought Kinder because Williams probably was raising so much hell about it that there was only one way to quiet him down, and that was get Kinder on his side.

I'll bet you a crisp $100 bill that Williams could tell you what the hell Kinder threw him the first time he ever saw Kinder. And he would tell you. You'd be talking about somebody, he'll start you out with a fastball then he'll throw you a breaking ball. Vern used to tell me about guys when I got out of the service. Vern knew all those guys. He'd tell me all about the sequence they'd be liable to throw. That taught me to do the same thing. But they had total recall. It was just a natural thing with him. Thirty years later he'd tell you what Kinder threw him. The only thing I could tell you thirty years later is a baseball.

But he was a good guy. He never changed, you know; I always stayed in touch with him. When I was the CEO of the players association, the benevolence association of pro baseball[37]—I did that for thirty-eight years after I quit playing. Ted was on the board with me the entire time. So we were in constant touch weekly or semi-weekly for the rest of our lives. And if the winter meetings were in Florida and Ted could make it, he'd drive into town, attend the meeting, and then go back home.

---

[36] According to retrosheet.org, Williams was 5–14 against Kinder, although the data is incomplete.

[37] Association of Professional Ball Players of America

When Ted was in Boston, we'd get out there early to watch batting practice. Everything stopped in the ballpark; not only the visiting ballclub, but the Boston ballclub, just to watch him hit. He was that impressive at the plate.

I remember him taking batting practice—it got to be a kind of a thing with me—I would look around and everybody stopped what they were doing to watch him while he was taking batting practice. Because he was Williams—normally you'd get into the batting cage and hit four or five, whatever the predetermined number was, then get out of there and the next guy would move in. It would just expedite the time you had. But Ted would get in there and take up homesteading rights. He'd swing until he got tired. The sequence was always: The first two or three swings were just singles; then the next two or three swings was him letting it out a little bit; then he'd begin to pump the ball; and the last four or five he'd swing at they might still be looking for 'em someplace. But that was always his routine. As I say, he stopped all activity, I don't care what ballclub he was playing against.

I often wondered . . . I always stayed close to [Joe] DiMaggio because of my job and we were in constant contact, and I often wondered if Joe stopped what he was doing. Did you ever stop to think of that? One of the greats looking at another great. Every time I was having dinner or something with DiMaggio, I always forgot to ask him. I would have if I had thought about it.

I'll tell you another story. We're playing in St. Louis, [and at that time] both the Browns and Cardinals used the same ballpark. By July or August, the infield was probably a little harder than Highway 40. It was *really* hard. So Williams is up at-bat, hits the ball, and pulls it into right field. It wasn't that far off the ground. I jumped and *just* made a fraction of contact with the ball and it got over my head by about 10 or 15 feet. It felt like it went off my uniform. And the ball hit and bounced way up in the air and we held him to a single, which is a victory in itself. Now, Eddie Rommel was umpiring first base. He was a really, really nice man, and everybody liked him. Williams said to me, "Damn, I hit that ball on the top half." That was why it bounded over my head and bounced so high. I turned to Rommel and I said "time." And I got right in Williams' face and said to him, "Are you telling me you can hit the damn ball on the bottom side or the top side?" And he said, "Sure." I can't repeat what I told him, but Rommel was hysterical [the entire time]. But he finally walks up to us and says, "Gentlemen, I wonder if we could get on with the ball game."

But Williams and Musial and those guys, they were endowed with a *tremendous* advantage in sight. Paul Waner told me—again, I asked him one time—how big did a baseball look to you? And he said, "Kind of like a softball." To me, the thing looked like an aspirin tablet. Those guys, they were amazing.

You know, Ted was Ted. You'd look out in left field and if he's po'd at the writers, he's liable to be giving them the middle finger or whatever. You never knew what he was going to do out there. But he was a very decent guy and was really, really interested in the well-being of the ballplayer. That was our obligation, and we quietly took care of people in our business that needed help and never divulged who they were to anybody, unless they wanted us to. And he was always concerned about the ballplayers, that he played with or against or heard of, that were in financial need.

He liked everybody on the ballclub and everybody liked him. Where Joe was always so quiet . . . because I was on an all-star ballclub in, oh boy, '50 or '51 over in Japan, and you just didn't bother Joe. You just didn't walk up and, like Williams, whack him on the back, that kind of thing, because you never knew if he was in a mood or not.

On that tour to Japan—it was during the Korean War, '51 as I remember—Joe and I are in a lobby, and a Japanese guy interrupts and wants to know if he can talk to me. So I go over, and it turns out he was a shirtmaker, and he was asking if I liked silk shirts. And they were dirt cheap [there], you know. He gave me his card, and it was on the Ginza in Tokyo. So he leaves and I tell Joe, "Man, we have to go down to this cat's place and load up, because the price is right." So Joe and I get into a cab and go down to the Ginza—that's the Broadway of Tokyo. We're walking down the sidewalk and looking at stores and one thing or another, and I hear, "DiMaggio, DiMaggio," and I look back, and there must have been a thousand Japanese people following us down the street. We get to the corner of this busy intersection, and I turn to Joe and say, "Geez, I get so tired of this. Here I am all the way in Tokyo, Japan, and they're following me [laughs]." There wasn't one guy in that thousand who knew who the hell I was. He hit me on the arm, kind of [threw me] off balance, and I went out in the street, and a cab comes within about a foot of me. So I go back and tell him, "Jesus, you almost got me killed in front of all of my fans." That was the first time I ever really saw him break up.

You must know, the entire atmosphere was so much different than it is now. Whether you were playing with or against—and I don't think there is that kind of concern now, because of the money denominator, than there was then. You made lifelong friends and you were always concerned about their well-being, whether you liked them or not, and I don't know if that exists today. I've been retired for ten, twelve years now, and I kind of lost the pulse of things, but it doesn't appear that the same kind of *that* feeling—you're a ballplayer, you're proud of the game, and you're beholden to the fans.

The thing we didn't know in school . . . Ted didn't have . . . I'm assuming because we didn't talk about it personally, but his home life must have been horrible. I suspect he had to overcome a lot. His mother was very religious, and I guess was passing out pamphlets and that kind of thing, and I don't know whether she carried that into the home, although I have since heard probably yes. But I can't say anything about the guy. And stop and think about that, we both know that he was a silver-tongued devil. You didn't turn him loose, but you never knew what some of those guys were going to say.

A funny story about Lem. I had announced my retirement after thirty-eight years, and Lem by this time was on a cane and a walker with circulatory problems, but I wanted him there. There were 500 people; big representation from the commissioner's office and one thing and another, but 500 to be exact; [Tommy] Lasorda and [Sparky] Anderson; the whole mob. Lem struggles to the microphone. I always emceed my own program, so I could keep it timely and get them in and out of there. He gets to the microphone—and I don't happen to be Catholic, but one of my dear friends is a monsignor of the local Catholic church in Long Beach where Lem and I grew up. He always did the invocation, and he was seated next to me. Lem gets the microphone and looks out at 500 people—all male—and said, "Good to see everybody, but I want to say this: Anybody that said the golden years are great is full of shit [laughs]." I looked down, and I have to prop the monsignor up in the chair because I was afraid he was going to fall out and hurt himself [laughs]. Things like that. And Ted would set that pattern. You know, if he got wound up, lordy knows what he's going to say . . . and he couldn't care less.

But he was a good guy. That's the most you can say; he was a caring guy. I think he probably would be identified with older players, probably more than anybody who stayed in touch with most of his old teammates . . . stayed in touch more than anybody I know . . . and did that until he died. The last few years John Henry pretty much kept him isolated, but before that he was a really, really gregarious guy.

Guys like Early Wynn and Lem and all of those people, they always had good things to say about him—until he walked to the plate. *Then* it got a little salty. But he was a marvelous hitter.

And then that gallop of his. When he was circling the bases, I've seen that many times; it looked like he was on a merry-go-round. That kind of lope he had.

Ted was a better hitter (than anyone else). When you're talking about the four dimensions—run, throw, hit, field—I don't think there's any contest, because the guy from New York did them all superbly. The guy from Boston, how many of the four would you give him?

It was an interesting time. And writers, again, called it the golden years. I have to go along with that. I think it was. Times were not good before the war, and then a lot of us volunteered there. Then after spending three or four years, most of us took a while to recover or readjust. But Ted, that didn't seem to bother him. It didn't look like he'd been away. I'm up there struggling to hit .250, and he's up there struggling to hit .400. And he had two interruptions like that. It was so natural with him, I reckon, that there wasn't anything that was going to get that swing or eye-hand-bat coordination ever disturb that. I think that was the reason he had all of that success. It was just a built-in thing. And he could still do it when he was nearing forty. Under normal circumstances, when a guy was forty, he was looking for the La-Z-Boy. Williams is still hitting .350. That pretty much well sums up my feelings on the guy. I respected him and loved his attitude. His ability to the ordinary ballplayer was absolutely awesome.

Once you saw him—and Musial was the same way with that unorthodox stance—you never forgot it. It was indelibly stamped. The first time I saw Musial, we had an off day, so we did something different and went to the ballpark to see the Cardinals play. And some left-hander with Cincinnati is out there—the guy could really pump—and he threw Musial a change, and I think Musial had committed a little bit for a fastball. He quickly adjusted on the change and laid one up against the left-center-field fence for a triple. And I'm thinking, uh-oh, I just saw a guy with a magic wand. And Williams could have done the same thing—and did.

Ted loved to talk hitting. Hell, he'd talk hitting to a sign post. The thing that always amused me about him . . . I sat in on a conversation with Williams, Musial, and two or three others, I think [Joe] Gordon, and they were talking about hitting. I'm thinking, here's three or four guys—[Johnny] Mize might have been in there [as well]—when they talk about hitting to me, it was always so natural for them, they had no sense of struggling at the plate. But the ordinary ballplayer, it was [always] a struggle. You're doing everything you can to maintain a presentable average, but those guys, they just walked out there and began to start whaling away—with great success. But it was interesting to listen to his conversation about hitting, because he made it sound so simple. And if you were able to apply all his theories, then everyone in the world would be hitting .400 and it wouldn't be any fun. And I think I told him that one time. He just looks at me like, "another dizzy left-hander."

Vern Stephens had the same ability—he was never a high-average hitter, but had great power for a shortstop. But once they hit against a pitcher, the sequence of the pitches they were shown that day was indelibly stamped. They never forgot it.

When he came to the plate—as you know, most hitters have a spot they can really cream the ball, low ball, high ball—Williams didn't have those weaknesses. So if you are pitching against him—and I can say this with all certainty—you would just go after him with the best you got. And obviously, most of the time it didn't work, because you're not going to throw a fastball by him. A breaking ball didn't worry him. The only pitch that would be difficult was maybe one low and in or high and away, but that was everybody's weakness.

The thing about Williams, he had great ability to keep that ball in the strike zone. If he did have a weakness, nobody knew it. You'd try everything on him, but everybody in baseball—and I never really asked him about it, what guys he had trouble with. The only guy I was aware of—because he'd was always moaning when he'd get down to first base—was Kinder.

Of course with the Browns, we didn't have too many guys you had to worry about anyway. Once in a while you'd come up with a guy that could pitch a little bit, and I guess make him work for it, but the rest of them were just struggling to get him out. He always did well against our ballclub. The only time I saw him look bad was in that World Series. He had probably just cooled off or was pressing, who knows. It happens to everybody. And I don't know if he ever went through a slump. Maybe he'd consider 1–4 a slump. Hell, 1–4, I figured I had a triumphant eye. He kept everything in the strike zone, and I'm sure the umpires knew that and were extra careful, which meant it had to be in the strike zone. There were no in-between calls against Williams. I'm sure that prevailed and rightfully so, because the umpire knew this guy had the eyes of an eagle, and he's going to raise hell if they make a mistake on him, which he did . . . quietly. I don't think he [often] showed an umpire up. It wasn't much in his nature. He didn't have to, because when you opened up the paper in the morning, he was always leading the league. That must have been utopia. When I opened up the paper in the morning, I looked to see if I was still in the league!

I was there from 1936, I guess, '35, '36, to the end. I think we graduated at the same time. I remember in '36 I guess, our ballclub, Long Beach Poly, where a lot of good players like Tony Gwynn and the like came from, knew we were going to play for the Southern California championship. They didn't have a state championship [at that time]. We had already clinched the spot for the final, and Ted's ballclub was playing Escondido, another Southern California town. I was the captain of the ballclub, and the coach took me and a couple of pitchers and drove us down to see the ball game. Ted was playing the outfield. He also pitched in school, but I never did see that . . . and his swing *never* changed. It was the same stroke as a kid that he had as a retiring adult. So that's pretty much the history of Williams.

It was a real privilege to see him at the plate. You know, it must be like the past generations when they saw people like [Ty] Cobb and

Charlie Gehringer, the second baseman, those classic hitters. It must have been the same feeling from that generation as ours, looking at Williams and DiMaggio. [That you get to watch somebody] you know is great, and will always be considered great.

Wayne Terwilliger

Second baseman

1949–51: .... **Chicago Cubs**
1951: ....**Brooklyn Dodgers**
1953–54: ....**Washington Senators**
1955–56: ....**New York Giants**
1959–60: ....**Kansas City Athletics**
Career Statistics: .... **666 games, 22 home runs,**
.240 batting average

I **"INTERACTED" WITH WILLIAMS** more than once, as I coached for him when he came back in 1969 to manage the Senators.[38] My memory isn't as good as I would like, but I do remember catching a line drive off him as a player one of the few times I played third base.[39] I was totally surprised, as Williams rarely hit it to the left side, but I caught it!

[As a manager], all he demanded was that you hustled and guys on the bench paid attention to what was going on in the field. He let his coaches do their jobs—he and Sid Hudson [the pitching coach] did a great job with so-so talent. I had free reign coaching third base—as to hit-and-run, steal, etc. He never questioned me. He would talk hitting to anyone who was really interested, no matter who it was. He had a great thirst to know the finer points of photography, real estate, you name it. I learned more about hitting [when he was coaching with the Senators] that, if I had still been playing, I probably would have improved my batting average by 50 points, or at least 40! For four

---

[38] Terwilliger coached with Williams on the Senators and Texas Rangers from 1969–72.
[39] Terwilliger played third base just fourteen times in his career. On September 24, 1954, in the second game of a doubleheader, with Terwilliger playing third, Williams lined out to third in the third inning. It is the only time Williams is credited with a line out to third in a game in which Terwillger played that position.

years, Ted talked and I listened to everything [he had to say] about hitting, pitching, and more. Ted's first years as manager of the Senators was 1969, and it was the greatest year in my career—he was named manager of the year.

Was he the best hitter I ever saw? Of course!

Ray Webster

Second base

1959:..**Cleveland Indians**
1960:..**Boston Red Sox**
Career Statistics:..............................**47 games, 2 home runs,**
.198 batting average

I THOUGHT HE WAS fantastic. He sort of took me under his wing, you know. Really treated me nice. I'd go into the dugout and sit down with him and we'd talk about whatever. It's been fifty-plus years ago. I think everyone looked up to him, as far as I know.

When I was with Cleveland in 1959, when he went into the batting cage everyone stopped everything and watched him hit and take batting practice.

He was an amazing guy, actually. I think he got some bad press, you know. I thought a lot of him.

What I loved about him, I'll never forget, he gave me . . . I think at that time he was a representative with Sears & Roebuck, and he gave me a fishing rod and poles to bring home. And I got some autographed balls from him. And at the time I should have had pictures taken with him, but I was only twenty-two or twenty-three, I can't recall exactly, and you don't think much about that at that time. You know, you're young and stupid.

I had scrapbooks when I was a kid growing up, and I was a Boston Red Sox fan. And I got pictures of him, and, oh God, I still got 'em. Pictures of him and I can't recall who else . . . Bobby Doerr and all those guys who played with Red Sox when I was a kid. So he was always my idol.

What got me was—you know I was playing utility mainly; wrong spot, wrong time—but anyway I got to Boston,[40] and he says, "I

---

[40] Webster was traded by the Indians to the Red Sox in January 1960.

remember when you got that double off Tommy Brewer and hit the ball off the left-field wall."[41] And here I was a nobody, you know what I mean. He had such a memory. That's just hard to believe, you know. But he was an amazing guy. I could not say anything bad about him.

He had a tremendous set of eyes. I just was honored to have the opportunity to meet the guy and play with him. Not many people can say they played with Ted Williams.

And he was a loner. Unfortunately in those days he couldn't go anywhere, a restaurant or what have you. He was the greatest at that time. That's about all I can say about him. He was a great guy.

---

[41] On September 14, 1959, Webster, then with Cleveland, singled to left field off Boston's Brewer at Fenway Park. Williams was on the bench that day.

INTERVIEWS

Bob Kline

Shortstop

1955: .... Washington Senators
Career Statistics: .... 77 games, 0 home runs,
.221 batting average

Q. Being an infielder, what was your defensive strategy against Williams, and how do you think you fared?

A. My defensive strategy against him was to pray a lot!

Q. Did your teams use the "Williams shift," and if so, did you like that and how did it fare? If not, do you wish they did?

A. My team used the shift and it helped.

Q. Recollections of any specific at-bats and/or plays vs. Williams.

A. My recollections about him: At his first at-bat on returning from Korea, I was [at] second base in the shift, and he hit a ground ball to me.

Q. What was the talk among other players on how to face Williams in pregame meetings or just in general?

A. There was no particular talk about Ted Williams between players on our team.

Q. Was he the hitter you feared the most in the field?

A. He was the hitter we feared the most on the field!

Q. Did you ever have occasion to interact with Williams? If so, what kind of guy was he like?

A. During batting practice, Ted and I had a good conversation about fishing, since he was a fisherman, and I was born and raised in Florida, where I fished all my life. We discussed different types of fishing lures and our love of fishing.

Ted Lepcio

Second base / Third base / Shortstop

1952–59: ....Boston Red Sox
1959: ....Detroit Tigers
1960: .... Philadelphia Phillies
1961: .... Chicago White Sox
1961: ....Minnesota Twins
Career Statistics: .... 729 games, 69 home runs,
.245 batting average

Q. Did your teams use the "Williams shift," and if so, did you like that and how did it fare? If not, do you wish they did?

A. Fortunately, I played with him most of my career. Outside of Cleveland, I don't remember many teams applying the shift. During my career, Ted hit balls so hard it didn't do much good to employ the shift.

There is no doubt in my mind that he could have hit .400 several more times if he wanted to. But, Ted was "Teddy Ball Game." They didn't come to see the greatest hitter bunt or hit a ground ball to left field when they played the shift.

Q. What was the talk among other players on how to face Williams in pregame meetings or just in general?

A. All players respected Ted.

Q. Was he the hitter you feared the most in the field?

A. Fielding against him was a nightmare. I played third base many times against him, so I didn't feel any fuzzy feeling.

Q. You played with Williams from 1952–59. Did you ever discuss hitting with him? What kind of guy was he like?

A. He always talked hitting and tried to help not only me, but other teammates.

Gene Verble

Second base/ shortstop

1951, 1953: ....Washington Senators
Career Statistics: .... 81 games, 0 home runs,
.202 batting average

Q. Being a middle infielder—playing second base and shortstop—what was your defensive strategy against Williams, and how do you think you fared?

A. Being a pull-hitter and left-hand batter, I played almost right behind first baseman Mickey Vernon. Was very successful at [it, and] one time he hit into a double play.

Q. Did your teams use the "Williams shift," and if so, did you like that and how did it fare? If not, do you wish they did?

A. Yes, it was a challenge.

Q. What was the talk among other players on how to face Williams in pregame meetings or just in general?

A. We knew he did not swing at bad balls, so tried to throw strikes all the time.

Q. Was he the hitter you feared the most in the field?

A. Yes

Q. Did you ever have occasion to interact with Williams? If so, what kind of guy was he?

A. He was a swell guy and was very helpful when he was asked for suggestions.

Section Four: Outfielders

Chuck Diering

Outfielder

1947-51: .... St. Louis Cardinals
1952: .... New York Giants
1954-56: .... Baltimore Orioles
Career Statistics: .... 752 games, 14 home runs,
.249 batting average

MUSIAL OR WILLIAMS? I don't try to distinguish between [players]. I played with so many good ballplayers all around, uh, God, I guess I'd have to say . . . I'd have to pick Stan because he was a better all-around ballplayer. Ted . . . well, he was a big home run hitter. When Stan had to become a home run hitter, he did, but Ted was a better home run hitter. He could hit them probably further, but all around, Stan could do everything. Of course, Ted was in the outfield, and I guess he was probably classified as a better-than-average outfielder, a good outfielder in that respect. I don't remember much about him being an outfielder when I played against him, but as a hitter, I can remember him calling his own balls and strikes, like all those good hitters did.

I played him in center field with that shift. That was part of the shift we used on him, and I guess the rest of the clubs did as well. Because he wouldn't . . . you could give him the whole left field and shortstop, and he wouldn't try to hit it out that way. He was strictly a hard pull-hitter. And he hit the line drives, and of course hit the long ball.

I played him a little deeper than normal, because if he hit the ball high enough, it was probably gone. But what I played him more for was low line drives—to catch them balls—because they would sink. With his type of swing, you're going out there and they'd sink, because he'd put that topspin on the ball. So that's the way I played him on defense. Because I could go back and get a ball—a long fly ball, while using that fence from right-center to the right field line. It was deep in center, but the right-field fence wasn't that deep. I think there was a little hill that you had to run up to the fence. I mean, I never had no trouble going back on a ball, in that respect, so I didn't play him as deep as some of them guys did. I played him more for those line-drive hits through the infield, over the infield.

You can cut off hits. You'd rather have him hit a single or double than a home run, but you're not going to hit 500 home runs a year. I don't know what the most he hit, 40? It isn't like today where you got eight guys on your ballclub and they all hit home runs. Back in our day, you only had one or two guys on a ballclub that hit home runs. It's just a different game than when I played.

He had a good eye; he got the benefit of the doubt. Yup, I've seen that happen many a time. The good power hitters, they pretty much have their own strike zone. You respected him, like a [Albert] Pujols, no denying that. The strike zone being so narrow, it was tough without putting it into an area where he could really rack one or get a base hit.

The only incident I had with Ted was when we had our first professional alumni . . . the retirement guys. And that was in St. Petersburg, Florida. I brought a bunch of bats down there and I wanted to get these guys to autograph for me. And I went up to Ted and said how about you autographing a bat for me? And he said, "Chuck, I can't do it." And I said, "Why not?" Musial autographed a bat for me. I was getting different signatures on one bat. I wasn't just asking for *his* autograph, but I wanted his signature on a bat with the other big stars. And he said, "I can't do it." And I said, "Why not, Ted?" And he said, "Because I got a contract." I was like, my God, I'm not going to sell the damn bat, I just want it with your name on it. He said, "I won't do it Chuck. I'll sign anything else, but I won't sign the bat." No thank you. And that was the last time . . . that was really probably the only time I recall having a conversation with the guy. Those big guys don't talk with rinky-dinks. That's what I called myself, a rinky-dink.

Joe Hicks

Outfielder

1959–60: .... Chicago White Sox
1961–62: ....Washington Senators
1963: ....New York Mets
Career Statistics: .... 212 games, 12 home runs,
.278 batting average

FEEL LIKE I didn't play against the "real" Ted Williams. It was 1960, his last year. Still he hit over .300 with almost 30 home runs and forty-one years old. Most all players would be pleased with stats like that, but it seemed like he was such a perfectionist that he was embarrassed by them. I'm sure the last player to hit .400 didn't want to play any longer when pitchers who he used to feast on were getting him out—he was just too proud to play the game any longer.[1]

---

[1] Williams batted .316 and hit 29 home runs in 1960, his last full year.

Jim Landis

Outfielder

1957–64:	Chicago White Sox
1965:	Kansas City Athletics
1966:	Cleveland Indians
1967:	Houston Astros
1967:	Detroit Tigers
1968:	Boston Red Sox
Career Statistics:	1,346 games, 93 home runs, .247 batting average
American League All-Star:	1962

Jim Landis said, in his era, no one compared to Ted Williams.

YES, HE IS definitely the best I ever saw. Oh my God, yeah.

One of the greatest things I think he did was study the pitchers. I mean, he had great ideas on all of them, and if you look at his record—records, I should say—he had some of his best luck against the greatest left-handers. He was just a knowledgeable man and he watched [everything].

And I'll tell you something—I was in a rut, so we were in the runway that both teams came down in the old ballpark of the White Sox, and Nellie Fox said, "I was going to ask him something." And Ted came down and Ted says—from left field now, remember this—it [my slump] had something to do with my hands. And he watched that from left field! That's how recognizable [he was] with things. I was totally amazed. But it helped, believe me!

I can tell you, I always went by Nellie Fox. He got along with Ted real well and liked him. I always figured if Nellie was that way toward him, then Ted had to be a pretty good guy.

I didn't talk to Ted, really. I was much younger,[2] and these guys were great vets like that. You just sort of looked at them and that was about it.

I definitely played him to pull and plenty deep. I don't care where you played him. He proved it by his averages it didn't matter where you played him.[3] You had three infielders to one side, play him to pull, whatever it was, it didn't matter.

I can remember one game and two balls in the same game, I took off towards right-center and thought *I got a shot at that ball,* and all of a sudden that backspin on that ball . . . and both of them went into the stands at the White Sox ballpark. What can you say about that? That's how good he was, and those fences were something like 350, 360, somewhere in that range.

I don't know what else to say about him as a hitter, my God. I think everything that he has in his averages, they speak for themselves. And like I said, he hit the best pitchers just as well. It didn't matter. And he studied them; he was very knowledgeable on all those pitchers.

I think the funniest thing I ever saw was Billy Pierce threw him a fastball—it looked like a strike, you know I'm out in center—and the umpire called ball four, and Billy Pierce jumped up about a foot in the air and straight back down. You know, you get a strikeout on that guy. . . . He probably did get a break, but give him credit.

---

[2] Landis was twenty-three when he broke into the majors in 1957; Williams would turn thirty-nine in August of that year.

[3] Landis was a five-time Gold Glove winner, from 1960–64.

He had such a goddarn good eye, too, they had to go along with that somewhat. What can you say but [he was] one of the greatest I'll ever see.

In my era, nobody compared to him. Nobody. I mean, I don't even know his stats to be honest with you, but I bet everything is outstanding. And if he didn't go into the service, my God, the home runs he would have hit. I'll always remember him as far as hitting the ball. You know, you always will remember some things, and Ted Williams will always come to my mind. I'm so glad that I got to see him. He was the greatest pure hitter ever. I just keep saying it, but that's what I feel. I haven't seen any better than him in all these days still, you know. Don't make me say it again!

Wally Westlake

Outfielder

1947–51: ....Pittsburgh Pirates
1951–52: .... St. Louis Cardinals
1952: .... Cincinnati Reds
1953–55: .... Cleveland Indians
1955: .... Baltimore Orioles
1956: .... Philadelphia Phillies
Career Statistics: .... 958 games, 127 home runs,
.272 batting average
National League All-Star: 1951

I HAD LITTLE ASSOCIATION with the "Big Guy." When I played with Cleveland, I was just a part-time player. My association with Ted, little as it was, was about the fly rod, not the bat. I do remember that when he walked into the batting cage, we all stopped to watch.

INTERVIEWS

Joe Durham

Outfielder

1954, 1957: .... Baltimore Orioles
1959: .... St. Louis Cardinals
Career Statistics: .... 93 games, 5 home runs,
.188 batting average

Q. When you played right field, what was your defensive strategy against Williams, and how do you think you fared?

A. Williams = play him extremely to pull.

Q. Did your teams use the "Williams shift," and if so, did you like that and how did it fare? If not, do you wish they did?

A. Yes, we did use the Williams shift.

Q. Recollections of any specific at-bats and/or plays vs. Williams.

A. No

Q. What was the talk among other players on how to face Williams in pregame meetings or just in general?

A. What can you say about a legend like Williams?

Q. Was he the hitter you feared the most in the field?

A. Yes

Q. Did you ever have occasion to interact with Williams?

A. No

Jim McAnany

Outfielder

1958–60: .... Chicago White Sox
1961–62: .... Chicago Cubs
Career Statistics: .... 93 games, 0 home runs,
.253 batting average

THANKS FOR THE opportunity to recall some very special memories. Ted Williams was my hero!

Q, When you played right field, what was your defensive strategy against Williams, and how do you think you fared?

A. I always played deep and ready to cut across on him.

Q. Did your teams use the "Williams shift," and if so, did you like that and how did it fare? If not, do you wish they did?

A. Yes, "the shift" fared well for us. One time Nellie Fox came almost all the way out to my position in right field to catch a ball off his bat— we were ready for him.

Q. Recollections of any specific at-bats and/or plays vs. Williams.

A. I recall one time catching a line drive off his bat that was the hardest ball I had ever caught. It stung for awhile!

Q. What was the talk among other players on how to face Williams in pregame meetings or just in general?

A. Pregame reminders: Keep the ball away and no good pitches.

Q. Was he the hitter you feared the most in the field?

A. He was the most feared hitter, and Mickey Mantle was next.

Photo courtesy of Jim McAnany

The minor-league and major-league batting average leaders from 1958—Jim McAnany and Ted Williams—pose before a game in 1959.

Q. Did you ever have occasion to interact with Williams?

A. I was a twenty-four-year-old rookie and still getting used to being a major leaguer.[4] I had won the Silver Bat for hitting .401 in Triple-A the previous year. Ted Williams won the Gold Bat that same year.[5] When the Red Sox came to play us, I was called out of the dugout before the game. I was asked to stand next to Ted Williams for a photo shoot. Each of us is smiling and holding a bat. A very memorable moment for me!

---

[4] Actually, McAnany was twenty-two as a rookie in 1959.
[5] In 1958, Williams led the American League in hitting at .328, while McAnany led all of the minor leagues with a .400 batting average for Colorado Springs.

Roy Sievers

Outfield / First base

1949–53: .... St. Louis Browns
1954–59: .... Washington Senators
1960–61: .... Chicago White Sox
1962–64: .... Philadelphia Phillies
1964–65: .... Washington Senators
Career Statistics: .... 1,887 games, 318 home runs,
.267 batting average
American League Rookie of the Year: 1949
American League All-Star: 1956, 1957, 1959, 1961

Q. What was your defensive strategy against Williams, and how do you think you fared? When you played first base, did you play especially deep?

A. I played Williams deep at first base.

Q. Did your teams use the "Williams shift," and if so, did you like that and how did it fare? If not, do you wish they did?

A. Yes, our team used the Williams shift. It worked fairly well at times.

Q. Recollections of any specific at-bats and/or plays vs. Williams.

A. Williams and I were going for the home run title. Playing in Washington, Williams' first at-bat—hit a line drive that missed going for a home run. If it happened, he would have been one ahead. My second time at-bat, I hit a home run to go ahead.[6]

---

[6] Sievers led the league in home runs in 1957 with 42. Williams finished in second with 38.

Q. What was the talk among other players on how to face Williams in pregame meetings or just in general?

A. We all talked about Ted Williams and what a great hitter he was.

Q. Was he the hitter you feared the most in the field?

A. Yes, he and Mantle. I didn't fear Williams—played him like most every player.

Q. Did you ever have occasion to interact with Williams, perhaps at first base? If so, what kind of guy was he like?

A. Williams was a great guy on and off the field. Back when I played, you didn't talk to the other players—especially during the game. Williams and I became good friends 'til he died.

Photo courtesy of Bob Wolff

Me interviewing Ted Williams and a young fan.

AFTERWORD

I STILL MARVEL AT the most unusual schedule of events that led me to the major leagues as a broadcaster. In my school days, playing sports was everything to me. My ambition was to make it as a major league baseball player, and didn't pay too much attention to the sports broadcasters. I knew that most were hired because of their voice, not their athletic ability. I was a fan of the big band era though—my family had a musical background—and my younger sister Margy and I harmonized on many of the New York City amateur shows where I also played my ukulele. Little did I realize that in my college days, I would sing with the college dance band and, when I became a sportscaster, would use my singing technique on the most exciting calls in sports.

I always felt, though, that the skill more important to broadcasting than a good voice was the content. That was particularly so in television, where one picture is greater than a thousand words. Content is the key to holding an audience, and still is. Content has to have appeal, though. One has to grip the audience through stories, revelations, humor, explanations, and personality—or being different in some fashion. Ted Williams had that mystique. He had his idiosyncrasies, and he was stubborn too. Ted believed in his baseball views and disdained many societal customs. Being different is an asset in attaining a TV audience, but what matters most is true talent. Ted had that.

Ted would never wear a tie and didn't believe in tipping his cap to thank those who were applauding him. A great hitter in olden days,

Lefty O'Doul, had told Ted never to change his classic swing. Ted never did, even when opposing teams used a defensive shift against him. With all the fielders on the right side, giving Ted the option of slapping the ball to left for an easy single or possible double, he decided to compete against this defensive strategy by lining hits to right field out of reach of the fielders or hitting long drives over their heads. One cannot quarrel with a player who, in 1941, had an astounding season, finishing with a .406 batting average. Baseball players are often superstitious. If the quirks helped Ted psychologically, who can complain?

I first met Ted Williams in Washington, D.C. I was the first television sportscaster in the city—the TV voice of the Washington Senators— and Ted was the most in-demand ballplayer of his era. It was vital for me to get him on the air. Ted seemed rather aloof in his relationship with the media, so I checked on his mood with a few of his teammates before approaching him for his first appearance with me. Ted agreed, and we had a most enjoyable session together. He seemed completely at ease answering my baseball questions, in fact appeared grateful at the opportunity to express his views. I always wanted my guests to leave our time together feeling as though they had an enjoyable experience. This certainly set the stage for future ones.

Whenever possible, I tried to spend some time with my guests in a social way without discussing an on-camera session. I learned what topics the potential guest enjoyed discussing and what made them smile, and Ted was no exception. I learned that he seethed with anger at himself if he didn't fulfill his own expectations on the ball field. When Ted stepped into the batter's box for practice swings, there was silence in the ball park. All players—both sides—as well as the media stopped what they were doing to watch the master in action. Fans always arrived early to enjoy this extra bonus.

Ted exhibited artistry at its finest with exploding line drives and a few towering homers; but occasionally, there were a few innocuous dribblers or routine pop-ups. Reporters learned on these occasions to move quickly out of the way when Williams started back to the dugout. Ted would get so mad at himself that he would not tolerate any questions or baseball banter before the game. I learned quickly to give him ten or fifteen minutes to cool off before resuming a lighthearted conversation; and luckily, it never interfered with our friendship. I was always surprised that practice could cause him such consternation. Maybe such intensity contributed to making him such a terrific player.

When it came to interviewing, whether the Virginia Slims Tennis matches, handlers at the Westminster Kennel Club Dog Show, or just athletes from the major sports, I always used my three-act system:

Act One was an unusual question which brought a laugh or a smile to make them relax.

Act Two was about something newsworthy they had performed in competition.

Act Three was something of a personal nature about them so we could conclude with a story ending on a happy note.

One day before a Red Sox game in Washington, I noted that Ted was in a good mood and asked him if I could spend a few minutes with a TV camera on him to just discus his baseball techniques. I said this would benefit young players who wanted to follow his beliefs, his examples. "Ok," said Ted, "let's do it right now." I motioned to my cameraman and we stood near the dugout on the first base side. I had the microphone in one hand and my stopwatch in the other. I never use notes in an interview; all I needed was my curiosity, as I had enough questions for a two-hour documentary. My technique is similar to having lunch with a friend. No one brings notes to start the conversation.

"Ted, I always notice that you keep flexing your fingers while you grip the bat. What's the purpose of that?"

"Bob, I use a lot of pine tar on my bat, and don't want the bat to slip out of my hands. But I don't want to hurt my swing because my hands are sticking to the bat, so I test my fingers all the time to make sure they're not going to stick there when I need them."

"Ted, you take a lot of pitches at the plate—including some good ones. Some other hitters usually go for the first pitch, believing it will be a fast ball over the plate and that the pitcher wants to get ahead in the count. What's your theory on this?"

"Bob, if it's early in the game and I'm not that acquainted with the pitcher's style or his stuff, this is my chance to look at what he's got. I don't want to swing at a slow curve and get angry at myself for swinging at his pitch, rather than one I can hit well. It's sort of a guessing game, but I'm always looking for a pitch I can drive well. Now the other night I took one pitch too many, but was ready for the next at bat and had learned what to look for. Figuring out what the pitcher is going to throw is important to hitting well."

"Ted, you seem to take batting practice very seriously. How important is that to how you'll do in a game?"

"Bob, it's an important dress-rehearsal. It's a final practice before the game. I'm saying to myself—need a fly ball to right—sacrifice fly to bring home a run—a line drive to center—or whatever. This time for me isn't to exercise my muscles; it's to do something specific to win games. The best hitters take it seriously."

This is just a sampling of my TV conversation—but with Ted, a perfectionist, batting practice was serious business—done with a purpose.

I remember another time when the Red Sox were warming up for a game; I was walking towards the Sox dugout with a mic in my hand. Ted was playing catch and I had no intention of interrupting him, as I already had my guests lined up. Ted scowled when he spotted the mic. . . . Guess he figured I wanted him for a show. I was taken aback when I saw the look on his face. The mic must have looked like a bayonet. There was not time for pleasantries, though, so I just kept walking.

After the game, I visited him in the clubhouse. "Ted, I came close enough to wave hello, but was concerned with your look of disgust.

I've always considered you a friend and I couldn't understand your facial reaction. What offended you?"

"Bob, it certainly wasn't you. I just didn't want to do another interview—I've had my fill this past week and I guess I overreacted."

"Understandable, Ted, so here's what I suggest. As a TV and radio guy, part of my job is interviewing players on the pre- and post-game shows, but you're doing me a favor by going on. So tell me when you'd like to do so and the rest of the time when I come by it'll just be to say hello, offer you a ride back to the hotel, or just to talk baseball."

Ted seemed to like the idea, so he said, "Tell you what, kid. If my average is around .330 or I've hit 20 home runs when I come in next time, you can count on me. The rest of the time, grab somebody else."

"That's great with me, Ted. I'll be pulling for you to hit those numbers whether you do the interview or not," and we shook hands.

The last series before Ted came to Washington; he was home at Fenway Park and made headlines there. Ted had become upset when he was booed after misplaying a windblown fly ball. When he came up to bat the following inning, Ted spit on home plate, thumbed his nose at the press box, was fined $5,000, and vowed after the game never to speak to the press, TV or radio, again. Ted's next stop was Griffith Stadium in Washington.

I got to the park early and saw Ted dressing for the game. After a warm greeting, I said, "Ted, I've got a problem. According to our agreement, you said you'd go on TV with me if you hit a certain batting average and the number of home runs you specified, and you've easily passed that amount. Here's my issue. I read that you were through doing interviews. To add to that, you're a good friend; so if you go on as promised, I'll have to ask you about your recent actions in Boston. I don't like asking those questions, but if I don't, the public will think I'm a bad reporter and my station will feel the same. So you can just refuse to go on with me despite our contract, and our friendship will still remain. But if you do go on, I'll have to ask you how you feel about it now—I can't avoid that. So it's your choice."

Ted then said, "Where do you want to do the interview and what time?" After telling him where and when, I said, "How about my questions?" Ted said, "Anything you want to ask."

The interview was done. Ted expressed his being contrite about his behavior. He also said that he could take criticism, but not when things were written about him that weren't true, and he hoped the fans would understand. I took that interview, added one with switch-hitter Mickey Mantle, in which the slugger confided that he was strictly a right-handed hitter and the only thing he could do lefty was wallop homeruns. No home run hitter was ever faster at beating out drag bunts. Like Ted, Mickey is an all-time great. With these two interviews as a pilot film, I went to New York and met with General Manager Lev Pope of Channel 11, where I telecasted Madison Square Garden events. They also carried the Yankee games at that time. We ended up selling Colgate-Palmolive my interview series with ballplayers from all clubs. This became the Yankees pre-game TV series, the Red Sox pre-game series, as well as Washington's and Kansas City's. The next year I formed my own production company and increased our coverage to the national scene.

The interesting thing about that interview was that it had been interrupted by an unusual happening; a hazard of live television. I did my best to make light of it, but hoped it would not changed the mood of the show. Let me explain that, in all my years of interviewing, I always did first-take shows. I have three important reasons for this:

1. All the players were on a busy schedule getting ready for the game. They couldn't wait for another try.
2. My schedule included doing a minimum of four interviews before each game, then pre- and post-game TV and radio shows, post-game taped, and then the play-by-play. No time to start re-scheduling.
3. First-takes are always more spontaneous. On second takes, laugh and smiles seem more rehearsed and not as genuine.

So about halfway through my filmed questioning of Ted, a fan climbed over the low ballpark barrier, came onto the field, walked right up behind me, and asked for my autograph. I didn't want to reveal my being upset on camera, believing that this important interview was being spoiled, so I smiled, explained I'd take care of the autograph a bit later, and continued speaking to Ted. The fan started to leave, and then returned to ask, "Is that Ted Williams with you?" Again a big smile, a "yes," and again, "please come back a bit later." This time the fan left.

I was afraid to look at the filmed result, so I stayed outside the viewing room, disheartened that this sought-after prized interview might no longer be good enough to use.

As the TV staff viewed it, I kept waiting for their verdict. Through the wall, however, I heard chuckles of mirth and then unrestrained uproarious laughter as they viewed my forced smile next to Williams' facial agony. The close-up of Ted showed him scowling, then enraged, and then his lips muttering a few swear words illustrating his wrath. This was visual proof of Ted's emotion, which was what the interview was about.

The true greats—in sports or otherwise—enjoy winning as we all do, but some become so used to praise that losing moments may have an even greater effect on them. Ted's reactions were genuine and honest, but sometimes resulted in far more coverage than his many good deeds.

The Williams interview remains one of my most cherished memories, particularly his last line in the interview. Ted said, "Bob, the reason I'm doing this with you is because you've always been so fair with me." I was flattered by his comment. Ted was certainly fair with me, and still I remain appreciative.

When Ted ended his career as a player and became manager of the Washington Senators, he had mellowed, realizing he could impart knowledge to his players—but not his talent. His players respected his advice and his patience with them.

Now at the age of ninety-two, I'm still talking on News 12 Long Island TV and am cited by the *Guinness Book of World Records* as the longest-running sports broadcaster in the world. I currently have no retirement plans—I enjoy working—but I do admire those who leave on a high note.

When Ted Williams announced his retirement as a player, he knew that his farewell game deserved a terrific ending. He provided that himself. On his final at bat, Ted put everything within him into stroking a pitch of his liking, smashing the ball into home run land at Fenway Park. That personified Ted the legend—a hall of famer who did it his way.

After serving in the Navy during World War II, I signed on as the Sports Director of the *Washington Post*. In 1947, I achieved my major league dream by becoming the Washington Senators' first TV play-by-play announcer. Sports Director Paul Jonas of the Mutual Broadcasting System signed me on to do national radio play-by-play, including bowl games and the Game of the Day. In 1954, I began a fifty-year run televising Madison Square Garden events, and in 1956, I broadcast my first of three World Series, which included Don Larsen's perfect game. I was also lucky enough to cover Jackie Robinson's last major league hit. In 1962, I became NBC-TV lead play-by-play announcer. My family and I have been thrilled by my inductions into the baseball and basketball Halls of Fame, the Madison Square Garden Walk of Fame, and the Sportscaster-Sportswriters Hall of Fame. Everything seemed to happen for the best. One can't ask for more. I've been more than fortunate and I'm truly grateful.

—Bob Wolff, December 2012

ACKNOWLEDGMENTS

AS WITH ANY project, there are a number of people to thank and recognize. First off, I'm not sure any of this would be possible without all the data compiled by the folks from retrosheet.org and baseball-reference.com. They certainly make the life of any baseball researcher—and fan—easier and a lot more fun. Also, Jack Smalling's *Baseball Address List* was an invaluable resource in contacting all these former major leaguers.

Even with all of this information at my fingertips, I still wasn't sure if this was a viable project or not. My gut said yes, but I guess I also needed some positive reinforcement. Enter two co-workers: Enrique Rodriguez and Sam Manchester. I innocently floated them my idea to get some feedback and both gave honest, enthusiastic, and positive responses that spurred me on to get started. In fact, Enrique was so enthusiastic that he not only kept asking me about updates on the project, but he also designed the graphics you see on these pages. I cannot thank him enough for his encouragement and enthusiasm, even though I try.

Jason Katzman with Skyhorse Publishing was aggressive and gung-ho about this project from the moment he called me. This book is in part a testament to his ideas, guidance, and pursuit of the best possible product.

And, of course, I have to thank each of the former major leaguers who corresponded back with me, whether they could help out or not.

FACING TED WILLIAMS

Although it's funny how many times a former player would tell or write to me that they couldn't offer much, whether due to memory or not having faced Williams often, and then go off and tell a great story. I thought I was really onto something early in the process when a few of them told me that this book is something that they'd really like to read. Boy, talk about feeling like hitting a game-winning home run when you hear something like that! Not to mention a lot of them just liked talking about Williams—he was a hero to many of them as well—and they would tell me that in those exact words. I had a couple of people thank me for allowing them to just discuss Williams for a few minutes. There was a definite reverence and respect for the man, not only as a ballplayer, but as a person.

Finally, and in cliché-speak, last and definitely not least, a giant thank you to my wonderful family. My boys, Laben and Kieran, keep alive my fire for the game of baseball with their enthusiasm and questions. My wife, Shelly, is always there encouraging me to forge ahead— even if she has no idea what the heck I'm talking about half the time. . . okay, three-quarters of the time. Without them, I don't know if I'd have the desire, passion, or energy to undertake a project like this. I love them, feed off their love, and in turn, love doing something like this.

By the way, I know Ted Williams didn't have much use for the media—and maybe even pitchers—but I can only hope he'd take some appreciation in reading this and learning what his colleagues thought of him. Heck, he might have even gotten a big laugh out of it.

Dave Heller

INDEX

A

Aaron, Hank, 104, 145, 200, 225
Aber, Al, 76
Adcock, Joe, 62
Air Force, 209, 256
All-Century Players, 56
Allison, Bob, 166
American Association (Baseball league), 148
American Sportsman, The, 4
Anderson, Sparky, 76, 278
Armed Services, 213
Association of Professional Ball Players of America, 274
Astrodome, 3
Astroth, Joe, 131
Avon Park, 68

B

Bailey, Ed, 64
ballparks.com, 128
Bard's Room, 136
Bauer, Hank, 104
Bauman, Bob, 68
Bell, Gary, 53, 81

Berra, Yogi, 23, 30, 69, 76, 87, 98, 111
Bertoia, Reno, 93
Bolling, Milt, 267
Bonds, Barry, 271
Borg, Bjorn, 228
Boston Record, 230
Boudreau, Lou, 48, 75, 132, 142, 223, 232, 258, 273
Brandt, Jackie, 145
Brett, George, 76, 206
Briggs Stadium, 76, 261, 262
Bruce, Bob, 27–28
Buddin, Don, 100
Bunning, Jim, 56, 240, 261, 262
Byrd, Harry, 213
Byrne, Tommy, 234

C

Carey, Andy, 51
Carrasquel, Chico, 138
Castro, Fidel, 30
childhood (of Ted Williams), 277–278
Chiti, Harry, 36, 107, 134

Chylak, Nester, 107
Clemente, Roberto, 104
Clinton, Lou, 42, 107
Coast League, 20
Cobb, Ty, 162, 232, 235, 281
Colavito, Rocky, 84, 194
collarbone injury, 223–224
Colledge, Sharky, 141
Collins, Joe, 223
Comiskey Park, 128, 142, 224
Connie Mack Stadium, 213
Courtney, Clint, 166
Cronin, Joe, 252
Crosetti, Frank, 229
Cullenbine, Roy, 48, 159

D
Damon, Johnny, 77
Dibble, Rob, 117
Dillinger, Bob, 138
DiMaggio, Dominic, 71, 138, 223, 233, 248, 261
DiMaggio, Joe, 48, 50, 69, 71, 74, 77, 188, 200, 225, 226, 233, 238, 251, 267, 268, 271, 275, 277, 282
Dobson, Joe, 137
Doby, Larry, 181, 211
Doerr, Bobby, 141, 233, 273, 285
Doubleday, Abner, 162
Dressen, Chuck, 259
Dropo, Walt, 40, 71, 251
Dyer, Eddie, 232

E
Easter, Luke, 104
Ed Sullivan Show, 51

Egan, Dave, 226, 230
elbow injury, 49, 224, 236
Eglin Field, 249
Elmira Pioneers (Red Sox), 1
Elson, Bob, 136
Embree, Red, 48

F
Feller, Bob, 46–50, 73, 77, 78, 209
Ferrell, Kerby, 83–84
fine (for obscene gesture), 161, 201, 315
Fisher, Jack, 170
Fitz Gerald, Eddie, 91
Ford, Whitey, 74, 77, 142
Fornieles, Mike, 30
Fox, Nellie, 16, 17, 48, 141, 181, 203, 298, 299, 306
Foytack, Paul, 28, 58–61
Francona, Tito, 145
Frick, Ford, 53

G
Galehouse, Denny, 140
Gammons, Peter, 6
Garbo, Bob, 273
Garcia, Mike, 208, 210
Gardner, Billy, 52
Gehrig, Lou, 162
Gehringer, Charles, 239, 282
Gernert, Dick, 147–148
Ginsberg, Joe, 161
Gold Bat, 307
Gold Glove, 299
Gomez, Lefty, 77
Goodman, Billy, 29, 122, 232

Gordon, Joe, 145, 280
Gowdy, Curt, 4
Graham, Jack, 273
Green Monster, 165, 168, 246, 251
Griffith Stadium, 167, 315
Grove, Lefty, 77
Guinness Book of World Records, 317
Gwynn, Tony, 10, 235, 237, 281

H
Hardy, Carroll, 152
Hegan, Jim, 138
Hemsley, Rollie, 122
Henrich, Tommy, 48, 233
Hey Kid, Just Get It Over the Plate, 103
Higgins, Pinky, 140, 152
Hitters Hall of Fame. See Ted Williams Museum
Hodges, Gil, 177, 204
Hornsby, Rogers, 10, 136
Howard, Elston, 23
Howser, Dick, 88
Hudson, Sid, 15, 203, 283
Hughson, Tex, 140
Hurley, Ed, 98

I
Irvin, Monte, 104

J
Jacksonville Naval Air Station, 239
Jensen, Jackie, 22–23, 81, 131, 166, 240, 261–262, 270

Jimmy Fund, 161, 199, 253
Johnson, Deron, 206
Joost, Eddie, 84, 132

K
Kaline, Al, 23, 40, 56, 90, 104, 151, 181, 194, 240
Kell, George, 72
Kennedy, Bob, 239
Keough, Marty, 108
Killebrew, Harmon, 23, 73
Kinder, Ellis, 273–274, 280
Kiner, Ralph, 224
Kingdome, 23
Klaus, Billy, 29, 119
Korean War, 25, 76, 159, 213, 225, 236, 266, 276, 289
Kuenn, Harvey, 23, 181

L
Labine, Clem, 27–28
Lang, Dick, 273
Larsen, Don, 109–112, 318
Lasorda, Tommy, 106, 278
Lavagetto, Cookie, 259
Lee, Thornton, 185
Lemon, Bob, 210, 273
Lillis, Bob, 145
Limmer, Lou, 132
Long, Dale, 62, 63
Lopat, Eddie, 69
Lopez, Al, 55, 127, 210
Lyons, Ted, 136

M
Madison Square Garden, 224,

316, 318

Major League Baseball Players Alumni Association, 73, 77, 296

Malzone, Frank, 32–33

managing career (of Ted Williams), 141, 153, 201, 211, 224, 283, 317

Mantle, Mickey, 8, 23, 30, 39, 71, 74, 81, 90, 98, 104, 115, 123, 139, 146, 154, 159, 165, 166, 186, 228–229, 233, 234, 244, 255, 262, 268, 269, 306, 309, 316

Marine Corps, 52, 236

Maris, Roger, 104, 115, 186, 228

Marrero, Connie, 217

Masi, Phil, 138

Mattingly, Don, 6

Mays, Willie, 23, 30, 39, 104, 165, 200, 233

Mazeroski, Bill, 62

McCarthy, Dave, 7

McDermott, Mickey, 92, 270

McDougald, Gil, 120, 250

McMillan, Roy, 63

military physical, 236–237

military service, 209, 249–250. See also Air Force; Korean War; World War II

Minoso, Minnie, 179, 194

Mitchell, Dale, 211

Mize, Johnny, 225, 280

Monbouquette, Bill, 23

Musial, Stan, 19, 55, 102, 108, 155, 188, 209, 224, 232, 243, 257, 260–261, 275–276   23, 64, 112, 120, 167, 200, 225, 240, 251, 262, 276, 279–280, 296

N

Napp, Larry, 35

National Baseball Hall of Fame, 4, 7, 8, 9, 30, 46, 74, 81, 84, 199, 261

Newhouser, Hal, 160

O

O'Doul, Lefty, 312

Old League Park, 48

Orlando brothers, 68

P

Paige, Satchel, 128–129, 263

Parnell, Mel, 106, 251

Passeau, Clause, 49

pepper (game), 33, 251

Perry, Gaylord, 159

Pesky, Johnny, 48, 71, 74, 106, 138, 142, 223, 261

Petrocelli, Rico, 148–150

Pierce, Billy, 299

Piersall, Jimmy, 44–45, 73, 113, 131, 154, 180, 213

Pillette, Herman, 126

pitching career (of Ted Williams), 38

player of the year award, 251

Pope, Lev, 316

Power, Vic, 84

Pujols, Albert, 233, 271, 296

R

Radcliff, Rip, 48
Ramirez, Manny, 77
Ramos, Pedro, 218
Raschi, Vic, 234, 237
Richards, Paul, 153
Richardson, Bobby, 263, 264
Rizzuto, Phil, 233
Roberts, Robin, 53
Robinson, Eddie, 141
Robinson, Jackie, 272–273, 318
Rommel, Eddie, 275–276
Rosen, Al, 90, 125, 211
Runge, Ed, 53
Runnels, Pete, 97, 100, 259,
    267, 271
Ruth, Babe, 162

S

salary, 265
San Diego Hall of Fame, 95
Schaive, John, 166
Science of Hitting, The, 1, 5, 10,
    231
Score, Herb, 24, 74, 77, 91, 250
Scott, George, 201
Scott, Jim, 93
Sears, 112, 119, 225, 262, 285
Sewell, Rip, 49
Shantz, Billy, 131
Shea Stadium, 97, 106
Sievers, Roy, 73, 308–309
Silver Bat, 307
Slaughter, Enos, 84
Soar, Hank, 208
Society for American Baseball
    Research, 68

Spahn, Warren, 142
Spence, Stan, 48, 136, 138
spitball, 35
Sports Illustrated, 6, 142–143
Spragins, Homer, 249
Staley, Gerry, 141
Stengel, Casey, 22, 98, 125, 229,
    232
Stephens, Vern, 122, 137, 138,
    273, 280
strike zone chart, 258
Sturgeon, Bob, 273
Sullivan, Frank, 29, 140
Summers, Bill, 161

T

Tasby, Willie, 97
Ted Williams Day (at Fenway),
    250
Ted Williams Museum, 6–7, 49,
    68, 160, 267
Temple, Johnny, 63
Thomas, Frank, 62, 63
Thome, Jim, 75
Tiger Stadium, 55, 60, 261,
Tighe, Jack, 261
Tipton, Joe, 250, 251
Tresh, Mike, 136
Triandos, Gus, 52
Tropicana Field, 6
Trout, Paul, 160
Trucks, Virgil, 10, 11, 106,
    156–162
Turley, Bob, 228–229, 230
Turner, Jim, 229
Tyndall Field, 249

U

University of Illinois, 136
University of Wisconsin, 130
Urban Shocker's Weblog, 125

V

Veeck, Bill, 128
Vernon, Mickey, 52, 73, 218,
    262, 268–269, 271, 291
Vincent, Fay, 69

W

Walsh, Ed, 93
Waner, Paul, 276
Washington Post, 318
Wertz, Vic, 107, 211
White, Frank, 206
White, Sammy, 230
Wight, Bill, 136, 138, 142,
Williams, John Henry, 49, 73,
    278

Williams, Sam, 52
World Series, 23, 232, 265, 281,
    318
World War II, 50, 225, 318
Wright, Taft, 48
Wrigley Field, 3
Wynn, Early, 210, 265–266, 278

Y

Yankee Stadium, 22, 84, 96,
    110, 225, 230, 234, 267
Yastrzemski, Carl, 117, 186
Yawkey, Tom, 264, 274
Yost, Eddie, 218

Z

Zarilla, Al, 232
Zernial, Gus, 213
Zoldak, Sam, 70
Zuverink, George, 119, 172–173

#1

VINCE LOMBARDI

There is little doubt that Vince Lombardi was the most compelling coach in the history of the NFL, and perhaps the greatest coach and leader in the history of all North American sports, let alone professional football.

His talent and prowess were not in his ability to draw up explosive and scintillating plays. There were many coaches who had far more to offer in that area, but when it came to getting his players to prepare well and execute at their best on an every-week basis, Lombardi set a standard that no other coach has been able to sustain.

Lombardi also had an eye for execution. When his teams practiced, he made sure that each player got it right before he moved on to the next play.

That was the Lombardi way, and those who played for him in Green Bay from 1959 through 1967, or in Washington in 1969, quickly learned that there was only one way to get things done. Those who chose to try to get by or to put one over on Lombardi did not last long under his watchful eye.

Lombardi had been the offensive coordinator of the New York Giants under Jim Lee Howell in the late 1950s. While Lombardi coached the offense, Tom Landry ran the defense and the two competed hard against each other, something that would play out quite a bit during the 1960s.

There was a strong impression that Lombardi would eventually become head coach of the Giants, and that would have pleased the New Jersey native quite a bit. However, the lowly Green Bay Packers came calling in 1959, and Lombardi seized the opportunity even though the Packers had not had a winning season since 1947.

It was assumed that Lombardi was inheriting a mess of a team, but he didn't see it that way once he arrived at training camp that year. Instead, he saw the Packers as a fairly talented team that had lacked direction and discipline.

Lombardi provided both of those characteristics and did it with gusto. He simplified the Green Bay offense and had his team work on the basic fundamentals of the game—blocking and tackling. The power sweep was his bread and butter play, and he would run it again and again in practice so that each player knew where he was supposed to be as a matter of instinct.

That play featured the offensive guards pulling out from the line of scrimmage and running toward the sidelines, where they would kick out opposing linebackers or defensive backs and seal off an alley for the running back to attack with gusto.

ning with their 2001 championship year, and they have been to the postseason in all but two of those seasons (2002 and 2008).

However, they could not win another Super Bowl title until 2014, when they rallied with fourteen fourth-quarter points to beat the Seattle Seahawks in Super Bowl XLIX.

Prior to that, they lost two Super Bowls to the New York Giants following the 2007 and 2011 seasons. The loss in 2007 was particularly noteworthy, because the Patriots were 16-0-0 in the regular season and had swept their playoff games before New York used a spectacular pitch and catch from quarterback Eli Manning to unheralded wide receiver David Tyree to key the upset.

While Belichick's consistent excellence has allowed him to become one of the sport's coaching greats, his career has been steeped in controversy.

Belichick has often been accused of pushing the rules to the limit. Both he and his team were fined and the Patriots lost draft picks after the NFL determined that New England illegally filmed opponents' practice sessions to give the team a strategic edge.

After the 2014 AFC Championship victory over the Colts, the "Deflategate" controversy blew up, as eleven of the twelve footballs used by the Patriots were reportedly not inflated to the proper standards.

At the time that this book went to press, no determination of guilt had been assessed by the NFL, but many observers believed that Brady, Belichick, or some other New England employee played a key role in deflating the footballs. Brady and Belichick denied any wrongdoing.

Belichick may not like to share his ways with the public or elaborate when he speaks to the media. However, when it comes to winning football games and championships and preparing for any and all possibilities, he walks shoulder to shoulder with Lombardi.

For the record

Bill Belichick
Regular-season record: 211–109–0, .659
Postseason record: 22–9, .710
Four Super Bowl victories

#3

TOM LANDRY

The man in the fedora and the impeccable suit stood on the Dallas Cowboys sidelines for the first twenty-nine years of the franchise's existence. Under his leadership, the Cowboys went from a laughingstock of an expansion team to America's Team.

The only professional sports rival the team has had in terms of popularity throughout the decades is the New York Yankees, and the Bronx Bombers had a long head start in which they had icons like Babe Ruth, Lou Gehrig, Joe DiMaggio, and Mickey Mantle represent them.

Landry shepherded the Cowboys every step of the way, and it was clear he was destined for greatness when he was named head coach of the expansion team prior to the 1960 season. Landry had been a defensive back with the New York Giants, and while he was still in uniform when playing for head coach Steve Owen, he was asked to implement the Giants "Umbrella" defense and became a coach on the field.

When Jim Lee Howell took over for the embattled Owen, Landry officially became a player coach and then a full-fledged defensive coordinator. While Landry was running the defense for the Giants, Vince Lombardi ran the offense. The association of Landry and Lombardi working together undoubtedly gave the Giants the best set of assistants any team has ever had.

Landry was more than ready to compete with the best minds in the game, but it took a while for the expansion Cowboys to get competitive. Owner Clint Murchison had Tex Schramm as his general manager and Gil Brandt as his head of personnel, along with Landry as his head coach, and those three turned the Cowboys into a formidable franchise.

The Cowboys suffered through five consecutive losing seasons through 1964, but they finished at .500 with a 7-7 record in 1965. After undergoing a 2-5 first half, the Cowboys reversed that record in the second half of the season and showed they were ready to become one of the NFL's elite teams.

They lived up to that promise the following year when they went 10-3-1 and finished first in the NFL's East Division. That success set them up for the championship game against Lombardi's Packers in the last year of the NFL's two-division setup.

The Packers were the league's dominant team at the time, and they came into the Cotton Bowl expecting to take care of the Cowboys with few problems. However, Landry's Cowboys were becoming an offensive juggernaut with Don Meredith at quarterback, Don Perkins and Dan Reeves at running back, and explosive Bob Hayes at wide receiver.

Landry had Lombardi in a cold sweat as the Cowboys had the ball on the doorstep of a tying touchdown in the final moments of regulation time. Meredith, harassed by Willie Davis and the Packers' defensive front, hurled the ball into the end zone, where it was intercepted by Tom Brown to preserve Green Bay's 34-27 victory.

The following year, the two teams met in perhaps the most famous NFL Championship game of all time in Green Bay. The temperatures dropped to a ferocious minus-16 degrees, and Landry's Cowboys had a 17-14 lead until the game's final play. That's when Green Bay guard Jerry Kramer bowled over Dallas defensive tackle Jethro Pugh, and quarterback Bart Starr followed the block into the end zone with the game-winning touchdown in a 21-17 triumph.

The Cowboys gained many new fans in that heroic defeat. They had played Lombardi's Packers nearly even in two championship games, and many thought the Packers were the greatest NFL team of all time.

Landry and the Cowboys would win consistently from that point forward. The Cowboys earned a playoff spot in sixteen out of seventeen seasons with Landry leading the way.

During his tenure, he had three outstanding quarterbacks in Meredith, Roger Staubach, and Danny White, and they led the Cowboys through their rise, their ascendant reign, and their decline.

Staubach was the quarterback who helped them win their two Super Bowl titles in the Landry era. He may not have had the arm strength of either Meredith or White, but his superb leadership skills meshed perfectly with Landry's demeanor and innovative ways.

The Cowboys finally won their first Super Bowl following the 1971 season, when they defeated the Miami Dolphins 24-3 in Super Bowl VI. The Cowboys performed almost flawlessly, as they took apart the up-and-coming Dolphins.

The game was a sharp contrast to the previous year's Super Bowl in which the Baltimore Colts had outlasted the Cowboys 16-13 in a game that would become known as the "Blunder Bowl" because the two teams combined for 11 turnovers.

"That game stayed with us throughout the offseason and into training camp," Landry said. "I knew that if we got back to the Super Bowl, we would not see that kind of game again. We got there and we were prepared for the situation."

The Cowboys would win the Super Bowl again following the 1977 season, when Landry's experienced team outclassed the Denver Broncos 27-10. Denver head coach Red Miller had a ferocious defense and an opportunistic offense led by former Dallas quarterback Craig Morton, but there was no way that Landry's defense was going to give the Denver offense a chance to find its rhythm.

The flex defense, designed by Landry during the 1960s, involved his defensive linemen changing their positions—flexing—an instant or two before the ball was snapped. This formation served to confuse quarterbacks who weren't sure which play would work against a defense that they knew would change before the ball was snapped.

That flex defense was instrumental in two more Super Bowl appearances in the 1970s against the Pittsburgh Steelers. The Cowboys would engage Chuck Noll's Steelers in two of the decade's most exciting Super Bowls, and Dallas came up a tad short in both of them.

While they could not defeat the Steelers, there was something heroic about the Cowboys' performances, considering the fact that the Steelers of the '70s would go down as one of the NFL's greatest teams of any era. The Steelers would win four championships in the decade.

Landry kept his emotions in check throughout his career on the sidelines, and that was a conscious decision. There were never any tears following the victories or the defeats. He didn't want to show any form of a perceived weakness, because he knew his players would follow his example.

But in masking his feelings for the majority of his career, he built walls between himself, his players, and his coaches.

Walt Garrison, one of his top running backs in the 1960s and '70s, was once asked if he had ever seen Landry smile. Garrison, always quick with the quip, gave a response that provided great insight into Landry's demeanor.

"No I haven't, but I've only been here nine years," Garrison said.

Keeping emotions and feelings in check was the way many American men conducted themselves at the time. While the strong, silent type is no longer the norm, it worked for Landry as a football coach.

The Cowboys started to lose their way in the 1980s, and they suffered through three consecutive seasons from 1986 through 1988. After the 1988 season, Arkansas oil man Jerry Jones bought the Cowboys. Jones appeared to know that Landry's time had passed.

He replaced him with college coach Jimmy Johnson suddenly and harshly.

The firing was widely criticized because Jones seemed to show no concern for the coach who had led the Cowboys from their first game. He later acknowledged his mistake and admitted that he should not have been so blatant in the move, but he had a plan and was quick to act on it.

Landry was angry and embarrassed, but he did not write a tell-all book, go on television, or try to get even with the owner who forced him out of a job he held for twenty-nine years.

Instead, he went to the Hall of Fame in 1990 having won 250 regular-season games and twenty more in the postseason. Only George Halas and Don Shula won more regular season games, and no coach has ever won more postseason games.

The sight of Landry stalking the sidelines in his trademark fedora remains one of the classic images of the NFL.

thirty-three years seems out of the question at this point, and it took a man of remarkable energy to last that long in the NFL.

Shula played in the NFL from 1951 through 1957 with the Browns, Colts, and Redskins before he began his coaching career at the University of Virginia and the University of Kentucky, respectively. He had his chance to move into the NFL as the defensive coordinator of the Detroit Lions, and he became one of the first coaches to use a zone setup. He helped the Lions build one of the toughest defenses in the NFL.

Carroll Rosenbloom, the owner of the Baltimore Colts, had taken notice of how well Shula had done in Detroit and could sense that he was fine head-coaching timber. While he had Weeb Ewbank on the sidelines, Rosenbloom grew tired of the team's mediocrity, and he fired his coach and replaced him with the thirty-three-year-old Shula.

Shula's first team in Baltimore finished with an 8-6 record in 1963, and the Colts players quickly learned how demanding their new coach was. A winning record was simply not good enough, and Shula let his players know, via his blunt language and fiery temper, that he was not satisfied.

Shula was fierce in his preparations and he worked his players hard. Hall of Fame quarterback Johnny Unitas said Shula made "enemies" out of some of his players because of his hard-driving ways, but they all knew he was an excellent coach.

The Colts came roaring out of the gate in 1964 and finished with a 12-2 record to gain first place in the West Division.

The Colts were heavily favored in the NFL Championship game against the Cleveland Browns, but Unitas & Co. simply could not get it done and they were drummed 27-0.

The Colts were bitterly disappointed with that loss, and they began the 1965 season with new determination. However, they could only tie the Green Bay Packers for first place in the West with a 10-3-1 record, and that meant the two teams had to meet in a playoff game to decide who would meet the Browns in the NFL championship.

Injuries had depleted both teams, and neither Unitas nor backup Gary Cuozzo could play for the Colts. They were forced to have running back Tom Matte play quarterback. The Packers' Bart Starr could not play, and he was replaced by backup Zeke Bratkowski.

It was a brutal war in Green Bay, and the Packers tied the game in the fourth quarter on a late field goal by Don Chandler. That kicker would end the game in overtime on a controversial 25-yard field goal that appeared to be wide of the goalpost, but was called good by the officials.

Shula and the Colts would have to bide their time while the Packers dominated through the mid-1960s, but the Colts put an overpowering team on the field in 1968. Baltimore would roll to a 13-1 record, as they had a ferocious defense led by huge Bubba Smith and nasty middle linebacker Mike Curtis.

The Colts defeated the Minnesota Vikings 24-14 in the divisional playoffs and embarrassed the Browns 34-0 in the NFL Championship game.

That victory gave the Colts the chance to represent the NFL in Super Bowl III against the American Football League's New York Jets.

The AFL had been beaten handily in the first two Super Bowls, and the Colts were an even heavier favorite over the Jets than the Packers had been against the Kansas City Chiefs and Oakland Raiders in the first two AFL-NFL Championship games.

Jets quarterback Joe Namath and his teammates didn't care what the oddsmakers thought and they were confident that they could not only stay with the Colts, but also find a way to beat them. When Namath was goaded by Baltimore fans at a pre-Super Bowl event during the week of the game, he offered his famous "guarantee" that the Jets would win.

Shula and his players were amused and perhaps annoyed with Namath's bold remarks, but they did not change anything in their game plan prior to the game. After all, they had won fifteen of

#5

BILL WALSH

Few coaches have ever taken a team that was at the bottom of the NFL heap and catapulted it to the top more dramatically than Bill Walsh did with the San Francisco 49ers.

Walsh was hired by the 49ers in 1979, after the team had gone 2-14 and was the laughingstock of the NFL. It didn't seem like Walsh would be much of a head coach, as the Niners repeated that 2-14 mark in his first year.

However, there was a huge difference between the 1978 team and the 1979 version. While they did not win any more games, Walsh gave them a game plan and an offensive scheme that would serve the team in an extraordinary manner over the next two decades.

Walsh had prepared to become a head coach by learning from two of the game's masters. His first job as a pro football coach had been with the Oakland Raiders, where he had been the running backs' coach on Al Davis's team. Davis, who had been trained under Sid Gillman, favored the vertical passing game. Walsh learned how Davis wanted to attack quickly and decisively, and he gained the foundation of an offense while with the Raiders.

Walsh would come into his own as an assistant coach with the Cincinnati Bengals from 1968 through 1975. Head coach Paul Brown was clearly one of the game's most innovative coaches, both with the Bengals and prior to that with the Cleveland Browns. Walsh teamed up with Brown to help transform the Bengals from an American Football League expansion team to an NFL winner.

However, when Brown retired prior to the 1975 season, Walsh was passed over for the head coaching job. Brown named Bill "Tiger" Johnson as his successor, and Walsh left the team in a huff.

Brown kept Walsh from getting an NFL head coaching job on numerous occasions after that by giving him lukewarm praise or offering critical comments when other teams called him to ask about Walsh. Brown was one of the most revered men in the NFL, and he was able to keep Walsh from getting ahead in his career. However, he couldn't stop the 49ers from hiring Walsh in 1979.

Walsh was not a typical coach who would work his players to a frazzle in training camp and practice. His philosophy was to build a team that was so skilled and smart that it would be able to run circles around its opponent on Sundays in the regular season.

He believed in concepts like strength, toughness, and physicality, but only to the point where his team was on even terms with opponents. He didn't want to overpower opponents; he wanted his team to have the edge in talent and skill. He was far more interested in winning the chess match with opposing coaches.

This was not an ego-driven goal for Walsh. He simply wanted to take the offensive principles that he had learned and then perfected and build the strongest team possible. He wanted to teach his principles to his players, and have them play at a nearly perfect level on the field.

Walsh would find success in his third year with the 49ers. After his 1980 team went 6-10, few thought the 49ers were ready to become contenders. However, Walsh had a brilliant quarterback in Joe Montana at the helm, and he had engineered a masterful draft that offseason that brought the 49ers four athletic, young defensive backs in Ronnie Lott, Eric Wright, Carlton Williamson, and Lynn Thomas.

Lott would go on to become a Hall of Famer and one of the best safeties in the history of the game, and the young foursome helped turn the Niners into one of the most aggressive defenses in the league.

But it was the offense that allowed this team to make its imprint. Walsh took the best of the offenses that he learned from Gillman, Davis, and Brown and put his own stamp on it to come up with his innovative West Coast Offense.

Instead of merely focusing on the deep ball as Davis had done with his vertical attack, Walsh spread out the defense and hit opponents with a game plan that allowed the Niners to find the weak spots on the flanks.

The key to the attack was having a quarterback who could read defenses expertly and throw the ball accurately. That description fit Montana to a T. He was able to diagnose what the defense was going to do before the snap and adjust his play call, if necessary, to take advantage of it.

The Niners knew they had something special brewing that season when the Dallas Cowboys came to Candlestick Park in Week 6. Walsh's team had a 3-2 record and they knew they were in for a test against Tom Landry's perennial power.

However, in this game, the Niners blew out the Cowboys 45-14. That game gave the 49ers the confidence to know they could play with and beat the best teams in the NFL.

"It was a great moment for us," Lott said. "We had a good mix of young players and veterans and we knew we were getting better. But to beat Dallas like that was a huge step. We all felt good going into that game because we knew we had a great game plan that would keep us in the game. But to blow them out like that had a long-lasting effect."

The 49ers were on a roll after that and would lose only one more game all season. However, they would find themselves right back at Dallas in the NFC Championship game at Candlestick Park.

The Cowboys would claim they overlooked the 49ers in the earlier meeting. That was obviously not the case in the championship game, with a Super Bowl appearance on the line.

The 49ers played well in that game, but the Cowboys had been just a tad better. The 49ers were trailing 27-21 late in the game, when Montana led them on an improbable drive that culminated with the quarterback throwing a game-winning touchdown pass to wide receiver Dwight Clark in the back corner of the endzone that gave San Francisco a 28-27 victory.

"The Catch" signified the rise of the 49ers and the demise of the Cowboys, who would struggle to maintain their elite position after that loss.

Walsh designed that play to give Montana options if he faced pressure. "That was a practiced play," Walsh said. "Now, we didn't expect three guys to be coming right at Joe, but he executed the play to perfection, as he put it, where only Dwight could catch it and nobody could deflect or intercept it."

Walsh had demanding standards for all his players in games and practices, but he also knew when to back off and lighten things up.

When the Niners arrived at the Super Bowl following their dramatic win over the Cowboys, Walsh greeted his players at the hotel in Detroit dressed as a bellman as he helped them with their luggage.

"It may have seemed like a strange thing to do, but Bill always did everything for a reason," Lott said. "He wanted his players to have fun and he wanted to make sure we didn't take it too seriously. He wanted us to relax in the spotlight, and he knew just the right thing to do to take the edge off the situation."

The ploy worked perfectly as the Niners were able to come up with a superb effort as they defeated the Cincinnati Bengals 26-21. It not only gave San Francisco its first NFL championship, but perhaps even more rewarding was the fact that it came against the team that Walsh seemed destined to coach until he had been bypassed.

While Walsh could motivate his team to come up with big emotional efforts, it was his ability to scheme, diagnose, and devise a game plan that made him one of the greatest coaches of all time. He was able to lead the Niners to three Super Bowl titles, and after he retired following the 1988 championship season, former assistant George Seifert led the Niners to two more titles.

Walsh was seemingly at the top of his game following the 1988 season, in which the Niners won the Super Bowl and again defeated the Bengals. But Walsh was no longer enjoying himself and he felt he was having a much harder time reaching his players.

The Niners were just 6-5 shortly after midseason, and they were not playing to their potential. Walsh saw this as an indictment against his coaching style. He was able to rally his team from that point, but he no longer thought he was the best man for the job and he left the Niners.

Walsh would go on to regret the decision. He had high standards for himself and his team, and he didn't understand why his team went through a rare slump. If he had been able to look at the big picture, he could have stayed longer and enjoyed even more success.

He later told the *San Jose Mercury News* that he had made a mistake. "I never should have left," Walsh said. "I'm still disappointed in myself for not continuing. There's no telling how many Super Bowls we could have won had I stayed."

Walsh would go on to try his hand at college coaching (at Stanford University), television analysis, and writing. He would never again reach the heights he had enjoyed with the 49ers.

Walsh's brilliance and talent helped turn a moribund team into one of the glamour franchises in the history of the NFL.

For the record

Bill Walsh
Hall of Fame, 1993
Regular-season record: 92–59–1, .609
Postseason record: 10–4, .714
Three Super Bowl victories

#6

PAUL BROWN

The New York Jets' victory over the Baltimore Colts in Super Bowl III (see chapter 4, Don Shula) is often viewed as the greatest upset in the history of professional sports. Joe Namath led the upstarts from the American Football League to an upset of the mighty Colts from the NFL, and thereby lifted the AFL and cut the older league down to size.

Well, as dramatic and exciting as that victory was, it was not unprecedented. In 1950, the NFL absorbed four teams from the rival All-American Football Conference, and it was expected that the NFL would trounce the Baltimore Colts, Cleveland Browns,

New York Yanks, and the San Francisco 49ers when they started to compete.

The Browns had been the champions of the AAFC, and they met the defending NFL champion Philadelphia Eagles in the 1950 season opener. However, instead of a one-sided win by the Eagles in front of their home fans, the visiting Browns trounced the Eagles 35-10.

The architect of that Cleveland victory was head coach Paul Brown, who had put together a superb team even though he didn't have the benefit of an NFL affiliation.

What Brown did have was superb coaching skill. Whether it was player evaluation, teaching a system, coaching players individually, or motivating them as a group, Brown was simply an A-plus leader.

Brown excelled as a head coach at all levels of the game. It started at Washington High School in Massillon, Ohio, where he went 80-8-2 and won six straight state championships. Brown moved to Ohio State for a three-year stint and won a national championship with the Buckeyes. After two successful years during the war with the Great Lakes Naval Station football team, Brown was named the coach of the Cleveland franchise in the newly formed AAFC.

Owner Mickey McBride wanted to name the team after his new coach and call it the Browns, but Brown rejected the idea. When the team settled on a nickname of the Panthers, the owner of a defunct franchise that had been called the Cleveland Panthers objected, saying he still had the rights to the name.

McBride didn't want a court fight on his hands, and Brown relented to McBride's original idea, so the team was called the Browns.

Brown built a dominant team in the AAFC. The squad went 52-4-3 in four seasons and won the championship every year. They had a sensational crew of players that included quarterback Otto Graham, fullback Marion Motley, wide receiver Mac Speedie, tackle Lou "The Toe" Groza, guard Alex Agase, and linebacker Lou Saban.

In addition to the talent, Brown was able to get the most out of his players. He did not do it with kindness and love in practice. It was clear that he was the unquestioned boss in every game he ever coached, every practice session he led, and every chalk-talk session he ever presented.

He was not interested in having his players like him, and he was only interested in having them play as he directed. If players made multiple mistakes in practices, Brown would greet them with an icy stare, followed by a sarcastic remark.

Remarkably, Brown would catch nearly every mistake and his players quickly realized they could not fool him at all. As a result, the only conclusion was for them to work diligently so they could do things right and avoid their coach's righteous indignation.

The razor-sharp Brown introduced many aspects of football that became staples in the game. Brown was the first football executive/coach to have a taxi squad of players who were not on the roster, but were ready when called upon.

When it came to giving his quarterback a play, he was the first coach to have a radio installed in his signal-caller's helmet. He was the first coach to grade game films and then go over those films with his players. He also was the first head coach to hire full-time assistant coaches and pay them to work for twelve months a year.

Brown was a master at scouting college players and finding the greatest talent. He introduced rudimentary athletic tests that included the 40-yard dash.

He popularized pocket passing, the draw play, and timed pass patterns that called for the quarterback to throw to a certain spot at a specific count, instead of when the receiver completed his route. This brought football to a new level, and other coaches throughout the league and in the college ranks followed his lead.

He had a finely tuned machine on his hands during the 1950 season. After Brown served notice in the ballyhooed season opener against the Eagles regarding the strength of his team, the Browns rolled throughout the season and finished with a 10-2 record.

They were pushed hard by the New York Giants and the Los Angeles Rams in the postseason, but won both games and earned the NFL championship in their first year in the league.

Brown was never satisfied with merely winning one championship. He wanted to dominate every year. The Browns followed with three seasons that included 11-1, 8-4, and 11-1 records, but they did not win the title in any of those years.

However, the Browns were 9-3 in the 1954 season and won the NFL's East Division title, and that put them in the championship game against the Detroit Lions. Interestingly, the Browns had closed the season with a 14-10 loss to the Lions and another close game was expected.

Nevertheless, Brown had saved something for the title game, and his team overwhelmed the Lions 56-10, as Graham threw three touchdown passes and ran for two more.

The Browns were not done at the close of that season, though. They followed with a 9-2-1 record in 1955 and another championship game appearance. This time they went out to Los Angeles and rolled over the Rams 38-14, after opening the game with a field goal from Groza and a 65-yard interception return for a touchdown from Don Paul. They were never threatened.

After ten seasons of coaching at the professional level, Brown's teams had won seven championships and the worst they had done was 8-4 in any season. He was innovative, clearly a brilliant teacher, and able to inspire his players.

The Browns endured their first losing season in 1956 when they went 5-7, but they bounced back in 1957 after he drafted running back Jim Brown from Syracuse. Jim was a powerful running back who had dominated in college, and Paul Brown made sure his game plan allowed the running back to show off his talents.

The Browns went 9-2-1 in '57 and 9-3 in '58, and made it to the playoffs in both seasons. However, they were stopped by the Lions in the '57 title game and lost to the Giants in the '58 tiebreaker after both teams finished with the same record in the East Division.

The Browns would not make it back to the postseason in any of their four ensuing seasons under Brown, but they did have a winning record every season.

Players, including Jim Brown (who thought his coach's offensive tactics had grown conservative), started to tune out the coach. At about the same time, young businessman Art Modell bought the team, and he wanted to learn more about football by getting inside the mind of his coach.

Brown would have none of it, and he rebuffed Modell's advances even though he owned the team. This went on for a couple of years and Modell eventually fired the coaching legend after the 1962 season.

Brown was out of football until the 1968 season, when he became owner and coach of the Cincinnati Bengals, an AFL expansion team. After two difficult opening seasons, Brown led the Bengals to the playoffs in 1970. The team's quick ascension showed that Brown still had many of his remarkable coaching skills.

He continued to coach the team through the 1975 season, when the sixty-seven-year-old Brown led the team to an 11–3 record.

His legacy should have ended there with great memories, but Brown had grown difficult and small-minded as he got older. He could have turned the Bengals over to assistant coach Bill Walsh, but he thought that Walsh was too eager and he passed him over for the more subservient Bill "Tiger" Johnson.

When Walsh felt the need to strike out on his own with a head coaching position, Brown tried to ruin his efforts by talking him down to every team he could. The 49ers ignored Brown's negative comments and hired Walsh, a move that turned the fortunes of that franchise around.

There was a demeaning edge to Brown's personality that grew in his final years, but it could not take away his remarkable coaching achievements. He had dramatic success at every level of the game, and that's a scenario that no other coach is likely to repeat.

For the record

Paul Brown
Hall of Fame, 1967
Regular-season record: 213-104-9, .672
Postseason record: 9-8, .529
Four AAFC championships, Three NFL championships

35

#7

BILL PARCELLS

The Big Tuna cast a big shadow over the game of football, and no coach has ever been so successful with so many teams.

Bill Parcells would have easily been a top-20 head coach if his career had come to an end after he decided to leave the New York Giants following his second Super Bowl victory with them in 1991. But that was not the end of his coaching career, as he would go on to do quite a bit more.

He would also have successful coaching stints with the New England Patriots, New York Jets, and Dallas Cowboys before he would walk away from the sidelines.

Parcells was a New Jersey guy, and he never tried to hide it. In the 1970s, there was a famous television commercial with actor Robert Conrad putting a battery on his shoulder, and looking into the camera for a solid second before he said, "Go ahead, I dare you. Knock it off my shoulder."

Conrad jutted out his jaw in a defiant act of toughness, and sent the message that anyone who tried to knock it off his shoulder was going to have to defend his actions.

Parcells took on much of that same kind of persona in his dealings with the media and, at times, his players. He was a tough guy, and he was going to let everyone know it. Nobody could disrespect Parcells and get away with it.

That was the most famous part of his personality, but it was not the only part. He was thoughtful, honest, and unafraid to change his mind if he thought that would help his team.

That was something he demanded from his assistants, players, and anyone he dealt with. Those who weren't straightforward with Parcells would not be forgiven.

Parcells got his chance to coach in the NFL with the Giants as an assistant on Ray Perkins's staff. During the 1981 season, Parcells was responsible for running the Giants' defense. That was the same season they drafted Lawrence Taylor out of North Carolina, and it was no coincidence that it was the first season that the Giants made it back into the NFL postseason since 1963.

Parcells knew from the first day of training camp that Taylor was special and that he would almost certainly become a game-changing player. He made sure Perkins knew how good Taylor was from the start, and Parcells was instrumental in Taylor becoming a star right from the start of the season.

Parcells would eventually become the Giants' head coach when Ray Perkins left the team to take over for the late Bear Bryant at Alabama. Parcells made mistakes that first year, and the Giants went just 3-12-1. He had a fiery, tough, and resolute personality, but he did not let it show that season.

His job was in jeopardy. Giants' general manager George Young knew ownership was not happy, and he had several conversations with Howard Schnellenberger of the University of Miami. If Schnellenberger had wanted it, he almost certainly could have been head coach of the Giants. That's what Parcells believed.

Schnellenberger did not become head coach of the Giants, and Parcells stayed. He put together a team that was founded on defense, a pounding offensive game plan that featured tough running, and special teams that didn't make mistakes and could force opponents into serious errors.

The Giants became a playoff team in 1984, as they gained a wild-card spot with a 9-7 record and beat the Los Angeles Rams on the road in their first playoff game under Parcells. Although New York lost in the next round to the San Francisco 49ers, Parcells had the core of his team.

In addition to Taylor, the Giants had Leonard Marshall, Carl Banks, Harry Carson, and Jim Burt on defense. Parcells also committed to Phil Simms at quarterback that season, and the move helped steady the offense.

The Giants were 10-6 in 1985 and back in the playoffs once again. This time the 49ers came east to play at Giants Stadium, and the marauding New York defense punished the Niners and shut down their vaunted attack, en route to a 17-3 victory.

Parcells and the Giants were feeling quite confident after the win, and they believed they could continue to advance in the postseason, even though they were going to Chicago to take on the 15-1 Bears. The confidence lasted all the way through kickoff, but once the game started, New York provided little competition for Mike Ditka's team. The Giants simply could not move the ball at all against the Monsters of the Midway and dropped a 21-0 decision on a brutally cold day at Soldier Field.

It was a painful defeat, but it also provided an important lesson for the Giants. They saw how the Bears attacked and dominated on defense, and Parcells got the message across to his players that they had to do the same thing if they were ever going to get to the Super Bowl.

The Giants were a nasty, hard-hitting, take-no-prisoners kind of team in 1986, and it appeared that Parcells message was taken seriously. They roared through the season with a 14-2 record, and appeared to be nearly as good as Chicago had been the year before.

Many were expecting an epic confrontation between the two teams in the NFC Championship game, but the Redskins ended up upsetting the Bears, and that meant Joe Gibbs was bringing Washington to Giants Stadium to decide the NFC Championship.

This time, the Giants would not be stopped. Despite playing in howling winds, the Giants dominated the game from start to finish on both sides of the ball and earned a 17-0 triumph.

That meant a Super Bowl date with the Denver Broncos and John Elway. Many thought the athletic and strong-armed Elway would be the difference in this game, but the Giants would have none of it. After enduring some first-half jitters, the Giants rolled to a 39-20 victory, as Simms completed 22-of-25 passes.

Parcells celebrated with his players, telling them that no matter what happened the rest of their lives, they would always be Super Bowl champions. "They can't take this away from you," he said in the locker room.

Parcells and the Giants would get back to the Super Bowl following the 1990 season. The Giants were 13-3 that year, but they appeared to suffer a crippling blow when Simms went down with a late-season injury. The Giants went into the postseason with backup Jeff Hostetler at quarterback.

Many thought that Hostetler had neither the arm strength nor the leadership ability to lead them past the Bears in the divisional playoffs.

However, New York rolled over Chicago by a 31–3 margin. Then they shocked the 49ers 15–13 the following week to earn a spot in Super Bowl XXV against the high-powered Buffalo Bills.

Buffalo was an offensive juggernaut that year, and they were coming off a monstrous 51–3 blowout over the Los Angeles Raiders in the AFC title game. The Bills were significant favorites to beat the Giants, and even Parcells knew his team did not have the fire-power to keep up with the Bills.

Instead, he told the offensive coordinator to "shorten the game." Parcells didn't just want the Giants to score, but also he wanted them to hold on to the ball, so Jim Kelly and the Buffalo offense were unable to find their rhythm. The Giants had possession for more than forty minutes and pulled out the 20–19 upset when the Bills' kicker sent the potential game-winning field goal wide right.

Parcells left coaching after that win, but he resurfaced with New England in 1993, and he quickly turned that team into a contender. The Patriots won the AFC in 1996, but they lost the Super Bowl to the Green Bay Packers.

Parcells wasn't satisfied in merely serving as the head coach of the Pats. He wanted to have a say in player personnel. This led to a rift with owner Bob Kraft, as Parcells famously made his case: "If you're good enough to cook the food, you're good enough to buy the groceries."

Parcells eventually went on to coach the Jets and Cowboys. He turned around both of those teams, which had struggled before he got there, with his straightforward approach.

Parcells left the sidelines after the 2006 season and moved on to a front-office position with the Miami Dolphins. He ultimately turned that team around before retiring as well.

Overall, he won two Super Bowl titles and left four teams better off than when he arrived.

Not bad for the ultimate Jersey guy.

For the record

> **Bill Parcells**
> Hall of Fame, 2013
> Regular-season record: 172–130–1, .570
> Postseason record: 11–8, .579
> Two Super Bowl victories

#8

CHUCK NOLL

B.C. has a different meaning in Pittsburgh than it does in the rest of the world.

In the Steel City, B.C. means Before Chuck, because the Pittsburgh Steelers were one of the most forgettable and inconsequential franchises in all of sports before they hired Chuck Noll as head coach in 1969.

But once Chuck Noll came aboard, the Steelers rose from the muck and mire of the NFL's bottom feeders and became perhaps the most glorious team in the NFL.

The Steelers have won six Super Bowl titles, and that's more than any other team in the league. They won the first four of those Super

Bowls under Noll, who found much of the talent that brought glory to Pittsburgh, trained it, and developed the team into the greatest winners the game has known.

The Steelers were a collection of mediocre stumblebums through the 1960s, and they were the type of team that would play aggressively every week but come out on the short end of the scoreboard. Opponents would often pay a price for playing the Steelers, but they would also come away with the win.

Owner Art Rooney was sick of that legacy and when he hired Noll to be his head coach in 1969, he had hope that this single-minded and determined coach would turn things around. "The Old Man" probably couldn't have dreamed how much success Noll would have over the course of his run at the helm of the Steelers from 1969 through 1991.

It wasn't immediate, as the Steelers were a putrid 1-13 in Noll's first season. But the disaster of 1969 was preceded by an event that would help Noll turn around the Steelers. They drafted defensive tackle Joe Greene out of North Texas with the fourth pick in the first round.

Greene would go on to become the foundation of the great Steel Curtain defense and one of the top players in the history of the game. The following year, the Steelers drew a lot of raised eyebrows when they selected Terry Bradshaw with the No. 1 pick overall. Bradshaw appeared to be straight off the set of *Hee Haw*, as he had "country bumpkin" written all over him.

But Bradshaw also had a magnificent arm, and Noll tutored him on the intricacies of the pro game. Bradshaw was often unhappy with Noll over the state of their personal relationship, but they formed one of the most productive partnerships in the history of the game.

Success in the draft would become the heartbeat for the Steelers in the Noll era. The Steelers had what is regularly acknowledged to be the best draft of all time in 1974, when they selected four future

Hall of Famers in Lynn Swann, Jack Lambert, John Stallworth, and Mike Webster.

The Steelers slowly improved in their first three seasons under Noll, but they still finished with a 6-8 record in 1971. However, the team would take a huge step up the ladder in 1972, when they won the AFC Central title with an 11-3 record.

Pittsburgh gained great confidence that season, and their first postseason game was a classic. They engaged in a brutal battle with the Oakland Raiders at a frigid Three Rivers Stadium. They carried a 6-0 lead until late in the fourth quarter, but Raiders quarterback Ken Stabler appeared to steal a win for John Madden and the Raiders when he skated thirty yards down the sidelines to score a touchdown in the final minutes that gave the Raiders a 7-6 lead.

The Raiders knew they were one defensive series away from winning the game and advancing to the AFC Championship game against the Miami Dolphins. The Raiders stopped the Steelers on three consecutive plays. On fourth down, Bradshaw ran for his life to escape the Oakland pass rush before he hurled the ball downfield towards backup running back Frenchy Fuqua. Raiders defensive back Jack Tatum blasted Fuqua and the ball in mid-flight, and it flew backwards.

But the play was not dead. Running back Franco Harris tracked the ball and caught it at his shoe tops while running at full speed. He made it all the way into the endzone and scored on a play known as the "Immaculate Reception."

While the Steelers, in turn, lost the AFC title game to the undefeated Dolphins, the image of the franchise changed dramatically with the miraculous win over the Raiders. The Steelers became legitimate contenders after that game.

Through those years, Noll was the consummate teacher. However, he wasn't just teaching his players. He was also teaching his coaches to do things in the manner that he demanded. So, if Noll wasn't directly instructing his players, he knew that his assistant coaches were delivering the message properly.

Noll appeared to keep his distance from his players. In the current era, it's common for coaches to be seen getting emotional on the sidelines. They will give their players high fives and often celebrate after a key play or dress down a player who has made a poor play or a mental mistake.

That was never Noll's style. He laid out his expectations for the team in his meetings. He let individual players know what he wanted from them in one-on-one meetings, and if he was disappointed, he let them know behind closed doors.

He kept an even demeanor on the sidelines and thus, just by looking at Noll's face, fans were unable to tell if the Steelers were ahead by 10 points or down by 10.

Noll was not the master of the pregame speech, either. He rarely got emotional when talking to his team, as his usual topic was the specifics of the game plan for that particular week.

However, when the Steelers got ready to face the Raiders in the 1974 AFC Championship game, Noll told his players that Oakland head coach John Madden had said the "two best teams in the league" met the previous week when the Raiders had defeated the Dolphins in the divisional playoffs. He took that as an insult and he wanted his players to do so as well.

Noll's team responded to that salt in the wound by beating the Raiders 24-13 in the Oakland Coliseum, and that allowed the Steelers to go to their first Super Bowl.

They dispatched a powerful and athletic Minnesota Vikings team with relative ease in registering a 16-6 win in Super Bowl IX.

In that game, and three other Super Bowl triumphs, Noll had his team mentally prepared and physically ready. "One thing about Chuck is that he was all business," said Hall of Fame defensive back Mel Blount. "It was a different era back then, as we didn't have the kind of media that followed every move.

"But I don't think it would have mattered because Chuck was so single-minded. He was only interested in getting us ready to play and understanding what the opponent was going to do. He was not interested in showing his hand to anyone else or creating an image. He just wanted to give us a chance to play our best game, and he did that nearly every week."

Noll's Steelers won nine AFC Central titles in addition to their four Super Bowl victories. The Steelers would win 10 or more games for seven out of eight seasons from 1972 through 1979.

Noll may have felt proud of himself in his private moments, but he was never one for self-congratulatory remarks.

"There was a good reason for that," Noll said to me in a 1990 interview. "There was always an opponent coming up and we always had future goals. No matter what game we won, that game was in the past as soon as it was over. You had to prepare for your next opponent. If you took time to say how great you were, there was always somebody ready to outwork you. I couldn't let that happen."

That philosophy allowed Noll to turn a franchise around and help the Steelers become one of the most respected organizations in all of sports.

For the record

Chuck Noll
Hall of Fame, 1993
Regular-season record: 194-143-1, .566
Postseason record: 16-8, .667
Four Super Bowl victories

#9

JOHN MADDEN

To millions of football fans, John Madden was the most memorable of all color commentators that has ever been seen on any NFL broadcast.

To millions of other fans, his Madden football video game is the best recreational video in the history of the medium.

Yes, Madden has proven to be a wildly successful businessman away from the game of football and a supersized personality who thrived for decades on the small screen. However, it's safe to say that none of those other ventures would have amounted to very much had he not been one of the game's greatest coaches.

Madden did not coach a long time—just ten years as the head coach of the Oakland Raiders—but he led with vision, consistency, and a strategic know-how that few coaches have ever matched.

Let's start off with the cold, hard facts. Madden coached the Raiders from 1969 through 1978. Among coaches who led their teams for 100 games or longer, Madden has the best winning percentage (.763) of all time (Vince Lombardi ranks second in that category). His Raiders won the first Super Bowl in the franchise's history, capturing Super Bowl IX with a convincing 32–14 victory over a strong Minnesota Vikings team.

His teams tallied a 103–32–7 record, and the Raiders teams played with a remarkable consistency. Madden excelled at diagnosing his team's strengths and then isolating them against their opponents. His strategic abilities often proved the difference between winning and losing throughout his tenure.

When Madden looked at film of his opponents prior to a game, he would not spend hours and hours trying to get to know his opponents. He looked for their weaknesses, so he could decide how to attack.

If he determined that the Raiders' opponents had problems in coverage, his game plan would feature Daryle Lamonica or Ken Stabler throwing over the top to receivers like Fred Biletnikoff or Cliff Branch. If he thought a team had problems stopping the run, he would have Clarence Davis, Mark van Eeghen, and Pete Banaszak soften them up with interior runs.

It was a simple process and Madden rarely got it wrong.

In addition to his strategic abilities, Madden was one of the best motivators of all time. At the time that he became a head coach in 1969, the head coach was usually a tough-minded disciplinarian who did not accept questions from his players or assistant coaches.

Madden was perhaps the forerunner of the modern coach. He was a great communicator who wanted to know what his players thought, and he was not going to threaten their jobs on a regular basis.

If he had to get tough to get his point across, he would do it. However, that was not the way Madden regularly did his business. He wanted his players to be happy, loose, and relaxed so they could play their best football.

The Raiders did things differently and were known for breaking molds. Madden's coaching style was a perfect match for owner Al Davis's "Just Win, Baby" philosophy.

"That's what it was all about," Madden explained during a 2005 interview. "That's why professionals play football and that's why coaches coach at the pro level—to win. Some guys get caught up in trying to show that they are the boss. I never understood it. We only wanted to win games and championships, and I never thought that yelling at guys was the best way to go about it. I still don't."

Madden's attitude and approach had a lot to do with the Raiders' fun-loving and rambunctious team personality. While other teams had dress codes when they went on the road and lengthy rules, Madden didn't push that on his players. He had two rules: Show up on time and play hard.

If players did that, Madden was happy.

Madden was a sharp assistant coach for the Raiders prior to being named head coach. The Raiders had fallen short in the 1968 AFL Championship game against the New York Jets, and that defeat was impossible for Davis to live with.

He did not think that the team had played its best game under John Rauch, and he fired his coach and brought in Madden to lead the team.

Madden was thirty-three years old at the time, and the youngest head coach in the game by a wide margin. Nevertheless, Madden was comfortable in the job from the start, and the Raiders remained competitive without any hiccups.

The Raiders were 12-1-1 in Madden's first season, and they appeared to be the best team in the AFL by a wide margin. They pummeled the Houston Oilers in the first round of the AFL play-offs, and that set up a meeting with the Kansas City Chiefs in the final AFL Championship game.

The Raiders had beaten the Chiefs in both of their regular-season meetings, and it seemed like they would be able to roll past them in the title game. However, veteran Kansas City coach Hank Stram and quarterback Len Dawson led the defensively sound Chiefs to a 17-7 victory. Kansas City recorded a 23-7 victory over the Vikings in Super Bowl IV, and that moment helped Madden stay focused throughout the rest of his coaching career.

He knew that a successful regular season was a wonderful achievement, but it didn't guarantee anything when a team got to the play-offs. Madden did not measure himself or his team by how many regular-season games the Raiders won. He wanted the championship, and that meant playing their best football in the postseason.

However, the Raiders had two problems. In the early 1970s, Don Shula's Miami Dolphins was the best team in the sport. Shortly after the Dolphins won back-to-back championships, the Pittsburgh Steelers started to assert their dominance.

The Raiders were nearly equal to both teams, but they suffered tough losses to both of those opponents. They lost to the Dolphins in the 1973 AFC Championship game, and they suffered a series of painful defeats to the Steelers in the divisional playoffs or in the conference championship game.

The most famous of those came in 1972, in the so-called "Immaculate Reception" game. The Raiders and Steelers engaged in a brutal defensive struggle on a nasty, cold day in Pittsburgh. The Raiders trailed 6-0 until late in the fourth quarter, when Stabler broke away down the sidelines and scored on a thirty-yard run.

When the Steelers were getting shut down on the next possession, it appeared the Raiders would walk out of Three Rivers Stadium with a 7-6 victory. However, on a fourth-and-long play, Pittsburgh quarterback Terry Bradshaw threw up a miracle—and his prayer was answered. His off-target pass ricocheted off defensive back Jack Tatum (and perhaps off Pittsburgh's John "Frenchy" Fuqua), and into the arms of Franco Harris.

The Steelers running back caught the ball off of his shoe tops and somehow raced into the endzone for the game-winning score.

It took nearly twenty minutes for the officials to determine that Harris's touchdown was legitimate, and many believed that only happened because they thought their lives would be at risk if they reversed the touchdown.

It was a defeat that Madden never got over.

But while that loss seared his soul and remained in his heart, Madden's team continued to win. They finally reached their peak during the 1976 season, when they were overpowering in building a 13-1 record.

Madden wasn't overly impressed with his team's regular-season record, but when they defeated the New England Patriots 24-21 in the divisional playoffs—a controversial win that went the Raiders' way—and the Steelers in the AFC title game, they had earned a spot in the Super Bowl.

It would be the team's first trip to the big game since Super Bowl II, and Madden knew his team was not going to let the opportunity pass.

They had beaten the Steelers on the biggest stage, and while Bud Grant had a fine team in Minnesota and a Hall of Fame quarterback in Fran Tarkenton, the Vikings were simply no match.

The Raiders' offensive line, led by Gene Upshaw and Art Shell, simply obliterated Minnesota's famous Purple People Eaters. The Raiders ran the ball with ease, made big plays through the air, and dominated on defense.

It was Madden's crowning moment.

"That's what you live for as a coach," Madden said. "You have a team, you know your goal, and you go out and achieve it against the best competition in the world. There could not be a better feeling in your professional life."

Madden coached two more seasons before deciding to retire. He had taken his team to the mountaintop, and he would leave the sidelines.

Madden broadcasted the game for far longer than he had coached, but there's no doubt that he was one of the game's greats during the ten years he roamed the sidelines for the Raiders.

For the record

John Madden
Hall of Fame, 2006
Regular-season record: 103-32-7, .763
Postseason record: 9-7, .563
One Super Bowl victory

#10

GEORGE HALAS

No individual had more to do with the existence and growth of professional football than George Stanley Halas did.

Halas was one of the founding members of the American Professional Football Association, and he was at the initial meeting at Ralph Hay's Hupmobile showroom in Canton, Ohio in 1920. From that point on, Halas either made or was involved in every key decision concerning the National Football League for the next forty-seven years.

Halas started with the Decatur Staleys in 1920, and the team moved to Chicago a year later. By 1922, the team was called the

Bears, and Halas had a number of partners until 1932, when he acquired complete ownership of the team.

Halas had four different coaching stints with the Bears, and each of them was quite successful. He coached them from 1920 through 1929, and stepped down that year when arguments with his partner Dutch Sternaman grew so frequent that he agreed to step aside from his coaching duties until they could be worked out.

Halas's teams had nine winning seasons in their first ten years, and they won their only championship of that decade in 1921.

After Halas gained full control of the team, he returned to the sidelines in 1933. He coached another ten years, and his teams won NFL championships in 1933, '40, and '41. All of those seasons were winning ones for the Bears, but he left the team after five games of the 1942 season because he went into the Navy.

He did not return until the 1946 season, and this time he remained coach through 1955, another ten-year stint. The Bears won their fifth championship under Halas in his first season back, but he endured back-to-back losing seasons in 1952 and '53.

Halas had gotten the Bears back on a winning track in 1954 and '55, but he felt it was time to step down after that season. Paddy Driscoll was his successor, and Halas saw the Bears reach the NFL Championship game in 1956 from afar, but they lost the title. When the Bears endured a losing season in 1957, Halas couldn't take being away from coaching the team any longer and returned to the sidelines.

He had one more ten-year stint, as he coached the team from 1958 through the 1967 season. Halas and the Bears would win a sixth title in 1963, and that would be his last hurrah as a head coach.

But while forty years of being a head coach in the NFL is an overwhelming legacy by itself, there is so much more to this man who had a hand in so many key decisions for the NFL.

His two most memorable championship teams came in 1940 and 1963. In 1939, he brought in Clark Shaughnessy to upgrade the Bears' offense, which had grown stale. He also acquired Sid Luckman to play quarterback for the Bears.

The combination of Halas, Shaughnessy, and Luckman turned out to be a brilliant one, as the Bears went 8-3-0 and won the NFL's West Division, finishing 1 ½ games ahead of the Green Bay Packers. Their last loss of the regular season had been a 7-3 defeat at the hands of the Washington Redskins.

Washington went 9-2 and won the East Division, and they appeared to be the better team when they met in Griffith Stadium for the NFL Championship. But the Bears had a surprise in store for the Redskins, as they eschewed their old single-wing formation and came out with the T-formation.

The Redskins were bollixed and confused on the defensive end and the Bears ran roughshod over them in a 73-0 victory. That remains the most one-sided triumph in NFL and championship game history.

Ten players combined for eleven touchdowns that day, as Halas and the Bears ushered the NFL into the modern era.

Halas had put together a defensive juggernaut in the early 1960s. The Bears had finished third in the West Division in 1962 with a 9-5 record, behind the 13-1 Green Bay Packers and the 11-3 Detroit Lions. Halas knew his team had a difficult assignment in front of them, because the Packers won the championship that year and there were no signs of weakness.

But the Bears had a defense that featured Doug Atkins, Bill George, and Ed O'Bradovich and an excellent supporting cast that took pleasure in not only stopping their opponents, but also pounding them unmercifully. The offense could not match the defense's intensity, but tight end Mike Ditka and wideout Johnny Morris gave them enough firepower to be a threat.

The Bears went 11-1-2 in '63, as they beat the Packers twice and took the division by ½ game over their rivals. Their only loss came at San Francisco in Week 6, and they had back-to-back ties in Weeks 11 and 12 against the Pittsburgh Steelers and Minnesota Vikings.

When they hosted the Giants in the NFL Championship game at Wrigley Field on a four-degree day, the Bears were in top form. The Giants opened the scoring on a fourteen-yard touchdown pass from Y. A. Tittle to Frank Gifford, but the Bears stopped New York from reaching the end zone after that and got two rushing touchdowns from quarterback Bill Wade to pull out a 14-10 win.

Halas still had energy after that win, but his team could not keep up with Vince Lombardi's Packers after that. Halas finally decided to call an end to his forty-year coaching career when he got angry at the officials in his last season.

Halas was known for his feisty attitude and cantankerous demeanor. Ditka, after a failed contract negotiation with Halas, said he "threw nickels around as if they were manhole covers."

But while Halas may have been frugal in his negotiations, he was a man who took care of his old friends and teammates, and was incredibly charitable.

Halas was more of a protector than a catalyst for NFL growth. He abhorred the idea of expansion, because that meant that more competitors would get more of a share of the NFL's income, and he never wanted to cut any more pieces of pie.

However, when the American Football League formed, he finally relented on expansion because the new league would have been able to command cities that the NFL wanted for itself.

Halas loved to say no to many proposals and ideas, but he did give his stamp of approval to Pete Rozelle when the league chose the brash public relations guru to be its commissioner in 1960. Rozelle, to his credit, never gave in to Halas after he became commissioner, and his strength in standing up to Halas won him respect around the league, and begrudgingly, from Halas.

Halas had many coaching rivals over the years, but his two most notable rivals were Curly Lambeau and Vince Lombardi in Green Bay.

Halas and Lambeau feuded famously, but despite their personal animus, Halas was instrumental in helping Lambeau get funding for City Field in Green Bay.

On the other hand, Halas loved and respected Lombardi, and the two embraced regularly after games and at league functions.

Lombardi said the only man who he called coach was Halas.

Halas ran the Bears after his coaching days ended, but when his son George "Mugs" Halas Jr. died of a heart attack in 1979, it was a brutal blow for Halas. He had wanted his son to take over for him.

Halas remained in control of the Bears until he died in 1983. One of his last major acts was to hire Ditka as his head coach, and it was a move that would help the Bears win their only Super Bowl following the 1985 season.

Although he passed away more than three decades ago, Halas's imprint remains all over the franchise and the NFL. He is truly one of the most influential figures in the history of North American professional sports.

For the record

George Halas
Hall of Fame, 1963
Regular-season record: 318-148-31, .682
Postseason record: 6-3, .667
Six NFL championships

#11

TOM COUGHLIN

There is little doubt that Tom Coughlin has both the credentials and the longevity to have earned a spot as one of the top coaches the NFL has ever seen.

But even more compelling than his achievements—he took a second-year expansion team to the AFC Championship game and he has won two Super Bowls with the New York Giants—is the personality change that Coughlin went through that allowed him to connect with his players.

That connection was likely the key that helped the Giants go from a talented team that tended to fade in key games to one that played its best football in the most important games.

Coughlin had started his coaching career as a college assistant and had made his most important stops at Syracuse and Boston College. During his time at Boston College, he had helped develop Doug Flutie into one of the most dangerous and charismatic quarterbacks in the nation.

That performance helped Coughlin earn a job as an assistant on the Philadelphia Eagles staff, but the players there did not embrace him. Coughlin was a demanding assistant who made sure that the athletes did things the right way on the practice field and never cut corners. Veterans referred to him as "Technical Tom," and they were relieved when he left Philadelphia after his second season in 1985 and moved on to Green Bay.

After two years with the Packers, Coughlin was hired by Bill Parcells, and he played a key role as the Giants won Super Bowl XXV over Buffalo following the 1990 season. Coughlin went on to become head coach at Boston College, and he helped turn the Eagles into a winning program.

Meanwhile, the Giants wanted Coughlin back as their head coach. Parcells had left the team in 1991 due to health concerns, and the Giants were unhappy with Ray Handley at head coach. They fired Handley and asked Coughlin to take his position, but he remained at Boston College for another year.

Then, when the NFL expanded to Jacksonville in 1995, Coughlin became the Jaguars' first head coach. It was expected that the Jaguars would follow the pattern of most expansion teams and suffer for several seasons with losing records and ill-equipped players, but Coughlin was not willing to go that route.

He gave many unproven veterans a chance to show that they could play, he drafted wisely, and he crafted a resourceful team. The Jaguars went 4–12 that first season, but they were ready to win games the following year.

Inexplicably, the Jaguars went 9–7 that season and earned a spot in the playoffs as an AFC wild-card team. They came into the playoffs with a five-game regular-season winning streak, and while that was impressive, few expected anything but a blowout when they went to Buffalo for their first playoff game.

The Jaguars fell behind by 7-0 and 14-7 margins, but the combination of quarterback Mark Brunell's passing and Natrone Means's running allowed the Jaguars to hang in with the Bills and they eventually pulled out a 30-27 victory.

The Jaguars were undaunted, and the coach pushed his team even harder as they went to Denver to take on the heavily favored Broncos. The Jaguars would fall behind by two touchdowns, but there was no give-up. The Jaguars roared back and shocked the Broncos by another 30-27 margin.

While the Jags were stopped by the Patriots in the AFC Championship game, based on the team's success, Coughlin had demonstrated that he was a formidable NFL.

Jacksonville would win eleven or more games during the next three seasons and get back to the AFC Championship game in 1999 after going a remarkable 14-2. However, they lost that title game to the Titans, and that was the end of Coughlin's hopes of getting to the Super Bowl with the Jaguars, who faded badly over the next three seasons, when the team's talent level diminished and players started to tune out their demanding coach.

Coughlin's run in Jacksonville came to an end with a 6-10 season in 2002, but he was rested and recharged when the Giants came back to him in 2004. New York had a talented team, but the Giants had been undisciplined under Jim Fassel. Coughlin quickly changed that with his hard-nosed rules and militaristic manner.

After a 6-10 season in his first year with the Giants in 2004, he turned things around quickly and they won the NFC East with an 11-5 record in 2005. They appeared to be in position for a decent playoff run, but the Giants were flat and were shut out at home by the Carolina Panthers 23-0.

The following season, the Giants slipped to 8-8, but they still managed to get into the playoffs and they were once again beaten in the first round. Coughlin's approach was wearing thin on a lot of key players and while most tried to keep their differences in house, veteran running back Tiki Barber made no attempt to hide his displeasure with the demanding coach.

While Coughlin initially dug his heels in when he got wind of the players' displeasure, a one-on-one conversation with Giants defensive end and leader Michael Strahan helped Coughlin relate to the players. Strahan urged Coughlin to show a more human side, and the plea worked during the 2007 season.

The Giants came together as the season progressed and they made the playoffs again as a wild-card team. But this time, they were energized as the postseason got underway and they reeled off road wins over Tampa Bay and Dallas to earn a spot in the NFC Championship game against the Packers.

Few expected the Giants to survive a game against Brett Favre in bitterly cold and brutal wind-chill conditions, but the Giants hung in there and forced the game into overtime. Coughlin resembled an icicle as the game concluded with New York placekicker Lawrence Tynes drilling a 47-yard field goal to win the game.

Coughlin had finally taken his team to the Super Bowl, and he had survived frozen Hell to get a shot at the undefeated New England Patriots. The Patriots were playing for a place in history as only the second undefeated World Champions of the Super Bowl era, and they had defeated the Giants in the regular-season finale that year.

But New York conceded nothing to Bill Belichick's Patriots, and the Giants trailed just 14-10 in the fourth quarter. They came through on their final drive, thanks to a spectacular throw and catch from Eli Manning to David Tyree, and the Giants upset the Pats 17-14 when Manning concluded the come-from-behind effort with a touchdown pass to angular wideout Plaxico Burress.

Four years later, the Giants and the Patriots met in the Super Bowl again, and New England remained the heavy favorite. The Giants played harsh defense and held New England in check throughout, and that allowed Coughlin and his players to come away with a 21–17 victory.

Strahan retired shortly after the first Super Bowl win over the Patriots, and he said Coughlin's personality change was the key reason for the success. "Sometimes people change a little bit here and there," Strahan said. "That's pretty much what I expected with Tom. But it was a dramatic change and he showed the players a completely different side, and it had a huge impact on his players."

Coughlin always understood how to formulate a game plan and what kind of attributes players needed to be successful. But until he could reach and relate to his players on an emotional level, he had no chance of being successful. Once that changed, the Giants won two Super Bowls.

They proved to be incredible road warriors, playing only one home game in those two championship runs.

Coughlin has remained head coach of the Giants through this book's printing (mid-2015). Though things have not gone as well for the Giants since their second victory over the Pats, Coughlin's legacy has nevertheless been fulfilled by his 2–0 record in the Super Bowl.

For the record

Tom Coughlin
Regular-season record: 164-140-0, .539
Postseason record: 12-7, .632
Two Super Bowl victories

#12

TONY DUNGY

For years, Tony Dungy appeared to be waiting for his opportunity to become head coach of an NFL team.

He served a long apprenticeship, becoming the youngest assistant coach in the league when he was hired by Chuck Noll as defensive backs coach for the Steelers in 1981. Dungy was able to rise to the defensive coordinator position within three years.

He later coached defensive backs for Marty Schottenheimer in Kansas City and then went with Dennis Green to Minnesota, where he was the defensive coordinator.

It seemed that Dungy was regularly mentioned as the top head coaching candidate among assistants who were looking to take that step up, but he often had a hard time getting interviews or serious consideration. Race appeared to be a factor, because every spot where Dungy had coached, players and other coaches marveled at his demeanor, preparation, communication ability, and teaching talent.

Eventually, Dungy got his opportunity to become a head coach when he was hired by the Tampa Bay Bucs in 1996. At that point, Tampa was a woeful organization. Prior to hiring Dungy, they had lost ten or more games in twelve of their previous thirteen seasons.

The first year was a difficult one for Dungy, as he had been anointed by the fans and media as something of a miracle worker when he took the job since so many of his coaching associates and former players had so many glowing things to say about him.

However, there were no miracles when he took the job with the Bucs. Dungy had a plan for the team to improve, but it did not include any quick fixes.

His team lost its first five games in 1996 before beating the Vikings for their first victory, but then lost three more games in a row to fall to 1-8. The last of those games was against the Chicago Bears. The Bucs dropped a 13-10 decision in Chicago even though they outplayed the Bears from a statistical point of view, and after the game the media surrounded Dungy in the cramped and steamy Soldier Field locker room.

Question after accusatory question was hurled at Dungy, and he handled each and every one of them in a calm and thoughtful manner. It was a situation that almost certainly would have caused many coaches to crack and get explosively angry, but Dungy knew what he was doing and he was not going to let a few setbacks upset him.

That calm demeanor started to rub off on his team, as the Bucs started to play much more efficient and mistake-free football. After that miserable start, the Bucs went 5-2 to close the season and served notice that their days of losing ten or more games every year were over.

The following season, the Bucs went 10-6 in the NFC Central and earned a spot in the playoffs as an NFC wild-card team. The Bucs beat the Lions 20-10 in the playoff game and held Detroit running back Barry Sanders in check.

The newly confident Bucs had designs on playing for the NFC Championship, but those dreams went out the window when Tampa Bay suffered a 21-7 loss at Green Bay in the divisional playoffs. The Packers would go on to beat the Carolina Panthers in the NFC Championship game and the New England Patriots in the Super Bowl.

Dungy had built a formidable defense with the Bucs in just two seasons, and they were regarded as perhaps Green Bay's most legitimate challenger. Players like Warren Sapp, Derrick Brooks, Hardy Nickerson, John Lynch, and Brad Culpepper had given the Bucs' defense a nasty edge that had been missing for years.

The Bucs slipped a bit in 1998, but they were a playoff team for the next three years. They lost in the 1999 NFC Championship game to the St. Louis Rams in a game that they nearly stole away from the eventual Super Bowl champions.

However, they lost to the Philadelphia Eagles in the wild-card round in each of the next two seasons because the Tampa Bay offense had not made any progress. While Dungy had turned the Bucs around overall, he made no progress with their offensive players. He was fired after the 2001 season.

It didn't take long for the Indianapolis Colts to come calling and hire him as head coach. On paper, it seemed like a match that would work well.

Dungy was a proven master at teaching and implementing strong defensive game plans. The Colts already had one of the game's best quarterbacks in Peyton Manning, and their offense was prolific. All Dungy had to do was improve the defense and let the offense take care of itself. If he could do that, the Colts would be a perennial championship contender.

Life is never that simple in the NFL. At the very least, the competition is always making moves to get better, and Dungy found the competition to be formidable in the AFC.

The Colts had no easy path to the Super Bowl. Instead, they found worthy rivals and nasty opponents in Bill Belichick, Tom Brady, and the New England Patriots.

The Patriots would prove to be difficult roadblocks for Dungy, Manning, and the Colts. Indianapolis would make the playoffs and win ten or more games in each of Dungy's first four seasons at the helm of the Colts. However, they lost to the Patriots in the AFC Championship game in 2003 and the divisional playoffs in 2004.

The Pittsburgh Steelers stopped the Colts in the divisional playoffs in 2005, and there was a belief in Indianapolis that Dungy and Manning would never make it to the Super Bowl together, as a duo.

The 2006 season had a much different feel for the Colts, as they came roaring out of the gate with seven straight wins. They went to New England in Week 8, and it seemed likely that their winning streak would come to an end in Foxboro against their archrivals. However, the Colts played a sensational game and defeated the Patriots 27-20 behind a 326-yard, two-touchdown effort from Manning.

The win gave the Colts the confidence they had been missing. As the Colts were enjoying their breakthrough season, Dungy went through the worst kind of personal crisis, as his oldest son committed suicide.

While nothing prepares any parent for that type of brutal pain, Dungy remained calm and in control, thanks to his spiritual and religious convictions.

He remained on the sidelines for the rest of the season, and the Colts defeated the Chiefs and Baltimore Ravens in the playoffs. A trip to the Super Bowl loomed if they could repeat their regular-season success and defeat the Patriots.

It looked like the season would once again end in heartbreak, as the Patriots built a 21-3 second-quarter lead. However, the Colts were undaunted as they came roaring back behind Manning's 349 total passing yards and ultimately secured a 38-34 win.

The Colts were going to the Super Bowl, where they would meet the Chicago Bears, who were coached by Dungy's former assistant Lovie Smith.

The two men were the first African-American coaches to lead their teams to the Super Bowl, and Dungy would get the best of his former student, as the Colts rolled to a 29-17 victory.

The win was the culmination of a sensational coaching career for Dungy. He coached the Colts to a 13-3 record in 2007 and a 12-4 mark in 2008, but they lost in the first round of the playoffs each time.

Dungy decided to retire after that '08 season. Dungy was an NFL head coach for thirteen years, went to the playoffs eleven times, and had just one losing season.

Dungy exhibited a serene confidence from the first day he stepped on the field to the last, and he always treated his players and fellow coaches with respect.

That peaceful strength became his legacy and helped make him one of the game's winningest coaches of all time.

For the record

Tony Dungy
Regular-season record: 139-69-0, .668
Postseason record: 9-10, .474
One Super Bowl victory

#13

SID GILLMAN

The fast-paced, high-powered passing game that is featured in today's NFL started in the fertile mind of Sid Gillman.

The Hall of Famer made a name for himself as the head coach of the powerful San Diego Chargers in the American Football League in the early 1960s, but the ideas for his high-powered, vertical passing game came when he was an end at Ohio State in the 1930s.

Francis "Close the Gates of Mercy" Schmidt was coaching the Buckeyes at the time, and he brought an explosive offense to Columbus. Once Gillman was done with his playing career, he decided to work with Schmidt as an assistant.

That's where Gillman developed his coaching ideas, and after working as an assistant coach at the University of Miami (Ohio) and Army, he got the chance to serve as head coach at the University of Cincinnati. He installed a highly evolved Split-T offense, and the Bearcats went 50-13-2 under Gillman.

The NFL took notice, and the Los Angeles Rams hired him as head coach in 1955. He brought them to the championship game against the Cleveland Browns in his first year, but his team suffered a 38-14 trouncing and never made it back to the championship game again, in his five-year tenure.

Gillman's 1958 team went 8-4, but he had a problem getting his message across to his players. Gillman was not very diplomatic in those days, and his personality rubbed many of his players the wrong way. He was very blunt with them, and Hall of Fame wide receiver Tom Fears criticized him for not getting his players to play hard for him, and accused him of "tearing down the franchise."

The Rams went 2-10 in 1959, and he was fired after that season.

But Gillman was able to get back on the horse quickly, because the American Football League went from Lamar Hunt's drawing board to an actual entity in 1960. Gillman accepted a head coaching job offer from the Los Angeles Chargers.

Gillman put all of his offensive theories into fruition with the Chargers, who would move to San Diego after one year in Los Angeles.

The Chargers were an early powerhouse in the wide-open league, winning the West Division in each of the AFL's first two seasons, but falling short in the championship game both times at the hands of the Houston Oilers.

The Chargers fell badly in 1962 and had a miserable 4-10 season, but Gillman was undaunted. He put together one of the best offensive teams of the 1960s the following year with Tobin Rote at quarterback, Paul Lowe and Keith Lincoln at running back, and the spectacular Lance Alworth at the wide receiver position.

The Chargers went 11-3 that season and scored 399 points during their fourteen-game season. They went into the AFL title game with full confidence against a Boston Patriots team that won the East Division with a 7-6-1 record after they beat the Buffalo Bills in a playoff game.

The Patriots simply did not have the weapons to compete with the Chargers, and San Diego rolled to a 51-10 win for the only title in the team's history.

At that point, the NFL barely recognized the AFL as anything but an annoyance, and the thought of the Chargers getting a chance to compete with the NFL champion Chicago Bears was not any consideration by NFL commissioner Pete Rozelle.

However, Gillman asked Rozelle for a chance to let his team play the Bears by sending him a telegram. Rozelle sent him a condescending dismissal.

That response helped solidify the AFL's competitive fire. From that point forward, the four-year-old league stopped thinking of itself as second-class and wanted to wage war against the NFL. That effort eventually paid off when the two leagues agreed to merge in 1966. The first championship game was played in 1967, and the AFL would play through the 1969 season before the NFL absorbed the AFL teams and divided into two conferences.

Many point to that '63 championship team that Gillman built as the igniter for the AFL's growth and ability to force the NFL's hand just a few years later.

Gillman's Chargers remained a strong team in the AFL after that, but they were eventually bypassed in the West by Al Davis's Oakland Raiders and Hank Stram's Kansas City Chiefs. The Chargers were equal to or better than the Raiders and Chiefs on offense, but they fell short on defense, and that's why they could not win another title game.

They made it back to the AFL Championship game in '64 and '65, but lost to the Buffalo Bills on both occasions. Jack Kemp, who got his start with the Chargers, led the Bills at quarterback, but Gillman eventually decided to go with Rote and the strong-armed John Hadl at quarterback.

Gillman seemed to be more obsessed with building an explosive and artistic offense than he was with winning championships, and that was his undoing. He would coach the Chargers intently, cutting a striking figure with his trademark bow ties on the sidelines.

Gillman had to leave the Chargers in 1969 due to a severe bout with ulcers, and he couldn't return to the team and reclaim his place as head coach until 1971. However, he did not have a hero's welcome when he returned. The Chargers were a mediocre football team at that point, and Gillman had a number of battles with team owner Gene Klein.

Gillman resigned after the first ten games of the season, and he left the team with a 4-6 record. The Chargers went into a tailspin shortly thereafter and struggled badly after he departed.

Still, he was one of the most respected strategists in professional football. Shortly after he left the Chargers, Tom Landry hired Gillman to be his quality control coach. The idea was that Gillman would study film and give Landry his game-plan suggestions based on the Cowboys' strengths and their opponents' weaknesses.

It didn't last long, and Gillman eventually became head coach of the Houston Oilers in 1973 and '74. The Oilers were an awful team when he took over four games into the 1973 season and went 1-9, but he was named coach of the year when he led that team to a 7-7 record the following season.

He stepped down after that, but remained in the game as an advisor and assistant coach at both the college and professional levels.

Gillman probably would not have thrived in the modern era when the bright lights of television and the media would have tracked his every step. He did not like to reveal much of his personality, other than the fact that he was obsessed by the game of football.

His ability to innovate on offense remained his passion for the remainder of his life. Gillman died in 2003, at the age of ninety-one.

For the record

Sid Gillman
Hall of Fame, 1983
Regular-season record: 122-99-7, .552
Postseason record: 1-5-0, .167
One AFL Championship

#14

JIMMY JOHNSON

Few coaches ever came into the NFL with more hype and hoopla than Jimmy Johnson did when he made his NFL debut in the 1989 season with the Dallas Cowboys.

All Johnson did was replace Tom Landry, who had coached every game for the Dallas Cowboys from their first season in 1960 through 1988. However, when Cowboys owner Bum Bright found himself in financial difficulties and put his team up for sale in 1989, he found an enthusiastic buyer in Jerry Jones.

Jones was an Arkansas-based oil millionaire, and he had dreamed of owning an NFL franchise. Once he got the keys to the car, he was not going to stand on ceremony and slowly warm to the task. He put his imprint on the Cowboys with the boldest possible move.

He fired Landry and he brought in Johnson as his head coach. The move was one that almost certainly had to be made because the Cowboys had grown stale in the final years of the Landry regime. However, Jones came across like an arrogant rube because of the callous way he dismissed Landry.

While the Cowboys had lost their way through the 1980s and it seemed clear that a change at the top was a good idea, Landry was one of the greatest coaches in NFL history and he deserved a bit of dignity.

Jones did not give it to him, and he was taken to task for that. One thing that Jones could not have been accused of was duplicity. He was direct in his approach and decisive in his move.

Johnson had been a top-level college coach at Oklahoma State, and that stint had prepared him for a run at national powerhouse Miami. He coached the Hurricanes to a national championship and the No. 2 position on two other occasions.

Johnson had also been a teammate of Jones when the two played college football together at Arkansas during the 1960s. The perception was that Jones hired his best buddy from college and they were going to attempt to turn the Cowboys back into an NFL power.

Johnson would do just that, but his level of friendship with Jones was greatly overstated. While they were tremendous "buddies" whenever they were on camera together, Jones's ingratiating nature tended to rub Johnson the wrong way. But the working relationship was a good one, and they brought the Cowboys back to prominence.

It wasn't an easy journey, as Johnson's first season in Dallas was a 1-15 disaster. But Johnson had a plan, and he was able to execute it when he was able to commandeer a trade with the Minnesota Vikings.

Early in that first season, he knew he had a team that wasn't going anywhere because the Cowboys didn't have enough good players who could contribute. However, they did have one brilliant asset in running back Herschel Walker, and Johnson knew that if he traded Walker he could get the kind of players who would help the Cowboys begin to climb up the NFL ladder.

He didn't know how much he could get for Walker, but he found a willing trade partner in Minnesota general manager Mike Lynn. Johnson made a complicated deal that involved trading Walker and several mid-to-late-round picks for Minnesota's first-round pick, six players, and six conditional draft picks.

When Johnson started waiving the players he acquired from Minnesota, that activated those conditional picks into actual draft picks. Johnson continued to move his picks on draft day, and eventually worked deals with fifteen different teams.

The Cowboys were able to remake their roster with talented young players. They already had wide receiver Michael Irvin, and Johnson was able to draft quarterback Troy Aikman and running back Emmitt Smith, and those "triplets" became the cornerstone of the Dallas offense.

The Cowboys made significant progress in 1990 when they nearly reached the .500 mark (7-9). NFC East opponents could see how strong the Cowboys were becoming and that they were going to be difficult to contend with in the years ahead.

The Cowboys made the playoffs as a wild-card team in 1991 with an 11-5 record, and won a playoff game against the Chicago Bears before they were defeated 38-6 by the Detroit Lions in the divisional playoffs.

That defeat steeled the Cowboys for a hard push from their head coach the next season. Johnson was a demanding task master who wanted to get the most out of his young, championship-caliber team. He threatened to bench or cut players any time he did not see a top effort being given on the field, and he carried out those threats without exception.

The Cowboys went 13-3, won the NFC East title, and were the odds-on favorite to roll through the playoffs. But Johnson was anything but a happy man. When his team lost a 20-17 late-season decision to the Redskins in Washington, Johnson ordered all his players to remain in their seats on the flight home and told the flight attendants not to serve food to any of his players.

His explosive temper was on display, and he did not want anyone to take their position on the team for granted. Two weeks later, the Cowboys closed the season with a 27-13 victory over Chicago, but the win was tarnished by sloppy play down the stretch that included two fumbles by backup running back Curvin Richards.

Richards was a talented athlete, but he had major issues holding onto the ball. Of all the sins a player could commit, Johnson thought nothing was worse than fumbling.

He was beside himself with anger after the game, and he cut Richards the next day. While that move was viewed as harsh from the outside, it helped Johnson make sure everyone on the team knew he was serious.

He was not impressed by a 13-3 record or a division title. He wanted a team that functioned smoothly and efficiently at all times, and he was not going to tolerate needless errors.

The Cowboys rolled by the Eagles in the divisional playoffs and beat the San Francisco 49ers 30-20 in the NFC Championship on the road.

That victory earned them a spot in Super Bowl XXVII at the Rose Bowl against the AFC Champion Buffalo Bills. Johnson knew he had the better team during Super Bowl week and that his players were superbly prepared for a maximum effort.

The normally high-strung Johnson was remarkably calm before the game, as his confidence was unshakable. Dallas pummeled the Bills by a 52-17 margin.

The Cowboys were nearly as good the following year and they once again beat Buffalo in the Super Bowl. While they were not quite as dominant as the year before, their 30-13 victory left little doubt that the Cowboys were the superior team.

The Cowboys were a dynasty, but when Jones tried to share the credit with Johnson, he was rebuffed and insulted by his coach. That was more than Jones could bear, and neither man could stomach working with the other any longer.

Johnson left the Cowboys "by mutual decision" and the Cowboys hired former Oklahoma coach Barry Switzer to take over.

The Cowboys eventually won a Super Bowl following the 1995 season under Switzer, but he received almost no credit for it because Johnson had left him with such a powerful roster.

Johnson returned to the NFL in 1996 and coached four more years with the Miami Dolphins, but he was unable to build a juggernaut in Miami.

Though he had a good team, his final game was a 62-7 playoff defeat to the Jacksonville Jaguars. It was an ignominious ending to a brilliant and tempestuous coaching career.

Johnson was more than happy to fade into the sunset, fishing in his boat off the Florida Keys and serving as an NFL analyst for the Fox network.

For the record

Jimmy Johnson
Regular-season record: 80-64-0, .566
Postseason record: 9-4, .692
Two Super Bowl victories

#15

MARV LEVY

The words have become his calling card. When Marv Levy was the coach of the Buffalo Bills, he would gather his team in the locker room, and look each of his players in the eye before a big game.

"Where else would you rather be, than right here and right now?" Levy would say, and those words would inevitably leave his team in a fired-up state.

But in many ways, Levy was an atypical head coach. He did not rule by fear and he was not known for his locker room talks to get his team prepared before a game or rally them when they were trailing at halftime.

Instead, he was a cerebral man who wanted to outthink and out-prepare his opponents. When it came to motivating his players, he was wont to do that with a single phrase or saying.

These were some of his favorites:

"It's not the will to win, it's the will to prepare."

"Persistence can change failure into extraordinary achievement."

"Football doesn't build character, it reveals it."

If ever Levy wanted to give a longer speech, he was partial to English poetry.

However, he was not going to march into the locker room and upbraid his players, question their manhood, and threaten their jobs. He was a gentleman football coach, an anomaly at a time when most coaches held long and demanding practices, treated their players like property, and paid any price in order for their teams to come away with a win.

Levy struggled throughout a large majority of his coaching career. Prior to being named as the Bills head coach in 1986, Levy had a five-year run in Kansas City from 1978 through 1982, and he had just one winning season before losing his job.

Levy was out of football for a year, but he returned at the professional level with the Chicago Blitz of the United States Football League. The Blitz had been coached previously by George Allen, and when he left to coach in Arizona, he took most of his players with him.

As a result, Levy's team had a 5-13 record, and both the team and the league eventually folded. Levy had worked with general manager Bill Polian in Chicago, and Polian came calling after he became general manager of the Buffalo Bills.

The Bills were stockpiling talent, and when Levy was hired in 1986, they were starting to get better. Levy's first two seasons in Buffalo saw the team improve and get better, but it didn't necessarily show in the record. The Bills were 2-7 after Levy took over in '86 and 7-8 in the strike-altered 1987 season.

But everything came together in 1988, as the Bills went 12-4 and finished first in the AFC East. The Bills defeated the Houston Oilers in their first playoff game before losing in the divisional playoffs to the Cincinnati Bengals, who would eventually make it to the Super Bowl.

The Bills had found their leader in quarterback Jim Kelly, and he had the kind of physical tools that all head coaches were looking for in their leaders. Kelly had the arm strength, quick release, and accuracy to become a great quarterback, but despite the team's record, Levy knew that something wasn't right.

Kelly had a 15-17 touchdown–interception ratio that season, and Levy knew that Kelly was simply much better than that. He was determined to make changes to his offense that would allow Kelly to join the ranks of the top quarterbacks in the game.

The biggest change came the following year when Levy hired mastermind Ted Marchibroda to become the team's offensive coordinator. Marchibroda, another thoughtful coach who rejected the typical football coach's mentality, redesigned the team's offense. He saw the talent the Bills had on offense with Kelly, running back Thurman Thomas, wide receiver Andre Reed, running back Kenneth Davis, and running back Ronnie Harmon, and he decided to up the tempo to put opposing defenses on their heels.

Levy had charged Marchibroda with designing a game plan that would help the Bills to become an offensive juggernaut, and he gave the Bills the "K-Gun" offense. While the Bills would not use this through the entire game, whenever they went to it, it seemed to throw opposing defenses into a state of panic.

"What you want to do as a coach is give your team a chance to be at its best," Levy said. "If it also puts the opponent at a disadvantage, that's a bonus. That's what we did with our K-Gun. I think it brought the best out of Jim, Thurman, and all the rest of our guys, and I don't think our opponents knew what to do. They knew we had options, and they couldn't figure out which option to stop first."

The Bills went 9-7 that season and won the division again, but they came into their own in 1990. They reeled off back-to-back 13-3 seasons in 1990 and '91, and went to the Super Bowl both years. While their record slipped to 11-5 in '92, they also won the AFC title that year and again in '93.

They went to the Super Bowl in four consecutive seasons, and they are the only team in NFL history to manage that feat. Unfortunately for Levy and his players, they lost all four of those Super Bowls.

They almost certainly should have won the first of those appearances when they faced the New York Giants in Super Bowl XXV.

That was the season that the Bills' offense was at its peak, as the Bills scored a league-best 428 points and gave up just 263, which was the sixth-best total in the league.

Kelly had a remarkable season, completing 63.3 percent of his passes for 2,829 yards and compiling a 24-9 touchdown-interception ratio. Thomas rushed for 1,297 yards and also caught 49 passes, while Andre Reed caught 71 passes and was a tremendous runner after the catch. On the defensive side, Bruce Smith had 19.0 sacks while linebacker Darryl Talley had a team-high 123 tackles.

The Bills beat the Dolphins 44-34 in the divisional playoffs, and registered a shocking 51-3 triumph over the Oakland Raiders in the AFC Championship game.

That victory left the Bills as heavy favorites to beat Bill Parcells's New York Giants, who came into the game with backup quarterback Jeff Hostetler under center because starter Phil Simms was injured.

The Giants knew they could not compete with the Bills' firepower, so they took the air out of the ball and tried to maximize each possession by working the clock with their running game.

That strategy served its purpose, as they held a 20-19 lead in the final seconds.

The Bills still had a chance, and if Scott Norwood could have connected on a 47-yard field goal on the Bills' final play, they would have won the game. While Norwood hit the ball squarely, it sailed wide to the right and the Bills were defeated in the game.

They went on to lose two Super Bowls to the Dallas Cowboys and one to the Washington Redskins. None of those games were close.

Obviously, the Super Bowl losses stung Levy and his players, but it didn't keep him from enjoying a Hall of Fame career. Levy would coach the Bills through the 1997 season before retiring from coaching.

The Bills have not been a consistent winner since Levy left, and the team continues to search for a coach who can find a winning formula in Western New York once again.

For the record

> **Marv Levy**
> Hall of Fame, 2001
> Regular-season record: 143-112-0, .561
> Postseason record: 11-8, .579
> Four AFC Championships

#16

BUD GRANT

Finally, he said yes.

The year was 1967, and Bud Grant had spent ten years in the Canadian Football League coaching the Winnipeg Blue Bombers. His team had played for six CFL titles and come away with the championship four times.

He knew, and the Minnesota Vikings knew, that he was ready to coach in the NFL. The Vikings had come calling previously. When the franchise had come into existence in 1961, Grant was asked to be the team's initial head coach. However, he knew he had a good thing going in Canada, and if he was good enough to be offered the job when he was thirty-four years old, he reasoned he would be good enough later on.

When the Vikings fired taciturn head coach Norm Van Brocklin in 1966, Grant was ready. The Vikings had the makings of a great team, and he knew he could bring out the best in them.

The first year was a struggle, as the Vikings finished the year with a 3-8-3 record, but after that the Vikings put winning season after winning season on the board. The Vikings went 8-6 in 1968, and made it to the playoffs for the first time when they won their last two games of the year—both on the road to the San Francisco 49ers and the Philadelphia Eagles—to earn a spot in the playoffs.

They were overmatched against the powerful Baltimore Colts, but they played a tough, close game before dropping a 24–14 decision.

That game may have lit the fuse for what followed. The Vikings had a 12-2 team in 1969, led by one of the best defensive lines in the history of the game.

That unit was comprised of Carl Eller, Allen Page, Gary Larsen, and Jim Marshall, and was nicknamed the Purple People Eaters. They played a devastating brand of football, and it was as if that unit took the baton handoff from the Los Angeles Rams' Fearsome Foursome and became the best defensive line in the game.

Offensively, the Vikings were ruffians. Running backs Bill Brown and Dave Osborne handled the bulk of the ground attack, but quarterback Joe Kapp was not afraid to take a hit or dish one out when he had the ball in his hands.

Kapp, another CFL import just like his coach, was not a classic pocket passer. In an era featuring some of the game's finest passers—Johnny Unitas, Sonny Jurgensen, Don Meredith, and John Brodie—Kapp was just as likely to throw a ball that traveled end over end as he was to throw a spiral.

It didn't matter to Grant or the Viking receivers as long as the ball got where it was supposed to go. The Vikings took on the personality of their defense and their quarterback as they rampaged through the NFL that year.

They also took on the image of their coach in Grant, who cut quite a memorable figure with his crew cut and chiseled features. Grant looked like the most serious man in the world and the image painted by the media was that of a tough guy who wanted things done his way … or else.

But image is not everything. Grant may have looked like he came directly out of central casting to coach a team in the heart of Minnesota's frozen tundra, but he was a thoughtful man who cared about his players as individuals and was more than willing to take part in a practical joke … or two.

He was serious about football, but he was not the kind of coach who would stay in his office for hours upon hours and demand the same things of his assistants. He wanted to do his job and do it well, and then he wanted to go home and enjoy his family and the great outdoors.

Early in the 1969 season, the Vikings served notice that it would be their year. They pounded the defending NFL champion Baltimore Colts in the second game of the season and that was the first of twelve straight wins. They wouldn't lose again until the regular-season finale against the Atlanta Falcons.

The Vikings were heavy favorites to dominate in the NFL playoffs and go on to represent the league in Super Bowl IV.

That's just what happened. The Vikings struggled before beating the Los Angeles Rams 23-20 in their first playoff game, but overpowered the Cleveland Browns 27-7 in the NFL Championship game. Kapp scored on a seven-yard run early in the game and then threw a seventy-five-yard touchdown pass later in the first quarter to Gene Washington, and the Vikings dominated from that point on.

The Super Bowl turned out to be a disaster. Minnesota was a double-digit favorite over the AFL's Kansas City Chiefs, and they were expected to dominate because of their supposed edge in toughness and skill.

The Chiefs would have none of it, and just like the Jets had done the year before to the Colts, they came into Tulane Stadium and shut down Grant's Vikings by a 23-7 margin.

Losing in the Super Bowl would unfortunately become a theme for the Vikings under Grant. They would make it back to the Super Bowl following the 1973 season, but Don Shula's Miami Dolphins would beat them in the second of their back-to-back championships. The following year, Minnesota would get another shot at the Super Bowl, but they had the misfortune of meeting the Pittsburgh Steelers.

Pittsburgh would become the team of the decade as they won four Super Bowls in the 1970s, and their first victim would be the Vikings.

Grant would get one more chance after the 1976 season, and they would meet another team in the Oakland Raiders that had been frustrated because they had never won a title despite their regular-season excellence in the AFC.

The Vikings, with Fran Tarkenton at quarterback, Chuck Foreman at running back, and wide receivers Ahmad Rashad and Sammy White, were a dynamic offensive team that could score in bunches. They still had the Purple People Eaters up front, and their defense was ferocious.

The Raiders, coached by John Madden and quarterbacked by Ken Stabler, were also loaded. The game had all the elements needed to become a classic.

However, the Raiders were loose and relaxed and played their best game. Grant's Vikings never found their rhythm, and they were badly outplayed. The Raiders pounded them physically and enjoyed a one-sided 32-14 triumph.

Grant's teams were winless in their four Super Bowl chances. While the Vikings fans were heartbroken, Grant was philosophical about the losses.

"You don't look back after any losing game," Grant said. "You look ahead. Life goes on. We never lost a conference championship game and we never lost when the Super Bowl was on the line."

Grant was admired and respected by his players. "Bud was one of the greatest coaches ever in the NFL," Foreman said. "He is a victim of the four losses we had in the Super Bowl, but that doesn't take away from the kind of coach he was. He told players what they needed to hear, not what they wanted to hear. He was fair with everyone, from the superstar to the guy on special teams. He treated every individual like a man."

Grant never brought home the Lombardi Trophy, but his record of consistency is matched by very few coaches. He knew how to get the most out of his players, and he did it without fail.

For the record

> **Bud Grant**
> Hall of Fame, 1994
> Regular-season record: 158-96-5, .622
> Postseason record: 10-12, .455
> One NFL Championship, Three NFC Championships

#17

JOE GIBBS

W hen the Washington Redskins hired Joe Gibbs to be their head coach prior to the 1981 season, it was not a move that had a big impact around the NFL. Gibbs had been an offensive coordinator with the high-powered San Diego Chargers, and while that team was lighting up scoreboards throughout the league, it was difficult to give Gibbs more than a minimal share of the credit.

The Chargers were loaded with talent on the offensive side of the ball with Dan Fouts at quarterback, and receivers like John Jefferson and Kellen Winslow. Gibbs certainly was helping these players, but they were great players on their own. Additionally, head coach Don Coryell had earned a reputation as one of the most thoughtful offensive-minded head coaches in the game, and he deserved quite a bit of credit for San Diego's explosive offense.

But the Redskins knew that Gibbs was smart, organized, and had been successful. They were willing to give him a chance to get their once-glorious franchise going in the right direction.

It was a rough start for Gibbs in the 1981 season, as they dropped their first five games and looked awful in the process. However, Gibbs kept an even keel and did not come close to losing his cool. He was confident that his team would learn the offense he was teaching and would get used to his coaching style.

It didn't take long for that to happen. As inconsistent as they had been in the early part of the season, the Redskins were the most improved team in the league by the end of the season, when they finished 8-8.

Quarterback Joe Theismann learned and adapted to Gibbs's offense, and he proved to be the ideal triggerman to lead the Redskins.

There were no missteps in the 1982 season, although that year the NFL was torn apart by a players strike and the season was shortened to nine games. The Redskins were the best team in the NFC with an 8-1 record, and that earned them the top seed in the NFL's post-season tournament.

They registered convincing postseason victories over the Detroit Lions, Minnesota Vikings, and Dallas Cowboys, and that earned Gibbs's team a spot in the Super Bowl vs. Don Shula's Miami Dolphins.

It could have been a spot for a second-year head coach to feel like he was in over his head, since Shula had already earned a reputation as one of the best coaches in the game's history.

"I suppose I could have been intimidated," Gibbs said. "But I wasn't blocking or tackling Don Shula. I knew I had all the talent I needed on my side and there was no way we wouldn't come up with a great effort against them. I didn't know how it would turn out, but I knew we had the team to compete for 60 minutes."

That's just what the Redskins did, and they came away with a 27-17 victory over the Dolphins in Super Bowl XVII. The Redskins had tremendous balance with Theismann throwing to wide receivers Art Monk and Charlie Brown, and John "Diesel" Riggins running it.

Riggins gave the Redskins the lead in the fourth quarter and took the heart out of the Dolphins with his 43-yard touchdown run.

The Super Bowl would be the first of three Gibbs would win with the Redskins, and he is the only coach to do it with three different quarterbacks. Gibbs's abilities as an offensive innovator made him one of the game's superior minds and it earned him Hall of Fame status in 1996.

Gibbs had developed his offensive philosophies while coaching under Coryell, but he added several of his own innovations.

Gibbs basically invented the position of the H-back position and he also popularized the one-RB set. He wanted to use his bigger, stronger offensive line to get his team's power running game going, and then he wanted to fool opponents with his "trips" and "bunch" formations that made it difficult for opponents to cover Washington's open receivers.

His technical superiority when it came to offensive strategy gave the Redskins a big edge on most opponents, even if the opposition was a more talented team.

Gibbs's goal as a gameplanner was to force the opposition to think about what the Redskins were going to do instead of just playing their game. "Offensively, I wanted to dictate the pace of the game," Gibbs said. "I want to use a fast-paced offense because that makes our team more aggressive and it forces the defense to react to what we were doing."

Gibbs won his other two Super Bowls with Doug Williams and Mark Rypien at quarterback. Each of his three quarterbacks had different strengths, and that speaks to Gibbs's abilities as a head coach.

Theismann was certainly the most accomplished of the three, but Williams had one of the strongest arms of any quarterback to play the game, while Rypien was a mountain of a man who was capable of absorbing big hits from the pass rush and not going down to the ground.

After his third Super Bowl championship following the 1991 season, Gibbs coached one more year before retiring.

After he left the game, Gibbs set up a NASCAR racing team, and he was also successful in that field, as he won three NASCAR cup series championships.

He seemed to be as far away from the NFL as he could possibly be, but Gibbs still maintained an interest in the game as a fan. He thought his coaching days were long over, but new Washington owner Daniel Snyder courted him on a nonstop basis and basically begged him to return to the team.

Gibbs finally relented, and he returned for his second tour of duty with the team in 2004—eight years after he had been named to the Hall of Fame.

The NFL was a much different world in 2004, and Gibbs did not get immediate results, as Washington was a 6-10 team that season. However, Gibbs seemed to have a bit of magic left, as the Redskins improved to 10-6 in 2005, and then made the playoffs.

While they beat Tampa Bay in the wild-card game, they dropped a 20-10 decision when they had to go to Seattle for a divisional playoff game.

The Redskins could not maintain that momentum, as they slipped to 5-11 the following year, which was the worst record of Gibbs's coaching career. They bounced back a bit with a 9-7 record in 2007 that earned them a spot in the postseason, but they got manhandled by the Seahawks once again in the playoffs.

That proved to be the end of Gibbs's career, as he made a final decision to retire.

Throughout his career, Gibbs had proven to be one of the top offensive minds of the game. It can be argued that Gibbs is at the top of the coaching chain when it comes to offensive innovation, and his three Super Bowl titles cement that status.

For the record

Joe Gibbs
Hall of Fame, 1996
Regular-season record: 154–94–0, .621
Postseason record: 17–7, .708
Three Super Bowl victories

#18

DON CORYELL

Don Coryell wanted to do one thing when he coached in the NFL. He wanted to attack with the passing game and confound opponents with his team's ability to score points in bunches.

Few coaches have ever had the kind of success at installing, developing, and fine-tuning the passing game that Coryell had, first with the St. Louis Cardinals and then the San Diego Chargers.

Today's NFL has largely followed the blueprint that Coryell was responsible for developing in the 1970s. When it came to movement, deception, multiple formations, and vertical pass patterns, Coryell's offense had it all.

"I believe in wide open offense," Coryell said when he was hired by the Cardinals prior to the 1973 season. "I like to throw the ball and I want to attack."

There was never a day in his coaching career that he was not true to his beliefs. He helped transform the unglamorous and ordinary Cardinals into one of the most exciting teams in the league and later turned the Chargers into one of the most explosive teams in NFL history.

Coryell was all about offense, and his attention to defense was not quite what it could have been. That's one of the reasons that his teams would often contend and get to the playoffs, but fail once they got there.

Coryell got a chance to develop his offensive philosophies at the college level first, as the coach at San Diego State. He knew his teams could not compete with national powers like UCLA and USC, so he built a dynamic passing game that often confused opposing defenses.

Coryell also proved adept at developing talented players and coaches. Quarterbacks Brian Sipe and Dennis Shaw came out of his program, as did wide receivers Gary "The Ghost" Garrison, Isaac Curtis, and Haven Moses. He also had top coaches like John Madden and Joe Gibbs on his staff.

When the Cardinals came calling in 1973, he needed a year to get his team turned around and to learn his offense. By 1974, the Cardinals had become one of the most prolific offensive teams in the NFL. Quarterback Jim Hart was a resilient leader and a rubber-armed passer, and he received magnificent protection from an offensive line that included Dan Dierdorf and Conrad "Dirty" Dobler.

They went 10-4 in '74 and followed that with an 11-3 record in '75. They won the NFC East Division title in both years, edging out the Redskins and Cowboys, respectively. Getting the edge on those two powers who were coached by George Allen and Tom Landry, respectively, earned Coryell a tremendous amount of respect among coaches.

However, the Cardinals lost first-round playoff games each year, and that sent Coryell back to the drawing board. He wanted to turn the Cardinals into a true powerhouse, but he rarely got the backing he wanted from the Cardinals' management and ownership.

Coryell grew exasperated when owner Bill Bidwill failed to sign star receiver and returner Terry Metcalf to a fair contract, and that caused Metcalf to abandon the team for the CFL. Coryell's relationship with the team fell apart after that and he left the Cardinals following the '77 season.

He was immediately hired by the Chargers, and they quickly adhered to the principles of Coryell's offense and mastered them. With Dan Fouts at quarterback, the Chargers became the most explosive team in the league. They rolled to a 12-4 record that season, won the AFC West title, and scored 411 points in the process.

However, the Chargers suffered the same playoff failures that Coryell's teams in St. Louis had, as they dropped a 17–14 decision to the Houston Oilers, on their home turf in San Diego.

While criticism started to rain down on Coryell for his playoff failings, Coryell was not daunted and he continued to press forward with his high-powered offense. The 1980 Chargers won the AFC West title again, and this time Coryell finally got his playoff win when the Chargers got the best of the Buffalo Bills in the divisional playoffs.

However, they dropped the AFC Championship game at home to the Oakland Raiders when the visitors played shutdown defense in the second half and held the Chargers to a field goal in the fourth quarter. That enabled the Raiders to win the game and go to the Super Bowl, where they defeated the Philadelphia Eagles.

That was a game that Coryell always felt his team should have been in, because he believed the Chargers were good enough to come away with the title.

The following year, Coryell went a long way to ridding himself of the reputation that he could not win the big game. The Chargers won their third consecutive AFC West title and they scored 478 points in the process. Their offense featured Fouts throwing the ball to Charlie Joiner, Wes Chandler, and tight end Kellen Winslow. They also had two brilliant running backs in Chuck Muncie and James Brooks, and were basically unstoppable with the ball.

The Chargers met the Miami Dolphins at the Orange Bowl in the first round of the playoffs, and this time they were in top form in the postseason.

They jumped out to a 24-0 lead in the first quarter, and they appeared to be running the Dolphins out of their own stadium. But Don Shula's team was nothing if not resilient, and they came back to make it a game by halftime.

The second half was a back-and-forth affair, and the game went into sudden death overtime. While the Dolphins had their chance to come away with the win, Rolf Benirschke's field goal in the extra session allowed the Chargers to win the game and move on to the AFC Championship.

That playoff game is widely recognized as one of the greatest games in NFL history.

The AFC Championship game was another matter. The Chargers were forced to go to frigid Cincinnati to take on the Bengals in the title game. The wind chill reached minus-57 degrees Fahrenheit, and the San Diego offense was frozen solid. The Bengals easily survived and won the game 27-7.

That basically took the heart out of the Chargers. While they made the playoffs again in 1982, that was their last trip to the postseason under Coryell. He continued to coach into the 1986 season before he decided to call it a career.

Coryell's teams never got to the Super Bowl and were just 3-6 in the postseason. But his abilities to come up with an innovative offense made him one of the greatest coaches in the game's history.

Madden, Gibbs, and Fouts have all backed him to become a Hall of Famer. He has reached the semifinals in the voting process from 2011 through 2014, but he has still not been admitted to the Canton shrine.

"It's just wrong that Don isn't in the Hall of Fame," Madden said. "There are some things that just don't make sense, and this is one of them."

For the record

> **Don Coryell**
> Regular-season record: 111–83–1, .572
> Postseason record: 3-6, .333
> Five division championships

#19

WEEB EWBANK

W eeb Ewbank didn't look like a tough football coach, and he was not known for making demands of his players and asking them to do everything he told them to do.

Even though he coached in an era when football coaches were often tyrants who could not be questioned by their players or assistants, Ewbank was more of the thinking man's coach who brought out the best in his players and helped them achieve great things.

Ewbank led two teams to perhaps the most symbolic and important victories in the NFL. He led the Baltimore Colts to the 1958 NFL Championship in a game that has often been described as the greatest game in NFL history.

The Colts had a marvelous team in 1958 that featured Johnny Unitas at quarterback, Alan Ameche running the ball, Raymond Berry at wide receiver, and a destructive defense. The Colts finished 9–3 that season and won the West Division by a game over the Chicago Bears and Los Angeles Rams, who both finished 8–4.

They earned a spot in the NFL Championship game against the New York Giants, who had finished in a tie with the Cleveland Browns for first in the East Division. The Giants had emerged victorious in a playoff game to decide the title, and they hosted the Colts at Yankee Stadium in the title game.

It was a back-and-forth bruising affair, and the Giants appeared to be on their way to victory when Frank Gifford scored a fourth-quarter touchdown after taking a fifteen-yard pass from Charlie Conerly.

However, the Colts tied it on a late field goal by Steve Myhra, and the NFL had the first overtime game in its history.

Unitas led the Colts on a historic march in the extra session, and they pounded the ball down the field. Finally, he stuck the ball in Ameche's belly, and the big fullback pounded into the end zone from a yard out and the Colts earned the championship.

That game, more than any one single event, is considered to be the game that turned professional football into America's national sport. The game captured the nation's attention, and it translated so well to the audience viewing the game on television that it triggered a love affair between a nation's sports fans and the sport.

Ewbank would lead the Colts to the NFL championship again the following year, and they would remain a competitive team after that, but they were supplanted by the Green Bay Packers as the best team in the West.

The Colts fired Ewbank after the team went 7–7 in 1962, and the decision angered Ewbank. He felt like he was being blamed even though he had led the Colts to two titles and the team was capable of bouncing back and competing again. He had also helped develop Unitas into perhaps the game's best quarterback.

But Ewbank was not out of work for very long. The American Football League started play in 1960, and that meant that there were eight more opportunities for head coaches to gain employment. The worst of those teams may have been the New York Titans, who went bankrupt after the 1962 season.

However, the team did not stay insolvent very long, and it was rescued by businessman Sonny Werblin, who renamed the team as the Jets, and the first big move that he made was to hire Ewbank as his head coach.

Shortly after hiring Ewbank, the Jets drafted Alabama quarterback Joe Namath, and Werblin was able to convince the star to sign with his team over the NFL's St. Louis Cardinals. Something about the Broadway lights appealed to Namath, and he got an even bigger boost as he gained the opportunity to work with Ewbank.

Namath was one of the most gifted passers to ever play the game. He had a rocket for an arm and one of the quickest releases that pro football observers had ever seen. Namath could throw the ball forty yards with a flick of his wrist, and the sound of the ball whizzing through the air was unlike the sound of any other quarterback in the game.

But Namath was far from a finished product. He was a raw talent with an ego. Ewbank had to convince him that he had a lot to learn about winning at the professional level and that he could give him the knowledge he needed to read defenses, call the correct plays, and help make his team a winner.

It was not an easy relationship, but Namath ultimately came around to embrace his teacher and absorb his lessons. The two would form one of the greatest coach-quarterback partnerships, as Namath would blossom into one of the best quarterbacks in the AFL.

The Jets had a brilliant 1968 season and won the AFL's East Division with an 11–3 record. They were expected to fall short in the AFL Championship game against the relentless Oakland Raiders, but the Jets hung tough on their home turf at Shea Stadium and managed a 27-23 victory when Namath hit wide receiver Don Maynard with the winning touchdown pass late in the fourth quarter.

That set the scene for Super Bowl III, in which the Jets were expected to be cannon fodder for the powerful Baltimore Colts.

The same team that fired Ewbank six years earlier was clearly the best team in the NFL that year, and the Jets didn't appear to have a chance.

The Colts were bigger, faster, and stronger physically, and appeared to have an edge at every position with the possible exception of quarterback, where Earl Morrall had taken over for the injured Unitas.

The oddsmakers installed the Colts as 18-point favorites, and nearly every prominent sportswriter of the day thought the Colts would win easily.

However, Ewbank had a bunch of true believers in the Jets' locker room, and they shocked the Colts 16-7. Namath did not have a huge statistical day, but he picked apart the Baltimore defense with short passes, and the Jets' running game with Matt Snell and Emerson Boozer confounded Baltimore.

Colts coach Don Shula was perplexed by the Jets, and his offense could never figure out the Jets' defense.

Ewbank described the victory in Super Bowl III as the most satisfying moment of his career. The Jets' victory was not only a win for the team, but also it was a major triumph for the AFL.

The NFL had regularly looked down its nose and pooh-poohed the younger league, and those associated with the older league did not think any AFL squad could compete with its top teams.

The Jets' win allowed the league to celebrate and feel good about itself. "I remember how happy I was when the Jets won that game," said Kansas City Chiefs quarterback Len Dawson. "We would win the Super Bowl the next year, but the Jets' win did so much for all of us. I had tears in my eyes. Weeb Ewbank just did some great job of preparing his team and coaching it."

Ewbank couldn't have been more satisfied. "I gave the AFL a win in the Super Bowl, and it was over Baltimore," Ewbank said. "That was certainly a moment to savor."

Ewbank's legacy was sealed when he led the Colts to consecutive NFL championships, but he became one of the game's greatest coaches when he steered the Jets to the greatest upset in the history of professional football.

For the record

Weeb Ewbank
Hall of Fame, 1978
Regular-season record: 130-129-7, .621
Postseason record: 4-1, .800
One Super Bowl victory
Two NFL championships

#20

MIKE HOLMGREN

When Mike Holmgren was named head coach of the Green Bay Packers in 1992, general manager Ron Wolf had every confidence that he had made the right choice to bring the organization back to the glory that it had not known since Vince Lombardi was at the helm in the 1960s.

Holmgren had been Bill Walsh's right-hand man in San Francisco for years, and he was the one with whom Walsh would discuss his offensive theories. It was not simply a case of Walsh teaching Holmgren; he was the beneficiary of Holmgren's knowledge and philosophy of offensive football as well.

Additionally, Holmgren had the kind of personality that allowed him to relate well to his players and reach them with a dynamism that Walsh never had. That's what Wolf had recognized, and that's why he knew that Holmgren would be successful.

"He fills a room with that presence that you just can't measure," Wolf said. "He has that Bill Walsh type of confidence where he just knows what he does is right."

It was clear that Holmgren knew the game like few others, and that knowledge was put to the test in 1992. Not only was that his first year as head coach with the Packers, but it was also the year that Wolf acquired a quarterback named Brett Favre.

Favre had been highly thought of when the Atlanta Falcons drafted him in the second round of the 1991 draft. However, head coach Jerry Glanville was not overly impressed with the strong-armed quarterback from the University of Southern Mississippi, and when the Packers inquired about trading for him, Glanville had no objections.

Holmgren and Favre would become tied at the hip shortly after he came to Green Bay. In his first training camp with the Packers, Holmgren saw the same thing that Glanville had seen in Atlanta—a raw prospect with overwhelming physical skills, but also a player who was largely undisciplined and mistake-prone.

Favre seemed confused by nearly all of the assignments he had in practice and the preseason, and he did not figure in the Packers' immediate plans as the '92 season began.

The Packers had Don Majkowski as their starting quarterback, who was known as "The Magic Man" for his ability to escape pressure when all seemed lost and then make a big play. That was overstating his abilities just a bit, but the ever-hopeful Green Bay fans had little to work with.

That would soon change, as Holmgren was forced to tap Favre on the shoulder when Majkowski got hurt in the third game of the season against the Cincinnati Bengals. Favre threw a fourth-quarter touchdown pass to Sterling Sharpe and then he got the ball back with his team trailing 23–17 in the waning moments. He fired a game-winning, 35-yard touchdown pass to Kitrick Taylor in the game's final moments, and Holmgren knew he had his quarterback.

Holmgren looked at Favre the way Michelangelo looked at the ceiling of the Sistine Chapel. He knew there was an overwhelming amount of work to be done, but he also knew he had the finest raw material he could ever hope to work with.

Holmgren was an offensive master who had earned the respect of Walsh, and now he had a quarterback with overwhelming arm strength, a quick release, and brilliant talent. That they came together in the NFL's smallest outpost in Green Bay didn't matter a bit.

The Packers had been one of the NFL's most frequent losers prior to the 1992 season, having endured twenty-one losing seasons in twenty-five years since Vince Lombardi had left the team after Super Bowl II. But the combination of Holmgren, Wolf, and Favre gave long-suffering Packers fans hope that a major change was at hand.

The Packers would finish with a 9–7 record in '92, and when Wolf pulled off a major coup and signed future Hall of Fame defensive end Reggie White as a free agent in '93, the Packers became legitimate contenders in the NFL.

Holmgren knew how to get the most out of his players. His first priority was to continue to work with Favre so that his raw talent could be turned into skill and ability. It was not an easy assignment, as Favre often made mistakes in practice that left observers and teammates smacking their foreheads in frustration.

Holmgren proved to be a knowledgeable, competent, and successful teacher. Favre would go on to hone his skills and turn into one of the greatest quarterbacks the game has ever known. The key for Holmgren was not just limiting Favre's mistakes. It was keeping his competitive and creative spirit alive.

Holmgren was also a skilled game planner who could look at an opponent on film, find their weaknesses, and then provide an attack plan that regularly resulted in victory. He also knew how to relate to his players with his fully developed personality.

He could laugh with them, joke with them, excoriate them, and make demands. He showed all sides of his personality to his players, and they responded well to him.

Holmgren's Packers made the playoffs in '93, as they beat Detroit in the wild-card game before losing to Jimmy Johnson's Dallas Cowboys. Favre was instrumental in both of those outcomes, as his remarkable forty-yard touchdown pass to Sharpe gave the Packers the winning points in the fourth quarter against the Lions, and his two interceptions played a key role in the loss to Green Bay.

The Cowboys would eliminate the Packers from the postseason following the '94 and '95 seasons as well, and there was a feeling that Favre's spectacular arm would continue to wow fans and impress the media, but that his mistakes would always find a way to be costly to the team.

Holmgren and Favre knew of that reputation, and they stepped up their game in the 1996 season. They rolled to a 13-3 regular season, and most of their wins were of the dominant variety. They humbled the San Francisco 49ers in the divisional playoffs and Carolina Panthers in the NFC Championship game, and that earned them a trip to the Super Bowl for the first time in twenty-nine years.

The Packers went to Super Bowl XXXI in New Orleans against the upstart New England Patriots, and it was a dream game for the Packers. Favre threw two touchdown passes and did not have an interception, White had three sacks, and explosive Desmond Howard had a ninety-nine-yard kickoff return for a touchdown.

The Packers won the game and brought the Vince Lombardi Trophy back home to Green Bay. Holmgren, Favre, and White were heroes in Wisconsin.

The Packers may have been an even better team the following year, and they went back to the Super Bowl following another 13-3 season. They were expected to beat a Denver Broncos team that was trying to break the AFC's twelve-game losing streak in the Super Bowl.

However, the Packers came up short in the game and dropped a 31-24 decision that shocked the football world.

Holmgren would coach one more season with the Packers before he decided to leave the team. Instead of merely coaching an NFL team, Holmgren had a great desire to be responsible for personnel procurement. He wanted to bring in his own players as well as coach the team.

He found that opportunity in Seattle. The Seahawks gave him the chance to build a team and coach it, and after an up-and-down six years, he turned the Seahawks into a Super Bowl team in 2005. While they dropped a brutally tough 21-10 decision to the Pittsburgh Steelers, Holmgren accomplished what he had set off to do when he left Green Bay.

Holmgren coached through the 2008 season, and his final season was a 4-12 disappointment. While his coaching career appears to have ended with a whimper, he put together a remarkable career that featured the rejuvenation of one of the NFL's flagship franchises and the development of one of the game's best quarterbacks.

For the record

Mike Holmgren
Regular-season record: 161-111-0, .592
Postseason record: 13-11, .542
One Super Bowl victory

#21

BUM PHILLIPS

Homespun and folksy from the top of his head to the tips of his toes, Bum Phillips had the opportunity to coach the Houston Oilers in the mid-1970s. At the time, the Oilers were a laughable team competing in the same division with the Pittsburgh Steelers, who may have put together the greatest team in the history of the game.

Phillips may have seemed like a laughable bumpkin, but he was one of the greatest coaches the game has ever known. He combined a personable manner with his superior instincts for football and he turned the Oilers into a spectacular team.

While they were never able to overcome Chuck Noll's Steelers, they carved out a niche and developed a loyal following that has rarely been reached.

Philips and the "Luv Ya Blue" Oilers became a national team in a 1978 Monday Night Football game against the Miami Dolphins. In that game, the Oilers rode a magical performance from Hall of Fame running back Earl Campbell to a 35–30 victory.

Campbell carried 28 times for 199 yards and four touchdowns, including an eighty-one-yard run down the sidelines that is one of the greatest plays in the history of the Monday night series.

Phillips had started his NFL career as the defensive coordinator for Sid Gillman's San Diego Chargers from 1967 through 1970. When Gillman became both general manager and head coach of the Houston Oilers several years later, he brought Phillips with him, and Phillips was the defensive coordinator for the Oilers in 1974.

Gillman left the Oilers in a dispute with owner Bud Adams after that season, and the owner then turned to Phillips to become his head coach. Phillips was a defensive specialist, but he used his time with Gillman well and learned the principles of developing a high-powered offense quite well.

The Oilers could throw the ball and attack with the big play. He was not hesitant to let quarterback Dan Pastorini cut loose and wing the ball, and his quarterback had one of the top wide receivers in the game in Ken "Double-0" Burrough catching passes.

The Oilers were an up-and-down team from 1975 through 1977, but when they added Campbell in 1978, it changed their personality, talent level, and made the rest of the league take notice.

"I became a much better coach once we drafted Earl Campbell," Phillips said. "One of the things I learned throughout my coaching days was that the more good players I had, the better a coach I became. That's pretty much the way it goes in this business.

You show me a good coach and I'll show you a coach with good players."

That obviously made sense, but Phillips was always quite modest about his own abilities and never liked taking credit for anything his players did.

However, he was quick to pay compliments to other coaches. His assessment of Hall of Famer Don Shula during the 1970s has stood the test of time and is one of the most memorable quotes in the history of the game.

"He could take his'n and beat your'n," Phillips said, "and then he could take your'n and beat his'n."

The line, delivered in his thick Texas drawl, may have been amusing to those outside of Texas because of his quaint delivery, but football people appreciated his ability to get to the heart of the matter quickly.

In an era when coaches held all the power and were often quick to use it by criticizing and castigating players in front of teammates or with the media, Phillips was never one to follow that game plan.

He hated confrontations with his players and he refused to get in their face or take complaints to the public. If he had a problem with the way an individual player was performing, he simply changed players. He did not get into a war of words or have feuds with his athletes.

He wanted everybody on the same page, and he was able to get his Oilers to play at a very consistent level. The Oilers may have been the second-best team in the league in the 1978 and '79 seasons, but the Pittsburgh Steelers were the best team in the league.

The Oilers were forced to go to Pittsburgh after both of those seasons to play Chuck Noll's Steelers in the AFC title games, and they couldn't beat them in either one.

Pittsburgh's defense was brutal throughout their championship run during the 1970s, but the 1978 and '79 teams were much better offensively than the two championship teams earlier in the decade.

The Oilers were very talented on both sides of the ball, but they just couldn't match up with the Steelers, no matter what Phillips did to get his team prepared. The Oilers were humbled in the 1978 AFC Title game by a 34-5 margin, and they played a bit better the following year before losing 27-13 in that title game.

He tried to get his team fired up for the '80 season by telling a crowd of supportive Houstonians in the Astrodome that the team was capable of doing better. "Last year, we knocked on the door," he said. "This year, we beat on it. Next year, we are going to kick the son of a bitch in."

The crowd roared its approval, but the Oilers were never able to live up to Phillips's promise. The team suffered some attrition, and Phillips developed problems with Houston general manager Ladd Herzeg.

Those difficulties ultimately led to Phillips's dismissal from the team, and it can be argued that the Oilers never recovered from the loss of their beloved head coach.

Phillips's players were enraged when he was dismissed. All-Pro linebacker Robert Brazile launched into a staunch defense of his coach, saying some players should have been cut and so should some of the team's management, but not Phillips.

"It's a joke," Brazile snorted. "For everything he's done for this team. He was a father to most players, not just a coach. He treated us like men."

Philips would go on to coach the New Orleans Saints for five seasons, but the best he could ever do in New Orleans was an 8-8 season in 1983.

His head coaching career came to an end following the 1985 season, but his son Wade became a respected defensive coordinator and a fine head coach himself.

The Phillips years were among the best in Houston Oilers history, and his ability to get the most from his players remains his legacy and best characteristic.

For the record

Bum Phillips
Regular-season record: 82–77–0, .516
Postseason record: 4–3, .571

#22

MARTY SCHOTTENHEIMER

The numbers explain that Marty Schottenheimer was one of the great coaches in the history of the game. He won 200 games as an NFL head coach, a figure that ranks him seventh on the all-time list. He's just behind names like Bill Belichick and Paul Brown, and just ahead of Chuck Noll and Dan Reeves.

But for all of Schottenheimer's success, his postseason struggles tormented him and underscored what may have been the weaknesses in Schottenheimer's coaching style.

Schottenheimer coached four teams during his coaching career that lasted from 1984 through 2006. He led the Browns, Chiefs, and Chargers to a series of successful campaigns, and he had one season in Washington that was rather forgettable, as his straightforward and demanding style didn't fit in with owner Daniel Snyder.

But going back to the beginning, Schottenheimer had a way about him that was always different from the mainstream, and he embraced those differences. He didn't try to go along with the latest trends or even know what they were. He was his own man and he didn't try to impress his peers, his players, the fans, or the owners.

He wanted to win and he did it his way. He liked to play a conservative brand of football that features a strong running attack, taking the ball away from his opponents and being sound in the kicking game.

These decidedly unsexy features may be the reason he had a 5-13 postseason record, but they are also the reasons his teams went 200-126-1 during the regular season.

When it comes down to it, his first playoff team in Cleveland was almost certainly the closest he ever came to taking one of his teams to the Super Bowl.

In the 1986 season, Schottenheimer was in his third season at the helm of the Browns. He had Bernie Kosar at quarterback, a pair of hard-nosed running backs in Kevin Mack and Earnest Byner, and one of the hardest-hitting and nastiest defenses in the NFL.

The Browns were a relentless team that knew how to put away an opponent when they got them down. While they did not have explosive superstars, they were a sharp bunch that took advantage of mistakes by their opponents. They won the AFC Central Division with a 12-4 record, and that mark also gave them home field advantage throughout the playoffs.

They were nearly upset in the opening round by the New York Jets, as they found themselves down by 10 points in the fourth quarter. However, a one-yard touchdown run by Mack and a field goal by Mark Moseley—the last of the NFL's straight-ahead kickers—sent the game into overtime.

The Jets and Browns slugged back-and-forth and accomplished nothing until Moseley booted a 27-yard field goal early in the second overtime to put the Browns in the AFC title game.

Cleveland's Municipal Stadium was a rabid Dawg Pound when the Denver Broncos came calling in January of 1987, and the Browns were much better than they had been the previous week against the Jets.

However, even though Kosar hit wide receiver Brian Brennan with a forty-eight-yard touchdown pass late in the fourth quarter to give the Browns a 20-13 lead, Schottenheimer knew his team was in anything but a safe position.

The Broncos had John Elway, and he was rapidly becoming one of the greatest quarterbacks in the game. He would make occasional errant throws and poor decisions, but he had the strongest arm in the game, brilliant athleticism, and a penchant for coming through when his team needed him most.

When the Broncos botched the ensuing kickoff and started the possession at their own two-yard line, it looked like the Browns were going to be making a trip to their first Super Bowl.

However, Elway was undaunted. He negotiated his team up the field, using his legs to escape the pass rush and firing hard strikes to his receivers.

The Cleveland crowd had been bawdy when Elway started the drive, but they grew quieter and quieter as Elway led his team upfield in the final moments.

Schottenheimer had no way of slowing Elway down, and the quarterback culminated the drive in the final seconds when he hit wide receiver Mark Jackson with a perfectly thrown five-yard touchdown pass that hit the receiver in the chest as he was going low to make the catch.

The air went out of the huge stadium after that play. Even though it only tied the score, everyone seemed to know what would happen in overtime.

It did. The Broncos moved the ball smartly down the field, and their barefoot kicker Rich Karlis drilled a thirty-three-yard field goal to send the Broncos to Super Bowl XXI and left the Browns and their fans to cry in their beer.

A year later, the two teams met in Denver for the AFC title, and the Broncos rolled to an early 21-0 lead that was still 28-10 in the third quarter. That's when the Browns mounted a huge comeback behind Byner's running prowess and Kosar's passing acumen.

Late in the fourth quarter, the Browns started a drive from their own two-yard line to tie the game, just as Denver had done the year before. However, this time the dream died in heartbreak.

Kosar stuck the ball in Byner's midsection and the Cleveland line gave him the hole he needed. Byner broke into the open and just as he was preparing to take the stride that would let him into the end zone, Denver defensive back Jeremiah Castille stripped the ball from him and the Broncos recovered the ball.

Schottenheimer coached one more season in Cleveland before moving on to Kansas City. He had nine winning years out of ten with the Chiefs, and his 1997 team won thirteen games. However, Schottenheimer's Kansas City teams were just 3-7 in the postseason.

It was more of the same in San Diego, as he had a 12-4 team in 2004 and a 14-2 team in his final season in 2006. However, the Marty Ball philosophy failed in the playoffs in both years.

Schottenheimer never altered his ways, and his stubbornness cost him in the end. He was clearly a brilliant regular-season coach, but his intractability cost him in the postseason.

It will probably prevent one of the most driven and organized coaches from ending up in the Hall of Fame.

For the record

Marty Schottenheimer
Regular-season record: 200–126–1, .613
Postseason record: 5–13, .278
Eight division championships

#23

HANK STRAM

There is a plethora of diva wide receivers, and quite a few who man the quarterback position.

But when it came to the diva as head coach, Hank Stram may be at the top of the list.

Stram was always perfectly tailored and looking sharp when he took the sidelines for the Kansas City Chiefs (or for the Dallas Texans or New Orleans Saints), and he always demanded that his players and assistant coaches looked good as well.

There was nothing casual about the Stram style, as he paraded the sidelines like a proud rooster.

But there was a lot more to Stram than making a statement with his looks and his clothes. He was one of the most innovative coaches of his time, and he was also exceptional when it came to player development.

Stram began his head coaching career when the American Football League came into existence in the 1960 season. League founder Lamar Hunt hired Stram to coach his Dallas Texans, and his team was a contender right from the start and won its first AFL title in 1963.

While the Texans were a strong team on the field, Hunt's AFL entry was not going to be able to compete long-term with the Cowboys on a financial basis, so he moved his team to Kansas City, where they became the Chiefs.

Stram had assembled a team of strong players that included Len Dawson at quarterback, Mike Garrett at running back, and Otis Taylor at wide receiver. The defense may have been even better, with stars like defensive end Buck Buchanan, middle linebacker Willie Lanier, outside linebacker Bobby Bell, and safety Johnny Robinson.

Stram was not content merely to play with the standard formations of the day. His offense would shift regularly to confuse opposing defenses and he would regularly use a 3-4 formation so his sensational group of linebackers could use their athletic ability to dominate games.

Stram liked to use two tight end formations long before they became popular in the NFL, and he would "stack" his defensive players so they could play without being bogged down by blockers. Instead of positioning his linebacker in the gaps between his defensive linemen, he would often place the linebackers directly behind a defensive tackle or end so they could play with freedom.

Stram explained his theories regularly to the media, and I interviewed him on several occasions. "With a player like Bobby Bell, why would I want to make him take on a blocker before he went after the ball carrier?" Stram asked rhetorically. "He was so fast and such a good athlete, I wanted him to take a direct line into the backfield or to the ball carrier. There was no reason to ask him to take on a blocker first if he didn't have to."

When Stram explained something, you always got the feeling that he believed anyone who didn't see it his way was lacking in intelligence.

Stram and his Chiefs won the AFL championship in 1966, when they beat the Buffalo Bills. That victory earned the Chiefs a spot in the first Super Bowl, a game that was known as the "AFL-NFL Championship Game" at the time.

The Chiefs played Vince Lombardi's vaunted Green Bay Packers, and none of the experts or oddsmakers figured the Chiefs would be anything more than cannon fodder in the game.

The final score was 35-10 in favor of the Packers, and it seemed like Green Bay was the dominant team from the end result. Though that may have been true in the second half, in the first half, the Chiefs played the Packers on nearly even terms and trailed by just a 14-10 margin.

Kansas City made mistakes in the second half, and the Packers took advantage of them to build a significant margin.

Lombardi damned the Chiefs with faint praise after the game. "Kansas City has a fine ball club," Lombardi told the media after the game. "But I think there are four or five teams in the National Football League that are better than they are. There, I said it."

Lombardi's remarks chafed Stram throughout the offseason. The AFL and NFL teams played exhibition games against each other for the first time in 1967, and when the Chiefs met George Halas and the Chicago Bears in the preseason, he decided to take on Lombardi's insult as a challenge.

The Chiefs beat the Bears up and down the field throughout the exhibition game, which they played as if it were a playoff game. The Chiefs ripped the Bears 66-14, and there was no let-up at any point in the game.

"This was no ordinary exhibition game," said former Chicago Bears linebacker, the late Doug Buffone. "They were out to make a point from the start, and they made it. We were there to play a preseason game, and they wanted to mop the field with us."

Stram and his Chiefs were an excellent team in 1967, but they were not quite as good as the Oakland Raiders, who won the AFL championship that year and also lost to the Packers in the Super Bowl. The following year, the Chiefs lost a playoff game to the Raiders after both teams finished with 12-2 records.

Despite seemingly superior personnel, the Raiders could not get past Joe Namath and the New York Jets in the AFL title game.

The Jets would go on to beat the Raiders in the AFL title game and then register perhaps the biggest upset in pro football history when they defeated the Baltimore Colts 16-7 in Super Bowl III.

It was a victory celebrated by every AFL member, including Stram. "I remember there was just this feeling of great pride when New York won the game," Stram said. "I knew we were doing something special in the AFL and there was not a doubt in my mind about that. But when I had a chance to see the Jets prove it on the field against their super team, it was wonderful.

"Of course, we wanted to go out there and do it ourselves."

Stram didn't have to wait long. The Chiefs beat the Jets in the playoffs and then defeated the Raiders in the final AFL Championship game before that league merged with the NFL.

That gave the Chiefs a chance to go back to the Super Bowl against the supposedly superior Minnesota Vikings. Minnesota was a huge double-digit favorite, and the Purple People Eaters were supposed to punish the AFL representatives for the humiliation the NFL had been handed the year before when the Jets beat the Colts.

If anything, the Chiefs were more dominant than the Jets had been, as they rolled past the Vikings 23-7 in Super Bowl IV.

That Super Bowl became one of the most famous games in NFL history, and helped make NFL Films a huge success. Stram agreed to wear a tiny microphone on his finely tailored suit, and everything he said during the game was captured for posterity.

The gregarious Stram was at his most colorful as his team played with poise and momentum. He urged Dawson and the offense to keep "matriculating the ball down the field" and when running back Mike Garrett scored a first-half touchdown on a running play, Stram played to the cameras by repeating the play call "64 toss-power trap" repeatedly.

Stram loved to strut and preen, but he had the substance to go with his style. His teams won three AFL championships and one Super Bowl, and he was among the most innovative coaches of his time.

Additionally, he helped open doors for African-American players that had been closed and he was always appreciated and loved by his players.

Bell said that Stram would often exasperate his players with his demanding ways in practice, but his players always thought of him with warmth and fondness. "We knew he cared about us," Bell said. "That was the bottom line. He cared about us as people, and that's why we always played for him."

Stram appreciated his players and he gave them inventive and innovative game plans. He built championship teams and helped write some of the most important chapters in the history of professional football.

For the record

Hank Stram
Hall of Fame, 2003
Regular-season record: 131-97-10, .575
Postseason record: 5-3, .625
One Super Bowl victory
Two AFL Championships

#24

CHUCK KNOX

By the time Chuck Knox got his first opportunity to become a head coach in the NFL, he had become an expert in what it took to be successful.

Knox had spent the start of his pro football career as the offensive line coach for the New York Jets under Weeb Ewbank, and the main part of his job was making sure that the line gave quarterback Joe Namath protection.

After he left the Jets and moved on to the Detroit Lions, it was more of the same thing. He needed to find a way to protect Lions quarterback Bill Munson, who had a strong arm but lacked mobility.

During a five-year run in Detroit under head coach Joe Schmidt, Knox picked up on what it took to put pressure on an opposing quarterback. Since it was his job to make sure his quarterback was protected and upright, he spent most of his time figuring out how to attack the pocket and then coming up with the game plan that would defeat the strategy.

By the time the Los Angeles Rams came calling so he could become their head coach in 1973, the forty-one-year-old Knox knew as much about attacking the pocket and protecting the quarterback as any coach in the NFL did.

He had immediate success with the Rams. His team went 12-2 in his first season, and they did it with flair. The Rams scored 388 points that season with John Hadl at quarterback, Lawrence McCutcheon running the ball, and Harold Jackson making big plays through the air.

The defense was just as accomplished, and a unit that featured Fred Dryer, Jack "Hacksaw" Reynolds, and Isiah Robertson gave up just 178 points. The plus–210-point differential was by far the best in the league, and the Rams went into the postseason as the odds-on favorite to represent the NFC in the Super Bowl.

But despite all the team's regular-season success, there was something wrong in the playoffs. The Rams lost 27–16 to the Dallas Cowboys. Dallas jumped to a quick 17–0 lead, and the Rams were never able to get back in the game.

Unfortunately for Knox, that first season would become a pattern that he and his teams would repeat regularly throughout the twenty-two years he coached in the NFL. The hard-nosed Knox would often get the most out of his team by building a powerful running attack, limiting turnovers, and creating pressure with its defense.

However, when the Rams continued to stick with their conservative strategy once they got into the postseason, they were relatively easy to figure out for top coaches like Tom Landry of the Dallas

Cowboys and Bud Grant of the Minnesota Vikings. If a team was going to load the box and go all out to stop the Rams' power running game, Los Angeles was going to be at a disadvantage.

Knox coached the Rams for five years, and while they made the playoffs every year, they never got out of the NFC Championship and made it to the Super Bowl.

Perhaps their best chance to make that happen came in the 1975 season when the Rams rolled to another 12-2 mark and easily dispatched Don Coryell's St. Louis Cardinals in the divisional round of the playoffs.

However, even though they were heavy favorites against the wild-card-winning Dallas Cowboys in the NFC Championship game, they got embarrassed badly by a 37-7 score. Even though the Rams were bigger, stronger, younger, and faster than the Cowboys, they got outplayed and outsmarted at every turn.

After five years of scintillating regular-season success and post-season disappointment, Knox and Rams owner Carroll Rosenbloom mutually decided to part company. Knox went to the struggling Buffalo Bills, and he turned that team around in his third year.

The Bills had back-to-back playoff seasons in 1980 and 1981. While they dropped a playoff game to San Diego in '80, they came back with a fire the following year.

Quarterback Joe Ferguson and running back Joe Cribbs gave them a formidable offense, and the Bills scored a thrilling 31–27 victory over the Jets in the wild-card round before losing in Cincinnati the following week.

Knox would leave the Bills after the strike-torn 1982 season and return to the West Coast. He headed the Seattle Seahawks operation, and he was bound and determined to take an undisciplined team and turn them into champions.

His first season in Seattle was a magical one. The Seahawks were a .500 team through fourteen weeks, and they needed to win their last two games to make the playoffs. They beat the New York Giants on the road and then hammered the New England Patriots 24-6 in the season finale to earn a playoff spot with a 9-7 record.

They met the Denver Broncos in the wild-card game, and Knox's Seahawks overpowered Denver 31-7. Considering the quarterback matchup of John Elway vs. Dave Krieg, most found the Seahawks' victory shocking.

Expectations continued to be low for the Seahawks, who were expected to be cannon fodder for Miami and Dan Marino in the next round. There was no reason to expect the Seahawks to stay close to the explosive Dolphins, but Krieg was sharp in his passing and running back Curt Warner (113 yards and two touchdowns) showed why he was one of the top running backs in the league. The Seahawks left Miami with a 27-20 victory.

The Seahawks met the Los Angeles Raiders in the AFC Championship game, and they had beaten the Raiders twice in the regular season. However, the Raiders were too deep and too strong and ultimately prevailed in a 30-14 decision.

Knox and the Seahawks were determined not to fall short in the following season. They rolled to a 33-0 victory over the Cleveland Browns in the season opener, but the Seattle locker room was like a morgue after the game.

Warner, perhaps the best running back in the game, tore up his knee and was lost for the season. Assistant coach Joe Vitt explained how Knox refused to let his team feel sorry for itself.

"Everybody's looking to Chuck for reassurance, and I'll never forget what he did," Vitt told the *Los Angeles Times*. "He comes out, gets the team together and says, 'Now we're going to find out who the believers are.'

"He says, 'Nobody is going to believe in this talent. There are teams around the league right now saying the Seahawks are finished. There are coaches and players right here who don't believe we're going to win. Now we're going to find out who the believers are.'

"Then he went out to practice and he was right in the huddle, running the plays, and he wouldn't let anyone feel sorry for themselves. I remember him challenging the defense. He had stepped up to another level, intensity-wise, and everybody out there realized he was in this thing to win. They joined him."

The Seahawks went on to win the AFC West that year with a 12-4 record. They found a way to beat the Raiders in the postseason, but they lost their chance to advance to the AFC Championship when the Dolphins ripped them 31-10.

But the 1984 season was vintage Chuck Knox. His team had suffered an injury that would have cut the heart out of most teams, and all the Seahawks did was play their best football.

Knox would coach the Seahawks through the 1991 season, and then return to the Rams for three more seasons before calling it a career after the 1994 season.

Knox never changed his approach, and while his hard work and run-first style never won a championship, it earned him 186 regular season wins, a figure that ranks tenth in NFL history.

For the record

Chuck Knox
Regular-season record: 186-147-1, .559
Postseason record: 7-11, .389
Seven division championships

#25

BILL COWHER

The hard-nosed, jut-jawed head coach of the Pittsburgh Steelers didn't appear to have much of a chance to make a name for himself in the NFL.

He was a linebacker out of North Carolina State, and he wasn't even drafted in 1979. He was invited to try out for the Philadelphia Eagles that year, and made it all the way to the final cut when head coach Dick Vermeil let him go.

Despite that rejection, he earned a spot with the Cleveland Browns and he eventually became captain of their special teams. The Eagles, who had cut him three years earlier, traded a ninth-round draft choice to reacquire him to lift their special teams play.

A knee injury ended his playing career in 1984, but he had demonstrated maximum effort every minute that he had worn an NFL uniform, and that impressed Marty Schottenheimer. He hired Cowher as an assistant coach in Cleveland, and Schottenheimer took the enthusiastic Cowher to Kansas City when the Chiefs hired him.

The apprenticeship served Cowher well, as he learned quite a bit about coaching from Schottenheimer, who was regularly viewed as one of the most prepared men in the NFL.

Cowher had the desire to be a head coach, and when Chuck Noll decided to call it a career after the 1991 season, Cowher wanted the position.

Cowher was decidedly old-school in his approach. The main thrust of his coaching philosophy that he expressed while he was seeking the job and once he had it was that he wanted the Steelers to be a tough football team.

"To me, that's what building a winning team was all about. I wanted to run the ball and I wanted to play defense," he said. "I knew you had to score and you had to pass, but toughness mattered at every turn in this game, and it still does. That's what I wanted my teams to be known for above everything else."

Cowher was true to his word from Day One. The Steelers certainly had plenty of toughness and a mean streak during the majority of Chuck Noll's reign as a four-time Super Bowl winner with the Steelers, but they seemed to lose a bit of that identity in his final years with the team.

The Steelers had turned into an ordinary team in Noll's last four years, going 5-11, 9-7, 9-7, and 7-9 from 1988 through 1991 and making the playoffs just once in that span. Cowher gave the team a spark that had been missing. The Steelers went 11-5 and finished first in the AFC Central.

While the roster did not have overwhelming talent—Neil O'Donnell and Bubby Brister handled the QB chores—the Steelers played with an energy and ferocity that had been missing. That regular-season success did not translate to the playoffs, as the Steelers were beaten decisively by the Buffalo Bills 24-3 at Three Rivers Stadium in the divisional playoffs.

The Steelers were a winning team nearly every year in Cowher's coaching regime, and they made the playoffs in his first six seasons at the helm. In 1994, the Steelers went 12-4 and pummeled the Cleveland Browns 29-9 in the divisional playoffs. That gave them the opportunity to win the AFC Championship at home against the San Diego Chargers.

Few thought San Diego had a chance in Pittsburgh in January. The Steelers had a ferocious team that featured Greg Lloyd, Levon Kirkland, and future Hall of Famer Rod Woodson. The Chargers had gotten hot over the second half of the season and featured a journeyman quarterback in Stan Humphries.

The Chargers could only muster three points well into the third quarter, but Humphries persevered and rallied San Diego to a 17-13 victory.

The heartbreak stayed with Cowher for a year, and looked as if it might be repeated in the AFC Championship again the following year.

The Steelers once again hosted that game after a strong 11-5 season and an overwhelming 40-21 win over the Bills in the divisional playoff games. All they had to do to get to their first Super Bowl of the Cowher era was beat the mediocre Indianapolis Colts, who finished the season with a 9-7 record.

The Colts didn't appear to have the talent to compete with the Steelers as they featured Jim Harbaugh at quarterback and a cast of no-names who had played hard for head coach Ted Marchibroda. Harbaugh was an ordinary quarterback throughout his NFL career, finishing with a 66-74-0 record and a 129-117 TD-interception ratio.

However, the Steelers couldn't put them away and were clinging to a 20-16 lead on the game's final play. Harbaugh floated a pass into the end zone that hit wideout Aaron Bailey in the midsection as he fell to the turf. Bailey tried to clutch the ball and keep it from hitting the ground, but he failed by inches. The Steelers had their AFC title and were going to the Super Bowl to take on the powerful Dallas Cowboys.

The Steelers had twice defeated the Cowboys in the Chuck Noll era, but this Cowboys team was not about to let another opportunity slip through their grasp. Dallas had Troy Aikman, Emmitt Smith, and Michael Irvin on the offensive side, and their defense was relentless.

The Cowboys did not play their best game, but they still came away with a 27-17 victory. Cowher was heartbroken with the defeat, but it was a setback that would not derail him.

He would continue to coach in the Steel City until he got back to the Super Bowl and won it.

That would take eleven more years. After getting to the Super Bowl in his fourth season as a head coach, Cowher wouldn't get back there until his 15th, following the 2005 season.

It didn't look like that was a possibility, as the Steelers were 7-5 with four weeks to go and had played inconsistently. But Cowher told his team they were champions and would not lose another game.

His players bought it, as they finished 11-5 and registered road playoff wins over the Cincinnati Bengals, Colts, and Denver Broncos to make it to Super Bowl XL against the Seattle Seahawks.

Cowher may have known he was getting close to the end of his reign in Pittsburgh, but he wasn't telling anyone. However, that was not the case with running back Jerome Bettis. "The Bus" made it clear the 2005 season was his last and that the Super Bowl— which was played in his hometown of Detroit—was to be his last game.

It ended in storybook fashion for Bettis, as the Steelers outlasted the Seahawks 21-10. It was a moment of sheer joy for Cowher, who celebrated tearfully with his family.

Cowher coached one more season and then decided to retire and move on to the television booth after an 8-8 year.

Many have expected Cowher to leave the CBS set and get back to the sidelines, but he has not decided to return to coaching yet.

Whether he does or doesn't make that decision, Cowher still has a legacy that includes 149 regular-season wins, twelve more in the postseason, and one Super Bowl title. Not bad for a former free-agent linebacker and special-teams ace.

For the record

Bill Cowher
Regular-season record: 149-90-1, .623
Postseason record: 12-9, .571
One Super Bowl victory

#26

DAN REEVES

There were few things that Dan Reeves didn't know about coaching by the midway point of his playing career with the Dallas Cowboys. Drafted out of South Carolina as a quarterback, Reeves never had the kind of arm that NFL teams wanted and he was quickly converted to running back.

Tom Landry loved Reeves's versatility because he could run inside, carry the ball on sweeps to the outside, block effectively, and catch passes. He also put his quarterbacking skills on display, as he could throw the option pass, and Landry was never afraid to call on those skills.

But more than simply executing as a player, Reeves learned the game like a coach under Landry and he was able to advise all of his offensive teammates where they were supposed to be on each play if they ever had any questions.

The die was cast when Reeves donned his No. 30 uniform for the Cowboys, and perhaps well before that. Reeves was going to be a football coach someday.

Reeves's knowledge and ability to communicate with his teammates was not lost on Landry. He made Reeves a player-coach in 1971. Eventually, Reeves became a full-time assistant for Landry and he stayed with the Cowboys until the 1981 season.

Reeves had been sought by several NFL teams and had been a legitimate head-coaching candidate, but that year the Denver Broncos came calling and named Reeves as their head coach.

Reeves tried to turn the Broncos into a winning team with the likes of Steve DeBerg and Craig Morton at quarterback. While the Broncos finished with a 10-6 record in 1981—and did not make the playoffs—they slipped back to 2-7 in the strike year of '82.

However, that put the Broncos in a position to obtain rookie quarterback John Elway from the celebrated quarterback Class of 1983.

Elway was actually drafted by the Baltimore Colts, and he had said prior to the draft that he would not play in Baltimore. Unlike most rookies, Elway had leverage since he also was a Major League Baseball prospect and was property of George Steinbrenner of the New York Yankees. When the Colts came to believe that Elway would not relent, they traded his rights to the Broncos.

Reeves and Elway immediately formed a winning combination, even though their relationship was often tempestuous. Elway's remarkable athleticism and awe-inspiring arm strength gave the Broncos a chance to win nearly every game. They finished 9-7 and made the playoffs in 1983, and were 13-3 the following year.

The Broncos were the No. 2 seed in the AFC playoffs behind the Miami Dolphins (14-2) in 1984, and it was expected that the two teams would meet in the AFC Championship game to see who represented the conference in the Super Bowl. However, the Broncos were eliminated in the divisional playoffs by a feisty Pittsburgh Steelers team that took command in the second half and beat the Broncos 24-17.

While the Broncos finished 11-5 in 1985, it would not be good enough to make the playoffs, and there were grumblings about the leadership of Reeves and Elway. It was hard for local fans to understand how this team could fall short of the postseason, and the situation was going to have to change quickly.

The Broncos responded in 1986, as Elway grew more experienced and learned how to finish games. This time an 11-5 record was good enough to win the AFC West title, and the Broncos outlasted the New England Patriots 22-17 in the divisional playoffs, putting Reeves and Elway in the AFC Title game at Cleveland.

The Browns were more than a worthy opponent, and they took a 20-13 lead late in the fourth quarter when Bernie Kosar hit wideout Brian Brennan with a forty-eight-yard touchdown pass. The Broncos botched the ensuing kickoff and had to start their drive from the two-yard line.

What followed was legendary, as Elway led the Broncos downfield with a series of on-the-money passes in the face of a brutal Cleveland pass rush. The Browns had several chances to stop Elway, but could not do it, and the game was propelled into overtime when Elway connected with wideout Mark Jackson on a five-yard touchdown pass in the final moments.

Reeves breathed a sigh of relief, as his quarterback had rescued the team from a most precarious position. The Broncos would complete the comeback when Rich Karlis connected on a field goal in overtime to send the Broncos to Super Bowl XXI against the Giants.

It was a thrilling moment for Reeves as a head coach. He was going into the Super Bowl with a team that had glorious momentum and perhaps the best quarterback in the game. However, the AFC champions would fall short in Super Bowl XXI against the New York Giants because New York quarterback Phil Simms completed 22-of-25 passes and the Giants' defense was simply too strong for Denver's ordinary offensive line. Even though Denver led at half-time, the Giants earned a 39-20 decision.

Losing in the Super Bowl would become a habit for Reeves and Elway. A year later, the Broncos found themselves back in the Super Bowl against the Washington Redskins, and after Denver jumped out to a 10-0 lead, the Redskins roared back with thirty-five second-quarter points and earned a 42-10 blowout win.

Reeves was proving to be a master at navigating the Broncos through the regular season, but they would fall apart in the Super Bowl. The same scenario took place following the 1989 season. The Broncos had a limited running game and an ordinary defense, but they won the AFC again. This time they would meet the San Francisco 49ers in the Super Bowl.

The game turned out to be the most lopsided game in the history of the series. The Niners rode the superb play of Joe Montana and Jerry Rice to a monstrous 55-10 triumph.

Reeves was humiliated by his Super Bowl record, and his relationship with Elway would grow more distant over the ensuing three years.

Elway drew a line in the sand with owner Pat Bowlen about Reeves following an 8-8 finish in 1992, and the owner sided with the quarterback. Reeves was let go and Mike Shanahan came to Denver.

Reeves was hired immediately by general manager George Young of the New York Giants. Reeves had been a candidate for the Giants' head coaching position while he was still an assistant in Dallas, and Young ultimately hired Ray Perkins to coach the team.

This time, there would be no other choice for Young to make. Reeves inherited a team that went 6-10, but he led them to an 11-5 record and a playoff spot in 1993. The Giants defeated the Minnesota Vikings 17-10 in the wild-card game, but got overwhelmed 44-3 by the 49ers.

Reeves could not get back to the playoffs in three more years with New York, and he would coach the Atlanta Falcons in 1998. While Reeves developed a reputation for a lack of creativity on offense in Denver and New York, he proved to be the perfect leader in Atlanta.

The Falcons became the "Dirty Birds" and rolled to a 14-2 record with Chris Chandler at quarterback and Jamal Anderson carrying the load at running back. The Falcons made it to the NFC Championship game at Minnesota, where they were expected to be pounded by the explosive Vikings.

Minnesota had a brilliant passing attack that year and set offensive records with Randall Cunningham at quarterback throwing to Cris Carter and Randy Moss. Reeves's team was not intimidated and pulled off a shocking 30-27 overtime victory.

Ironically, the Falcons met Elway and the Broncos in the Super Bowl. The game proved to be Elway's last as an NFL player, and he directed Denver to a 34-19 win over his former coach's team. Both men had tried to play down the rift in their relationship, but it was a bitter defeat for Reeves.

His Falcons teams would never make it back to the Super Bowl and would only make it to the NFL playoffs once in the next six seasons.

Reeves would end his coaching career after the team went 3-10 in 2003.

Reeves won 190 regular season games during his coaching career, and that's the second-most of any head coach who did not win a championship, trailing only Marty Schottenheimer's mark of 200.

Reeves may never have developed the kind of rapport with Elway that he wanted, but he kept the team focused and winning, and his consistency allowed him to take three teams to the playoffs.

For the record

Dan Reeves
Regular-season record: 190–165–2, .535
Postseason record: 11–9, .550
Four conference championships

#27

ANDY REID

Andy Reid learned his lessons well as an assistant coach in college football. He coached at five schools between 1982 and 1991 before he got his first big break and was called by Mike Holmgren to begin his pro coaching career as a tight ends and offensive line coach with the Packers.

Reid eventually worked his way up to quarterbacks coach in 1997, and he quickly developed a reputation as an up-and-comer while working with Brett Favre. Teams around the NFL started to make inquiries about Reid, and the Packers thought they were protecting themselves when they named Reid as an assistant head coach.

However, that did not stop the Eagles from pursuing him hard prior to the 1999 season. Philadelphia had endured a brutal 1998 season, and the team was lacking in talent at the skill positions and depth at nearly everywhere else.

One of the first moves of the Reid regime was the drafting of quarterback Donovan McNabb in 1999. While the move was not looked at favorably by long-suffering Eagles fans who had wanted the team to draft Texas running back Ricky Williams, McNabb was a smart leader and Reid could teach him the West Coast offense.

The Eagles struggled with a 5-11 record in '99, but Reid had put his system in place and the team was ready to make a move up the standings the next year. The Eagles went 11-5 and won a spot in the playoffs as a wild-card team. The Eagles trounced the Bucs 21-3 in their first playoff game, but they were stopped 20-10 in the divisional playoffs by the Giants.

The Eagles would become a consistent playoff team under Reid, making the postseason five straight years. However, the Eagles seemed to be a limited team, and their weaknesses would usually come to the forefront during the postseason.

While McNabb developed into a solid quarterback who was capable of diagnosing opponents' weaknesses and exploiting them, he did not have a stellar crew of receivers and the running game was not first-rate.

As a result, the Eagles regularly came up short in the NFC Championship game. They were not expected to beat the St. Louis Rams following the 2001 season, but they were favored each of the two following seasons against the Bucs and Panthers.

Even though they had been a dominant team at home, they couldn't use their Veterans Stadium advantage constructively. Both the Bucs and Panthers walked into the Vet and beat the Eagles convincingly.

Just when it looked like the Eagles would never get to the Super Bowl under Reid, they added superstar wideout Terrell Owens prior to the 2004 season and they rolled to an NFC-best 13-3 record.

After beating the Vikings 27-14 in the divisional playoffs, the Eagles found themselves back in the NFC Championship game for the fourth consecutive season. While the atmosphere around Philadelphia was frought with doom and gloom as many pessimistic fans thought they would get stopped short of the Super Bowl once again, the Eagles dominated the Falcons 27-10 and earned a spot in Super Bowl XXXIX against the New England Patriots.

The game was tied 14-14 after three quarters, but when Corey Dillon scored a touchdown and Adam Vinatieri kicked a field goal in the fourth quarter, the Patriots had a ten-point lead and appeared to be in control of the game.

However, McNabb threw a thirty-yard touchdown pass with 1:55 remaining, and the Eagles got the ball back with forty-six seconds remaining. They could not do anything with their final possession and the Patriots were celebrating their third Super Bowl title at the end of the game.

Owens had been a huge factor in the Eagles' improved offense as he caught seventy-seven passes for 1,200 yards and fourteen touchdowns, but he was also a huge divisive factor within the locker room. Owens was the personification of the wide receiver as diva, and he also blamed McNabb for the team's loss in the Super Bowl.

The Eagles became a divided team, and they fell to 6-10 in 2005, before bouncing back with another division title in 2006. Reid knew that his team was starting to get old, and he began to make major changes to the roster.

The Eagles remained a contender and made the playoffs three consecutive years from 2008 through 2010, but they could not maintain that success and the Eagles slipped to 8-8 in 2011 before capitulating with a 4-12 season the following year.

The 2012 season was particularly brutal for Reid, as his oldest son, Garrett, died of a heroin overdose during the Eagles' training camp. Reid tried to carry on, but his team was no longer responding to him. The Eagles fired Reid after that painful season.

Many thought that he would remain on the sidelines for at least a full season so he could address his personal loss and take stock of his career. But Reid wanted no part of that. The Kansas City Chiefs had an opening, and when they offered him the head coaching position, he accepted it willingly.

Reid acquired quarterback Alex Smith, instituted a powerful running game, and the Chiefs went 11-5 and went to the playoffs as a wild-card team. The Chiefs built a 38-10 lead on the road over the Indianapolis Colts, but the defense fell apart and Kansas City ended up dropping a 45-44 decision.

The Chiefs remained competitive in 2014 with a 9-7 record, but losses to the Tennessee Titans in the opener and the Oakland Raiders in mid-November ruined their playoff chances.

Still, Reid has re-established himself as one of the best coaches in the game, and he demonstrated that he still has one of the best offensive minds in the business.

He has made just one Super Bowl appearance and his team lost that game, but his teams have won consistently and he has regularly been able to out-scheme opposing coaches. That's not likely to change any time soon.

For the record

> **Andy Reid**
> Regular-season record: 150-105-1, .588
> Postseason record: 10-10, .500

#28

CURLY LAMBEAU

There's only one reason an NFL franchise was given to the Northern Wisconsin hamlet of Green Bay. It was due to the strength, skill, persistence, and desire of one Earl L. "Curly" Lambeau.

Lambeau was the head coach of the Packers from 1921 through 1949, but in addition to leading them on the sidelines for more than three decades, he founded the franchise, played for the Packers, got backing for them when times were tough, and helped them win championships.

Lambeau grew up in Green Bay and was a high school football star. He played college football at Wisconsin and Notre Dame, but he had to leave both schools because he had to work at his father's construction business.

Lambeau continued to play football while working at the family business, and in 1921 he urged the Green Bay football team to apply for membership to the American Professional Football Association. That organization was the forerunner to the NFL, and they accepted Green Bay as a member team.

The club got backing from the Indian Packing Company, which was soon taken over by the Acme Packing Company. However, when Acme decided to pull out of its sponsorship, it was left to Lambeau to keep the operation running.

He did so with the help of *Green Bay Press-Gazette* sportswriter George Calhoun and *Press-Gazette* publisher Andrew Turnbull. Calhoun helped publicize the team and raised money to keep it running, while Turnbull came up with the idea and executed a stock sale that allowed locals to buy stakes in the team.

Lambeau became the team's star player and its coach during the 1920s. He threw 24 touchdown passes during his playing career, which was an impressive total at that time. He also came up with the plays, organized the team, and decided which players would be on the field and who would come in as a substitute.

The Packers won regularly during the early years of the league, and they earned three consecutive NFL championships between 1929 and 1931. In those days, there were no playoffs or even a championship game. The Packers simply became league champions because they had the best record during the regular season.

Those championship teams were led by Cal Hubbard, Johnny Blood, and Mike Michalske. The Packers returned to championship form when they signed a slick wide receiver from Alabama named Don Hutson.

Hutson came aboard in 1935, and the Packers won their fourth NFL title a year later. Green Bay had a 10-1-1 record that season, and won the NFL's West Division. They traveled east to play the Boston Redskins in the NFL Championship game. When the Redskins could not sell enough tickets to the game in Boston, it was moved to New York City's Polo Grounds. Nearly 30,000 fans saw Lambeau's Packers trounce the Redskins 21-6.

Arnie Herber threw two touchdown passes in that game, and one of them was to Hutson, who caught five passes for seventy-six yards. Lambeau had built one of the first modern offenses; his team was as efficient as any team in pro football at the passing game.

The Packers made it back to the NFL title game in 1938, but this time they lost to the New York Giants by a 23-17 margin. The following year, the Packers rolled to a 9-2 record to win the West, and they got their revenge on the Giants by beating them 27-0 in the championship game.

That gave Lambeau five championships for his career, and he won one more following the 1944 season when they had an 8-2 regular season record and then beat the Giants 14-7 in the championship game.

Six NFL titles put Lambeau in a tie with George Halas for the most championships won in a career. Halas and Lambeau appeared to be bitter rivals on the field, and both had curmudgeonly personalities off of it. The two men never shook hands in the middle of the field after any Packers-Bears game, but when the Packers needed money for their new City Stadium, it was Halas who helped them raise the funds. That act was indicative of the true respect between the two legendary coaches.

Lambeau was an innovative head coach who initiated the idea of leading his team in daily practice sessions to prepare for each upcoming game. Lambeau also used movie cameras to film games, so his teams could see their mistakes and then work on them in the practice sessions.

Lambeau was a driven man as a coach, and he would push his players hard in their practice sessions and games. He did not care at all if his players liked him; he simply wanted them to be winning football players. He was known as the "Bellicose Belgian" because he yelled at his players with such alarming frequency.

But Lambeau did win games. He had twenty-six winning seasons as head coach during his first twenty-seven years with the Packers, and that's clearly a record that no modern coach will ever get close to.

He struggled in his final two years with the Packers as he was slow to change his ways. His teams stuck with the Single-Wing formation long after the T-formation became standard in the NFL. As a result his team had losing records in 1947 and '48, which was his last season in Green Bay.

Lambeau moved on to become the coach of the Chicago Cardinals for two years, and followed that by coaching the Washington Redskins for two years.

He had a winning 6-5-1 record in his final season as a head coach in 1953. However, his most notable activity in Washington was getting into a shoving match with owner George Preston Marshall that left his players laughing in celebration.

As the years went by, the Packers struggled badly without him, and he was angling to return in the late 1950s. However, when Green Bay hired New York Giants assistant coach Vince Lombardi in 1959, that was the end of Lambeau's coaching career.

It was Lombardi's name that would become synonymous with the franchise. However, the Packers never would have existed in the first place or survived their rocky early years if not for the strength and drive of Lambeau.

For the record

Curly Lambeau
Hall of Fame, 1963
Regular-season record: 226-132-22, .631
Postseason record: 3-2, .600
Six NFL championships

#29

JIM MORA

He may be best known for a viral video that includes his incredulous facial when asked a question about his team's chance of gaining a spot in the playoffs, but Jim Mora's coaching career is worthy of recognition even though his success in the postseason was nonexistent.

Mora got his start in coaching at Stanford under head coach John Ralston, and that came after a three-year stint in the Marines. Ralston was struck by Mora's command and drive, and he said he had the "executive ability to run General Motors. He's highly intelligent, disciplined, and with a great grasp of what it takes to succeed."

Mora quickly moved through the college ranks and became an NFL assistant coach with the Seattle Seahawks and the New England Patriots. He moved on to the head coaching ranks when the United States Football League opened its doors in 1982, and he signed on with the Philadelphia Stars.

While the new league had an array of problems, many scouts were impressed with the talent level in the new league, and there were quite a few competitive franchises. The best of them was Mora's Stars, who made it to the championship game in all three years of the league's existence, winning the title in two of those years.

When the league went out of business, the NFL snatched up its top players like Herschel Walker, Jim Kelly, and Reggie White quickly. Mora had also made a name for himself in the USFL, and he was a hot coaching commodity.

The New Orleans Saints came calling, because they had never had a winning season in their history, and they were hoping that Mora could change that. General manager Jim Finks was impressed by Mora's straightforward approach and he had confidence that the coach could turn around the Saints' losing history.

The Saints finished 7-9 in 1986, but there was a big difference between how the team went about its business from the previous year. There was greater discipline and organization, and it seemed like a sense of confidence was developing.

The Saints were an energized and talented team in 1987, and Mora's crew finished with a 12-3-0 record, and that gave the franchise a second-place finish in the NFC West. It also earned the team its first playoff appearance.

It was a remarkable year for the franchise because the success was sudden and explosive. The Saints were just 3-3 after their first six games, and their third loss was a 24-22 decision to the 49ers that featured a disappointing comeback that fell just short.

But the Saints would not lose another game in the regular season, as they reeled off nine straight wins behind the accurate passing of USFL refugee and Cajun native Bobby Hebert, the running of Dalton Hilliard and Rueben Mayes, and the receiving of Eric Martin and a glue-fingered tight end named Hoby Brenner.

While none of those players were All-Pros, they functioned at an efficient level under Mora's leadership. Hebert did not have a strong arm, but he was an accurate short- and medium-range passer and he got the ball away quickly.

The defense was the backbone of the 1987 Saints, and it featured linebackers Rickey Jackson, Pat Swilling, Vaughan Johnson, and Sam Mills. Many NFL observers thought Jackson was the second-best linebacker in the NFL behind Lawrence Taylor of the New York Giants, and the foursome was almost certainly the best in the league.

The Saints announced their presence among the NFL's elite when they went on the road in November and beat the Los Angeles Rams and 49ers, and then came home and defeated the defending champion New York Giants.

Many thought the red-hot Saints would be the team to beat as the playoffs got underway, and they were cocky favorites when they hosted the 8-7 Minnesota Vikings in the wild-card round of the playoffs.

The Saints started the game in impressive fashion when Hebert hit Martin with a ten-yard touchdown pass in the first quarter, but the Vikings scored forty-four of the next forty-seven points to humble them in the Superdome.

The defeat stung Mora and his players, and while the Saints posted a winning record each of the next two years, they did not make it back to the playoffs.

They were an ordinary 8-8 in 1990, but that record was good enough for them to grab the final wild-card spot in the playoffs. This time, Mora's crew was forced to play at Chicago against Mike Ditka's veteran Bears, and the Saints could not contend with the twenty-one-degree temperature and dropped a 16-6 decision.

The Saints returned to the playoffs in '91 after winning the NFC West with an 11-5-0 record, but they were upset at home by the Atlanta Falcons.

Mora and his Saints made it to the postseason again the following year, and they appeared to have a chance to finally win a game when they hosted the Philadelphia Eagles. The Saints led the game 17-7 at halftime, and when superb placekicker Morten Andersen added a forty-two-yard field goal early in the third quarter, the Superdome fans were raucous and let the visiting Eagles hear it.

However, the Eagles had a pass rush that included Hall of Famer Reggie White and running mate Jerome Brown. They turned up the intensity and punished Hebert throughout the second half with a vicious pass rush, and the Eagles outscored them 26-0 in the fourth quarter and rolled to a 36-20 victory.

Mora and his team never got over that defeat. He would remain with New Orleans for four more seasons, but their talent level and confidence eroded over that period.

Mora left the Saints following the 1996 season and after spending a year away from the sidelines, he was named head coach of the Indianapolis Colts in 1998.

The Colts had drafted quarterback Peyton Manning that year, and they struggled to a 3-13 record. However, they turned that around the following season and went 13-3 to earn first place in the AFC East. The Colts had a home playoff game against the Tennessee Titans, and they could not contend with Titans running back Eddie George, who gashed the Indianapolis defense for 162 yards. The Colts dropped a 19-16 decision.

It seemed like Mora would finally get his playoff victory the following year. The Colts made the postseason as a wild-card team with a 10-6 record. They played a near-perfect road game against the Dolphins, and took a 17-10 fourth quarter lead when place-kicker Mike Vanderjagt boomed home a fifty-yard field goal with 5:01 remaining.

The Indianapolis defense had been strong throughout the game, but it gave up the game-tying touchdown with forty seconds remaining, and the two teams went to overtime. Vanderjagt had a chance to win the game with a forty-nine-yard attempt in overtime, but he could not convert, and the Dolphins won the game on a seventeen-yard touchdown run by Lamar Smith.

That defeat was the last of Mora's six attempts to win postseason games, and his team had failed in all of them. He never made excuses and he always assessed his team openly and honestly when mistakes were made. He took responsibility for his own issues and never tried to excuse them.

His blunt assessments and pronouncements were often captured on camera. He spared no one, including the media. "You think you know, but you don't know. And you never will."

His famous "playoffs" rant remains popular on football broadcasts and YouTube.

Mora had taken struggling teams in New Orleans and Indianapolis and turned them into consistent regular-season winners, but that's where it ended. He was not able to succeed in the playoffs, and those defeats are part of his legacy.

However, if he had not been such a competent and strong-willed coach, the Saints and Colts would have taken much longer to become successful teams.

For the record

> **Jim Mora**
> Regular-season record: 125-106-0, .541
> Postseason record: 0-6, .000
> Two division championships

#30

JOHN FOX

J ohn Fox may coach in the modern era of professional football, but he does it with a mentality that would make coaches from older eras like Vince Lombardi, Don Shula, and Chuck Noll smile broadly.

Fox has a conservative outlook to his game, and he wants to take care of the basics whenever he has been put in charge of a team. He wants his team to run the ball. He wants his team to stop the run. He wants his team to pressure the opponent's quarterback.

Do all three of those things, Fox believes, and your team is going to win a lot more games than it loses.

Fox never played professional football, but he was a hard enough hitter in the San Diego State secondary during his college days to earn the nickname "Crash."

He started his coaching career shortly thereafter, and it's no surprise that a guy who loved to deliver the big hit would gravitate towards coaching defense. That would eventually become his specialty, and he had a long run as a college assistant coach until Noll plucked him to coach the Pittsburgh Steelers' defensive backs in 1989. After spending three years with the Steelers, he moved on to the Chargers and coached two years under Bobby Ross.

By that time, Fox had earned a reputation as one of the sharpest defensive coaches in the league, and Oakland Raiders head coach Art Shell hired him to be the team's defensive coordinator. His tenure with the Raiders was a short one, because Fox saw how things operated within the franchise.

Owner Al Davis was still a man of great influence, and he did not hesitate to tell Raiders' coaches what he thought of their game plans and what changes needed to be made. Fox did not see this as one of the game's most innovative minds offering up his knowledge. Instead, he saw Davis as the worst kind of meddler and he abruptly quit because he simply couldn't abide it.

That decision may fly in the face of Fox's general perception from the image he has projected because he seems like such a likable and agreeable individual. However, dealing with an owner who wouldn't let coaches do what they were paid to do rubbed Fox the wrong way and he stood by his principles.

The New York Giants took notice, and they hired him as their defensive coordinator. He got consistent results, as the Giants finished in the top 10 in points allowed in each of his five seasons there.

The Giants won the 2000 NFC Championship, as they ripped the Minnesota Vikings 41-0 in the conference championship game, and Fox earned a great deal of credit for the way his defense shut down what had been a very explosive Minnesota offense.

While the Giants were obliterated by the Baltimore Ravens in the Super Bowl, Fox had established his reputation as one of the top defensive coordinators in the NFL. It would be just a matter of time until he got an opportunity to become an NFL head coach.

That chance came in 2002, when the moribund Carolina Panthers hired him to make immediate repairs on a team that had finished a dreadful 1-15 the previous year under George Seifert, and looked hopeless.

Fox changed that immediately, as the Panthers became a respectable team and finished 7-9. Fox was not a complex head coach who came up with game plans that were designed to force opposing coaches into mental gymnastics. He merely wanted both of his lines to win the battle in the trenches and he wanted his running game to exert his will on opponents.

The Panthers not only played respectable football in 2002, but they also established a reputation for toughness, and the holdover who had suffered through the dreadful 2001 performance were believers. The 2003 season saw the Panthers get off to a shocking 8-2 start, as the offense had a versatile attack with quarterback Jake Delhomme, running back Stephen Davis, and wide receivers Steve Smith and Muhsin Muhammad.

While the offense moved the ball consistently, the defense often locked down opponents and made big plays at key moments.

They finished first in the NFC South Division and beat the Cowboys by a convincing 29-10 in the wild-card round of the playoffs. Despite that victory, they were not expected to give the explosive St. Louis Rams much of a battle in the divisional playoffs on the road. Instead, the Panthers extended the game to double overtime, and they beat the Rams when Delhomme hit the explosive Smith with a sixty-nine-yard game-winning touchdown pass.

The Panthers pulled off another upset in the NFC Championship game when they punished the Philadelphia Eagles 14-3 on the road, and that gave Fox an opportunity to take his team to the Super Bowl in his second season.

Carolina had a daunting task in trying to beat the New England Patriots, but they stayed in the game for sixty minutes and tied the score when Ricky Proehl caught a game-tying touchdown pass from Delhomme with 1:14 remaining. However, Fox's dreams of glory dissolved into teams when Adam Vinatieri hit a game-winning forty-one-yard field goal.

Two years later, the Panthers made it back to the NFC Championship game, but they lost an opportunity to get back to the Super Bowl when they dropped a 34-14 decision to the Seattle Seahawks.

Fox kept the Panthers competitive through the 2009 season, but they fell apart in 2010 and Fox was fired after Carolina slipped to 2-14.

The Denver Broncos wasted no time in hiring him, and even though they had a substandard offense and an ordinary defense, they made the playoffs in 2011 as they won a very poor AFC West with an 8-8 record. Most expected a blowout in their playoff game against the Steelers, but quarterback Tim Tebow threw a game-winning touchdown pass in overtime to shock Pittsburgh.

There would be no magic the following week at New England, and neither Fox nor general manager John Elway had any belief that Tebow was a viable alternative at quarterback.

The Broncos made a bold move and signed Peyton Manning in free agency, and even though he was coming off neck surgery that caused him to miss the 2011 season, the Broncos turned over their offense to him.

The results were spectacular, as the Broncos went 13-3, 13-3, and 12-4 over the next three seasons. They parlayed their explosive offense and hard-hitting defense into a Super Bowl appearance following the 2013 season, but the Broncos played poorly in the championship game and were blown out by the Seahawks.

When Denver lost its divisional playoff game the following year at home against the Indianapolis Colts, the Broncos and Fox decided to part company. While Elway announced the decision as mutual, there were behind-the-scenes disagreements between Fox and Manning as well as Fox and Elway that led to the change.

Fox was pursued immediately by a Chicago Bears team that played pitiful football in 2014. They took a look at Fox's track record and saw how successful he had been when he took over a brutal team in Carolina, and believed he was the right man for the job. He was hired by Chicago days after leaving Denver.

Fox knows how to coach defense, eliminate errors, and find a way to win. While he may have fallen short of winning the Super Bowl, he has the ability to get the most out of a team and the Bears are counting on him to return them to respectability.

For the record

> **John Fox**
> Regular-season record: 119-89-0, .572
> Postseason record: 8-7, .533

#31

GEORGE SEIFERT

Do you know who Phil Bengtson was?

Even some of the most devout, long-time (non–Green Bay Packers) fans have no idea who Bengtson was or what he did.

But he has a page in the history of pro football and even his own chapter in the Packers' lengthy history. When Vince Lombardi decided to retire from his position as head coach of the Green Bay Packers, Bengtson was named to take over.

While the Packers were starting to get older, many thought Bengtson would merely take the handoff from Lombardi and the team would continue to contend for championships.

But running a championship team is not easy, and the Packers quickly became also-rans.

George Seifert could have been to the Niners what Bengtson was to the Packers—a footnote in team history—following head coach Bill Walsh's retirement.

Walsh was the genius who had been the architect of the Niners' rise to prominence. They couldn't possibly succeed without him. How could the quiet and expressionless Seifert follow one of the greatest and most inventive coaches in the history of the game?

Here's what Seifert did. He coached the 49ers for eight seasons, and he won double-digit games in all of them. He won the Super Bowl in his first year as head coach and he won it again five years later. He had a regular season record of 114-62-0 with the Niners and his teams won six NFC West championships.

But when most people think of the game's greatest coaches, Seifert doesn't even get a sniff.

It's time for them to think again.

Seifert may not have been a genius like his predecessor, but he was a perfectionist with the 49ers. He had started with Walsh as his secondary coach in 1980, and a year later he had three rookies starting in the defensive backfield when the Niners won their first Super Bowl

Three years later, he was named the Niners' defensive coordinator. The 49ers would go on to win their second championship of the Walsh era following the 1984 season as they rolled to a 15-1 record and hammered the Miami Dolphins in the Super Bowl.

However, Joe Montana and the Niners offense were not unscathed that season. During practice every day, Walsh's offense would go up against Seifert's defense. Seifert's defense often got the best of those battles.

When Walsh stepped down following the Niners' heart-stopping victory over the Cincinnati Bengals in Super Bowl XXIII, there was an air of a letdown surrounding San Francisco. The story of

Bengtson was a bit fresher in 1989 than it is now, and most expected that Seifert did not have the coaching skill or personality to follow Walsh.

Some of those thoughts came from Walsh. He respected Seifert and knew he was a good coach, but he wanted to protect his own legacy. Walsh had many insecurities, and he was not above raising questions about his successor.

Many picked up on Walsh's thoughts and questioned Seifert's overall ability. Seifert was well aware of the whispering campaign.

"There was no way I couldn't be aware of it," Seifert said. "There were a lot of things being said, but I concentrated on coaching the team and preparing for each game as much as I could. I developed the most as a coach under Bill. I have always held him in the highest regard."

Seifert clearly took the high road.

He may not have shown it on the sidelines, but Seifert knew how to coach football. For one thing, he raised the morale inside the 49ers locker room.

The players were used to the regal Walsh, and his uncommunicative ways. Walsh would talk to players he perceived as his leaders, but he would often ignore many others.

Seifert talked to everyone and let them know his expectations and where they stood. He might not have been cracking jokes and he might not have been the players' buddy, but he let them know in an honest fashion where they stood with him.

Seifert came in with a spectacular 14-2 season, and the 49ers were even better that year in the postseason. They dominated the Minnesota Vikings 41-13 and then punished the Los Angeles Rams 30-3 in the NFC Championship game.

They continued their mission of destruction in Super Bowl XXIV against John Elway and the Denver Broncos. The Niners scored two touchdowns in every quarter and they pounded the Broncos 55-10 in the most one-sided game in Super Bowl history.

As well as Montana played throughout the 1989 season, he was nearing the end of his time with the 49ers. When Montana was seriously injured in the 1990 NFC Championship game against the Giants, Seifert knew that it was time to turn the team over to Steve Young on a full-time basis.

There was no controversy at first, because Montana was not healthy enough to play in the 1991 season, but when he came back in 1992, Montana's supporters barked their support.

Seifert was strong enough not to make a move. Young remained as a starter, and Montana would be traded to the Kansas City Chiefs after the '92 season.

A weak coach would not have been able to stick to his guns. But Seifert knew that Young was a brilliant quarterback in his own right and he was just coming into his own.

Young would lead the Niners to one of their best seasons in 1994. They rolled to yet another NFC West crown with a 13-3 record, and were an unstoppable force during the playoffs.

San Francisco humiliated the Chicago Bears 44-15 in the divisional playoffs, and that set up a confrontation with the defending Super Bowl champion Dallas Cowboys in the NFC Championship.

This may have been the most worthy team the 49ers faced in their championship years, but they did not let this game get away. They rolled to a 38-28 victory as Young's passing and the 49ers' active defense frustrated the Cowboys at every turn.

Another Super Bowl appearance would prove fruitful for Seifert and Young. The upstart San Diego Chargers had shocked the football world by beating the marauding Pittsburgh Steelers in the AFC title game, and some thought of Bobby Ross's Chargers as a team of destiny.

That title disappeared in the early moments of the first quarter. The Niners scored two touchdowns before the game was five minutes old and rolled to a 49-26 victory.

Young threw a record six touchdown passes in the win and famously wrestled the monkey off of his back. Prior to that win, many critics said Young simply could not win "the big one." He ended that reputation in remarkable fashion.

Seifert coached two more seasons with the Niners, and went 11-5 and 12-4 in those seasons. However, the Niners did not want him around any longer and he resigned, as the organization had been giving him the cold shoulder.

He would return to coaching in 1999 with the Carolina Panthers, and after two non-descript seasons, he had a brutal 1-15 year in 2001 to close his career.

It was a tough way to go out, but it doesn't change the fact that Seifert was one of thirteen NFL coaches to win multiple Super Bowls and have eight seasons in which he won ten or more games.

He may have been in a good position to work under Walsh for so many years, but he established his own legacy as a brilliant defensive mind and one of the game's best coaches.

For the record

> **George Seifert**
> Regular-season record: 114-62-0, .648
> Postseason record: 10-5, .667
> Two Super Bowl victories

#32

JON GRUDEN

To many NFL fans, Jon Gruden is the pointed analyst on *Monday Night Football* who has a tendency to go to extremes when describing plays on an every-week basis. "This Peyton Manning, this Tom Brady, this Philip Rivers, this Cam Newton … this Ryan Fitzpatrick …"

… According to Gruden, they are all the greatest.

While he is fairly accomplished at breaking down plays, and slightly palatable since he stopped fighting for air time with Ron Jaworski, it's easy to pick up on the fact that this former coach would like to be back on the sidelines.

Jon Gruden

Gruden has certainly been through the wars and created an even bigger impression when he was on the sidelines for the Oakland Raiders and the Tampa Bay Buccaneers. He nearly took the Raiders all the way to the Super Bowl, and he got there with the Bucs and led them to their only championship.

But that's more the climax of the story. Gruden started his NFL coaching career with the San Francisco 49ers in 1990. Mike Holmgren, who was the offensive coordinator under George Seifert, hired Gruden as a quality control assistant.

With that one year of experience, Gruden was able to get an assistant coaching job at the University of Pittsburgh. From there, it was back to the NFL and Holmgren when he was named head coach of the Green Bay Packers in 1992. After working with Brett Favre as the Packers' quarterback coach, Gruden took an offensive coordinator position with the Philadelphia Eagles in 1995.

While the Eagles did not have stellar offensive personnel—Ty Detmer and Rodney Peete shared the quarterback duties—Gruden built one of the top offenses in the league. Many around the league took notice, including Raiders owner Al Davis.

Gruden, a practitioner of the West Coast Offense, was hired by Davis to coach the Raiders. Davis had long favored using an offense that featured a downfield passing attack, but his team had been struggling and backsliding, so he gave Gruden the chance to build his own attack in an attempt to raise the Raiders' level of play.

Gruden quickly became known around the league for his quirkiness and sideline antics. In a league where many coaches worked long hours so they could figure out opponents' tendencies and build a winning strategy, Gruden decided he was going to get a jump on the competition by coming in to work at 4 a.m. Gruden made it a point to let everyone know how early he was arriving, and the media soon picked up on it.

He also had a tendency to make strange faces on the sidelines when referees' calls went against the Raiders or one of his players made a mistake. His facial contortions and diminutive stature appeared to have an odd resemblance to the wooden doll character "Chucky" from the fright movie *Child's Play*. Thereafter, Gruden was regularly referred to as Chucky in a demeaning way.

While Gruden did not embrace the nickname, he slowly built the Raiders into one of the better teams in the league, and that eased the pressure that Davis put on him.

The Raiders were 8-8 in Gruden's first two seasons, but the 2000 Raiders turned the corner and went 12-4, finishing first in the AFC West. With Rich Gannon handling the quarterback duties, the Raiders completely eschewed Davis's downfield passing game and became an effective West Coast team.

The Raiders won seven of eight games in the middle of the season, and that included back-to-back road victories over the 49ers and the Kansas City Chiefs. Nothing made Davis happier than beating his cross-bay rivals and then his team's traditional AFL rival.

The Raiders rolled into the playoffs with a head of steam and easily dispatched the Miami Dolphins 27-0. The ease of that victory made them favorites over the Baltimore Ravens in the AFC title game, but the Baltimore defense was playing at the highest level the NFL had seen since the 1985 Chicago Bears, and they came into Oakland and squashed the Raiders 16-3.

The Raiders were solid again in 2001, and defended their AFC West title. After beating the New York Jets in the wild-card game, they earned a date with the New England Patriots in the divisional playoffs. The Raiders seemed to have that game locked up when Raiders defensive back Charles Woodson forced a late fumble from Tom Brady, which gave the Raiders the ball in the final moments.

Since the Raiders had a 13-10 lead at the time, it appeared all they would have to do was run a few plays and grind out the final moments. But before that could happen, the officials got together and decided Brady's arm was coming forwards as he fumbled and the officials determined this to be a "tucking" motion, which made it an incomplete pass.

The Pats held on to the ball, and placekicker Adam Vinatieri kicked the tying field goal and then won the game with another three-pointer in overtime. The game, played in a New England snowstorm, became one of the most legendary NFL games ever played.

It would also be the last game Gruden would ever coach for the Raiders. After the back-to-back seasons, Gruden wanted a substantial raise, and Davis was not about to give it to him. He actually traded Gruden to the Tampa Bay Bucs for two first-round draft choices, two second-round picks, and $8 million.

Gruden was taking over a Tampa Bay team that had perhaps the best defense in the league at the time. What they didn't have was a competent offense, and that's why they went after Gruden.

It turned out to be a brilliant move. Gruden found a solid quarterback in Brad Johnson, and he turned the Bucs into a competent offensive team. They went 12-4 and won the NFC South Division.

Still, few thought they would be able to accomplish much in the playoffs. The Bucs and Gruden didn't care about what outsiders thought. They were peaking as the playoffs got underway, and they overpowered the San Francisco 49ers 31-6 and then went to Philadelphia to play Andy Reid's Eagles in the NFC Championship game.

At the time, the Bucs had never won a game in their history when temperatures were below the freezing mark at 32 degrees. Few expected that to change in Philadelphia, where they were forced to play in 20-degree conditions.

After the Eagles scored the first touchdown, it appeared the Bucs would offer little competition. But they stiffened and outscored the Eagles 27-3 the rest of the way and earned a spot in Super Bowl XXXVII against none other than the Raiders.

On paper, it looked like a fairly even matchup, with the Raiders having the better offense and the Bucs having the better defense. However, Gruden gave the Bucs a huge strategic advantage. He knew the Raiders so well that he could advise his defense of each player's tendencies down to the smallest detail. In practice prior to the game, Gruden played the role of Gannon and showed the Raiders how he tended to look to his right and pass to his left, or look to his left and pass to his right on a play called Sluggo Seam.

Additionally, Gannon would pat the ball with his left hand an instant before he got rid of it.

This intimate knowledge of the opposition left the Bucs with overwhelming confidence. They played like it and rolled over the Raiders 48-21 in the game. The Bucs' defense knew Gannon so well that they returned three interceptions for touchdowns in the game.

After that brilliant first year in Tampa, Gruden was unable to match that performance again. They experienced just two more playoff appearances in the next six years, and Gruden was fired after the 2008 season.

He has enjoyed a high profile as the Monday night expert analyst, but Gruden still has a desire to coach again if he can find the right situation. His name is often rumored to be in consideration for head coaching openings, but he has not gone back into the battle since his last season in Tampa.

For the record

Jon Gruden
Regular-season record: 95-81-0, .540
Postseason record: 5-4, .556
One Super Bowl victory

#33

MIKE McCARTHY

It was all right there, so close that Mike McCarthy and his Green Bay Packers could reach out and touch it. Then it all disappeared with a harshness and suddenness that will leave lifetime scars.

The Packers had the defending Super Bowl champion Seattle Seahawks all but beaten in the final moments of the 2014 NFC Championship game, and when Morgan Burnett intercepted a Russell Wilson pass with 5:13 remaining in the fourth quarter with the Packers holding a 19-7 lead, the high fives and congratulatory looks and handshakes began on the Green Bay sideline.

They shouldn't have, because the Packers breathed life into the Seahawks from the point that Burnett wrapped his hands around the ball.

McCarthy deserved his share of the blame, because the Packers were playing conservative football throughout much of the fourth quarter even though they were at their best when attacking with Aaron Rodgers at the quarterback slot.

As the game disintegrated and the Seahawks came back to win the game in overtime, McCarthy and his players wore stunned looks that belied the team's humiliation. No matter what happens in the future, the Packers will long feel the pain of the opportunity they let slip away in 2014.

While it will always hurt, McCarthy has proved to be one of the best coaches of his generation and deserves credit for being one of the best offensive minds in the game.

McCarthy paid his dues as a college assistant and got his first chance to work in the NFL as an assistant on Marty Schottenheimer's Kansas City Chiefs. From there he moved on to Green Bay, New Orleans, and San Francisco, and it was with the Saints that he showed he had the kind of offensive knowledge and teaching ability that would make him an excellent head coach.

Prior to the 2000 season, his first in New Orleans, McCarthy urged the Saints to pick up third-string quarterback Aaron Brooks. Under McCarthy's tutelage, Brooks became a starter and the Saints won the NFC South and a wild-card playoff game. McCarthy won assistant coach of the year honors for his ability to guide Brooks and help him develop into a winning and competitive quarterback.

McCarthy was on the head coaching radar after that, and his chance came in 2006. There were questions in Green Bay, where fans wanted an established winner, but general manager Ted Thompson was convinced that McCarthy had the personal skills as well as the X's and O's knowledge to lead the Packers back to glory.

McCarthy produced immediate results, as he helped the Packers improve from 4–12 in 2005 to 8–8 in his first year.

Green Bay came roaring out of the gate in 2007, and rolled to a 13–3 record. That allowed them to claim the No. 2 seed in the NFC, and they defeated the Seahawks 42–20 in the divisional play-offs.

Since the top-seeded Dallas Cowboys had lost their divisional playoff game to the Giants, the Packers were able to host New York in the NFC title game. It looked like Green Bay and quarterback Brett Favre would earn a trip to the Super Bowl, but the long-time Packer legend's last pass in overtime was intercepted and set the Giants up for the game-winning field goal.

That play began an important trial for McCarthy and Thompson. By the end of the season, they were convinced that they wanted Rodgers to take over at quarterback and that it was time for Favre to retire (preferably) or move on.

Favre began a retirement dance that would go on for several years, but McCarthy and Thompson never wavered. They ultimately let Favre go so he could continue his career with the New York Jets (and then the Minnesota Vikings), and that gave Rodgers the opportunity to take over as the starting quarterback.

While Favre had become the greatest quarterback in Green Bay history and one of the legendary franchise's most beloved icons, McCarthy, Thompson, and Rodgers were ultimately able to win the public relations battle in the eyes of the public because they never vacillated, while Favre seemed to behave like a diva.

Ultimately, Rodgers would prove to be every bit as effective as Favre, and he gave the Packers sensational accuracy and leadership.

Green Bay struggled to a 6–10 record in 2008, but rebounded to 11–5 the following season and that allowed McCarthy's team to make the playoffs. It ended in shocking fashion, as the Packers went up and down the field but lost a 51–45 decision in overtime to Arizona when Rodgers lost a fumble and Cardinals linebacker

Karlos Dansby picked up the loose ball and returned it 17 yards for a game-winning touchdown.

The 2010 season would have a much better finish for McCarthy and the Packers. While they needed a Week 17 win over the Chicago Bears to earn a wild-card spot, they took advantage of that magical opportunity to go on a brilliant postseason run.

They defeated the Eagles, Falcons, and Bears on the road, and earned a spot in Super Bowl XLV against the Pittsburgh Steelers. Rodgers and the Packers built a solid 21-3 lead late in the second quarter and held on to record a 31-25 victory.

The partnership of McCarthy and Rodgers had won as many Super Bowls for Green Bay as Favre had during his legendary run, and the feeling was that Rodgers would continue to improve under McCarthy's tutelage.

McCarthy was able to continue his advanced teaching with Rodgers, and the quarterback became an artist with the football in his hands.

Rodgers developed the best footwork in the league and his passes were more precise than any other quarterback.

While the Packers regularly struggled on the defensive side of the ball, it was clear that nobody wanted to get into shootouts with Green Bay. That included New England QB Tom Brady, who played a brilliant game in Week 13 of the 2014 season, but came up on the short end of a 26-21 loss at Green Bay because Rodgers was even better.

That's one of the reasons that NFC Championship loss to Seattle was so painful for McCarthy and the Packers. Green Bay had already beaten New England in the regular season, and the team had full confidence it could do it again in the Super Bowl.

That would have given McCarthy his second Lombardi Trophy as a head coach, which would have put him in rare company.

However, he still has built a solid career that still appeared to be in its prime as the 2014 season came to an end.

For the record

Mike McCarthy
Regular-season record: 94-49-1, .666
Postseason record: 7-6, .538
One Super Bowl victory

#34

STEVE OWEN

The New York Giants have been one of the NFL's bedrock franchises for decades, and they have cultivated a certain image that has stayed with them most of their successful years.

They play rock-hard defense, they run the ball, and they don't make a lot of mistakes. They play simplistic football, yes, but effective football nonetheless. This was the game plan followed by long-time head coach Steve Owen, who headed the Giants from 1931 through 1953, and 17 of those 23 seasons were winning ones.

Owen gave the Giants franchise consistency and an identity, something that was lacking when he came aboard.

The Giants were a winning team when owner Tim Mara hired him, but there was a mutiny brewing because the players couldn't stand head coach Leroy Andrews. They revolted, went to Mara, and said they couldn't play for the intractable Andrews any longer and the owner went along.

He gave the position to Owen, and he did so with the marching orders that the infighting would stop. Mara was not worried about the Giants' performance on the field because he could see that he had a talented roster. He wanted a coach who would treat his players like men, listen to their issues, and then figure out a way to fix problems. He was sick and tired of players coming upstairs and bothering him. He wanted a coach who could command the locker room with respect.

That's what he got with Owen, who was tough-minded but reasonable throughout the majority of his years with the Giants.

He was also a devotee of defensive gameplanning, and that's how he would help the Giants become one of the top teams in the NFL. Four of his teams allowed the fewest points in the NFL, and the Giants were in the top three in that category ten times. Nasty, hardhitting, and effective defensive play was his calling card as coach of the New York Football Giants. (They were regularly referred to that way to avoid confusion with the baseball team by the same name. The baseball Giants moved to San Francisco following the 1957 season.)

Owen didn't mind if an opponent drove the field on his defense and had to settle for three-pointers. It was part of Owen's bend-but-don't-break philosophy.

Owen believed that if he could prevent offenses from making big plays and force them to drive the field, they would make mistakes. His goal was to have his defense in a position to take advantage of those mistakes and take the ball away from his opponents.

Owen was one of the first coaches to pay serious attention to defense in practice every day, and his "Umbrella" setup with four defensive backs playing in the secondary became the forerunner of the base 4-3 defense that remains one of the staples of modern defensive play.

Owen laid the foundation for the Giants in his first two years with the team when they were quite ordinary. However, by the 1933 season they had absorbed his lessons and became a consistent championship contender. From 1933 through the 1946 season, the Giants played in eight NFL Championship games.

While they won only two of those games, both of those championship teams were quite legendary. The 1934 Giants won the East Division with an 8-5-0 record, and that allowed them to host the championship game against George Halas's Bears, who had ripped their way through the league with a 13-0 record. The Bears had rocked the Giants 27-7 in Chicago during the regular season, and nobody expected the Giants to reverse that outcome even though they were playing in New York at the Polo Grounds. Nevertheless, Halas knew that whenever his team played the Giants, it was going to feature great defensive play that was all about keeping the Bears out of the end zone and making them settle for field goal attempts.

Throughout the first three quarters of the game that was played in icy conditions at the venerable stadium, the Bears dictated the pace and built a 13-3 lead. But the Giants were not about to surrender. At the start of the fourth quarter, they changed their footwear from ineffective spikes to conventional gym shoes. Giants end Ray Flaherty had suggested to Owen that the players would be more effective in basketball shoes that gripped the surface, so Owen had an assistant retrieve nine pairs of the shoes from nearby Manhattan College.

Suddenly, the Giants came to life at the start of the final quarter as quarterback Ed Danowski threw one touchdown pass and ran for another, while running back Ken Strong had two touchdown runs. By the time the final fifteen minutes had concluded, the Giants had outscored the Bears 27-0 and ended the Bears' eighteen-game winning streak. Halas and his players were flabbergasted. That championship contest would live on in NFL history as "The Sneakers Game."

The Giants would meet the Green Bay Packers in the 1938 title game after winning the East Division with an 8-2-1 record. The Giants were surging, as they went 7-0-1 to finish the regular season after starting with two losses in three games. They had a solid offense led by Danowski and Tuffy Leemans, but the Packers were a more explosive offensive team, with Cecil Isbell passing and Arnie Herber running the ball.

The Giants would outlast Green Bay 23-17, as Owen's defense forced three turnovers to seal the deal for New York.

Owen's conservative nature was an issue in the Giants' other championship game appearances. While he was content to try to establish the run in those games, opponents came up with more innovative offenses and that put the Giants at a disadvantage.

He would come around and later start to use the T-formation that nearly all of his opponents had installed years before, but Owen would never embrace that offensive formation. He preferred to tinker with the defense, and didn't take advantage of the skill that his faster players had.

As the years went along, Owen followed a practice held by many veteran coaches. He trusted his long-time players and looked on rookies and other less experienced players with disdain. That caused a rift between him and his younger players, and that showed in the Giants' 41-40-3 record over the final seven years of his tenure in New York.

Eventually, Owen was fired by Wellington Mara after the 1953 season. Owen always thought that football was a series of one-on-one battles, and the team with the stronger and tougher men would win the majority of those battles. He tended to ignore strategy that would take advantage of speed and quickness.

While it was a tough way for his career with the Giants to come to an end, few coaches were ever able to build teams that played as consistently as Owen's Giants. They played with so much ferocity on defense, and that's the legacy that got him elected to the Hall of Fame in 1966.

For the record

> **Steve Owen**
> Hall of Fame, 1996
> Regular-season record: 151–100–17, .602
> Postseason record: 2-8, .200
> Two NFL championships

#35

MIKE SHANAHAN

J ohn Elway was desperate after the 1994 season. He had been playing in the NFL since 1983 and had gotten close to winning the Super Bowl three times.

He had been the triggerman for three AFC Championship teams, and each one of those teams had lost in the Super Bowl. Each of those defeats had been more humiliating than the one before, and Elway did not want his career to conclude without a Super Bowl ring.

Many players feel the same way, but are often powerless to do anything about it. Elway may have been the best quarterback of his generation and there were no doubts about his physical gifts.

Elway had spent the majority of his career working with Dan Reeves to bring the Broncos a title, but when that relationship ran its course after the 1992 season, Reeves was sent packing by owner Pat Bowlen at the urging of the quarterback.

The Broncos were ordinary the next two seasons under Wade Phillips, going 9-7 and then 7-9. Phillips was relieved of his coaching duties, and Elway was sure who he wanted to coach the Broncos.

He went to the Super Bowl following that season and sought out Mike Shanahan, who was the offensive coordinator of the San Francisco 49ers. San Francisco was days away from winning the Super Bowl title against the upstart San Diego Chargers, and Elway went to Miami to convince Shanahan to become the next head coach of the Broncos.

Shanahan had been an offensive coordinator with the Broncos, and Elway loved his offensive creativity. That aspect of the Broncos offense had been put asunder by Reeves's conservative nature, and Elway knew in his heart that if he was going to win a Super Bowl in the final years of his career, he needed a great mind like Shanahan's to lead him to it.

Shortly after the Niners annihilated the Chargers, Shanahan became head coach of the Broncos, and Elway could not have been more relieved.

He knew there were no guarantees that the Broncos would get to the Super Bowl and win it, but he knew that Shanahan represented his last and best chance to get there.

Shanahan took the job, the second NFL head coaching position of his career. He had coached the Los Angeles Raiders in 1988 and into the '89 season, but that position fell apart when he started bumping heads with Al Davis. Shanahan's tenure with the Raiders ended four games into his second season with them and it was an ugly divorce that resulted in disdain between the two for twenty years.

By the time he became the Broncos' top gun, he was a fully mature coach who had his own game plan, could communicate it to his players, and excelled at teaching the game.

He laid the groundwork for his coaching tenure in 1995 during an 8-8 season, but the Broncos became an elite team after that. They were 13-3 in 1996 and the top seed in the AFC playoffs, and they were expected to roll through the postseason.

Strangely and shockingly, the Broncos lost a divisional playoff game to the upstart Jacksonville Jaguars, a defeat that left the city of Denver shaking and wondering if the team would ever win a championship.

But Shanahan was not shaken. He knew the talent was there and that the Broncos would continue to contend for the title. In addition to Elway, Shanahan had upgraded the Broncos' offensive line and drafted a sensational running back in Terrell Davis.

Elway had never had a viable running game to support him in the past, but Davis changed that. He was a powerful between-the-tackles runner who had the speed to run away from tacklers once he got to the second level.

Davis rushed for 1,538 yards in '96, and he followed that up with a 1,750-yard season and 15 touchdowns in '97. That ability to run the ball gave the Broncos' offense a dynamic quality that had been missing from other Broncos' teams in the past.

Elway was more than happy to take advantage of the newly found versatility of the running game. At the age of thirty-seven, Elway was still a gifted quarterback with a powerful arm, but he was no longer the swift athlete who could outrun the defense consistently. The presence of Davis meant opponents were forced to defend the run, and not just pay lip service.

So the defeat in the '96 postseason may have been painful for everyone within the organization, but it just steeled Shanahan more for the '97 season. After a 12-4 season, the Broncos were back in the postseason and their first opponent was Jacksonville once again.

There would be no repeat of the previous year's debacle. The Broncos rolled to a 42-17 triumph, and that victory gave them confidence to move forward.

The Broncos followed up with road triumphs over the Chiefs in the divisional playoffs and came up with a huge upset over the Steelers in Pittsburgh that earned them a trip to Super Bowl XXXII against the Green Bay Packers, in San Diego.

Green Bay had won the championship the year before and the combination of head coach Mike Holmgren and Brett Favre appeared to be an unbeatable one. Additionally, NFC teams had won a remarkable twelve straight Super Bowls, and the Packers were huge favorites to win this game as well.

Green Bay had confidently swaggered around San Diego in the days before the game with an edge that bordered on conceit. The Packers came out on fire, as Favre hit Antonio Freeman with an early twenty-two-yard touchdown pass, and many thought the rout was on.

However, it was just the first blow in a heavyweight fight. The Broncos hit back with a big play every time Green Bay made one, and that seemed to shock the Packers. Davis and Elway scored first-half touchdowns to give the Broncos the lead, but the game was tight throughout.

Shanahan had helped his team stand up to what many thought was a superior opponent, and they got the inspiration to win the game when Elway converted a crucial fourth down by taking two big hits and running for a first down late in the third quarter. When his teammates saw him make that play, they were not about to lose.

Davis scored the go-ahead touchdown in a 31–24 victory, and the defense stopped Favre on his final drive when his fourth-down pass to Mark Chmura was batted away.

The Broncos and Elway had their title, and Shanahan was the architect.

The Broncos defended that title the following year by beating the Atlanta Falcons, who were coached by Reeves.

In turn, Elway retired with two consecutive championships.

Shanahan coached the Broncos for ten more seasons and made four more playoff appearances, but the team could not get back to the Super Bowl. Shanahan and the Broncos parted company after the 2008 season, and he was often criticized for never winning another Super Bowl without Elway on his side.

However, it should be noted that Elway never won a Super Bowl without Shanahan.

Shanahan moved on to the Washington Redskins and spent four seasons with them, making the playoffs once. His tenure in Washington never had the even flow and consistency that it did in Denver, and the 2013 season was his last.

Shanahan's discipline, preparation, offensive creativity, knowledge of personnel, and ability to bring about the best from his players allowed him to win back-to-back Super Bowls and earn one of the most respected reputations in the game.

For the record

> **Mike Shanahan**
> Regular-season record: 170-138-0, .552
> Postseason record: 8-6, .5718
> Two Super Bowl victories

#36

GREASY NEALE

Alfred Earle "Greasy" Neale was a part of sports history long before he became head coach of the Philadelphia Eagles in 1941.

As an athlete, he was a major league baseball player in addition to a college football and basketball star. His most noteworthy athletic achievements came as a baseball player for the Cincinnati Reds. Neale played outfield for the Reds from 1916 through 1924, and batted .259 over that span.

While his overall play was average, he played a starring role for the Reds in the 1919 World Series, when he batted .357 with 10 hits in 28 at-bats against the Chicago White Sox. Few remember that Series for anything other than the fact that the heavily favored

White Sox infamously threw the series at the behest of gambler Arnold Rothstein.

That didn't impact Neale, who lashed line drives throughout the series.

But Neale's heart was in football, and he coached college football even as he played in the major leagues. His big break appeared to come when he was hired to coach at West Virginia in 1931, but he struggled to win with the Mountaineers and moved on to Yale in 1934, where he served as the team's backfield coach.

Neale had been known as an innovative coach throughout his twenty-five-year run as a college coach. One of his most important moves was to give defensive linemen an alternative to charging straight ahead and attempting to overpower offensive linemen on every play.

Instead, Neale had his inside linemen loop to the outside before charging into the backfield, with his defensive ends looping to the inside. Neale devised these "stunts" to confuse opposing blockers and give his defensive line a chance to gather momentum before they attempted to stop plays in the backfield.

Owner Lex Thompson hired Neale to coach the Philadelphia Eagles in 1941. Thompson was a Yale alumnus who was quite impressed with Neale's knowledge of the game and his coaching ability.

However, Neale inherited a poor team that had never had a winning season, and he knew he couldn't win with the players he had on his roster. A year after he was hired, the World War II effort took away many of the Eagles players—as it had from other teams throughout the league—and that prevented Neale from making any significant moves with the roster.

However, the team grew steadily stronger, and by the time the war ended, Neale had a team that included quarterback Tommy Thompson, end Pete Pihos, and running backs Steve Van Buren and "Bosh" Pritchard.

Neale was a demanding coach on the practice field who would not tolerate mistakes. He was bold, loud, and intimidating, and he had an amazing ability to pick out the slightest flaw he saw on the practice field, explain it to his players, and correct it immediately.

Unlike most coaches who came across as disciplinarians on the field, he was not afraid to show another side to his personality off the field. He was friendly and gregarious away from the football field, and the same players that he upbraided on the field a few hours earlier genuinely enjoyed spending time with him off of it.

That helped the Eagles become a close-knit team. He led them to their first winning record in 1943, and they never had a losing record throughout the rest of his tenure, which ended in 1950.

Neale helped the Eagles build one of the NFL's most consistent offenses throughout the 1940s. Like many other football coaches, he was shocked and impressed when the Chicago Bears destroyed the Washington Redskins by a 73-0 margin in the 1940 NFL Championship game with their innovative T-formation.

Neale studied Chicago's format and gave the Eagles an improved version. While the Bears had concentrated on running the ball between the tackles, Neale made sure his team also had the option of taking plays to the outside. As he perfected the Eagles' version of the T, he also built a counter formation for his defense.

He knew that nearly all of his competition would be running some version of the T, so building a defense that could stop it was essential to winning. Neale devised a 5-4-2 format, which was quite naturally called the Eagle defense.

Additionally, Neale originated the concept of man-to-man coverage in defending the pass, and then putting as many as nine men on the line in a goalline defense. Teams did not stack the line of scrimmage when opponents were threatening until Neale came up with the concept.

By the 1947 season, the Eagles were functioning at a very high level. They tied the Pittsburgh Steelers with an 8-4 record, good for first in the East Division, and whipped Pittsburgh 21-0 to earn a spot in the NFL Championship game against the Chicago Cardinals.

The Eagles were playing catch-up throughout the game, and when Chicago's Elmer Angsman ran seventy yards for a touchdown in the fourth period, Chicago took a 28-14 lead. The Eagles closed to within seven points when Russ Craft scored on a one-yard run, but they could get no closer.

The Eagles were sharper and even more focused the following year when they rolled to a 9-2-1 record. They faced the Cardinals again in the 1948 season opener, and dropped a 21-14 decision, but they were nearly unbeatable from that point forward.

When the Cardinals came to Philadelphia for an NFL Championship game rematch, the two teams were forced to play in a brutal snowstorm. It was nearly impossible for either team to sustain an offense, but Van Buren scored the only touchdown in the fourth quarter and the Eagles had their first NFL title.

The Eagles were even better in 1949, as they rolled to an 11-1 record. They were clearly the best team in the league, but the NFL did not offer home field advantage to the team with the best record in the league. Since they had hosted the NFL Championship game as the East Division champion against the West Division's Cardinals the previous year, they were forced to play at the West Division champion's home field in 1949.

It was a trip that Neale and his players enjoyed thoroughly. Instead of playing in cold and snowy Philadelphia, the Eagles went to sunny Los Angeles to play the Rams. The Eagles had defeated Los Angeles 38-14 earlier in the year and they treated the game like a vacation. The Rams offered little resistance as Philadelphia won its second consecutive title by a 14-0 margin, thanks to a Pihos touchdown pass from Tommy Thompson and a blocked punt for a score.

The Eagles played the most significant Opening Day game in the history of the NFL at the start of the 1950 season. The NFL had allowed the Cleveland Browns, San Francisco 49ers, Baltimore Colts, and New York Yanks from the All-American Football Conference to join the NFL. The Browns had been the dominant team in that league, and Paul Brown's team met Neale's Eagles in the opener.

Once again, the Eagles had a cavalier attitude towards their opponent from a supposedly inferior league. But head coach Paul Brown had the redoubtable Otto Graham at quarterback and the Browns came into Philadelphia and trounced the Eagles 35-10.

That defeat resounded with the Eagles, who had grown older and less efficient. They fell to 6-6-0 that season, and when Lex Thompson sold the team to a syndicate headed by temperamental James Clark, Neale lost his job security.

Clark barged into the locker room following a late-season defeat at the hands of the Giants and criticized Neale in front of his players. Neale responded back in kind, and he was let go by the Eagles at the end of the season.

Neale's run with the Eagles represented the glory years in Philadelphia. They would win another title in 1960, but they have not won another one since then.

Neale was a sharp and innovative coach who turned the fortunes of the Eagles around in a dramatic fashion.

For the record

Greasy Neale
Hall of Fame, 1969
Regular-season record: 63-43-5, .594
Postseason record: 3-1, .750
Two NFL championships

#37

JEFF FISHER

Jeff Fisher was slated to play a key role with the 1985 Chicago Bears, perhaps the greatest defensive team in the history of the NFL.

Fisher was a defensive back with Chicago and also a solid punt returner, and he thought through the game like a coach on the field from the time the Bears drafted him in 1981. However, Fisher hurt his ankle and he was placed on Injured Reserve prior to the start of that season, and he had to watch that great defense play from the sidelines.

Fisher had already impressed Bears defensive coordinator Buddy Ryan with his knowledge of the game prior to 1985, but it became obvious to Ryan and others that Fisher's future was on the sidelines.

When Ryan was named head coach of the Philadelphia Eagles prior to the 1986 season, he took Fisher with him as one of his defensive assistants. He became the Eagles' defensive coordinator by 1988, and there was little doubt that he was one of the fastest-rising coaches in the business.

When the Eagles parted company with Ryan after the 1990 season, they interviewed Fisher as one of the top two candidates for the head coaching job. However, in a decision that would prove to be one of the worst in Eagles history, they went with offensive coordinator Rich Kotite instead of Fisher.

Fisher continued to hone his coaching skills with the Los Angeles Rams under John Robinson, and then he became the Houston Oilers' defensive coordinator.

Fisher was itching for a head coaching position, and he finally got his opportunity when the Oilers parted company with veteran head coach Jack Pardee. They turned their miserable 1-9 team over to Fisher, and he was not able to do much as the Oilers finished the season by winning just one of their last six games.

However, Fisher established his coaching style over those final weeks of the 1994 season, and he became one of those rare individuals who could speak honestly to his players without losing them.

Fisher has always been blunt in his assessments, but he has the gift of being able to speak the truth without his players or assistant coaches hating him for telling them exactly where they stood. Many players will say they want someone who will tell them the truth and let them know where they stand, but they get uncomfortable or insecure when they actually hear it.

More than anything, Fisher's players have always worked hard for him and respected him because he doesn't lie to them. Many head coaches speak around the truth, but few will actually look their players in the eye, tell them exactly what they need to do, and then hold the players and themselves accountable to those requirements.

That's exactly how Fisher has done his job, even through his present-day job as coach of the St. Louis Rams, a team that has gone through some bad years. "In a way, it has been easy for me to treat players that way," Fisher said. "I know how I wanted to be treated as a player and I know that the best coaches are dead honest with them. That's what I believe that nearly every player wants and that's how I treat my players."

Fisher's Oilers showed immediate improvement as they went 7-9 and 8-8 in 1995 and '96, but owner Bud Adams left Houston after that year and took his squad to Tennessee in 1997. It was one of the most difficult years in NFL history for any team, because the squad's new headquarters was in Nashville, but the team played its first season in Memphis, some 212 miles away.

In many ways, the newly named Titans played 16 road games in 1997, and that was a big reason why the team went 8-8. They had to do the same thing in '98, and had another .500 season.

However, they finally moved into their new stadium in Nashville in 1999, changed their name from the Oilers to the Titans, and went 13-3.

In most years, that kind of record would earn a team a division title and a likely bye in the first round of the NFL playoffs. However, the Titans finished second in the AFC South to the 14-2 Jacksonville Jaguars and were forced to travel the wild-card route in the playoffs.

The Titans were tested in the first round by the Buffalo Bills, and it seemed that the Bills would walk out of the Adelphia Coliseum with a 16-15 victory when Buffalo placekicker Steve Christie connected on a forty-one-yard field goal with twenty seconds left on the clock.

But the Titans had been well-prepared by Fisher to overcome the desperate straits in which they found themselves. Tight end Frank Wycheck picked up the kickoff and ran a few steps to his right before turning 180 degrees and lateraling the ball back in the direction he came from. The ball landed in the midsection of speedy return specialist Kevin Dyson, who turned upfield with excellent blocking in front of him and ran seventy-five yards for the game-winning touchdown.

That play became known as the "Music City Miracle."

The Titans used that play to spur them on a great postseason run. They defeated the Indianapolis Colts 19-16 in the divisional play-offs before going to Jacksonville to take on the Jaguars. The Titans were supremely confident they would win that game because they had defeated Jacksonville twice in the regular season. Tennessee rolled behind quarterback Steve McNair, running back Eddie George, and a hard-nosed defense and earned the AFC title with a 33-14 victory.

The Titans faced the St. Louis Rams in the Super Bowl, where they fell behind Dick Vermeil's explosive team 16-0 before mounting a dramatic comeback that allowed them to tie the score at 16-16. The Rams rebounded to take the lead, but the Titans had a chance to score the tying touchdown. On the game's final play, McNair hit Dyson with a short pass and the receiver appeared to be going into the end zone for the tying touchdown. However, St. Louis line-backer Mike Jones brought Dyson down at the one-yard line and the Titans absorbed a crushing defeat.

Fisher has never gotten back to the Super Bowl. His Tennessee teams made four more playoff appearances, but they never had quite enough offensive balance or consistent quarterback play to get to the top of the football world.

Fisher eventually resigned following the 2010 season, and took a year off before resurfacing with the Rams. While he has not brought the Rams back to glory, they are respected as a hard-nosed and honest team that plays nasty and aggressive defense.

Fisher has been a head coach for twenty years, and his honest, straight-forward approach has made him one of the most successful and popular head coaches through the 2014 season.

For the record

Jeff Fisher
Regular–season record: 162–147–1, .524
Postseason record: 5-6, .455

#38

BUDDY PARKER

It is so common today that most football fans can't remember a time when teams didn't run a fast-paced, no-huddle offense at the end of the half or at the conclusion of the game when it was trying to catch up and valuable seconds were draining off the clock.

However, the two-minute offense is not just a part of football the way that gravity is a part of daily existence. It was not born with the game.

It was, in part, an invention of the fertile mind of Raymond "Buddy" Parker. However, Parker did not come to invent the two-minute offense by himself. In fact, he never would have come by it if it had not been for the prowess of Bobby Layne, Parker's quarterback in Detroit.

Not only was Layne way ahead of his time, but he also was a hard-living man who loved to chase women and drink off the football field, and he didn't like to be reined in by football coaches or game plans.

When Layne walked on to the football field, he wanted to call the plays that best suited him and his teammates. After all, he was the one on the field, and it was his body and career that were on the line. He didn't see any reason to comply with a coach's suggestion.

Except that he understood that he was the employee and the coach was the boss, and most of the time he worked under the parameters of the offense, even if he didn't like it. Most of the time. Not all of the time.

Parker also had an ego similar to Layne's, and the two butted heads often. He thought of Layne as a rule breaker who wanted to do what he saw fit on the football field, and that did not make Parker happy.

However, Parker also saw that Layne was one of the most accomplished quarterbacks in the game and he was perhaps the best leader at his position in the NFL. So while they didn't always agree during Parker's tenure as head coach of the Detroit Lions between 1951 and 1956, they also worked well together and forged consistent success with the Lions.

Parker led the Lions to three straight NFL Championship games between 1952 and 1954, and they won two of those games. He also was the first coach to use a "two-minute offense" in the final stages of either half. Layne would rush his team to the line of scrimmage, and either run the play that was called or audible out of it in a matter of seconds.

The quarterback did this with Parker's approval and urging. It was very successful, as the Lions won twenty-eight of thirty-six regular-season games in those seasons.

Parker was a colorful coach from Texas, who got his first chance as a head coach in the NFL with the Chicago Cardinals. He was initially one of Jimmy Conzelman's trusted assistant coaches and he basically handled much of the offensive coaching.

When Conzelman left after the 1948 season, Parker and Phil Handler were named co-coaches of the team, but the team booted Handler upstairs prior to midseason and let Parker handle the head coaching duties. He led the Cardinals to a 4-1-1 record in the second half, which gave them a 6-5-1 record for the season.

But instead of preparing for his first full season as the team's lone coach, Parker decided to quit the Cardinals. He could not stomach the front office's meddling ways, and he figured that if he could not coach the team his way without interference, it wasn't a job he wanted.

Parker immediately went to the Lions as an assistant to "Bo" McMillin, and that turned out to be a fateful move. The Lions players liked Parker and they despised McMillin, and he was fired at the end of the 1950 season.

Layne, Doak Walker, and Cloyce Box, the three stars of the Lions, were thrilled by the move because they saw Parker as a coach who could help them win. Mainly, they liked him because he was not McMillin.

Parker did not have a lot of rules for his players off the field. He did not give them a curfew, and that suited Layne just fine. He also turned over much of the defense to his trusted friend Buster Ramsey, and Ramsey was able to build a unit that ranked in the league's top three defenses four times during his tenure.

That allowed Parker to spend much of his time building an explosive offensive team. While Layne would often do as he pleased on the field, Parker was able to offer suggestions to the quarterback that turned out to be successful. That's because Parker spent much of his time studying film of the opposition, and he could find weaknesses that weren't so obvious to the other coaches.

Layne knew that Parker was gifted in this area, particularly when the coach would make adjustments at halftime. Those adjustments were not based on feel or gut instincts that were the hallmark of Layne's career, but on the study and hard work that Parker had done by watching film.

Parker was one of the most successful coaches of his era while he was with the Lions, but he abruptly quit the team prior to the start of the 1957 season. At the time he stepped down, he claimed the team had looked awful in training camp and was not capable of winning consistently.

Some reporters claimed that that wasn't the real reason, but rather that Parker had been negotiating a new contract with the Lions, and when the process got bogged down and he didn't get the deal he wanted, he decided he was not going to do any more talking.

Weeks later, Parker was hired as head coach of the Pittsburgh Steelers. At the time, Pittsburgh was a moribund team that lacked star players and endured losing season after losing season.

Parker was able to help the Steelers play much more respectable football. He coached the Steelers from 1957 through 1964, and he led them to five seasons (out of the eight that he was there) in which they were .500 or better.

He was quirky and superstitious, and he liked to have a controlling hand on personnel. This proved to be his undoing. During training camp prior to the 1965 season, he tried to trade Chuck Hinton and Ben McGee to the Philadelphia Eagles. Hinton and McGee were two of the team's top defensive linemen, and when owner Art Rooney heard he wanted to do this and get Philadelphia backup quarterback King Hill, he rejected the deal.

Parker quit in a huff and never coached in the NFL again. However, he basically invented the two-minute drill and honed his game-planning by studying film as it had rarely been done before.

That gave Parker a legacy that made him one of the top coaches of his era.

For the record

> **Buddy Parker**
> Regular-season record: 104-75-9, .581
> Postseason record: 3-1, .750
> Two NFL championships

#39

DICK VERMEIL

Dick Vermeil shed more tears in his coaching career than a room full of brides do.

He shed tears of sadness, tears of happiness, and tears of joy. Vermeil was a brilliant coach who set trends and precedents throughout his career, and celebrated every one of them.

Vermeil was smart, thoughtful, and organized to begin with, and he began to make a name for himself as an assistant coach on John Ralston's Stanford staff in the 1960s. George Allen, who was head coach of the Los Angeles Rams at the time, took notice of Vermeil, and hired him to become the first special teams coach in NFL history.

It was a move that all pro teams quickly copied, because Vermeil did the job so well that it was quite clear that getting the advantage on special teams could make a huge difference. Vermeil became a trusted assistant coach in both the NFL and college, and that allowed him to earn his first head-coaching position when he was hired at UCLA in 1974.

Vermeil turned the Bruins into winners and he became one of the most sought-after NFL head coaching prospects when he led UCLA to a Rose Bowl upset over Ohio State.

The Philadelphia Eagles organization was the most persistent suitor and eventually hired Vermeil prior to the 1976 season.

Many people thought Vermeil had lost his senses because the Eagles were a brutal team that had not had a winning record in nine seasons. The Eagles were loaded with out-of-shape players, and drug use was rampant.

Vermeil got rid of those players and turned over the roster. He didn't care about a player's previous accomplishments. He just wanted hard-nosed players who had a single-minded determination to play winning football.

It wasn't enough for Vermeil to find the players. He had to put everything he had into the job, and that often meant staying in the office overnight or working as many as twenty hours per day.

His efforts began to pay off in his third year with the team when the Eagles finished with a 9-7 record. Players like Ron Jaworski, Wilbert Montgomery, Herman Edwards, and Carl Hairston helped get the Eagles going, and they gave their emotional coach everything they had.

The 1979 season saw the Eagles earn a playoff spot with an 11-5 record. They defeated the Chicago Bears 27-17 in the wild-card game, but they dropped their divisional playoff matchup to the Tampa Bay Buccaneers.

That game stayed with Vermeil and the Eagles through the off-season and it was their motivation in 1980. The Eagles became a legitimate Super Bowl contender, winning the NFC East with a

12-4 record, because they held a tiebreaker edge over Tom Landry and his Dallas Cowboys.

The Eagles earned the right to host the NFC Championship game when they defeated the overmatched Minnesota Vikings 31-16.

The Cowboys had upset the Atlanta Falcons and they came to Philadelphia with a mind to do the same thing to the Eagles. Landry and the Cowboys were football royalty, and many assumed their pedigree would get them over the top in this crucial game.

But the Eagles proved nastier, tougher, and meaner, as they came through with a 20-7 triumph behind the spectacular running of Montgomery, who scored the opening touchdown of the game on a forty-two-yard run and finished with 194 yards.

The Eagles went to the Super Bowl for the first time and they faced the wild-card Oakland Raiders, who had defeated the Houston Oilers, Cleveland Browns, and San Diego Chargers to become the first wild-card team to get to the Super Bowl.

The Eagles seemed to be the bigger, stronger, and more physical team, but the Raiders were more opportunistic and were savvy. Linebacker Rod Martin intercepted three of Jaworski's passes, and quarterback Jim Plunkett threw three touchdown passes as the Raiders came away with a shockingly easy 27-10 triumph.

That loss stayed with Vermeil for years, and his Eagles started to backslide. They made the playoffs the following year, but were eliminated by the New York Giants in the wild-card game, and they fell badly the following year.

Vermeil quit after that season, as he had gotten so emotional that he had a difficult time adjusting to family life. "I'm my own worst enemy," Vermeil said upon leaving the Eagles. "I am far too intense and far too emotional."

Vermeil was burned-out when he left the Eagles, and that term became part of the national lexicon shortly thereafter.

Still, few expected Vermeil to stay away from coaching for more than two years. Yet, that's just what he did. He became a college football analyst and stayed away from the NFL for fourteen years. It seemed he would remain in the TV booth and grow wine grapes in Napa indefinitely.

However, he still had a desire to get back to coaching, and he took a job coaching the Rams in 1997. It appeared Vermeil had little left, as the Rams had two consecutive losing seasons.

However, Vermeil knew his team was loaded with talent as it prepared for the 1999 season. The Rams took what appeared to be a devastating blow when starting quarterback Trent Green suffered a season-ending knee injury in the preseason, but backup Kurt Warner was there to answer the bell.

Warner, a former Arena Football League quarterback, turned out to be one of the most accurate passers in NFL history.

He led "The Greatest Show on Turf" to a first-place finish in the NFC West, and the Rams rolled through the playoffs and earned a spot in Super Bowl XXXIV against the Tennessee Titans. With the scored tied 16–16 late in the fourth quarter, Warner hit wide receiver Isaac Bruce with a seventy-three-yard touchdown pass to give the Rams a 23–16 lead.

The desperate Titans fought back, but Rams linebacker Mike Jones tackled Tennessee wide receiver Kevin Dyson on the St. Louis one-yard line on the game's final play.

The Rams and Vermeil had their Super Bowl title, and the tears flowed for Vermeil. He hugged and kissed his family members, he hugged and kissed his players, and he hugged and kissed his coaches.

He retired again from coaching, but this time he came back in just two years to lead the Kansas City Chiefs in 2001.

He helped turn the Chiefs into a winning team, but they never had the playoff glory that either of his other teams had.

Vermeil retired again following the 2005 season.

His last team went 10-6, and the emotional coach left on his own terms. He was beloved by many of his players from all three teams, and his legacy of hard work, dedication, and long hours remains intact.

For the record

Dick Vermeil
Regular–season record: 120–109–0, .524
Postseason record: 6–5, .545
One Super Bowl victory

#40

GEORGE ALLEN

It's a fairly common story to hear that modern NFL coaches spend twelve, fourteen, or sixteen hours a day during the season working on game plans and preparing to compete against an opponent.

George Allen was the first of these single-minded coaches who put so much of his time into preparing for a game. He did this because he was obsessed with not losing.

The obsession was not with winning. When Allen's team won games, he would jump for joy, lead his teams in cheers, and celebrate with his beloved vanilla ice cream. But when it was over, he would begin the process anew.

However, if his team lost, Allen was crestfallen and deeply disturbed. "Every time you win, you are reborn," Allen said. "But when you lose, you die a little."

Allen came into his own when he was hired by George Halas to serve as a scout in the 1958 season. Specifically, Halas wanted Allen to scout the Los Angeles Rams. Allen gave Halas and his players a report that was so thorough and cogent that it gave the team a succinct game plan to follow.

Halas, a curmudgeon who was never easily impressed, realized that Allen was one of the sharpest men he had ever worked with and he hired him to be an assistant coach with the Bears. In addition to that job, Halas also asked Allen to do all the preparation work for the Bears' drafts, and run those as well.

During the time that Allen was in charge of the Bears' college player procurement, they drafted Mike Ditka, Dick Butkus, and Gale Sayers. Those were not only Hall of Fame players with dominant ability, but also three of the greatest players who have ever played the game.

Halas was now thoroughly impressed, and he made Allen his defensive coordinator in 1963, a move that his players applauded. Allen installed a defensive scheme that was based heavily on the zone blitz, and the results were remarkable.

The Bears finished 11-1-2 that season and won the NFL's West Division. They had a mundane offense that featured Bill Wade at quarterback and running backs Joe Marconi and Ronnie Bull. Neither Marconi nor Bull topped the 500-yard mark, while Wade threw for 2,301 yards and had a 15-12 touchdown-interception ratio. Ditka was the star of the offense, as he caught 59 passes for 794 yards and eight touchdowns.

However, the defense was simply remarkable, and it allowed just 144 points in fourteen games. Overpowering players like Doug Atkins, Ed O'Bradovich, J. C. Caroline, Rosey Taylor, Richie

Petitbon, and Davey "The Weasel" Whitsell pounded opponents and regularly took away the ball from them.

The Bears beat the New York Giants 14-10 in the 1963 NFL Championship game at Soldier Field, and that would be the last title the team would win under Halas.

Shortly after that, Halas told Allen he would become head coach of the Bears after he retired. However, Halas was still coaching the Bears through the 1965 season, and he did not offer any indications that he would be leaving in the foreseeable future.

As a result, Allen left the Bears to become head coach of the Rams. Subsequently, Halas grew angry that Allen would not remain with the Bears and patiently continue to wait. Halas held a grudge against Allen from that point on, a grudge that he never got over.

Allen's meticulous ways worked wonders with the Rams. He took over a team that had been 4-10 in 1965, and immediately started making trades and personnel moves. Allen did not think the Rams had the kind of personnel that could win in the NFL, and he was determined to make sure they improved quickly. If that meant trading draft picks for veteran players, he was more than willing to do just that.

The Rams became a winning team in 1966 with an 8-6-0 record, but that was just the beginning. They finished 11-1-2 in 1967, and they closed the regular season with seven straight wins. The final two wins of the season came against Vince Lombardi's Green Bay Packers and Don Shula's Baltimore Colts.

Wins over those two brilliant coaches raised Allen's status in a powerful way, and the Rams went into the postseason with full momentum. Some thought the Rams would be able to repeat their earlier win over the Packers, but when they were forced to go to Lambeau Field and play Lombardi's team in its preferred element, the Rams fell short by a 28-7 margin.

Still, Allen had come a long way in a short period of time because his team had tremendous pass rushing abilities, thanks to its "Fearsome Foursome" that included "Deacon" Jones, Merlin Olsen, Roger Brown, and Lamar Lundy. The Rams' offense was quite conservative, but the defense was reckless and exciting.

The Rams continued to be one of the better regular-season teams over the subsequent three years, but only made the playoffs once, and they lost that game to the Minnesota Vikings.

Allen's quirky style and failure to build an exciting offense angered team owner Dan Reeves, and the 1970 season became Allen's last with the Rams.

The Washington Redskins wasted no time in bringing Allen aboard. They had also been an ordinary team prior to Allen's arrival and had finished 6-8-0 in 1970 with the nondescript Bill Austin at head coach.

Allen immediately started making the same kind of personnel moves with the Redskins that he had with the Rams, as he had an eye towards immediate improvement and was not concerned about anything but the present and the immediate future.

He traded rookies and draft picks for solid veterans, and the Redskins suddenly became competitive. They finished 9-4-1 in 1971, and he sang, danced, and whooped it up when the Redskins won. When reporters asked him what his team would do in the future without all their first-round draft picks since he traded them every year, he didn't hesitate. "The future is now," he declared.

Allen brought his team to the precipice of a championship in 1972. After they finished first in the NFC East Division with an 11-3-0 record, Allen's team won its first playoff game when the Redskins defeated the Packers 16-3.

That relieved a great deal of pressure for Allen, and he got his team prepared as it had never been the following week in the NFC

Championship game against the archrival Dallas Cowboys. The Redskins dominated, with Billy "The Kid" Kilmer throwing the ball and Larry Brown running it, and they pounded Tom Landry's team 26-3.

The victory was so impressive that the Redskins were slight favorites to defeat the Miami Dolphins in Super Bowl VII—even though the Dolphins were undefeated. Miami kept its perfect season intact and won the game by a 14-7 margin.

The Redskins would never get back to the Super Bowl under Allen, and they would never win another playoff game. His teams played consistently in the regular season, but Allen's simplistic offense was fairly easy for opponents to figure out in the postseason, and he never adjusted. Allen left the Redskins when his contract concluded after the 1977 season.

Allen was particularly demanding and difficult to work with, and few teams considered hiring him at that point. However, the Rams once again came calling under new owner Carroll Rosenbloom. Yet Allen did not even make it through the preseason and he was fired after two exhibition games because he was simply too overbearing.

He coached years later in the United States Football League with some success, but he never made it back to the NFL. At one point he tried to smooth things over with Halas, but his old boss refused his attempts at a rapprochement.

Still, Allen had a huge imprint on the NFL. He became the first coach to devote the majority of his hours to looking at film and diagnosing his opponents' weaknesses. He excelled at picking them out and installing the right game plan to take advantage of them.

While he later came to eschew the draft, his ability to find Hall of Famers like Ditka, Butkus, and Sayers is unparalleled. Allen's 2002 induction into the Hall of Fame was most deserved.

For the record

George Allen
Hall of Fame, 2002
Regular-season record: 116-47-5, .712
Postseason record: 2-7, .222
One conference championship

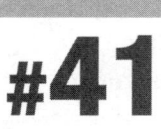

#41

BRIAN BILLICK

If you took the 2000 Baltimore Ravens and put them in a tournament with the best teams that ever played the game, they would be the team that nobody wanted to play.

The Ravens wouldn't win that tournament because they had a quarterback in Trent Dilfer who lacked all the characteristics needed to be dynamic, but they would have punished any team that they played.

Simply put, the Ravens had one of the greatest defenses the game has ever seen, one that might be bettered by the 1985 Bears and the Steelers of the 1970s, and few others. The defense was, without a doubt, their bread and butter.

That's the irony of Brian Billick's coaching career. When he was hired by the Ravens prior to the 1999 season, he got the job because he was one of the brightest offensive minds the game has ever seen. He was the offensive coordinator for Dennis Green and his explosive Minnesota Vikings teams in the late 1990s, and he helped take a team that seemingly had a different quarterback every season and turn it into one of the greatest offensive juggernauts in NFL history.

Under Billick, the 1998 season was a remarkable one for the Vikings. They went 15-1 during the season and scored an NFL record 556 points. Billick had an offense that included Randall Cunningham at quarterback, wide receivers Randy Moss and Cris Carter, and explosive Robert Smith at running back, and it was a virtual track meet every week.

The Vikings toyed with most opponents and they outscored opponents by 16 points per game. This may have been one of the best teams the game has ever seen, but they didn't get to the Super Bowl. They lost the NFC Championship game at home to the Atlanta Falcons in one of the most shocking upsets in the last twenty years.

But the pain for Billick was only temporary, as the Baltimore Ravens came calling and wanted him to take over their non-descript team. The Ravens were just 6-10 that season, and owner Art Modell knew he had to do something to help his team start to jell.

The Ravens were 8-8 in 1999, but Billick found a spark late in the season. The Ravens were 4-7 and looking quite miserable after dropping a 30-23 decision at home to the Jacksonville Jaguars. However, they won their next four games in impressive fashion, including a 31-24 win in Week 14 at Pittsburgh.

That game helped the Ravens gain confidence, and they were an eye-opening and marauding bunch in the 2000 season.

They weren't doing much with their offense, but they had a bone-jarring defense led by Ray Lewis, Rod Woodson, Peter Boulware, and Jamie Sharper that just shut opponents down.

Still, the Ravens were having problems early in the year, as they were getting nowhere with Tony Banks at quarterback. Baltimore had a 5-3 record at midseason after dropping a 14-6 home decision to the Tennessee Titans. That matchup marked the fourth straight game that the Ravens had not scored a touchdown.

Billick had seen more than enough, and he sat Banks on the bench and made Dilfer his starting quarterback. Dilfer had endured many difficult seasons with the Tampa Bay Bucs before coming to the Ravens and he had little on his resume that would indicate he could do anything but lose games in the NFL, but Billick had a feeling he could steady the team and help it win.

"I never expected any miracles with Trent at quarterback, but I didn't think we needed anything like that," Billick said. "I just wanted him to take advantage of what the defense gave him and not turn the ball over. If he could do that, I thought our defense would get the job done."

The Ravens' streak of touchdown-free games continued the following week when they dropped a 9-6 decision to the Steelers at home, but they turned things around in Week 10 when they drummed the Bengals 27-7. The Ravens did not lose again during the regular season, and they made the playoffs as a wild-card team.

They put on an impressive show in beating the Broncos 21-3 in their first playoff game, but they didn't appear to have much of a chance against the Titans on the road in the divisional playoffs. The presence of Steve McNair and Eddie George gave the Titans a big edge on offense, and there was only so much the Ravens could do.

Nobody explained that to Lewis, who pounded George on every occasion. He wrestled the ball away from the running back just past the midway point of the fourth quarter and took it fifty yards for a touchdown that clinched a 24-10 decision.

Baltimore then went across the country and punched Jon Gruden's Oakland Raiders in the mouth for sixty minutes, earning a trip to the Super Bowl with a 16-3 victory.

The Ravens had turned into a defensive juggernaut by that time, and they were overflowing with confidence when they met the New York Giants in Tampa. New York had an impressive offense led by quarterback Kerry Collins, but it was a brutal defeat for New York.

By the time Collins came off the field following the 34-7 defeat, his face was ashen. He tried to mouth postgame answers to the media, but his body was bruised and his psyche was shattered.

"That's how we play football," Lewis said after the game. "We are going to hit you and we are going to hurt you. The Giants were the best team in the NFC, and they found out today what Ravens football was all about. Punishment. Pain. Non-stop."

In many ways, that championship was a moment of brilliance for Billick. However, the irony of having a spectacular defense was not lost on him.

"The reason I became a football coach was to develop a game plan and give the offense a chance to score every time it had the ball," Billick explained. "It worked quite well with Minnesota, but it never came together in Baltimore."

"Don't get me wrong, because we had a spectacular championship team that was at its best when it mattered most. We shattered people and played overwhelming defense. I couldn't have been prouder."

But it was clear that Billick wanted to have the same kind of offensive success with the Ravens that he had in Minnesota. It never happened.

He had several more good teams in Baltimore and went to the playoffs three more times, but none of his teams were able to recapture the magic of the 2000 Ravens.

Billick never developed the quarterback or the offense he wanted in Baltimore, and the 2007 season was his last with the team. He has since become a color analyst for FOX Sports on the network's NFL broadcasts. While it may have been a frustrating run taken as a whole, Billick had one of the most imposing and intimidating teams of the Super Bowl era, and it helped him earn a spot as one of the top fifty coaches of all time.

For the record

> **Brian Billick**
> Regular–season record: 80–64–0, .566
> Postseason record: 5–3, .600
> One Super Bowl victory

#42

SEAN PAYTON

Sean Payton helped usher in the modern era of the NFL that emphasizes big plays through the pass at the expense of nearly every other aspect of the game. While he won a Super Bowl with the New Orleans Saints in his fourth season as head coach of the team—and that was clearly a brilliant achievement—his devotion to the passing game may be his ultimate legacy as an NFL head coach.

Payton was an Arena Football League quarterback before he got a chance to play in the NFL as a member of the Chicago Bears' replacement team during the player strike of 1987. But once the NFL players returned to action, Payton's playing career was over and he began his coaching career shortly thereafter.

He had college coaching experience at San Diego State (working with Marshall Faulk), Indiana State, Miami of Ohio, and Illinois before he was selected by Ray Rhodes to coach quarterbacks in Philadelphia in 1997. Jim Fassel eventually went after Payton and he became the Giants' offensive coordinator in 2000. However, Fassel took Payton's play-calling responsibilities away from him in 2002, so Payton eventually joined Bill Parcells with the Dallas Cowboys.

Payton was thought of as an up-and-comer prior to his association with Parcells, but he became one of the most desirable coaching candidates during his time in Dallas. He was a coaching finalist in Green Bay and New Orleans in 2006, and while the Packers settled on Mike McCarthy, he was given a chance to turn the Saints around.

The 2006 season was a bit of a miracle for the organization and the New Orleans region, as both were trying to come back from the raging Hurricane Katrina that had torn apart the city a year earlier.

The Saints won their first two games on the road that season, and came home to play their home opener at the Superdome. The Saints' home crowd had always been loud and raucous, but the fans brought it to a new level against the archrival Atlanta Falcons and the Saints recorded a 23-3 victory.

It was a win that let the NFL know that these were not the same old Saints, and that the combination of Payton and free-agent quarterback Drew Brees would take the organization to a new level. Brees had been a solid and resourceful quarterback during his previous five years with the San Diego Chargers, but Payton saw a quarterback who had the talent to play at a superstar level.

That's one of the reasons that Brees chose to continue his career in New Orleans. Payton told the quarterback that he would build his offense around Brees, include all the plays that he had excelled at with the Chargers, and then add more that would help him become even better. That was all Brees needed to hear in order to join forces with the Saints.

New Orleans would go on to win the division title in 2006, and Brees would go on to throw for 4,418 yards with a 26-11 touchdown-interception ratio.

Prior to Payton's arrival, the Saints had won one postseason game in their history. Payton helped change the organization's image, as the Saints earned a bye into the divisional playoffs, where they defeated the Philadelphia Eagles 27-24 and moved on to the NFC Championship game against the Chicago Bears.

Chicago's defense was led by middle linebacker Brian Urlacher, and it held Brees's offense in check until the Saints scored in the final minute of the first half. While New Orleans had momentum playing on the road, it trailed 16-7 at halftime. The Saints threw a further scare in Chicago when Brees connected with speedy Reggie Bush on an eighty-eight-yard catch and run for a score, but the Bears' defense reasserted itself and Chicago advanced to the Super Bowl with a 39-14 victory.

Payton continued to refine his offense and he attempted to build a tough and opportunistic defense. The Saints had a pair of ordinary seasons in 2007 and '08 in which they failed to make the playoffs, but they found their stride in '09 when they played consistently explosive football and dominated the NFC South Division with a 13-3 record.

They went into the playoffs that season as the top seed and they overwhelmed the Arizona Cardinals 45-14, as Brees threw three touchdown passes and Bush returned a punt for a touchdown. That victory gave them home field advantage in the NFC Championship, and Saints fans were delirious at the thought of their team going to the Super Bowl if they could beat Brett Favre and the Minnesota Vikings.

The Vikings tied the score late in regulation and had a chance to win it when they had the ball in New Orleans territory in the closing seconds, but instead of settling for a field goal attempt, Favre tried to throw the ball late and across the middle and his pass was picked off by Tracy Porter to send the game into overtime.

Garrett Hartley connected on a forty-yard field goal to send Payton and the Saints into the Super Bowl against Peyton Manning and the Indianapolis Colts.

It was widely expected that Manning would end the Saints' dreams in a painful manner and the great quarterback would lead his team to its second Super Bowl title. However, Payton had other plans, and he put them boldly into action at the start of the second half.

The Saints trailed 10-6 and were kicking off to start the final thirty minutes. Payton did not want Manning to lead the Colts on a long drive and increase the deficit, so he ordered kicker Thomas Morstead to attempt an onside kick. The Saints recovered the ball and took the lead when Brees hit Pierre Thomas with a 16-yard touchdown pass to give the Saints a 13-10 lead.

That shocking onside kick, recovery, and subsequent touchdown spurred the Saints to a 31-17 victory and gave them the only Super Bowl championship in their history.

While the Saints have had a rather inconsistent defense throughout Payton's run in New Orleans, their offense has regularly been among the best in the league. That unit was never better than in the 2011 season, when the Saints went 13-3 and scored 547 points.

Brees threw for 5,476 yards, completed 71.2 percent of his passes, and had a remarkable 46-14 touchdown-interception ratio. While many expected the Saints to reach the NFC Championship game in an epic confrontation with the equally prolific Green Bay Packers, they were stopped by the 49ers 36-32 in a heart-stopping game in the divisional playoffs.

The Saints thought that another Super Bowl season was at hand after that, but defensive coordinator Gregg Williams was brought down in the offseason by the "Bountygate" scandal, in which Williams rewarded players for laying big hits and injuring opposing star players.

Payton's reputation was also damaged in the fallout from the scandal, as he was suspended for the 2012 season. It was a painful blow for Payton and the Saints, but they came back strong in 2013 with an 11-5 record and a 26-24 victory over the Eagles in the wild-card round. While they were stopped by Seattle in the divisional playoffs, it was an important rebound season for Payton.

He has shown his ability to build one of the most prolific offenses in NFL history, and his teams have been able to rebound from poor defensive seasons quite well. Payton has one of the top offensive minds in the game, and he has shown that his teams almost always have a chance to come back and win any game.

For the record

Sean Payton
Regular-season record: 80-48-0, .625
Postseason record: 6-4, .600
One Super Bowl victory

#43

JOHN HARBAUGH

It would take a lot for any of the modern-day NFL coaches to stay in the business and lead their teams for as long as Tom Landry, Don Shula, or Chuck Noll headed their teams during their Hall of Fame coaching careers.

However, if there's one coach who has shown the consistency in his approach, demeanor, game-planning, and player relations, it's John Harbaugh. He has led the Baltimore Ravens to the postseason in six of his first seven seasons, and his teams have always won at least one playoff game in each of those appearances.

Harbaugh and the Ravens won a Super Bowl following the 2012 season, when his team earned a victory in Super Bowl XLVII over the San Francisco 49ers, a team that was coached by his brother Jim Harbaugh.

John Harbaugh earned his chance to become a head coach in the NFL by climbing the ranks as a college assistant coach and then getting called up to the professional ranks. Harbaugh established a reputation as a coach who understood the details needed to excel at each position, and a talent for building game-changing special teams.

Once word of his work at Morehead State, the University of Cincinnati, and Indiana got out, he got a call from Philadelphia Eagles head coach Ray Rhodes. Philadelphia had endured misery with their special-teams play in 1997, and Rhodes needed a strong, smart, and tough special teams coach who could turn that situation around quickly.

Harbaugh did just that, but the Eagles played awful football in 1998 and Rhodes was fired. However, new coach Andy Reid was impressed by Harbaugh and kept him on the staff. The Eagles' special teams ranked among the best in the league each year. Harbaugh would eventually get moved up the Eagles coaching ladder to defensive backs coach, and Reid knew that Harbaugh would most likely be leaving Philadelphia because he deserved a chance to become a head coach.

The Ravens came calling in 2008, and while Harbaugh did not have much of a reputation for building excellence on the offensive side of the ball, the Ravens were convinced Harbaugh was the right man for the job because of his thoroughness and his ability to remain on even keel even when circumstances called for panic.

The Ravens had a powerful defense at the time, and they were led by stars like linebacker Ray Lewis and safety Ed Reed. However, the offense was rather inconsistent and the team's quarterback play was below average.

That changed during Harbaugh's first year as head coach when the Ravens drafted strong-armed Joe Flacco out of the University of Delaware. While Flacco had the kind of physical tools to make all the throws needed in the NFL, he had not played against upper-level competition with the Blue Hens and he would need time and tutoring to develop into an elite professional quarterback.

Harbaugh understood this from the start, and he never stopped teaching Flacco or believing in him. As a result, the quarterback and the coach became partners in the NFL, and their success was tied to each other.

The Ravens had a very solid season in 2008, recording an 11-5 mark and earning a spot in the playoffs as a wild-card team. The Ravens were 6-4 through their first ten games, but they rolled to a 5-1 finish and were one of the hottest teams in the league at the start of the postseason.

They won postseason road games at Miami and Tennessee before dropping a hard-fought 23-14 decision to the Pittsburgh Steelers in the AFC Championship game.

The Ravens garnered respect with their showing that season, but nobody thought that the Harbaugh-Flacco combination would become a dominant one. The Ravens struggled with their consistency in 2009 and were just 9-7, but that was good enough to earn a postseason appearance.

Nobody expected them to survive their wild-card game against the Patriots, but they went into Foxboro and ran Bill Belichick's team out of its own stadium as they recorded a 33-14 blowout. The Ravens lost the following week at Indianapolis, but Harbaugh had impressed NFL observers with the way he was able to get his team prepared and keep them from getting intimidated against a high-powered opponent like the Patriots.

Harbaugh did an excellent job of establishing firm control of his veteran team, while getting players like Lewis and Reed to buy into his leadership. Harbaugh would never have had an opportunity to become an upper-echelon coach if he had come in with a "my way or the highway" kind of demeanor, but he couldn't give his players the same kind of loose rein that former Baltimore coach Brian Billick had given his team.

It was a delicate balancing act that Harbaugh had to endeavor, and he pulled it off brilliantly.

The Ravens had tremendous confidence as Harbaugh prepared for his third season in 2010, and they continued to play consistently with a 12-4 record. After they rolled to a one-sided 30-7 wild-card victory at Kansas City, their season once again came to an end at the hands of the Pittsburgh Steelers.

The Ravens continued to climb the ladder in 2011, as they won the AFC North title and rolled over the Houston Texans in the divisional playoffs before meeting the Patriots on the road in the AFC Championship game.

Unfortunately for the Ravens, they missed a chance to send the game into overtime when placekicker Billy Cundiff missed a short field goal late in the fourth quarter, and that allowed the Patriots to hold on for a 23-20 victory.

Harbaugh's team came to training camp with a new determination in 2012, and they rolled to a 9-2 start. However, unlike previous Ravens teams, they struggled down the stretch and lost four of their last five regular-season games.

Nobody expected them to do much in the postseason, but the Ravens overpowered the Colts before beating Denver and New England on the road to go to the Super Bowl.

The matchup with the 49ers presented a remarkable brother vs. brother confrontation between the Harbaugh coaches.

The contrast between the two brothers was vital, as John seemed steadier and more mature, while Jim was more emotional and perhaps a touch more creative.

John's Ravens built a big lead and held on to earn a 34-31 victory. Flacco had been brilliant for the Ravens, completing 22-of-33 passes for 287 yards with three touchdowns and no interceptions. Flacco had absorbed much criticism throughout his career, but

Harbaugh had always maintained faith in his quarterback. He was rewarded for that faith with a Super Bowl triumph.

The Super Bowl earned Harbaugh elite status, and his team has been able to win more playoff games on the road than any other team in the Super Bowl era.

Harbaugh's steady demeanor has been one of the key factors for the Ravens, and that's why he has a chance to go on a long run and perhaps join Landry, Shula, and Noll as an institution among head coaches.

For the record

> **John Harbaugh**
> Regular–season record: 72-40-0, .643
> Postseason record: 10-5, .667
> One Super Bowl victory

#44

MIKE DITKA

It all began with a handwritten letter.

Mike Ditka had been one of the great tight ends in the history of the NFL, and he had been a key player for the Chicago Bears when they won their last NFL championship in 1963 under George Halas.

Ditka not only helped carry the Bears offense on his broad shoulders, but he also helped redefine the tight end position with his big-play ability.

It didn't end well in Chicago, though, as Ditka grew annoyed by Papa Bear's penurious ways. He was traded to Philadelphia in 1968—"the worst year of my life"—before he finished his career with the Dallas Cowboys. He was on Tom Landry's 1971 Super

Bowl-winning team, and later became an assistant of the great coach's staff.

As Ditka grew as a coach, he had one aspiration. He wanted to be a head coach in the NFL, and he wanted it to be for the Chicago Bears. He wrote his old boss a long letter in which he explained his aspirations, apologized for his past feelings, and told Halas how much he wanted to be a Bear once again.

The two had one meeting, and by the time it was over, Ditka was named as the head coach of the Bears prior to the 1982 season.

So began the most raucous era in Chicago Bears history. Ditka was a roaring volcano of a coach, demanding that his players and assistants do things the right way at all times.

He was an old-school disciplinarian who had learned at the feet of Halas and Landry, and he was bound and determined not to let either man down.

The 1982 Bears had endured losing seasons in their previous two years, and Ditka was determined to turn the team around quickly. He pushed his team hard in training camp and began the process of getting rid of slackers. The Bears were 3-6 in that strike-shortened season, but showed signs of progress the following year when they finished .500.

That 8-8 season only fueled Ditka's fire, and he pushed his team harder than ever in 1984. With Jim McMahon at quarterback and Walter Payton running the football, the Bears had a credible offense. However, it was the defense that was really taking shape.

Defensive coordinator Buddy Ryan had a unit that included Dan Hampton, Steve McMichael, Richard Dent, Mike Singletary, Wilber Marshall, Otis Wilson, and Gary Fencik.

The defense was so fast and so aggressive that it was quite brutal to attempt to play against them. Perhaps the best example of this came in Week 9 of that season, when the Bears hosted Archie Manning and the Minnesota Vikings.

Manning had reached the late stages of his career, and his escapability was not what it had been during the prime of his career. The Bears went after him all day, and sacked him eleven times. It was a brutal beating that hastened the end of Manning's career.

It also spearheaded the Bears to a 10-6 record that earned them a spot in the playoffs.

Despite their defensive talent, nobody thought they would be able to give Joe Gibbs's favored Washington Redskins much of a battle in the first round of the postseason. However, the Bears came out of RFK Stadium in Washington with a 23-19 upset. The defense stopped the Redskins and quarterback Joe Theismann when it mattered most, and the Bears earned a trip to San Francisco to face Bill Walsh and his high-powered San Francisco 49ers.

This may have been the best of Walsh's teams, and they laid a 23-0 beating on Chicago. The 49ers would go on to win their second Super Bowl title as they overwhelmed the Miami Dolphins in Super Bowl XIX.

But Ditka would never forget the insult that he perceived Walsh had laid on him in that NFC Championship. Walsh used 300-plus-pound guard Guy McIntyre as a blocking back to help put the game away in the fourth quarter.

Ditka would never forget this, and he would use it as inspiration the following season. The Bears had gotten a taste of success in 1984, but they wanted the full smorgasbord in 1985.

They would run through the NFL in a season that would never be forgotten and would earn the '85 Bears a place in history.

It was a magnificent season that would see the Bears become recognized as perhaps the greatest one-year champions of all-time.

McMahon, though injury-riddled, made it a habit of making big plays when the Bears needed them most. He came off the bench in Week 3 to rally the Bears from a 17-9 deficit at Minnesota to a 33-24 victory by throwing three second-half touchdown passes.

But most of the time, the Bears did not need to rally to win games. They simply pounded opponents with their Payton-led running attack and a ferocious defense that held twelve opponents to ten points or less.

Defensive coordinator Buddy Ryan ran the Bears' 46 defense, and while he and Ditka had little regard for each other as individuals, they formed a remarkable coaching duo.

Ryan's philosophy was to have the defense attack the quarterback at all costs, and the Bears had given him remarkable athletes to accomplish that feat.

The Bears went 15-1 in the regular season, dropping a Monday night game in Miami that remains the highest-rated game in the history of that series.

The Bears had dreams of matching the 1972 Dolphins by going undefeated, but the disappointment of losing in the Orange Bowl did not result in any hangover. They shook the loss off, recorded a video called the Super Bowl Shuffle the next day, and continued their stampede through the league.

Ditka remembered the Walsh move of putting the huge McIntyre in the backfield. He went Walsh one better by putting 325-pound William "The Refrigerator" Perry in the backfield and letting him carry the ball.

"The Fridge" became a cartoon-like symbol for the team, and he was also a fine run-stuffer in the middle of the defensive line.

The Bears shut out the New York Giants and Los Angeles Rams in their two playoff games, and then savaged the New England Patriots 46-10 in Super Bowl XX in New Orleans.

As the Bears were piling up score after score, Payton never got his chance to get into the end zone. That troubled the Hall of Fame running back and Ditka for many years.

"It's something that I wish I could change," Ditka said. "If I knew how much it meant to Walter, I would have given him the ball. But you can't change the past, and you can't live in it."

The powerful Bears would continue to have regular season success as they went 14-2, 11-4, and 12-4 the following three seasons, but they could not get through the playoffs.

Ditka's teams had remarkable talent, but they could not repeat their dramatic regular-season success.

That's part of the reason that Ditka sits at 44th on this list of the best coaches. He had perhaps the greatest team of all time, but he could only coach them to one championship.

The rest of his tenure was disappointing, because championships were the team's only goal and they fell short every year that followed.

But for one year, Ditka was the right coach at the right time to lead one of the greatest teams ever.

For the record

Mike Ditka
Hall of Fame, 1988
Regular-season record: 121-95-0, .560
Postseason record: 12-6, .667
One Super Bowl victory

#45

PETE CARROLL

A Super Bowl win following the 2013 season and a loss in that game the following year have allowed Pete Carroll to raise his professional reputation dramatically.

Prior to the 2013 season, the Seattle Seahawks were moving in the right direction and coming off an 11-5 season that saw them win a wild-card playoff game over the Washington Redskins and fall just short in the divisional playoff game against the Atlanta Falcons.

However, that performance did little to change Carroll's reputation as an excellent college football coach who just did not have all the capabilities needed to win championships at the NFL level.

Carroll heard the doubters, and he knew they existed from the time he was named as the head coach of the New York Jets in 1994. At that time, the Jets responded to Carroll's infectious personality and enthusiasm by winning six of their first eleven games and looking like a possible playoff participant. Instead, the team took a painful defeat at the hands of Dan Marino's Miami Dolphins when the legendary quarterback executed his famed "fake spike" play and threw a game-winning touchdown pass.

The Jets didn't win another game, and Carroll was fired and replaced by (gulp) Rich Kotite, who led the Jets to two of the worst seasons in team history.

Carroll rebounded from the firing and was hired by the San Francisco 49ers as their defensive coordinator. He was successful and parlayed that position to get an offer from Robert Kraft and the New England Patriots. Kraft had just parted company with Bill Parcells, and the owner wanted a coach who was easier to communicate with and less demanding than Parcells.

Carroll fit the bill, and he was immediately welcomed by the Patriots players, who were relieved to be rid of the demanding Parcells.

The Patriots went to the playoffs in each of Carroll's first two years, but they fell to 8-8 in his third season, and the team was trending in the wrong direction. Those same players who celebrated Carroll's arrival in Foxboro soon took advantage of his relaxed attitude. Instead of getting the most out of his players, Carroll's team made multiple mistakes and the two sides parted company.

Carroll took a season off before he was hired at USC, and coaching college football appeared to be the perfect environment for his personality and talent. For one thing, the college game offered Carroll plenty of opportunity to show off his creativity when it came to play-calling and game-planning, and his strong defensive background meant that it would be relatively easy for him to build a team that knew how to stop opponents.

But it also gave him the opportunity to develop his own style. While Carroll never admitted that older, professional players had taken advantage of his relatively easygoing (compared to Parcells and other hard-nosed coaches) nature, he knew he had to alter his ways to prevent that from happening again.

College players were not about to challenge his leadership, and the Trojans were stellar under his leadership, recording an 83-19 record that included a thirty-four-game winning streak and two national championships.

As Carroll grew older and more experienced, he wanted to return to the NFL and conquer a world where he had shown promise but never quite delivered.

The Seahawks came calling prior to the 2010 season, and while it took some time for the Seahawks to turn the corner, they were clearly climbing to elite status.

Carroll's team reached significant heights in 2012, and he knew that his team was capable of winning the NFC West and being able to make a run at the Super Bowl.

Carroll and Seattle general manager John Schneider built the NFL's best defense, and young quarterback Russell Wilson proved to be the perfect triggerman. He was selected in the third round of the 2012 draft, and while few teams saw him as anything more than a backup or a project, Carroll realized that Wilson had all the intangibles—leadership, intelligence, courage—to become a consistent winner.

The only questions were about his physical skills. Wilson was short at 5-11, and there was an impression that quarterbacks under 6-0 could not win. Carroll ignored that, and when he saw that Wilson was accurate, athletic, could throw on the move, and had a strong enough arm, he did not hesitate to make him his starting quarterback.

Wilson was solid as a rookie in 2012, and his play improved significantly in 2013. He completed 63.1 percent of his passes that season and he had a 26-9 touchdown-interception ratio while rushing for 539 yards.

The Seahawks won their division, and they defeated the New Orleans Saints in the divisional playoffs and the San Francisco 49ers in the NFC Championship game.

That game was a huge step, because not only did it get the Seahawks to the Super Bowl, but also it represented a personal triumph for Carroll over San Francisco head coach Jim Harbaugh, his archrival. Harbaugh had been a college coach at Stanford when Carroll was at USC, and they used each other as a measuring stick.

Once the Seahawks survived that battle—a 23-17 win before the team's adoring home fans in Seattle—it was on to the title game.

The Seahawks knew they had been tested severely by the Niners, and they privately doubted that the AFC Champion Denver Broncos would be able to come close to them. They paid the Broncos and quarterback Peyton Manning full respect in the two-week build-up, but they overpowered Denver and rolled to a 43-8 triumph.

Carroll and his players were obsessed with winning a second straight Super Bowl in 2014, but the team was sluggish in the first half of the season. The Seahawks fell to 6-4 after dropping a 24-20 decision at Kansas City.

Carroll got back to basics on offense at that point and turned the offense over to Wilson and power running back Marshawn Lynch, while the defense played back to the form it had in 2013.

The Seahawks won their final six regular-season games, and they dispatched the Falcons 31-17 in the divisional playoffs.

Seattle needed to beat Green Bay in the NFC Championship game at home to get back to the Super Bowl, but all seemed lost late in the fourth quarter when Wilson threw a late interception as the Packers held a 19-7 lead.

Packers players were congratulating themselves at that point, but the Seattle defense stopped Green Bay from earning even one first down, and Wilson scored on a one-yard touchdown run with 2:09 left. The Seahawks recovered the ensuing onside kick and Lynch gave the Seahawks a late lead with a twenty-four-yard touchdown run.

While the Packers would tie the score on a last-second field goal, Seattle won the game in overtime when Wilson hit receiver Jermaine Kearse with a game-winning thirty-five-yard touchdown pass.

The Seahawks were challenged fully in the Super Bowl by Tom Brady, Bill Belichick, and the New England Patriots, but it appeared they would win their second straight title when they had the ball at the New England one with just seconds remaining.

Instead of having Lynch—the game's most ferocious short-yardage back—run the ball in, Carroll had Wilson throw the ball inside to receiver Ricardo Lockette.

It could have been the game-winning touchdown, but New England rookie defensive back Malcolm Butler would have none of it. He undercut Lockette's route and intercepted the pass, giving New England the Super Bowl victory.

Carroll faced criticism regarding the decision head-on and he explained his thought process. He saw the Patriots in what he believed was a goal line defense, so he wanted to take advantage of it by throwing the ball.

Despite this explanation, after the game, the reaction to the play call was immediate and harsh. Many observers described it as the worst play call ever.

Nevertheless, there is no arguing the fact that Carroll has won a Super Bowl, been to another, and won two NCAA championships. As a result, he ranks as one of the NFL's most impressive coaches.

For the record

Pete Carroll
Regular-season record: 83-61-0, .576
Postseason record: 8-5, .615
One Super Bowl victory

#46

BUCK SHAW

Anyone who watches the NFL on even a casual basis knows that professional football is a win-at-all-costs kind of game. Coaches tend to ignore their own players—even their superstars—when they get hurt. When an opponent suffers an injury, there may be some lip service to the media about hoping that player recovers, but there is little sympathy.

It's just the way business is done.

The exceptions to this practice are few and far between. However, Lawrence Timothy "Buck" Shaw was nothing like the standard head coach that stalks the sideline. He was a compassionate man who wanted to win, but he wanted to do it the right way.

Shaw coached the San Francisco 49ers from 1946 through 1954, and held the same position for the Philadelphia Eagles from 1957 through 1960. He was a winning coach with both teams, but his character and decency came out in a late-season game when the powerful 49ers were playing the Cleveland Browns in a key 1948 All-American Football Conference game.

The 49ers and the Browns were the league's two best teams, and the Niners seemed to have the advantage. Not only was the game played at old Kezar Stadium in San Francisco, but also Browns quarterback Otto Graham was playing on an injured knee and was clearly not at his best.

Shaw was not one for speeches to rally his troops—even though he had played college football at Notre Dame under Knute Rockne—but on this day he gave his team instructions on how to play against Graham.

"I want you to rush him hard but fair," Shaw said, in an anecdote reported in *The Eagles Encyclopedia*. "No one is to twist his leg or rough him up. I want us to win this game as much as you do, but there would be no pleasure in victory if we had to cripple Graham in order to win."

The 49ers lost the game 31-28, as Graham threw four touchdown passes. The Browns finished 14-0 that season and won the AAFC's West Division, finishing two games ahead of the 12-2-0 49ers. The Browns completed their undefeated season by beating the Buffalo Bills in the league's championship game.

Shaw's players always had full respect for their coach, even though his priorities seemed to put winning on a lower pedestal than many others. There was an honest, decent, and fair approach to life that very few other leaders in any field—let alone football—came close to matching.

"I played for a lot of coaches in the NFL," said former Eagles receiver Tommy McDonald. "But I can say without a doubt that Buck Shaw was at the top of the ladder. To me, he was the best of them all."

Shaw's 49ers were an excellent team in the four years of the AAFC, but they were beaten regularly by the Browns. San Francisco went 9-5, 8-4-2, 12-2, and 9-3 from 1946 through 1949, and the only year they earned a spot in the postseason was '49.

The Niners beat the Bills in their first-round playoff matchup 31-21, and had a chance to play the Browns in the league's final title game. San Francisco held Graham in check and limited him to 7-of-17 through the air for 128 yards, but Cleveland won the game 21-7.

The Niners struggled to a 3-9 record in their first season in the NFL, but Shaw got them going again in 1951, as they finished with a 7-4-1 record, which was good for second place behind the Los Angeles Rams in the National Division.

The 49ers would continue to win regularly in the NFL for several seasons, but they could never get past the Rams or the Detroit Lions, and did not make it to the championship game. The 49ers appeared to have the best offense on a year-in, year-out basis as they led the league in scoring three times.

They also had a plethora of dominating skill-position players in quarterback Y. A. Tittle, along with running backs Hugh McElhenny, Joe Perry, and John Henry Johnson, but they did not have a balanced team, as their defense often left them short.

San Francisco owner Tony Morabito got tired of watching his team come close but fall short, and he blamed Shaw for the team's inability to win the big games. When the 49ers finished 7-4-1 and slipped to third place in the West Division in 1954, Morabito fired his coach. "It's time we tried something else," were his parting words to Shaw.

Shaw combined college coaching with non-football business interests from 1955 through 1957, but he was lured back to the NFL in 1958 as head coach of the Philadelphia Eagles. Shaw would not take the job until the Eagles acquired veteran quarterback Norm Van Brocklin because he did not want to take the time to teach young quarterback Sonny Jurgensen the nuances of the game.

Shaw almost regretted his decision because the Eagles were awful in '58, going 2-9-1. He was disgusted with his players, many of whom appeared to be mistake-prone, inefficient, lazy, and out of shape, and that was proven by their record. When the Eagles dropped the season finale 20-0 at Washington, Shaw told his players to look around the locker room, because "most of you" will not be back here.

Shaw did as he said in the offseason, and the newly remade Eagles were a hard-working and hustling team that finished 7-5 and earned second place in the East Division.

Prior to 1960, Shaw knew he was tired of coaching in the NFL. He had enough energy to give it one last go-around, but he would not coach in the NFL after that. Van Brocklin came to the same conclusion, announcing that '60 would be his last season as an NFL quarterback.

The Eagles made that year count, as they went 10-2 and won the NFC East by a game and a half over the 10-3-1 Browns. The Eagles had earned a spot in the NFL Championship game against Vince Lombardi and the Green Bay Packers.

Lombardi was in the process of establishing his team as one of the greatest of all time. However, the Packers were a good team at this point in their development and not at their peak. Most observers thought the Packers would come into Franklin Field in Philadelphia and beat the Eagles, but the game was expected to be a close one.

It was close, but it was the Eagles who pulled out the 17-13 decision. Rookie fullback Ted Dean scored the winning touchdown on a seven-yard run with 5:21 remaining, and the Eagles withstood the final Green Bay possession to win the 1960 NFL championship.

The game ended with Philadelphia's powerful linebacker Chuck Bednarik wrapping Green Bay fullback Jim Taylor on the Eagles' nine-yard line as the clock ran out.

"It was the greatest tackle I ever made," Bednarik said.

It also gave Shaw the only championship of his career, as the gentleman coach went out a winner on football's biggest stage.

For the record

Buck Shaw
Regular–season record: 90-55-5, .621
Postseason record: 3-2, .600
One NFL championship

#47

DENNIS GREEN

W hen the career of Dennis Green is up for discussion, one incident comes up more than any other.

As head coach of the Arizona Cardinals in the 2006 season, his team was making a rare appearance on *Monday Night Football* against the 5-0 Chicago Bears. While the Cardinals were just 1-4 at the time, the Cardinals felt they knew the Bears very well because they had played them in the third preseason game that year.

Perhaps even more importantly than knowing the Bears, though, the Cardinals were dominating the game. They built a 20-0 half-time lead, and when placekicker Neil Rackers connected on a twenty-nine-yard field goal with 1:52 left in the third quarter, they had a 23–3 lead.

Under most circumstances, the Cardinals would have been safe to assume that they had secured a victory. Their defense was overwhelming Chicago quarterback Rex Grossman, and the Bears could not move the ball. However, the Bears got two touchdowns from their defense and another on special teams when Devin Hester returned a punt eighty-three yards.

The Bears managed a miraculous comeback and won the game 24–23.

Green was obviously upset that his team blew a chance to knock off an undefeated squad and gain some momentum in the process. He met the media after the game, and as he sat down to answer questions, nothing looked unusual.

But as he began to speak and analyze the game, Green lost control of his emotions. "The Bears are who we thought they were," Green said. "That's why we took the damn field. Now if you want to crown their asses, crown them! But they are who we thought they were. And we let them off the hook."

Green's postgame rant came in the last season of his coaching career, and perhaps all his frustrations came spilling out in that one postgame session. But instead of being a coach who lacked the ability to control his emotions as he was at that moment, he was just the opposite for the majority of his career.

Green had been a college assistant coach at Stanford before he became a head coach at Northwestern in 1981. After a five-year run with the Wildcats, he joined Bill Walsh's 49ers' staff for three years and helped them win a Super Bowl in 1988. From there, he became head coach at Stanford, and took the Cardinals to a bowl game in his third season.

He was viewed as an outstanding coach offensively who also had the skills to become a solid NFL head coach. The Minnesota Vikings came calling in 1992 and made him the second African-American head coach in the modern era.

Green was inheriting a team that had gone 6-10 and 8-8 in the previous two seasons. The Vikings were viewed as a group of selfish malcontents at the time, and Green's goal was to instill an unselfish attitude and promote a team spirit.

Green's enthusiasm set the tone for his new team and the Vikings turned it around immediately. They beat the Packers 23-20 in overtime in the season opener, and they took the momentum from that game to reel off an 11-5 record and win the NFC Central division.

It was a storybook regular season, but the playoffs turned out to be a nightmare. Despite having homefield advantage in their wildcard matchup with the Washington Redskins, the Vikings fell flat and dropped a 24-7 decision.

Losing in the playoffs would become a theme for Green's Vikings. They earned playoff spots in each of the next two seasons, but they went down in the first round to the Giants and Bears in both of those seasons.

Green was undaunted, even after an 8-8 season in 1995 that kept Minnesota out of the postseason. They returned to the playoffs in '96 and lost to the 49ers, but they finally got a playoff victory following the '97 season.

The Vikings were just 9-7 that year and finished fourth in the NFC Central, but that was good enough to earn a spot in the playoffs. Little was expected when they arrived at Giants Stadium to take on the Giants. However, the Vikings roared back from a 19-3 deficit to edge the Giants 23-22 when Eddie Murray connected on a game-winning twenty-four-yard field goal.

While the Vikings lost in the next round to the 49ers, it marked a big accomplishment for Green, as he proved he could finally win a playoff game.

The next season proved to be the Vikings' high point. They already had an accomplished offense with Randall Cunningham at quarterback, speedy running back Robert Smith, and All-Pro wide receiver Cris Carter catching everything he could get his hands on, but the Vikings went to a much higher level when they drafted explosive wide receiver Randy Moss in 1998.

There was no need for Moss to spend time getting acquainted. Green and offensive coordinator Brian Billick quickly recognized that Moss had generational talent, and he caught 69 passes for 1,313 yards and an amazing 17 touchdowns in his rookie season.

Moss was brilliant from start to finish, but he put on his most eye-catching performance on Thanksgiving Day, when he caught three touchdown passes of 51, 56 and 56 yards against the Dallas Cowboys. Moss had turned it up a couple of notches because the Cowboys had bypassed him in the draft and he wanted to show them they had made a mistake.

He clearly made his point.

The Vikings were basically unstoppable that season, as they reeled off a 15-1 record and became the highest-scoring team in league history as they scored 556 points, averaging 34.8 points per game.

They were expected to roll through the playoffs and return to the Super Bowl for the first time since the 1977 season, when they dropped their fourth Super Bowl appearance.

The Arizona Cardinals challenged Minnesota in the divisional playoff game, but the Vikings earned a 41-21 victory.

There were prohibitive favorites over the Atlanta Falcons in the NFC Championship game, and they had a 20-7 lead late in the first half. However, when the Falcons scored in the final minute of the second quarter to make it 20-14, the Vikings appeared to be in shock. They were not expecting a close game.

Late in the fourth quarter, the Vikings sent placekicker Gary Anderson onto the field to turn a 27-20 lead into a two-score advantage. Anderson had not missed a field goal all season, but he hooked a thirty-eight-yard field goal attempt.

The Falcons took advantage by scoring to send the game into overtime, and then completed the upset when Morten Andersen kicked a game-winning field goal and sent the Vikings and their fans home for the season.

Green had two more winning seasons with the Vikings, but it unraveled in the 2001 season. He would take two years off before joining the Cardinals. However, he could not find a winning formula in the desert and he was done at the conclusion of the 2006 season.

The failure of the Vikings to win a championship in 1998 was something Green could not get away from. All the frustration of that defeat came spilling out one Monday night after his team fell apart against the Bears.

It shouldn't obscure the fact that he had a 113-94-0 regular-season record and led his team to the playoffs eight times in the first ten years of his thirteen-year coaching career.

That's an accomplishment that ranks with the top coaches in the game's history.

For the record

> **Dennis Green**
> Regular-season record: 113-94-0, .546
> Postseason record: 4-8, .333
> Four division championships

#48

MIKE TOMLIN

Mike Tomlin was a sharp college assistant coach at Cincinnati in the late 1990s, and his Bearcats went from 111th in the nation in pass defense to 16th. That was all that Tampa Bay head coach Tony Dungy had to see.

He immediately hired Tomlin to coach the secondary in Tampa Bay in 2001, and even though Dungy left the Bucs to take the Indianapolis head coaching position a year later, Tomlin held on to his job.

Jon Gruden was hired as the Bucs' head coach, and he was impressed enough by Tomlin to keep him on his staff. The Bucs went on to win the Super Bowl that season, when their secondary performed expertly.

That got Tomlin noticed around the league, and he was eventually hired as the defensive coordinator by the Minnesota Vikings in 2006. It was just one year later that Bill Cowher retired from the Pittsburgh Steelers, and the confident Tomlin interviewed with the Steelers ownership for the head coaching job.

Many thought he was simply too young—thirty-six—and inexperienced to have a real chance at the position. Many thought that veteran offensive coordinator Ken Whisenhunt had the inside track for the job, but Tomlin blew away the Pittsburgh brain trust—led by owner Dan Rooney—and was named head coach.

Tomlin hit the ground running with his veteran team. One of his key decisions was to retain defensive coordinator Dick LeBeau, who did not have a strategic philosophy similar to Tomlin's. However, the young coach realized that LeBeau had been both highly successful and respected in the Steelers locker room, and he was not about to ignore his attributes in order to show everyone that he was boss.

The Steelers had gone 8-8 in Cowher's last season and many thought the team was on its way toward mediocrity. However, they rebounded to 10-6 in Tomlin's first season, and won the AFC North title.

While they dropped a 31-29 heartbreaker to the Jacksonville Jaguars in the playoffs, Tomlin had given the Steelers a spark.

Quarterback Ben Roethlisberger came of age that season and completed 65.3 percent of his passes, and had a powerful 32-11 touchdown-ratio. Roethlisberger credited Tomlin with much of his development, and the Steelers went into the offseason with a boatload of momentum.

The Steelers went on a roll in 2008, but it was not the result of Roethlisberger's brilliance. He struggled throughout much of the season, and his completion percentage slipped to 59.1 percent.

He also had a hard time hooking up with his receivers on big plays, as he was held to 17 touchdown passes.

But the Steelers made up for the lack of a passing game with a nasty, hard-hitting defense led by James Harrison, who forced seven fumbles that year. The Steelers were a solid 6-3 shortly after the midway point of the season, but they simply caught fire in the second half. They only lost one more game as they rolled to a 12-4 record and another first-place finish.

They picked up hard-earned victories over the San Diego Chargers and Baltimore Ravens in the playoffs to earn a spot in the Super Bowl, and they earned a remarkable 27-23 victory thanks to two spectacular plays.

Late in the first half, the Cardinals were threatening to score and turn a 10-7 deficit into a 14-10 lead. However, Harrison intercepted quarterback Kurt Warner's pass and made an incredible 100-yard return through the Cardinals for a touchdown and a 17-7 halftime lead.

Then, in the final minute of the fourth quarter, Roethlisberger hit Santonio Holmes with a six-yard touchdown pass that proved to be the game-winner.

In just two seasons, Tomlin had taken the Steelers back to the top and he had his Super Bowl. He achieved in two years what Cowher had needed fourteen years to do.

The Steelers missed the playoffs in 2009, but they got back to top form the following year and won the division with a 12-4 record. They beat the arch-rival Ravens in the divisional playoffs 31-24, and then survived a physical duel with the New York Jets to get back to the Super Bowl.

However, the Steelers had a huge assignment in trying to slow down Green Bay's brilliant Aaron Rodgers. While Pittsburgh kept it close and trailed 21-17 early in the third quarter, Rodgers responded with a fourth-quarter touchdown pass and another late drive as Green Bay pulled out a 31-25 triumph.

Few coaches have been to two Super Bowls in their first four years, but that's what Tomlin managed to achieve. His ability to find favorable matchups for his team to exploit was one of his greatest strengths, and he also excelled at firing up his players but not letting them get to the point where they committed foolish penalties that put the team in a hole.

It hasn't been quite so easy in the ensuing four years. While two of Tomlin's teams have made the playoffs, they have not recorded a win since their Super Bowl.

However, there has been a resiliency to both his team and his coaching style. The Steelers have slipped quite a bit on the defensive side of the ball, and LeBeau eventually resigned after the 2014 season.

Tomlin made adjustments to make sure his team was still competitive. The passing game improved, with Roethlisberger throwing to explosive wide receiver Antonio Brown, and the Steelers became a team that showed it could light up the scoreboard nearly every time it took the field.

The Steelers also had a productive running game that could make big plays and take time off the clock.

"In this game you have to make constant adjustments," Tomlin said. "Your players are competing against the best in the world, and we are coaching against the best and most experienced minds in the game. Just because you have had success doesn't mean it will continue. You have to adjust your game plan and then plan your next move. It never stops, and that's the way it always is and always will be."

After the 2014 season came to a conclusion with a wild-card loss to the Ravens, Tomlin said that his passion and feeling for the game was as strong as ever.

"It's still very painful," Tomlin said. "When the journey comes to an end, it should be elation or bitter disappointment, and it is that. We don't run away from that. I embrace that."

He still has many more years to fight for that elation.

For the record

> **Mike Tomlin**
> Regular–season record: 82–46–0, .641
> Postseason record: 5–4, .556
> One Super Bowl victory

#49

TOM FLORES

There were few coaches who had a more difficult assignment going in than Tom Flores when he was named as head coach of the Oakland Raiders.

First, there were the obvious factors. Legendary head coach John Madden had retired after the 1978 season, and all Madden had done in his ten years with the Raiders was become the all-time winningest coach by percentage (.763) in the history of the game. No NFL coach who had been on the sidelines for 100 games or more had ever won with more frequency than John Madden.

The second issue was having Al Davis as his owner. Davis almost certainly knew more about the game than any owner in the history of the league (with the possible exception of George Halas) and he made his feelings known to every coach the Raiders ever had. Many of Davis's thoughts were insightful and invaluable, but what kind of coach can get the job done the right way when his boss is offering his suggestions and input on nearly everything impacting the organization?

But it didn't stop there with Flores. In addition to the pressure of working for one of the most popular and successful teams in the history of the sport, Flores also had to deal with the fact that the Raiders were not the same team when he took over as they had been throughout the majority of the 1970s.

They were getting significantly older, and the difference between the Raiders and their competition in the AFC was growing smaller. The Raiders went 9-7 that year and finished in a tie for third place in the division with the Seattle Seahawks. The San Diego Chargers and Denver Broncos occupied the top two spots in the division, and the Raiders did not even make the playoffs.

Obviously, that did not sit well with Davis, and the 1980 season did not seem like it would be much better. Veteran quarterback Ken Stabler was in New Orleans, and former Houston Oiler Dan Pastorini appeared to have a grip on the quarterback job.

But the Raiders had also brought in thirty-three-year-old Jim Plunkett to compete for a job as a backup quarterback. There were no guarantees Plunkett would even make the team. The former Heisman Trophy winner from Stanford had endured an up-and-down career with the New England Patriots, and while he had a powerful arm, few thought he had the ability to be a winning quarterback in the NFL.

But Flores was happy to have him on board, and when the Raiders got off to a 2-3 start that season, Flores turned to Plunkett to handle the quarterback chores. "He worked with me a lot, to make sure I was confident and comfortable," Plunkett said. "He had been a backup quarterback who had spent a lot of time on the sidelines, so he knew what I had gone through. He helped me and helped our team quite a bit. We were really prepared every time we went on the field."

After Plunkett started to play, the Raiders picked it up considerably throughout the rest of that season. They went 9-2 the rest of the way, and that was good enough to earn them a spot in the post-season as a wild-card team.

They beat the Houston Oilers in the wild-card game by a convincing 27-7 margin, but they appeared to have a rough assignment when they went to Cleveland to take on the Browns. Cleveland was at its best at cold, dank, and cavernous Cleveland Municipal Stadium, but the Raiders were undaunted and pulled off the upset.

They did the same the following week when they upset the explosive Chargers 34-27 in San Diego. Plunkett threw two touchdown passes in that game and also ran for another.

That put the Raiders in the Super Bowl against Dick Vermeil and the Philadelphia Eagles. The Eagles had been the best regular-season team in the NFL that year, and they had beaten the Raiders earlier in the year in a midseason game.

However, the Raiders were a loose, happy, and confident bunch when they went to New Orleans for Super Bowl XV. They knew they had enjoyed a great season and that they were also playing their best football at the time.

While the Raiders were in New Orleans, Flores wanted his players to enjoy themselves as well as prepare for the game. The Raiders practiced hard, but this marauding bunch that included characters like Ted Hendricks, Jeff Barnes, Kenny King, Matt Millen, Lester Hayes, and Todd Christensen also partied hard.

The Eagles did not enjoy the same kind of atmosphere under Vermeil. He wanted his team to be in pristine shape for the Super Bowl, and he ran tight, clock-driven practices and had mandatory curfews for his team.

The Eagles were a finely tuned bunch when they arrived at the Superdome, but the minute they made their first mistake—resulting in a Ron Jaworski interception—the air went out of the balloon.

The Raiders took advantage of every Philadelphia error and pushed the pace throughout the game. The Raiders built a 14-0 first quarter lead on two Plunkett touchdown passes—one of which was an 80-yard catch and run by King—and the Eagles were never able to climb back in the game. The Raiders won 27-10, and in many ways the victory came because Flores had outprepared the meticulous Vermeil.

The Raiders won a second Super Bowl under Flores following the 1983 season. Once again, the Raiders had Plunkett at the helm, and they were a dominating team on both sides of the ball.

After winning the AFC West with a 12-4 record, the Los Angeles Raiders rolled over the Pittsburgh Steelers 38-10 in the divisional playoffs and then beat the Seattle Seahawks 30-14 in the AFC Championship game. That game was particularly satisfying for Flores because the plucky Seahawks had beaten the Raiders twice in the regular season, but could not do it when the money was on the table.

The Super Bowl was expected to belong to Joe Gibbs, Joe Theismann, John Riggins, and the Washington Redskins, who were trying to defend the title they won the year before. The Redskins went 14-2 in the regular season and had destroyed the Los Angeles Rams 51-7 in the divisional playoffs. They faced a tougher test from the San Francisco 49ers in the NFC title game, but they got by Bill Walsh's team 24-21.

The Super Bowl was expected to be a coronation for the Redskins, but it turned out to be a 38-9 blowout for the Raiders. The defense smothered Theismann and Riggins, while Plunkett and Marcus Allen were able to punish the once-formidable Washington defense. Allen ran for 191 yards, and his 74-yard touchdown run late in the third quarter remains one of the all-time great Super Bowl plays.

Flores became one of just thirteen coaches who have won two or more Super Bowls. Flores left the Raiders after the 1987 season, but he returned to coaching in 1992 with the Seattle Seahawks. He had three non-descript seasons before retiring for good.

While his years in Seattle were not successful, his legacy was intact. He had proven himself in his tenure with the Raiders—both in Oakland and Los Angeles—and he earned his status as one of the game's top coaches.

For the record

Tom Flores
Regular-season record: 97-87-0, .527
Postseason record: 8-3, .727
Two Super Bowl victories

#50

BLANTON COLLIER

The man should be a legend in Cleveland for what he accomplished while leading the Browns.

As nearly every sports fan knows, Cleveland is one of the hungriest sports cities in the United States. Cleveland fans love their Cavaliers and have a great desire to see the Indians return to glory. However, no team means more to Clevelanders than the Browns, and their fans still have great memories of 1964.

That's the year that the Cleveland Browns won their last NFL championship. They were a smart, athletic, and gifted team, led by the cerebral Blanton Collier.

Collier had been named head coach of the Browns prior to the 1963 season. The team had a relatively young and new owner named Art Modell, who wanted to learn about football from the inside.

Modell thought he had the ultimate insider to learn from in Paul Brown, the team's legendary head coach and the man the franchise had been named after. However, Brown was not interested in sharing his knowledge or his game plan with the team's owner.

Modell was filled with resentment toward his coach. Collier had been Brown's assistant for many years, and Brown respected his knowledge of the game and his ideas. However, when Collier wanted to give Cleveland quarterbacks the option of calling audibles and changing Brown's play calls at the line of scrimmage, the autocratic head coach shot down that idea with fervor.

Modell knew what was going on between Brown and Collier, and he asked the assistant to explain his idea to him. When Collier not only told Modell but showed him on film why the Browns had to give the quarterback the ability to change play calls to defeat the opponent's blitz, the owner was transfixed.

Not only was he learning football from the inside, but also he saw that Brown's old ways were no longer as effective as they had been in the past.

Modell shocked the football world when he fired Brown at the end of the 1962 season and named Collier as his head coach.

Brown had been one of the most innovative head coaches in his prime, and he had a hard time accepting the fact that he could be fired.

But while there was shock in the Brown household and outside of Cleveland, the move was a welcome one inside the Cleveland locker room.

Nobody was happier to see the move made than Jim Brown, the team's outstanding running back. Brown and Collier had an outstanding relationship, and the two thoughtful men had held many discussions about football and all other aspects of life.

Paul Brown had not treated Jim Brown in that kind of manner. The coach treated the superstar running back with little respect as an individual. He treated most of his players in that manner, and that's the way that many coaches treated their players in that era.

However, Jim Brown resented that kind of treatment from his coach, and when Collier was named head coach, the running back felt as if a huge burden had been lifted.

"I loved talking to that man," Brown told Cleveland sportswriter Terry Pluto. "[Collier] had a way of making you feel important. He allowed you to breathe, to grow."

Collier also treated Brown far better than his previous coach had treated him. If the running back needed to rest in practice, he was allowed to do so, without receiving any dirty looks or questions about it.

Collier may not have been the kind of coach who attempted to befriend all his players, but he certainly would make life easier for the players, who were the team's superstars and most important in determining the outcome of games.

Once Collier became the head coach of the team, he helped usher in the modern era of the game. He instituted his audible system, and he had in Frank Ryan one of the brightest quarterbacks the game has ever known running the show.

Ryan was studying for a Ph.D. in mathematics, and numbers were his life before, during, and after his football career. While he played, Ryan appreciated the opportunity to change plays based on the way he saw the defense line up.

Ryan almost always made the right decision when he changed the play call, and that didn't surprise Collier a bit.

The Browns were a strong team in Collier's initial season as head coach, as they finished with a 10-4 record and second in the NFL's East Division. Yet in those days, there was no playoff system. The winner of the East met the winner of the West for the NFL championship, and everyone else went home. That's where the Browns went.

But they were just a tad better the following year, as Cleveland finished with a 10-3-1 mark in 1964 and won the East by a game over the St. Louis Cardinals, who finished 9-3-2.

The Browns earned a spot in the NFL title game against the heavily favored Baltimore Colts, who were coached by Don Shula, the NFL's boy wonder at the time.

The Colts had a team that included Johnny Unitas, Lenny Moore, Raymond Berry, and a ferocious defense led by defensive end Gino Marchetti. The Colts had finished with a 12-2-0 record, and none of the other West Division teams could come close to them. The Green Bay Packers and Minnesota Vikings tied for second with 8-5-1 records.

The Colts came into Cleveland Municipal Stadium with a full head of steam and determined to stop Brown from beating them by running the football. They discounted Ryan and his passing attack. That was a huge mistake.

Ryan threw three touchdown passes that day to wide receiver Gary Collins, and the Colts did not come close to stopping Brown. He carried the ball 27 times for 114 yards, as the Browns were able to move the ball at will.

The Browns also got two field goals from legendary Hall of Famer Lou "The Toe" Groza.

While that was going down, the Cleveland defense did the unthinkable—they blanked Unitas & Co. The final score was 27-0, and Cleveland has been reliving that championship ever since.

There was never any letup from the Browns during the Collier era. They went 11-3-0 the following season, but this time their first postseason opponent was the Green Bay Packers. Vince Lombardi's team had tied the Colts for the West Division title as both teams went 10-3-1, but the Packers emerged from a playoff game to break the tie as they edged the Colts 13-10 in overtime.

The wise guys thought the rested Browns would have a big advantage over their exhausted rivals. In addition to getting the previous week off, the Browns had homefield advantage over the Packers.

It mattered little, as the Packers used the double-barreled rushing attack of Jim Taylor (96 yards) and Paul Hornung (105 yards) to take the Browns down by a 23-12 margin. Jim Brown was held to 50 yards in the final game of his professional career.

Brown's sudden retirement would have caused most coaches to go into shock, but Collier barely batted an eye. He had an exceptional running back in Leroy Kelly, and the Browns continued to win games through the 1960s, even without the greatest back the game has ever known.

The Browns never had a losing season under Collier, and they remained strong contenders. While they lost some of their luster to the up-and-coming Dallas Cowboys, Collier's Browns beat the Cowboys in the newly expanded NFL playoffs in 1968 and '69. However, they were ultimately humbled by the Colts in '68 and the Vikings the following year in the postseason, and those defeats kept them from getting to the Super Bowl.

The Browns slipped to 7-7-0 in 1970, and that was Collier's final year on the sidelines.

He finished his coaching career with a 76-34-2 regular-season record, and his .691 winning percentage is one of the best in history.

Collier was quiet, bespectacled, and to many looked more like a professor than a football coach, but he helped usher in the modern era of football with his stellar coaching.

For the record

Blanton Collier
Regular-season record: 76-34-2, .691
Postseason record: 3-4, .421
One NFL championship

INDEX

Adams, Bud 109, 189
Agase, Alex 32
Aikman, Troy 75, 131
Allen, George 23, 79, 95, 197, 202–207
Allen, Marcus 251
Alworth, Lance 69
Ameche, Alan 99
Andersen, Morten 150, 242
Anderson, Dick 22
Anderson, Gary 241
Anderson, Jamal 137
Andrews, Leroy 173
Atkins, Doug 55, 203
Austin, Bill 205

Bailey, Aaron 131
Banaszak, Pete 48
Banks, Carl 38
Banks, Tony 210

Barber, Tiki 61
Barnes, Jeff 250
Bednarik, Chuck 236
Belichick, Bill 7–12, 19, 61, 66, 113, 220, 232
Bell, Bobby 119
Bengtson, Phil 157–159
Benirschke, Rolf 96
Berry, Raymond 256
Bettis, Jerome 131
Bidwill, Bill 95
Billick, Brian 208–212, 221, 241
Bledsoe, Drew 9–10
Blood, Johnny 144
Boozer, Emerson 101
Boulware, Peter 209
Bount, Mel 45
Bowlen, Pat 136
Box, Cloyce 194
Bradshaw, Terry 43–44, 51

Brady, Tom 9-11, 66, 162, 164, 170, 232
Brandt, Gil 14
Bratkowski, Zeke 4, 21
Brazile, Robert 111
Brees, Drew 214-216
Brennan, Brian 115, 134
Brenner, Hoby 149
Bright, Bum 73
Brister, Bubby 129
Brodie, John 84
Brooks, Aaron 168
Brooks, Derrick 65
Brooks, James 96
Brown, Antonio 246
Brown, Bill 84
Brown, Charlie 90
Brown, Jerome 150
Brown, Jim 33-34, 254-255, 257
Brown, Larry 206
Brown, Paul 25-26, 30-35, 113, 254-255
Brown, Roger 205
Brown, Tom 4, 15
Bruce, Isaac 10, 200
Brunell, Mark 60
Bryant, Bear 37
Buchanan, Buck 119
Buffone, Doug 121
Bull, Ronnie 203
Buoniconti, Nick 22
Burnett, Morgan 167-168
Burress, Plaxico 61

Burrough, Ken 109
Burt, Jim 38
Bush, Reggie 215
Butkus, Dick 203, 206
Butler, Malcolm 232
Byner, Ernest 114, 116

Calhoun, George 144
Campbell, Earl 109
Caroline, J.C. 203
Carroll, Pete 228-232
Carson, Harry 38
Carter, Cris 137, 209, 241
Castille, Jeremiah 116
Chandler, Chris 137
Chandler, Don 21
Chandler, Wes 96
Chmura, Mark 180
Christensen, Todd 250
Christie, Steve 189
Clark, Dwight 27
Clark, James 186
Collier, Blanton 253-257
Collins, Gary 256
Collins, Kerry 211
Conrad, Robert 37
Conzelman, Jimmy 194
Coryell, Don 88, 93-97, 125
Coughlin, Tom 58-
Cowher, Bill 128-132, 244
Craft, Russ 185
Cribbs, Joe 125
Csonka, Larry 22

Index

Culpepper, Brad 65
Cundiff, Billy 221
Cunningham, Randall 137, 240
Cuozzo, Gary 4, 21
Curtis, Isaac 94
Curtis, Mike 21

Danowski, Ed
Dansby, Karlos, 170
Davis, Al 25–26, 49, 70, 153,
    163–165, 178, 248–249
Davis, Clarence 48
Davis, Kenneth 80
Davis, Stephen 154
Davis, Terrell 179–180
Davis, Willie 15
Dawson, Len 50, 101, 119, 122
Dean, Ted 236
DeBerg, Steve 134
Delhomme, Jake 154–155
Den Herder, Vern 22
Dent, Richard 224
Detmer, Ty 163
Dierdorf, Dan 94
Dilfer, Trent 208, 210
Dillon, Corey 141
DiMaggio, Joe 13
Ditka, Mike 38, 55, 57, 149,
    203, 206, 223–227
Dobler, Conrad "Dirty" 94
Dryer, Fred 124
Dungy, Tony 63–67, 243
Dyson, Kevin 190, 200

Edwards, Herman 198
Eller, Carl 84
Elway, John 39, 115, 126,
    133–138, 155, 159,
    177–181, 215
Ewbank, Weeb 20, 22,
    98–102, 123

Fassel, Jim 60, 214
Faulk, Marshall 10, 214
Favre, Brett 104–106, 139, 163,
    169–170, 180
Fears, Tom 69
Fencik, Gary 224
Ferguson, Joe 125
Finks, Jim 148
Fischer, Pat 6
Fisher, Jeff 187–191
Fitzpatrick, Ryan 162
Flacco, Joe 219–220
Flores, Tom 248–252
Flutie, Doug 59
Foreman, Chuck 86–87
Fouts, Dan 88, 95, 97
Fox, John 151–155
Freeman, Antonio 180
Fuqua, Frenchy 44, 51

Gannon, Rich 164, 166
Garrett, Mike 119, 122
Garrison, Gary 94
Garrison, Walt 17
Gehrig, Lou 13

George, Bill 55
George, Eddie 190, 210
Gibbs, Joe 39, 88-92, 97,
    225, 251
Gifford, Frank 56
Gillman, Sid 25-26, 68-72, 109
Glanville, Jerry 104
Graham, Otto 31, 186,
    234-235
Grant, Bud 51, 83-87, 125
Green, Dennis 63, 209,
    238-242
Green, Trent 200
Greene, Joe 43
Griese, Bob 22
Grossman, Rex 239
Groza, Lou "The Toe"
    32-33, 256
Gruden, Jon 162-166, 210, 243

Hadl, John 71
Hairston, Carl 198
Halas, George "Mugs" 57
Halas, George 17, 53-57, 120,
    145, 174-175, 203, 206,
    223, 249
Hampton, Dan 224
Handler, Phil 194
Handley, Ray 59
Harbaugh, Jim 130, 219,
    221, 231
Harbaugh, John 218-
Harmon, Ronnie 80

Harris, Franco 44, 51
Harrison, James 245
Hart, Jim 94
Hartley, Garrett 216
Hayes, Bob 14
Hayes, Lester 250
Hebert, Bobby 149
Hendricks, Ted 250
Herber, Arnie 145
Hester, Devin 239
Hill, King 195
Hilliard, Dalton 149
Hinton, Chuck 195
Holmes, Santonio 245
Holmgren, Mike 103-107,
    139, 163, 180
Holt, Torry 10
Hornung, Paul 3, 257
Hostetler, Jeff 9, 39, 81
Howard, Desmond 106
Howell, Jim Lee 2, 14
Hubbard, Cal 144
Huff, Sam 6
Humphries, Stan 130
Hunt, Lamar, 69
Hutson, Don 144-145

Irvin, Michael 75, 131

Jackson, Mark 115, 134
Jackson, Rickey 149
Jaworski, Ron 162, 198,
    199, 251

Jefferson, John 88
Johnson, Bill "Tiger" 25, 34
Johnson, Brad 165
Johnson, Jimmy 73-77, 106
Johnson, John Henry 235
Johnson, Vaughan 149
Joiner, Charlie 96
Jones, Deacon 205
Jones, Jerry 17, 73-74, 77
Jones, Mike 190, 200
Jurgensen, Sonny 6, 84. 235

Kapp, Joe 84-85
Karlis, Rich 116, 135
Kearse, Jermaine 232
Kelly, Jim 40, 80-81, 148
Kelly, Leroy 257
Kemp, Jack 70
Kiick, Jim 22
Kilmer, Billy 206
King, Kenny 250
Kirkland, Levon 130
Klein, Gene 71
Knox, Chuck 123-127
Kosar, Bernie 114-116, 135
Kotite, Rich 188, 229
Kraft, Robert 40, 229
Kramer, Jerry 5, 15
Krieg, Dave 126

Lambeau, Curly 57, 143-146
Lambert, Jack 44
Lamonica, Daryle 48

Landry, Tom 2, 13-18, 19, 26,
    71, 73-74, 95, 124,
    133-134, 199, 222, 223
Lanier, Willie 119
Larsen, Gary 84
Layne, Bobby 193-195
LeBeau, Dick 244, 246
Levy, Marv 78-82
Lewis, Ray 209-211, 219-220
Lincoln, Keith 69
Lloyd, Greg 130
Lockette, Ricardo 232
Lombardi, Vince 1-6, 14-15,
    19, 48, 56, 103, 105, 120,
    146, 151, 157, 204,
    236, 256
Lott, Ronnie 26-28
Lowe, Paul 69
Luckman, Sid 55
Lundy, Lamar 205
Lynch, John 65
Lynch, Marshawn 231-232
Lynn, Mike 75

Mack, Kevin 114
Madden, John 44-45, 47-52,
    86, 97, 248
Majkowski, Don 104
Manning, Archie 224-225
Manning, Eli 11, 61
Manning, Peyton 65, 67, 150,
    155, 162, 231
Mantle, Mickey 13

Mara, Tim 173

Mara, Wellington 175

Marchetti, Gino 256

Marchibroda, Ted 80, 130

Marconi, Joe 203

Marino, Dan 24, 126, 229

Marshall, George Preston 146

Marshall, Jim 84

Marshall, Leonard 38

Marshall, Wilber 224

Martin, Eric 149

Martin, Rod 199

Matte, Tom 21

Mayes, Rueben 149

Maynard, Don 101

McBride, Mickey 31

McCarthy, Mike 167–171

McCutcheon, Lawrence 124

McDonald, Tommy 234

McElhenny, Hugh 235

McGee, Ben 195

McIntyre, Guy 225–26

McMahon, Jim 224–225

McMichael, Steve 224

McMillin, Bo 194

McNabb, Donovan 140–141

McNair, Steve 190, 210

Means, Natrone 60

Meredith, Don 4, 14–15, 84

Metcalf, Terry 95

Michalske, Mike 144

Millen, Matt 250

Miller, Red 16

Mills, Sam 149

Modell, Art 34, 209, 254

Monk, Art 90

Montana, Joe 26–27, 136, 158, 160

Montgomery, Wilbert 198–199

Moore, Lenny 256

Mora, Jim 147–151

Morall, Earl 22

Morris, Johnny 55

Morris, Mercury 22

Morstead, Thomas 216

Morton, Craig 16, 134

Moseley, Mark 115

Moses, Haven 94

Moss, Randy 137, 209, 241

Muhammad, Muhsin 154

Muncie, Chuck 96

Munson, Bill 123

Murchison, Clint 14

Murray, Eddie 240

Myhra, Steve 99

Namath, Joe 21, 30, 100, 121, 123

Neale, Earle "Greasy" 182–186

Newton, Cam 162

Nickerson, Hardy 65

Noll, Chuck 16, 42–46, 63, 109–110, 113, 129, 151, 218, 222

Norwood, Scott 82

O'Bradovich, Ed 55, 203
O'Donnell, Neil 129
Olsen, Merlin 205
Osborn, Dave 84
Owen, Steve 14
Owen, Steve 172–176
Owens, Terrell 141

Page, Allen 84
Parcells, Bill 36–41, 59, 81,
    214, 229
Pardee, Jack 188
Parker, Buddy 192–196
Pastorini, Dan 109, 249
Payton, Sean 213–217
Payton, Walter 224, 226
Peete, Rodney 163
Perkins, Don 14
Perkins, Ray 37, 136
Perry, Joe 235
Perry, William "The
    Refrigerator" 226
Petitbon, Richie 203
Phillips, Bum 108–112
Phillips, Wade 111, 178
Pihos, Pete 183, 185
Plunkett, Jim 199,
    249–251
Pluto, Terry 255
Porter, Tracy 216
Pritchard, Bosh 183
Proehl, Ricky 155
Pugh, Jethro 15

Rackers, Neil 238
Ralston, John 147
Ramsey, Buster 194
Rashad, Ahmad 86
Rausch, John 49
Reed, Andre 80–81
Reed, Ed 219
Reeves, Dan (Rams' owner) 205
Reeves, Dan 14, 113,
    133–138, 178
Reid, Andy 139–142, 165, 219
Reid, Garrett 142
Reynolds Jack "Hacksaw" 124
Rhodes, Ray 214, 219
Rice, Jerry 136
Richards, Curvin 76
Riggins, John 90, 251
Rivers, Philip 162
Robertson, Isiah 124
Robinson, Dave 4
Robinson, John 188
Robinson, Johnny 119
Rockne, Knute 234
Rodgers, Aaron 169, 245
Roethlisberger, Ben 244
Rooney, Art 43, 195
Rooney, Dan 244
Rosenbloom, Carroll 20,
    125, 206
Ross, Bobby 160
Rote, Tobin 69
Rothstein, Arnold 183
Rozelle, Pete 56, 70

Ruth, Babe 13
Ryan, Buddy 187–188, 224, 226
Ryan, Frank 255
Rypien, Mark 90

Saban, Lou 32
Sapp, Warren 65
Sayers, Gale 203, 206
Schmidt, Francis 68
Schmidt, Joe 124
Schneider, John 230
Schnellenberger, Howard 38
Schottenheimer, Marty 63, 113–117, 129, 168
Schramm, Tex 14
Scott, Jake 22
Seifert, George 28, 153, 157–161
Shanahan, Mike 177
Sharpe, Sterling 105
Sharper, Jamie 209
Shaugnessy, Clark 54–55
Shaw, Buck 233–237
Shaw, Dennis 94
Shell, Art 51, 153
Shula, Don 4, 17, 19–24, 30, 50, 86, 89, 101, 110, 204, 222
Simms, Phil 38–39, 81, 136
Singletary, Mike 224
Sipe, Brian 94
Smith, Alex, 142
Smith, Bruce 81

Smith, Emmitt 75, 131
Smith, Lamar 151
Smith, Lovie 67
Smith, Robert 209, 241
Smith, Steve 154
Snell, Matt 101
Snyder, Daniel 114
Speedie, Mac 31
Stabler, Ken 44, 86, 249
Stallworth, John 44
Starr, Bart 3, 5, 15
Staubach, Roger 15
Steinbrenner, George 134
Strahan, Michael 61–62
Stram, Hank 50, 70, 118–122
Strong, Ken
Swann, Lynn 44
Swilling, Pat 149
Switzer, Barry 77

Talley, Darryl 81
Tarkenton, Fran 51, 86
Tatum, Jack 44
Taylor, Charley 6
Taylor, Jim 3, 236, 257
Taylor, Kitrick 105
Taylor, Lawrence 9, 37, 149
Taylor, Rosey 203
Tebow, Tim 155
Theismann, Joe 89–91, 225, 251
Thomas, Lynn 26
Thomas, Pierre 216
Thomas, Thurman 80–81

Index

Thompson, Lex 183, 185–186
Thompson, Ted 168–169
Tittle, Y.A. 56, 235
Tomlin, Mike 243–247
Turnbull, Andrew 144
Tyree, David 11, 61

Unitas, Johnny 4, 20, 84, 99, 256
Upshaw, Gene 51
Urlacher, Brian 215

Van Brocklin, Norm 84, 235–236
Van Buren, Steve 183
van Eeghen, Mark 48
Vanderjagt, Mike 150
Vermeil, Dick 128, 190, 197–201, 250
Vinatieri, Adam 141, 155
Vitt, Joe 126

Wade, Bill 56
Walker, Doak 194
Walker, Herschel 75, 148
Walsh, Bill 24–29, 34–35, 103–105, 158–159, 225, 239, 251

Warner, Curt 126
Warner, Kurt 10, 200
Washington, Gene (Minn.) 85
Webster, Mike 44
Werblin, Sonny 100
Whisenhunt, Ken 244
White, Danny 15
White, Reggie 105–106, 148, 150
White, Sammy 86
Whitsell, Davey 203
Williams, Doug 90
Williams, Gregg 216
Williams, Ricky 140
Williamson, Carlton 26
Wilson, Otis 224
Wilson, Russell 167, 230–232
Winslow, Kellen 88, 96
Wolf, Ron 103–105
Woodson, Charles 164
Woodson, Rod 130, 209
Wright, Eric 26
Wycheck, Frank 189

Young, George 38, 136
Young, Steve 160–161